DARK EYES ON AMERICA

DARK EYES ON AMERICA

The Novels of Joyce Carol Oates

GAVIN COLOGNE-BROOKES

Louisiana State University Press BATON ROUGE

Published by Louisiana State Univeristy Press
Copyright © 2005 by Louisiana State University Press
All rights reserved
Manufactured in the United States of America
Louisiana Paperback Edition, 2009

DESIGNER: AMANDA MCDONALD SCALLAN
TYPEFACE: WHITMAN
TYPESETTER: G&S TYPESETTERS, INC.

Grateful acknowledgment is made to Joyce Carol Oates for permission to print brief excerpts from her correspondence, published works, and unpublished materials.

Library of Congress Cataloging-in-Publication Data
Cologne-Brookes, Gavin, 1961–
   Dark eyes on America : the novels of Joyce Carol Oates / Gavin Cologne-Brookes.
    p.cm.
   Includes bibliographical references and index.
   ISBN 0-8071-2985-2 (hardcover : alk. paper)
  1. Oates, Joyce Carol, 1938—Criticism and interpretation. 2. National characteristics, American, in literature. I. Title.
ps3565.a8z585 2004
8139.54—dc22

                                                                            2004011736

ISBN-13: 978-0-0871-3530-3 (paper : alk. paper)

The paper in this book meets the guidelines for permanence and durability of the Committee on Production Guidelines for Book Longevity of the Council on Library Resources. ∞

For Xenatasha and Anastasia

I make my way up through marrow
through my own heavy blood
my eyes eager as thumbs
entering my own history like a tear
balanced sacred on the outermost edge
of the eyelid
—"Iris into Eye," 1970

By degrees, days
and years,
another voice
intrudes.
Another presence.
—"The Time Traveler," 1989

America is my home; the place of my soul.
—Correspondence, 16 January 1998

CONTENTS

Acknowledgments xi
Introduction 1

1. MIRRORS AND WINDOWS 19
2. ABSTRACTION INTO ACTION 55
3. REWRITING THE NOVEL 90
4. LOOK BACK TIME 133
5. DARK EYES ON AMERICA 175

Afterword 229
Notes 241
Selected Bibliography 261
Index 273

ACKNOWLEDGMENTS

MANY PEOPLE DIRECTLY or indirectly helped this book get written. Gregory Fitz Gerald introduced me to upstate New York, where, on the sunny afternoon of my first visit to Brockport in 1983, I saw a videotaped interview with Joyce Carol Oates in the Brockport Forum collection and so began to read her work. Greg's support was also instrumental in securing my scholarship to the State University of New York college at Brockport to study for a master of arts degree in 1984–85, and I will always value the people I met during that perspective-shaping year. Most prominent among them, in terms of this book, is Bill Heyen, who brought me into contact with contemporary American poets and poetry. Since then Bill has provided a wealth of material, including many books, much inspiration, and considerable insight into an American intellectual outlook he and Joyce Carol Oates help to shape. In the summer of 1998, Bill and Hannelore took me to visit Joyce's parents, Frederic and Carolina, at their home outside Millersport. This proved invaluable in furthering my understanding of her writings. That same day, Mary Brennan drove us around Lockport and showed me something of Joyce's early environment.

At Syracuse University Library, Kathleen Manwaring, manuscripts supervisor in the Department of Special Collections, was friendly and efficient during visits in 1995 and 1998 and by mail and e-mail. Kate Flaherty organized the *Prairie Schooner* Conference in Lincoln, Nebraska, in October 2001 that gave me the opportunity to put some faces to names, not least Greg Johnson and Randy Souther. Both Greg's biography and Randy's Joyce Carol Oates Home Page, *Celestial Timepiece*, have been especially useful sources of information. Susan Shillinglaw and Ruth Prigozy organized a John Steinbeck Conference at Hofstra University, New York, in March 2002, where, as in Nebraska, I was able to give a paper and meet a number of old and new acquaintances, including Jackson Bryer, John Ditsky, Hilary Hensler, and Budd Schulberg. I am also indebted in terms of hospitality during my 1998 and 2002 visits to Matt Martin and Elizabeth Reingold (not to forget Daniel and Erin) in New York, and Bill and Rose Styron on Martha's Vineyard and in Roxbury, Connecticut. Matt also sent me several books on request. Bill freely gave his insights into American writing. My other main hospitality debt is to Maggie, David, Elizabeth, and Abby Christensen, for my week in Nebraska.

Joyce Carol Oates herself has been extraordinarily helpful, responding graciously, swiftly, and in detail to my questions by mail, and finding time to discuss her work in Princeton in July 1998 and during the *Prairie Schooner* Conference.

In Britain, I would like to thank the British Academy for an award that funded my trip to Princeton, Lockport, and Syracuse in the summer of 1998. Various colleagues at Bath Spa University College helped the book toward completion. In particular, Tessa Hadley and Paul Edwards read several sections of the manuscript. Tessa also helped me find time to write despite extensive teaching commitments, while Paul reminded me to apply for British Academy funding. Colin Edwards and Jan Relf provided information. Richard Francis and Tracey Hill provided inspiration. Jeff Rodman and Neil Sammells secured some research funding. Many BSUC students have helped shape my sense of Joyce Carol Oates's literary significance through their reactions and insights. Finally, my love and thanks go to my wife, Nicki, for allowing me time to write the book, and to Xenatasha and Anastasia. Many people have been in my mind during the writing of this book, but none more so than my daughters.

DARK EYES ON AMERICA

> Speak your latent conviction, and it shall be the universal sense;
> for the inmost in due time becomes the outmost.
> —EMERSON, "Self-Reliance"

INTRODUCTION

"WRITING A NOVEL is an experience that evolves," runs one of Joyce Carol Oates's journal entries. "The novel is its own experience and its subject is always the evolving of consciousness . . . that of the reader, the author, the characters." As with an individual novel, so with Oates's writing career. "In many writers," she says, "it comes to seem over a lifetime that a complex and essentially unknowable drama is working itself out by way of the individual." Unknowable as that drama may be to the writer, in Oates's case commentators have begun to unravel its complexities. But for all the illuminating books and articles on Oates's work by sympathetic critics, Linda Wagner-Martin's 1990s view still seems valid. In the wider critical sphere, Oates remains "strangely marginalized. The value of her fiction keeps getting displaced, subsumed under arguments about who she is, what her concerns as a writer really are, what role her fiction plays in the paradigm of current literature." One area where the reverse is true is in the vigorous body of scholarship concerned with Oates's feminist convictions. Not only has her feminism become more apparent in recent decades but much has also been done to reassess her earlier work in light of this.

My reading of Oates is in broad agreement with these recent reassessments, and acknowledges her assertion, from novel to novel, that, in Wagner-Martin's phrase, "culture is male-determined." But I also agree with Wagner-Martin that the fact that Oates "is a woman writer is probably less significant than that she draws from all kinds of belief and knowledge." For a writer as diverse as Oates, observes Ellen Friedman similarly, "the category 'woman writer'—even when most generously defined—simply feels too constraining."[1] Oates's achievements are indisputable for anyone who has read her work extensively. Her body of novels, let alone her work in other genres, is among the most wide-ranging in contemporary writing. But whether, and if so why, it is among the most important, and which novels are most significant, remain the key questions. My contention in Dark Eyes on America is that while many of Oates's earlier novels are chiefly valuable in revealing her path to artistic maturity, her novels since the 1980s suggest that she is the nearest America could currently have to a national novelist. Over more than forty years, but most convincingly since Bellefleur, she has climbed the precipices of the American psyche, crossed its plains and valleys, delved into its crevices, and dredged its waters, all with energy, skill, and thoroughness, and in several genres. Where, we can now ask, has her "evolving of consciousness" led her, and where might it lead the reader? What does the best of her work tell us about ourselves, and what does it offer us as we push on into our new century?

It is, then, Wagner-Martin's question of the *value* of Oates's writing—here, most specifically her novels—that this book ultimately addresses. After all, to ask what use we can make of it is surely the most appropriate question when assessing a writer so obviously in tune with American pragmatism. Several critics have looked at aspects of William James's influence on Oates, and some attention has been paid to her interest in such precursors of pragmatism as Schopenhauer, Emerson, and Nietzsche, if less to a figure who, like Schopenhauer, was another key influence on Nietzsche: Pascal. But even with James, assessment has tended to appear in articles of necessarily limited scope. Since I agree with Wagner-Martin that Oates's writings mine all manners of creed and wisdom, I am not concerned exclusively with the pragmatist connection, except to say that it is in the nature of pragmatism to do exactly as Oates has done. Indeed, it is the glorious pluralism of her writings that helps define their value. Paradoxically or otherwise, her writings exude this pragmatist spirit in their very elusiveness when it comes to labeling. Nor do they reveal her to be a mere dramatizer of "authoritative" ideas, but rather an intellectual who has taken key tendencies in classical American philosophy in her own unique directions. Her reflections on American society dovetail with and develop convictions evident in the writings of founding pragmatists, of those who influenced them, of later pragmatists such as John Dewey, and of contemporary commentators like Richard Rorty and Charlene Haddock Seigfried. Not least in the feminist dimension to her work, but also in the fact that she *does* draw from and explore "all kinds of belief and knowledge," Oates has effectively become a pragmatist in her own right.[2]

To a greater or lesser extent, all these figures inform this study, and not least in terms of my sense that Oates is involved in a profound attempt to revise American language: to rewrite the way Americans talk about themselves, and therefore to help alter American realities. In "Feminism and Pragmatism," Rorty cites Marilyn Frye describing her own writing as a "flirtation with meaninglessness," a dance "kept aloft by the rhythm and momentum" of her own motion as she tries "to plumb abysses which are generally agreed not to exist." Frye might as easily have been writing about *Childwold, Bellefleur, Broke Heart Blues,* or any of the other novels, stories, poems, or plays through which Oates seeks new forms and languages to fill in what Frye refers to as "cognitive gaps and negative semantic spaces." "Meaninglessness," continues Rorty, "is exactly what you have to flirt with when you are in between social, and in particular linguistic, practices—unwilling to make use of an old one but not yet having succeeded in creating a new one." Oates has certainly risked opacity at times, even as she has sought to revise old practices and to create new ones. Writing "all over the aesthetical map," as John Barth remarked, she has been especially adept at renegotiating whatever conventions or ideas she adopts. Her writings exemplify, indeed amplify, Rorty's view that "the human self is created by the use of a vocabulary rather than being adequately or inadequately expressed in a vocabulary."[3] Her use of authoritative thinkers, then, informed by her inherently pragmatic aesthetic of experimentation, is a proactive, living process of adaptation and revision rather than any kind of static traditionalism.

Many aspects of Oates's worldview—most notably her belief that we are all artists in the broadest sense—can not only be traced back to Nietzsche but also bear comparison with ideas prevalent in poststructuralism. "Nietzsche stands as the founder of what became the aesthetic metacritique of 'truth,'" writes Allan Megill, "wherein 'the work of art,' or 'the text,' or 'language' is seen as establishing the grounds for truth's 'possibility.'" Plainly, then, there is as direct a line from Nietzsche to Foucault and Derrida as there is from Nietzsche to William James. "What ties Dewey and Foucault, James and Nietzsche together," says Rorty, is "the sense that there is nothing deep down inside us except what we have put there ourselves." There is "no criterion that we have not created in the course of creating a practice, no standard of rationality that is not an appeal to such a criterion, no rigorous argumentation that is not obedience to our own conventions." But what aligns Oates finally with pragmatism is that, unlike Nietzsche or Heidegger, pragmatists write out of a belief in the possibilities of social change. The pragmatist believes that, even if we accept language as a work of art in itself, and so an imperfect medium that leaves meanings open and plural, what count are the practical consequences of what we write, say, or do. "To accept the contingency of starting points," as Rorty puts it, "is to accept our inheritance from, and our conversation with, our fellow human beings as our only source of guidance." What matters in the end, pragmatists tell us, "is our loyalty to other human beings clinging together against the dark, not our hope of getting things right." Oates's career, for instance, has epitomized Dewey's view of the intellectual's main task. Whether by philosophy or any other discipline, he writes, "there is a kind of intellectual work to be done which is of the utmost importance." That task is to clarify people's ideas about "the social and moral strifes of their own day," to become "an organ for dealing with these conflicts." The links between the philosophy that Oates's novels ultimately express and the approaches of James, Dewey, or, latterly, Rorty, testify to the accuracy of John Stuhr's claims for pragmatism's ongoing importance. And, just as Wagner-Martin urges us to discuss "the value" of Oates's fiction, so Stuhr reminds us that to ask what we can *do* with such ideas—as found in this case in the writings of Oates—"is *the* pragmatic question."[4]

To see Oates as a pragmatist in her own right, rather than as simply indebted to pragmatism among other ideas, is to take on board the pragmatist worldview. Pragmatism has never been about kowtowing to dead thinkers, however admirable their thoughts. By definition, it is an ever-evolving philosophical tool to be reshaped according to the task at hand. In James's words, it "has no dogmas and no doctrines save its method," and that method is "only an attitude of orientation." As Stuhr writes, American pragmatism "has a living, as well as historical, importance. Today it speaks directly, imaginatively, critically, and wisely, to our contemporary global society, its massive and pressing problems, and its distant possibilities for real improvement." Seen, then, in the context of her breadth of intellectual awareness, the references and allusions to, say, Pascal, Schopenhauer, Emerson, Nietzsche, James, or Dewey in Oates's work signal a meandering but traceable path of intellectual thought. But it is also true that Oates is no more likely to be wholly formulaic or consistent in her ideas than were Nietzsche or James, so such figures are, from another perspective, merely indicative of her general approach. She will use whatever tools—whatever "beliefs and knowledge"—suit, in Mary Kathryn Grant's words, "her awesome sense of the responsibility of the writer who, by raising the consciousness of the age, creates history and the future."[5] Rather than being merely influenced by such figures, Oates's open approach makes a certain family resemblance inevitable.

Not just in her subject matter but also in her determination to experiment with old and new forms and to embrace all kinds of possibilities, Oates is the most American of writers, and classical American philosophy, as Stuhr points out, "is classically American." It is the self-aware articulation "of attitudes, outlooks, and forms of life embedded in the culture from and in which it arose." Like other pragmatists, Oates's writing tends to be "revisionist."[6] Her work stresses fallibility, especially the fallibility of dogma: uncertainty rather than certainty. It emphasizes the extent to which individual selves are created by and in the social realm. But it also celebrates pluralism and individuality over classification and system. And while Oates is still occasionally depicted as a writer of bleak, violent novels that stem from a "nightmare vision" of modern America, she could never be accurately called a pessimistic writer.[7] Certainly the influences of the likes of Pascal and Schopenhauer complicate her American optimism. From the beginning, Schopenhauer in particular looms large. The endless striving that so characterizes Oates's prolific career, as well as many an individual novel, seems infused with the logic of *The World as Will and Idea*. "Trust your emotion," writes Emerson with ebullient hope, whereas for Oates in some moods "the storm of emotion constitutes our human tragedy."[8] But in common with other pragmatists, her overall vision is melioristic, stressing the importance of individual behavior as the only way to facilitate improvements in collective behavior. "'Madness in individuals is rare; in nations, the norm,'" she replied when asked if she believed that humankind might make an evolutionary leap in terms of behavior. In contemporary times, "violence in the Mideast, in Bosnia, in Africa, and, perennially, in Northern Ireland, suggests the profound, bleak truth of this remark of Nietzsche's. 'Evolution' seems a possibility for individuals rather than groups. Writers address individuals, and we posit our hope in them." A writer concerned with community, she nevertheless knows that communal health depends upon individual adaptability. In James's words, "[t]he melioristic universe is conceived after a *social* analogy, as a pluralism of independent powers. It will succeed just in proportion as more of these work for its success."[9]

In keeping with her melioristic vision, Oates is an aesthetic risk taker. While writing *Blonde*, she described it as "an experimental novel." But, since she believes that only through risk taking can consciousness evolve, almost all her work in all genres is experimental. This openness to radical experimentation has led to some artistic failures. She is willing to balance on the edge of impossibility, to take chances, and so expose her work to opportunities for ridicule. If James can be described as "a process philosopher," Oates is the consummate process writer, following James in "assessing the journey, the flow," to be all important, even if concentration on the flow means that some of the results are less impressive—less stimulating—than others.[10] After all, the product itself only "lives" while being read or discussed or thought about, and thereby continuing to be a journey, an evolving of consciousness, for its reader. If skeptical critics have been known to shake their heads at the uneven quality of Oates's output, for sympathetic critics the temptation is to overpraise her artistic failures. An experimentalist aesthetic strews debris as well as marvels. And while the wake of that process may have produced *Expensive People*, *The Assassins*, and *Angel of Light*, those examples of apparent detritus have surfaced alongside *Bellefleur* and *You Must Remember This*; *Black Water* and *What I Lived For*; *We Were the Mulvaneys* and *Middle-Age: A Romance*. Of course, readers will dispute which novels are flotsam and which are treasures; Oates's experiments, as well as the diversity of her subject matter, attract and repel diverse groups of readers like shoals of fish darting around a meandering whale. But even those novels that seem (to some of us) demonstrably inferior as art can remain interesting—even of value—in terms of their role in the "evolving of consciousness" that constitutes her, and in the end the reader's, artistic journey. Experimentation is inherently pragmatic, and vice versa. If we hang back, we may never know our capabilities or the extent to which our sense of the parameters of the possible is dictated by the restrictive assumptions of convention or supposed authority. (And what seems flotsam to one reader at one time may be of value to other readers—or indeed to that same reader—at other times.)

The stream of Oatesian novels is also the *reader's* artistic journey, in the sense that pragmatists—adapting the strain of aestheticism traceable from Nietzsche—understand us all to be artists, actively involved in the creation of our own lives and identities. We are all, as David Bromwich puts it, "Novelists of Every Day Life." Like James, Rorty, and others, Oates is a pragmatic idealist with a self-reliant, and self-creating, approach to existence. She consequently constructs her characters, and sees her readers, in the same light. In John McDermott's words on James, such intellects admit to "the existence of the world in its sheer physicality," but at the same time affirm "the source of meaning for that world to be dependent on the creative imagination of the human mind." Again and again, Oates's writing expresses this belief that the poetic imagination pervades all areas of human endeavor, shapes our behavior, and allows us to revise, as daringly as we wish, the meanings by which we live. "I am not afraid to take risks," says Marvin Howe in *Do with Me What You Will*.

> I've taken many risks in the past, following my instincts, my dreams. Why not? I don't fear making mistakes. Being laughed at. Being ridiculed. I want to stretch the boundaries a little, push the world out into another dimension, distort it, change it; I'm like anyone who takes chances and isn't afraid: let's say like great conquerors, religious leaders, madmen. They told the great explorers of the oceans their ships would sail off the edge of the world—and the explorers replied, Why stay home because of that? Why not sail off the edge of the world?

For all her differences from such a monomaniacal character, Oates's words beyond the novels can sound remarkably similar. "If subject matter is difficult for me," she has said, "I would be drawn to it as a challenge." Indeed, she seeks as difficult a task as she can "undertake without courting absolute failure." Things that are easy for her, she describes as "not much tempting."[11] The risks of failure, therefore, are endemic to her experimental aesthetic. What matter are not authoritative discourses, but innovation, creativity, and the possibilities of new forms of language and so new perspectives. And failure or "meaninglessness," to repeat Rorty's terminology, is exactly what you must flirt with if you "are in between social, and particularly linguistic, practices."

Since I admire this pragmatic approach, and since reading Oates has led me back and forth between her work and that of these various other writers, inevitably the perspective articulated in *Dark Eyes on America* has itself evolved in broadly pragmatist terms. For instance, on the odd occasion that I analyze a given novel experimentally it is because I hope to reveal some aspect of it beyond the language of a more conventional assessment. My use of biographical information is similarly pragmatic. To borrow Oates's definition of her links with Marya Knauer in *Marya: A Life,* part of my aim is to trace some "inner kernel" of emotional and intellectual discovery taking place from novel to novel, so inevitably the recorded events of Oates's intellectual/emotional life sometimes seem relevant. Like Brenda Daly, and Oates herself (who follows Jorge Luis Borges in saying this in her brief essay "JCO and I"), I recognize that the "Joyce Carol Oates" of the texts has only a tangential relationship with the actual person who wrote the words. Books, as Mikhail Bakhtin puts it, are no more than the "sclerotic deposits of an intentional process."[12] But in common with previous studies, the novelist's life shimmers in the language of the work here, not exactly fictionalized but textualized, *recreated*—as all information is when viewed from the logic of Nietzschean aestheticism—into a pattern that facilitates discussion of the novels' social, cultural, and historical contexts. While taking it as given that writing creates its own reality, I follow the pragmatists rather than Nietzsche in believing that utility creates its own kind of truth. We all know that language, like any other form of selectivity, distorts, but if it usefully addresses the task at hand, then that is one of a number of forms of verification.

"The natural drama of the earth is Time," reflects "Anellia," the self-christened and otherwise unnamed narrator of Oates's second novel of 2002, *I'll Take You There*. As well as the practical wisdom careful readings of the best of her novels can reveal, this book tracks her novels through the years as, indeed, an intellectual drama, tracing the changes in the kinds of knowledge Oates chose to pursue as her insights evolved. If this, too, posits some kind of authorial presence, however symbolic, from a pragmatic perspective, such a "presence" is simultaneously an illusion and a practical necessity, not least in the case of a writer who approaches her art with an aesthetic of such intense emotional immersion. Indeed, Oates's attempts to distance herself from "JCO" seem necessary only because she is the kind of writer who feeds so much of her own emotional experience through the thresher of her art. She assumes it to be self-evident that the artist plunders her own life and massages personal facts into literary form. "It remains a surprising (and disturbing) fact to many literary observers that writers should, upon occasion, write so directly from life, that they should 'cannibalize' and even 'vampirize' their own experiences," she says in *(Woman) Writer*. But she sees this as inevitable because "the artist is driven by passion; and passion most powerfully derives from our own experiences and memories." She identifies with writers like Yeats and Lawrence, whose work is witness to "an immense emotional reality," so that Yeats's poetry "*is* Yeats," as she put it to the *Ohio Review*, or at least a "part of his life story." With a writer like Oates, to ignore the personality projected by the novels would therefore be odd indeed since the mystery of personality is a fascination that has remained fundamental to her writing even as other concerns have evolved. Indeed, she sees subjectivity—the fact that we "know the world only through the prism of self" yet know that our consciousness is as inaccessible to others as theirs is to us—as "the most profound mystery of our human experience."[13] Here as elsewhere, my rule of thumb is to use whatever evidence proves useful to the practical task of drawing meaning from the work.

Oates's assertion of authorial "personality" yet denial of an authorial "self" feeds this book's basic argument. To oversimplify: Oates's novels contain competing impulses that have shaped not only individual novels but also the trajectory of her writing career. Most evident and significant in the earlier novels is the struggle between an inward-looking urge that involves intense self-scrutiny and an outward-looking urge to be a social chronicler and to deny the significance of that very self so often under such intense examination. Her novels have always developed out of the Emersonian supposition that "the inmost in due time becomes the outmost."[14] Looking inward, she has sought to project her own perspective outward. This has meant that individual identity has always been a preoccupation, even when its significance or even existence has been denied. But, while this tension in Oates's aesthetic may be detrimental to some of the earlier novels, her eventual working through of the emotional and philosophical issues connected with personality freed her to use those insights to pinpoint the characteristic ills and virtues of American culture. Moving away from intense if disguised introspection, and an abstract and finally self-defeating contemplation of consciousness, her later novels are marked by an acceptance of the limitations of metaphysical and neurological inquiry, and a more pragmatic approach to life's problems and possibilities. From the start, all Oates's novels give voice to different kinds of Americans in diverse contexts. But her later work renders the sociohistorical subject matter with greater focus and effectiveness. Moreover, the later novels' stances on the relationship between the personal and the public subject matter employ a greater ironic distance from the characters' struggles. The "artist's conviction that he or she is born damned"—as she expresses it in *(Woman) Writer*—seems to be a major driving force of the introspective aspects of her first phase, up to and including *Son of the Morning*. But even in novels like *The Assassins* and *Childwold*, a psychological freeing-up from the abstract metaphysical entanglements of earlier work heralds what will become the very different—often more playful, usually more convincing—tone of her novels of maturity. The evolution of the writer's own consciousness ceases to be such an issue because Oates's novels have worked through the various complexities connected to the mystery of selfhood. In doing so, they abandon the traditional philosophical quest for definitive answers in favor of an acceptance of contingency and a determination to create art of practical use. "Is there any mystery," muses Felix Stevick, in Oates's 1987 novel *You Must Remember This*, "like who you finally turn out to *be*."[15] In a sense, *that* mystery is over for Oates by the late 1980s, because she has *become*. Further attempts to fathom, as opposed to examine and illustrate, the mystery of personality are shelved because of the self-defeating nature of teleological pursuit. As a result, these later novels have a very different feel, and a different *kind* of value—one in which her pragmatic critique of American culture in all its multifarious complexity holds unambiguous dominance over any further pursuit of selfhood.

This is not to claim that Oates is ever anything less than a social commentator and self-contemplator. Rather, the self-contemplator becomes less evident, and the doomed pursuit of certain kinds of questions less important. For instance, in philosophical terms, much of Oates's early work seems to epitomize precisely "the neurotic Cartesian quest for certainty" (in Rorty's phrase) that the pragmatists sought to relieve us of, even as in other ways it shows a burgeoning pragmatism. Not entirely sure of the intellectual territory she would come to inhabit, Oates was nevertheless already putting into place aspects of her mature position. By the time *Son of the Morning* appeared, she had decided which avenues of inquiry into the enigma of the self were worth pursuing further. Her views on Emily Dickinson and Walt Whitman, like so much of what she writes, say a lot about her own work. They "have come to represent the extreme, idiosyncratic poles of the American psyche," she remarks, "the intensely inward, private, elliptical and 'mystical' (Dickinson); and the robustly outward-looking, public, rhapsodic and 'mystical' (Whitman)." This is perhaps the best characterization of Oates's writing. It flickers between an inward-looking, private vision, and an outward-looking, dispassionate exploration of American society, both of which are driven by a sense of the mystical. She sees herself as "an artist in the service of an ineffable vision, before which the mere 'self' seems inconsequential." But the evidence of the work suggests that self-negation was not so much an inborn conviction as a verdict arrived at by way of her early work. While the struggle between what she calls "delirium and detachment" has been a major energy source galvanizing her career, the ironic detachment provided by ever-broader experience and perspective has resulted in an art of far greater assurance.[16]

Another way of stating this dichotomy in her art, and the way her novels have become more sophisticated in latter decades, is to apply Rorty's description of two very different creative impulses. Rorty divides writers into those who are exemplars of "private perfection" (including figures Oates has written on, such as Nietzsche and Nabokov) and others (like Marx, Mill, Dewey, and Habermas) who are "fellow citizens rather than exemplars," "engaged in a shared social effort." For Rorty, these two kinds of writing, one "necessarily private, unshared, unsuited to argument," the other "necessarily public and shared, a medium for argumentative exchange," are "equally valid yet forever incommensurable." There is, he thinks, no answer to the question of how you decide "when to struggle against injustice and when to devote yourself to private projects of self-creation."[17] Yet such words could as well be used to describe the net effect of Oates's writing. Her early novels in particular seem simultaneously strengthened and compromised by just such a conflict, as if two different writers were competing for the same novel-space. The "exemplar" competes with the "fellow citizen," as if for the young novelist's artistic soul, as she pursues her intellectual and emotional attempts to discover a working sense of the relationship between the inner artistic drive and its outer manifestations. These early novels often read as if they are not quite about their purported subject matter but almost abstract experiments designed to discover the forms and subjects that she will address with such conviction and clarity in the novels of her artistic maturity.

As with her depiction of the artistic enterprise as a dual process of "delirium and detachment," Oates has often expressed herself, in both her art and her commentary, in split terms, and makes numerous references to twins and doubles. There are the many doubles she employs, from Trick Monk in *Wonderland* to Teague or Tyde in *What I Lived For,* and even (as I will argue) the merging of Marilyn Monroe and Princess Diana in *Blonde,* a working title for which was *Gemini.* There are such literal twins as the strange Damm and Vann, of whom Jack Wells dreams in "The Brothers"—one of Oates's extraordinary stories from the 1996 volume *Will You Always Love Me?*—as well as symbolic twins like Ian McCullough's successive wives, Glynnis and Sigrid, in *American Appetites.* There have been—until her adoption of a second pseudonym, Lauren Kelly, for *Take Me, Take Me with You* (2004)—the two names she has used in writing novels: not only Joyce Carol Oates, but Rosamond Smith, under which semi-pseudonym (her married name being Smith) she has written, among others, *Lives of the Twins, Soul/Mate,* and *Double Delight.* (Indeed, all her Rosamond Smith novels explore the kinship of twins and alternative selves.) There are her roles, discussed in depth by Eileen Teper Bender, as both a university professor and a writer. In Oates's words, "my exterior life, as it might be called, is an exact balance to my sometimes rapacious interior life; as the height of a tree is said to be balanced by its root system beneath the ground. Otherwise the tree would be blown over, or wither away and die."[18]

If in later years Oates has become more relaxed about this split nature, her early novels present this tussle between introspection and social commentary in raw, sometimes messy, form. Novels that are undoubtedly intended to be about various American scenarios at times lapse into abstract musing about the relationship between the self and the world, the process of novel writing, and the trails the novelist might blaze out of the traditions of the form. While this inward examination helps energize the novels, it perhaps in turn accounts for their less-obvious social value compared with some later work. Also, it may shed light on how and why Oates's novel writing came to change direction and emphasis before returning, in artistic maturity, to similar subject matter through defter approaches.

Rorty's dichotomy has, indeed, a further use. If it is true that Oates's writing expresses itself in both these "incommensurable" modes, this may help explain diverse readings of her work, but also lead us some way toward understanding its social and aesthetic value. "The notion that the world is a work of art," argues Megill, echoing Rorty, "can and does lead in two radically different directions. On the one hand it leads in the direction of passive contemplation." If we see the world as a work of art in a narrow sense—or indeed our own career as an "artist" as socially divorced or as a form of escape—we might be tempted to view it as we do other such "precious" works. But, says Megill, "aestheticist ontology" can also lead us in "an activist direction," where "not contemplation but radical creativity comes to be stressed."[19] In other words, Oates can be seen to have always had much the same recognition of the irreducible significance of the poetic imagination. But she quickly broadened her definition of artistic activity from the Schopenhauerean notion of art as escape, via the Nietzschean notion of art as all-pervasive, into the pragmatic belief that, precisely because we are all "artists," we are able to recreate ourselves and help recreate our society. Suitably, given that pragmatism so often stresses such adaptability, the latter part of Oates's career has amounted to a process not only of intellectual advancement but also of revision. If there is a resemblance between her early realist novels and her later ones, any formal or thematic similarities are best understood as acts of renegotiation, rather than repetition. They are separated by an evolution of consciousness most immediately manifested in her period of extraordinary experimentation, dominated by the unique *Bellefleur*.

To reflect this split in Oates's novel-writing career, this book divides into five chapters, the first two covering the earlier part of her career, chapters 4 and 5 the latter part, and the middle chapter, chapter 3, covering that period of radical experimentation. All five chapters trace the "evolving consciousness" evident through the four decades of Oates's artistic productivity from the 1960s into the present. But while some sense of gradual evolution is traceable through the four decades, the novels published between 1964 and 1978 and then 1985 onward belong to comparatively different sensibilities, and the middle period is where that process of change is most apparent. No single moment constitutes a sharp break, but through much of the 1980s Oates's work stresses transition. Oates herself signals that transition in the near-synonymous titles of the two cusp novels, *Winterthurn* and *Solstice*. These novels appeared in the mid-1980s, in the wake of the *Bellefleur* period and prior to *Marya: A Life,* in which Marya's reunion with her mother promises to split her life in two. But signs of a shift are traceable much earlier, just as early ideas can still be found much later. If Oates is indeed keenly aware of her culture's "seismic shudders," the novels, together with biographical details that I touch on in chapter 1, suggest that she experienced seismic shudders in her own consciousness as early as the 1970s, culminating in the relative earthquake of *Bellefleur*.[20] Meanwhile, the aftershocks this change generated never allowed her novels to settle back into quite their original terrain. So while I recognize that such divisions schematize the more contingent and chaotic actuality of the stream of novels, and that other arrangements would be equally justified, they seem the best way to open up further debate.

Another element of the book is my attempt to show, in very general terms, how Oates's work in other genres reflects this change. From the start of her career, Oates has produced poetry, stories, and essays. Since 1967, but most notably in the 1990s, she has also published plays. While *Dark Eyes on America* is primarily a study of her novels, awareness of how her work in other genres has developed aids our understanding of the evolving consciousness evident in those novels. There have been several studies of her stories, notably by Greg Johnson, Katherine Bastian, P. Sreelakshmi, and Monica Loeb—indeed, in the wider critical community, regard for her short stories often surpasses regard for her novels—but far less has been written about her essays, poetry, or plays. For this reason, while I tend to confine myself to references to collections and brief analyses of certain stories in relation to the novels, small pockets of the study broaden the discussion to include her work in these other genres. To read Oates's mature poetry and her plays of the 1990s can be an astonishing experience. Overall, the poetry traces much the same path as the novels, from predominantly private, introspective writing to predominantly social, multivoiced writing, but the gulf between the tone and subject matter of her early and later poetry is greater, if anything, than that between her early and later novels. The claustrophobic obsessions of her first collection, *Anonymous Sins and Other Poems,* stand in stark contrast to the vigor, variety, inventiveness, and humor of such later volumes as *Time Traveler* and *Tenderness.* Early efforts such as *Ontological Proof of My Existence* and *Miracle Play* notwithstanding, Oates came to extensive playwriting when she had already found her multivoiced maturity. But it remains true that the works collected in *Twelve Plays, The Perfectionist and Other Plays,* and *New Plays,* most of which appeared in the 1990s, aptly illustrate the engaged social commentary that best characterizes her later novels.

Equally significant, in terms of understanding the pragmatist's emphasis on fluidity that informs many of the novels, is an awareness that, very often, what she designates as a story can look much like a poem, and what she calls a play can be read as a poem or story. Often, too, Oates has written a piece both as prose fiction and a play (such as *The Triumph of the Spider Monkey, Imperial Presidency*—part of the collage-play *American Holiday*—and *Black Water*) or as a play and a poem (as with "A Report to the Academy"). Moreover, her revisions of stories by Joyce, Chekhov, and others, as Sreelakshmi notes, can equally be seen as "textual critiques": examples of art as criticism or criticism as "an art form."[21] Indeed, some of her most experimental work can be found, throughout her career, in these cross-genre excursions that defy simple categorization as defiantly as does her oeuvre. Where appropriate, therefore, I comment on the nature of her achievements and developments in these other genres as the study of the novels unfolds.

Chapters 1 and 2 look at the first phase of Oates's novel-writing career up to her 1978 novel *Son of the Morning.* Beginning with discussion of Oates's 1974 essay collection, *New Heaven, New Earth,* and her 1969 poetry collection, *Anonymous Sins,* chapter 1 looks at the early novels from *With Shuddering Fall* to *Wonderland.* These often claustrophobic and—for all their social and historical subject matter—strangely abstract novels seem now to be both of their time yet in some ways curiously detached from the recognizable landscapes of America in the 1960s and 1970s. The characters and their experiences suggest varying degrees of self-absorption that echo Oates's reference to the artist's conviction of being born damned and redeemed only through art. Compared with later work, there is less sign of playfulness, aside from that in *Expensive People*. But even that novel's "playful" metafictional aspects seem more a reflection of what Brenda Daly calls "anxious authorship" than a relaxed carnivalization of the novel form.[22] Oates's early work reads like a prelude to and then a reaction to a crisis that peaks in the time after the publication of her exploration of consciousness, *Wonderland*. One novel in particular, however, the National Book Award–winning *them*, clearly involves a dialogue between old and new approaches as Oates seeks to find appropriate formal innovations for her subject matter, and so shows her working toward what will become her pragmatic perspective. For instance, her interest in the "art" of identity clearly echoes James, even if that aestheticist ontology seems in the early novels to lean rather more toward abstract contemplation than social action.

Chapter 2 examines Oates's later novels of the 1970s in terms of her burgeoning pragmatism. Taking "A Theory of Knowledge," from *Night-Side*, her 1977 story collection, as its cue, the chapter shows how *Do with Me What You Will*, *The Assassins*, *Childwold*, and *Son of the Morning* all marked new directions in Oates's art and in her developing sense of her role in the community. In particular, these novels experiment with first- and third-person narrative and, in doing so, question conventional approaches to point of view. As with some later work, they focus on illusory battles between the self and the world that are really internal battles on the part of characters who have created or inherited idioms, and so perspectives, that are self-defeating. Oates's novels of this period show her working through a necessary, but ultimately limited and limiting, phase toward something new and more liberating, both for the novelist and for her readers.

Chapter 3 describes the interlude between the early and later parts of her career. Starting with a brief discussion of Oates's essays of the time, and poetry up to and including *Invisible Woman*, it looks at the novels that confirmed a transition away from her early claustrophobic tendencies toward the assured originality of her later work. The pivotal period includes *Bellefleur*, *A Bloodsmoor Romance*, and *Mysteries of Winterthurn*, ending with *Solstice*. *Bellefleur*, which had been gestating through the 1970s, brought artistic release from the self-contemplative issues so evident in earlier work. As several critics note, the *Bellefleur* phase also reveals a new consciousness of gender that helps us to align Oates with other feminist revisionists and that renders redundant earlier criticisms of her work as antithetical to feminism. I use Charlene Haddock Seigfried's analysis of the links between feminism and pragmatism to help show how Oates's pragmatism merges with her feminism as she adapts the ideas of William James and others to serve, in Wesley's phrase, "her own revolutionary intention."[23] Rather than include the 1981 novel *Angel of Light* in this discussion, I comment on *My Heart Laid Bare*. Even though it was not published until 1998, it was conceived, along with the unpublished *The Crosswicks Horror*, as a companion to the *Bellefleur*-style works. *Angel of Light*, in contrast, which other critics have commented on in detail, seems to me not only less successful than many of Oates's other novels but something of an anomaly in this period and to the evolving of consciousness that I trace.

Chapters 4 and 5 look at Oates's mature work in terms of the significance and consequences of this change of approach and perspective—a change apparent not only in her novels but, more generally, in her much-neglected yet highly inventive plays and in her mature poetry and essays. From the late 1980s into the early years of the new century, Oates has returned to realism and reexamined her own background. These novels of her artistic maturity, even while practicing the conventions of realism, both revise and renew them, presenting characters who likewise tend to reassess and renegotiate their life-purpose. Chapter 4 begins with a discussion of two of Oates's four play collections of the 1990s, *Twelve Plays* and *The Perfectionist and Other Plays*, to illustrate how her expanding interest in theater at that time reflected the development of her mature vision. It then assesses *Marya: A Life, You Must Remember This, American Appetites*, and *Because It Is Bitter, and Because It Is My Heart* as novels that dramatize the paradoxical fact that the pursuit of desires is also a kind of death wish. Where, in early novels, characters ran to escape their backgrounds and situations, in these later novels they chase goals that, on another level, and often on reflection, they realize they would rather not achieve. All four novels, in different ways, investigate various forms of individual and cultural ambition and the bittersweet complexities of the successes and failures that result.

Finally, chapter 5 groups together Oates's major novels since 1992. *Black Water, Foxfire, What I Lived For*, and *We Were the Mulvaneys* are as much about maturity as they are in themselves mature works that intervene on a wide range of issues pertinent to contemporary American society. *Broke Heart Blues, Blonde*, and *Middle Age: A Romance* bring us into the twenty-first century with Oates's pragmatism in full bloom, dealing in particular with the role of myth and nostalgia in American life and in Western culture more generally. Where the first focuses on the school reunions of a group of classmates and their mythologizing of one classmate in particular, and the third, too, deals with the mythologizing of one member of a small community, *Blonde* explores the phenomenon of worldwide fame and, especially, of the blonde icon. Written in the wake of the death of Diana, Princess of Wales, about whom Oates wrote an essay for *Time*, it also serves as an incisive commentary on the cult of celebrity in contemporary global culture. But where *Broke Heart Blues* and *Blonde* offer the pitfalls of contemporary icon worship, *Middle Age* takes us all the way back to Socrates—regarded by James as the quintessential pragmatist—to provide an altogether more uplifting and enabling prescription for remedying twenty-first-century ills. As such, it epitomizes Oates as a pragmatic novelist who depicts the social and moral strifes of our age. The book then ends with a broader discussion of Oates's work as a whole within the context of contemporary American writing and culture.[24]

In the spirit of pragmatism, my reading of Oates's novels assumes that all arguments—to the extent that they claim coherence—fabricate, and that consistency is not always the same as accuracy. I have tried to avoid assertions of certainty, but, in any case, to push forward. "If you're certain, you're certainly wrong," said Bertrand Russell, despite his dismissive attitude toward Jamesian pragmatism, yet "one ought to be able to act vigorously in spite of that doubt." No contemporary writer does this more than Oates. She drives forward whatever her doubts or others' opinions, unworried as to whether, in William Heyen's words, "all criticisms that could be lodged against a piece are answered within it." Seeing consistency as a form of artifice, she celebrates uncertainty, contradiction, unpredictability, and above all movement. "For what is life, its myriad surprises," muses Anellia in *I'll Take You There*, "except *what's to come*?" Our Apollonian urge to construct illusory forms of coherence may be unstoppable, but life itself exists in the creating, not merely the product; in the living, not the having lived. "When we are awake we also do what we do in our dreams," writes Nietzsche. "We invent and make up the person with whom we associate—and immediately forget it."

The livingness of human relations, in this context, includes those between writers and writing, readers and readings, and, as many of Oates's characters learn, individuals and themselves. But while I acknowledge Oates's sense of all human activity as consistent only as flux, flow, motion, I recognize that to have "no false chronology, no lying emphasis upon one fact at the price of excluding others" (as Kasch demands in *Childwold*) would be self-defeating, if not impossible. Just as, in Oates's words, "the artist imposes his vision upon his material" and "necessarily distorts it because he cannot include everything," so must the critic. Faithful as this book is to its sources—including Oates's archives at Syracuse University, correspondence, and conversations with Oates in Princeton in 1998 and in Lincoln, Nebraska, in 2001—it aims to reveal aspects of the novelist's vision in a coherent, convincing, but above all useful way. It therefore makes a "story" out of Oates's novels, but one written in a spirit of provisionality and intended to help mediate Oates's own pragmatic vision of American society. All creeds, theories, and formal precepts, wrote another pragmatist, George Santayana, "sink in the estimation of the pragmatist to a local and temporary grammar of action." "To know things as a whole," he said, "is not only beyond our powers, but would prove worthless, and perhaps even fatal to our lives. Ideas are not mirrors, they are weapons." Following Santayana part way, I conceive of *Dark Eyes on America* neither as a mirror nor as a weapon, but more as a means of discovery. If it allows other readers to make better use of what they find in Oates's novels and to revise and remake them in their own images and to the benefit of their own and others' lives, then it will have done its job.[25]

> The artist must be a therapist to the race, and not simply to himself.
> —JOYCE CAROL OATES, *New Heaven, New Earth*

1   MIRRORS AND WINDOWS

MANY CRITICS OF Oates's early novels read them primarily as social chronicles. Harold Bloom, for instance, is moved by Oates's "immense empathy with the insulted and injured, her deep identification with the American lower classes," and sees her as a "true proletarian novelist." Linda Wagner sees her as a "perceptive social observer." Mary Kathryn Grant argues that the thrust of Oates's work is "to force her readers to examine in detail their own lives."[1] Overall, Oates's novel-writing career confirms such observations, and the early novels are clearly meant as social commentaries. *With Shuddering Fall* (1964), *A Garden of Earthly Delights* (1967), *them* (1969), *Wonderland* (1971), and, if less so, *Expensive People* (1968) begin very much as social realism. Yet there is also something dreamlike about not only the characters but also the American settings through which they move.

"Oates's America is an experience, not a place," noted Gary Waller in the late 1970s. "Typically, automobiles and highways dissolve into the evocation of an interior landscape, while the speaker's state of mind, thrust at the reader through the breathless ejaculations of the sentence, becomes the primary focus of our attention." In Oates, echoes Samuel Coale in the mid-1980s, "the outside world, however created with a Dreiserian thirst for details, remains vague, curiously distant, remote," and sometimes "entirely evaporates." Donald Dike, Oates's former professor to whom she dedicated *With Shuddering Fall*, observed in a 1974 essay that the movements of Oates's early figures seem strangely similar and unfocused, regardless of their ostensible social contexts. For Dike, her major characters are typically "running away or wanting to run away," but with little emphasis, on Oates's part, as to what exactly they are running toward. This, he says, explains "the striking effect of blind, haphazard, undirected motion" in these early novels, "and of the evidently meaningless course such motion describes." Dike also notes that this motion occurs through a landscape that, however "recognizably referential," "persists in being strange, alien, sometimes inhuman."[2] Waller's, Coale's, and Dike's insights seem as accurate as any depiction of these early novels as social chronicles. Social commentary here invariably competes with a more abstract, introspective discourse about the nature of the self, and ultimately about the purpose of the artistic enterprise. Novels that seem intended to depict various American scenarios slip into abstraction or philosophical speculation some way removed from their ostensible subject matter.

Oates first distances herself from her early preoccupation with issues of self-contemplation and abstract musing in her second essay collection, *New Heaven, New Earth* (1974), published the year after her sixth novel, *Do with Me What You Will*. Perhaps it is significant that many of these essays were written from early 1972 onward, after her "mystical vision" that revealed to her the illusory nature of a unified self: that "the 'I' doesn't exist" but "behaves as if it does, as if it were one and not many."[3] For, as Bloom has noted, her comments on other writers at this stage of her career seem as much to "intimate her own convictions" as to illuminate the writers in question. "To some artists there falls the difficult task," Oates writes in *New Heaven, New Earth*, "of standing between two worlds—one the visible, material, 'real' world, the other a world no less real, but not physically demonstrable." "By this attempt to synthesize both worlds," she argues, "or to explain poetically why the two worlds (the 'physical' and the 'spiritual') are not two at all, but one," the artist "may create an art that is very disturbing, because it is foreign to ordinary experience."[4]

In fact Oates's own art would become increasingly "disturbing" in the years after this, only returning to deal with "ordinary experience" from 1985 onward, when she followed *The Mysteries of Winterthurn* with *Solstice*. If that publication was to prove the re-turning point, *New Heaven, New Earth* coincided with the original turning point that would lead her art away from its earliest manifestations. Unlike her first essay collection, *The Edge of Impossibility*, extensive sections of *New Heaven, New Earth* discuss the limits of introspective writing. The general assumptions in the essays of *The Edge of Impossibility*, all written in the 1960s, suggest the very opposite of social engagement. "Art is built around violence, around death," writes Oates; "at its base is fear." Art, she says, alluding to Schopenhauer, "is a transcendence of time, but it is also a suicidal gesture." The artist, that "most intense of human beings," is by definition "asocial." "He has no clear relationship with society."[5]

In contrast, the Oates of *New Heaven, New Earth* seems to have been redefining herself, by implication, as an artist who does have, or wants, a "clear relationship with society." For instance, she distances her own emerging agenda from that of Henry James and Virginia Woolf, whose novels she sees as "characterized by an extraordinary blocking out of vast areas of life and a minute, vivid, at times near hallucinatory obsession with psychic experience" (24). Such writers "represent the furthest limits of the traditional English novel," in terms of "their preoccupation with interior details" (34). She distances herself, too—despite the obvious influence of both poets on her own poetry—from Sylvia Plath and the later Wallace Stevens, as lyric poets given to solipsistic tendencies that, in her view, it might be wiser to fight against. Plath, she writes, "did not 'like' other people because she did not essentially believe that they existed" (118). "The mirror and never the window," she argues, "is the stimulus for this art" (127). Instead, she aligns herself with Yeats and Lawrence, whom she sees as synthesizing the two worlds. In Lawrence, "inner and outer reality are confused, rush together, making up a pattern of harmony and discord, which is Lawrence's basic vision of the universe and the controlling aesthetics behind his poetry" (51). For the Oates of *New Heaven, New Earth*, such writers provide a way forward, whereas James, Woolf, Plath, and Stevens offer her roads inward that she prefers not to pursue farther. "After James and Woolf," she writes, "after the experiment of the mind's dissection of itself, and its dissociation from the body, perhaps we are ready to rediscover the world" (45).

The young author's misrepresentation of writers who clearly influence her may be deeply uncharacteristic of the mature author, but it is all the more fascinating for that. *New Heaven, New Earth* reads now very much like a stocktaking of how Oates's consciousness had evolved up to that point, and a blueprint for change. Her essay on Plath, "The Death Throes of Romanticism," seems especially pertinent less for its assessment of Plath than for what it suggests of Oates's own early writing. Waller describes Oates's early aesthetic as "so clearly a neo-romantic celebration and evocation of flux and the human potential of unpredictability that it is intriguing to discover the mixture of hostility and homage she has towards Sylvia Plath, perhaps the supreme embodiment of the self-obsessive confessionalism of mid-twentieth century romanticism."[6] Oates's comments on Plath do indeed suggest that the need to break free of self-destructive solipsism struck a chord with the young writer. In the essay, she distinguishes (despite always having been both) between the lyric poet and the novelist. "Most lyric poets," she says, "explore themselves endlessly," determined to discover the "problem of their personalities" when perhaps their only problem is "this insane preoccupation with the self and its moods and doubts, while much of the human universe simply struggles for survival." "If the lyric poet believes—as most people do—that the 'I' he inhabits is not integrated with the entire stream of life, let alone with other human beings, he is doomed to a solipsistic and ironic and self-pitying art."

Unlike "the small enclosed form of the typical lyric poem," Oates argues, the novel form is much better suited to investigating "the foreign/intimate nature of other people." When "not addressed to the same self-analysis as the lyric poem, it demands that one look out the window and not into the mirror; it demands an active involvement with time, place, personality, pasts and futures." The novelist's obligation, therefore, "is to do no less than attempt the sanctification of the world—while the lyric poet, if he is stuck in a limited emotional cul-de-sac, will circle endlessly inside the bell jar of his own world, and only by tremendous strength is he able to break free." The implications of her essay, she goes on to say, "are not that a highly self-conscious art is inferior by nature to a more socially committed art" (132–33); it is that a highly self-conscious art is a risk to the poet's own survival. Plath's poetry, for instance, most convinces when it is "most troubled, most murderous, most unfair," because it stirs in us "memories of our own infantile pasts," rather than provoking us "into a contemplation of the difficult and less dramatic future of our adulthood" (133–34). "So unquestioningly is the division between selves accepted, and so relentlessly the pursuit of the solitary, isolated self," argues Oates of this form of poetry, "that stasis and ultimate silence seem inevitable." It is "a risk because it rarely seems to open into a future: the time of lyric poetry is usually the present or the past" (135).

There is a striking similarity between what Oates says here and Rorty's ideas about the dichotomy between private perfection and social engagement. But where Rorty is talking as a commentator from outside the creative process, Oates is very clearly writing as a practitioner, both as novelist and poet. Since she sets up the writing of poetry and novels as somehow reflective of these opposing modes, it is enlightening to look through Oates's first poetry collection, *Anonymous Sins*. In the afterword to *Invisible Woman: New and Selected Poems, 1970–1982*, Oates explains that in aiming to select poems that struck her as recognizably her own, she ended up omitting most of her early poems, including this "entire first book." She was not, she wrote, rejecting them as poems, but because she failed "to recognize [her] own voice in them." She felt "no kinship, no sense of continuity. That aspect of the past" was "finally *past*." It would be inaccurate to claim that social commentary does not exist in any of these poems. "Lines for Those to Whom Tragedy Is Denied," for instance, is about middle-class American housewives living stunted lives while "their husbands account for the success of airlines / And the thick red carpets of certain restaurants." "You are educated, or were," says the poet, but with nothing to do now but wear "the pelts of animals killed for you," fail to control "your children," and be "liberal about Negroes." Indeed, there are a number of such poems about aging wives and empty lives. But there are also several poems that merge introspection with an opacity that suggests personal meanings to which readers can have no access. "A Rising and Sinking and Rising in My Mind," for instance, involves someone glimpsing an underground stream "where the pebbles in mud are turned gently," with patterns on them "unreadable" as snail trails. "Silence bursts heavily in this cold water," we are told, and "a thought rises shrilly in someone's mind: you cannot / change your life, or anything." Other such poems—"An Internal Landscape," "A Girl at the Center of Her Life," "Of the Violence of Self-Death"—continue this introspective vein. The collection ends with "Vanity," a bleak contemplation of the "vanity" of love and the impossibility of true human intimacy that is not deeply colored by personal projection. "Hard as strangulation are the decrees / of the beloved and remote," the poem opens:

>Across this distance songs cry,
>Composed for distance.
>The beloved is a cage
>you cannot enter.

The poet assures us in the final lines:

>If you lie at night with someone
>it is always with someone else.
>The distance between you
>fills slowly with time and snow.
>Years are field grass whining.
>Even in dreams the beloved is
>nimble of foot and vain
>and immortal.[7]

What is indeed most notable about the poems of *Anonymous Sins* is how sharply they differ from Oates's mature poetry in the narrow range of their subject matter and the comparatively unvaried nature of the poetic voice. They are mostly about the enigma of relationships and personal identity, and constantly muse on the self and the self's relationship with others. "How do you get a personality?" we are asked in "And So I Grew Up to Be Nineteen and to Murder," and several of the poems, not least "Three Dances of Death," suggest the randomness of named identity.[8] All this anticipates many of her later novels' depictions of changeable identities in all manner of Americans, but there is little, here, of the daring confidence, the playful wisdom that will later enable Oates to experiment so widely in voice, tone, and subject matter in her mature poetry. My point, however, has less to do with the relative quality of these poems than with why Oates herself felt distanced from them in compiling her 1982 selection. The downbeat tones, together with the introspection—indeed solipsism itself in "Vanity"—call to mind precisely those comments in New Heaven, New Earth about lyric poets' tendency to try to discover the "problem of their personalities" when perhaps their only problem is "this insane preoccupation with the self." Social commentary is certainly one impulse in these poems, but introspective self-analysis is clearly another.

The implications of New Heaven, New Earth with regard to Oates's own early novels, as with her early poetry, then, are that the young writer was realigning her own sense of the artist's relationship with society, and the uses of art. Written so soon after her crisis and revelation about the nature of the self, these ideas provide a way into exploring the difference between the novels prior to that experience and those written and published subsequently. Such an exploration reveals that, for all their variety of subject matter and approach, the early novels invariably contain a great deal of introspective, abstract analysis of the relationship between the self and others and the self and creativity. Novels that are on one level socially committed also provide veiled opportunities for the self-examination that the Oates of New Heaven, New Earth will assert as being more the territory of lyric poetry. "Technique" has perhaps always been for Oates a question of digging and building "the dams, dikes, ditches, and conduits that both restrain emotionally charged content and give it formal, and therefore communal, expression." But these early novels may best be viewed as examples of a young author sifting through modes of expression for folding those personal obsessions into socially useful subject matter. In other words, running from a childhood "partly obscured by pockets of amnesia, as by patches of fog" and toward a future sunlit with fulfilled ambition, Oates seems to have used these early novels to find a balance between those incommensurable impulses of private perfection and social effort.[9]

For all their differences, *With Shuddering Fall* and *A Garden of Earthly Delights* (and my concern here is only with the 1967 original, not Oates's rewrite, published in 2003) are remarkably alike in starting out as novels that seem to be wholly of the world of social realism, yet follow their protagonists on a journey that becomes altogether more abstract and introspective. Both novels contain the seeds of Oates's later work. Karen Herz of *With Shuddering Fall* and Clara Walpole of *A Garden of Earthly Delights* are prototypes for Marya Knauer of *Marya: A Life* in their sense of social alienation and need to escape their backgrounds, and their paternal estrangement is similar to Marianne Mulvaney's in *We Were the Mulvaneys*. On each count, these essential dramas are replayed in as recent a novel as *I'll Take You There*. Both protagonists take up with an older man, a taciturn stranger-on-the-move of the kind often seen in Oates's early stories, who seems to stand for, among other things, brute Schopenhauerean Will. There seems to be nothing to Shar, Karen's lover, a racing driver, except "Shar's will, the deadly whimsical rage of his desire." Lowry, meanwhile, seems to spend his life just driving "aimlessly across the country" as if "in an invisible, insatiable striving."[10] Karen's affair with Shar, like Clara's with Lowry, anticipates Enid and Felix's relationship in *You Must Remember This*. Perhaps less obviously, both these early relationships also prefigure those between Monica and Sheila in *Solstice*, Jinx and Iris in *Because It Is Bitter, and Because It Is My Heart*, and Anellia and Vernor Matheius in *I'll Take You There*. But in contrast to most of those later novels, the meticulous early details of the settings are subsequently overtaken by the dreamlike abstractions of these relationships.

In the end, even while nominally dressed as dramas about representative American citizens in specific contexts, these works come across as much more the author's relationship with her muse. The decision to run off with a mysterious figure reads like a decision to plunge out of social life and into an art that, while masquerading as life, is in fact anything but life: whether we read this to mean a form of transcendence or symbolic suicide. For if the male figure is in both cases a lover, he is also a death figure, and the courtship is more akin to the kind Emily Dickinson evokes in "Because I could not stop for Death" than to one between two human beings. It is as if the young author felt that to opt for art was in some way to renounce life: to take art as a religion, to strive for an "after" life. Art is presented as a lonely, isolated, alienated occupation—"a suicidal gesture," as she calls it in *The Edge of Impossibility*—in striking contrast to her later sense of it as a pragmatic, socially engaged activity. Both novels may show the novelist attempting to look "out the window" and involve her art "with time, place, personality, pasts and futures," but both novels contain, and in some ways give themselves up to, the impulse toward private perfection that keeps the outer world at bay.

With Shuddering Fall is the story of Karen Herz and Shar Rule, mutually obsessive lovers who exhibit notably similar forms of "lyric-poet-like" introspection. While Oates has said that With Shuddering Fall was in ways "very autobiographical," the autobiographical figure seems to be as much Shar as Karen. To look at one is largely the same as looking at the other since both provide what Eileen Bender calls "dramas of the self."[11] For much of the novel, the alienated Karen seems to concur with the judgment of a previous boyfriend that she is as cold as her "family up in the graveyard" and "might as well be dead" (52). Preoccupied with the gap between inner and outer selves, she is the first in a line of mirror gazers, from Clara and Swan in *A Garden of Earthly Delights*, through Jesse in *Wonderland* and Yvonne in *The Assassins* to Iris in *Because It Is Bitter, and Because It Is My Heart*. She is preoccupied, to use that phrase from Oates's Plath essay, with the self's "moods and doubts." As Pamela Smiley suggests, far from looking outward to try to depict "a realistic portrait of American life," *With Shuddering Fall* focuses primarily on Karen's isolation and self-alienation, which seems born of an abnormal degree of "masochistic self-martyrdom" and cannot, therefore, be regarded as socially representative.[12]

Prior to meeting Shar, Karen feels kinship with absolutely no one. Most company bores her. She is "proud of her ability to withdraw from the presence of others" (31). Brought up a Roman Catholic, if she has an emotional focus it is the "secret ecstasy" and "breathless power" of her prayers, which excite her in a way that ordinary relationships cannot (42). Karen has quit school and so "surrendered most of her life outside her home," and is even "jealous of the drain of energy the routines of life" demand (44). When the thirty-year-old Shar visits her home, she is attracted by a coldness she shares. Set apart from the "safe past" as from the "static present," he is like "a creature of another species" (46). The only emotion either shows is toward one another, but the mingling of fiery love with icy hatred makes for a tepid concoction. Only Shar gets Karen's heart thudding, but it is Shar who reveals to her that "hatred charged her, nourished her, prodded her along." She hates "all strangers," along with "the vast, strange world" that she and her family cannot control

(158). "Feverishly isolated," she seems to reserve her most potent hatred, however, for her "mirrored self—a face unrelated to her, to her soul," a mockery of whatever self resides within (161).

Turning from Karen to Shar, there is little to distinguish the desperately bleak worldview they represent. His self-obsession manifests itself in his passion for racing, which he experiences as ego-driven ambition that excludes meaningful, social communion. In Dike's words, "speed and then greater speed, the pedal pushed to the floor, makes the landscape rush past, abstracts the driver from circumstances, in the exhilaration of a private danger gives him momentarily back to his secret self."[13] Shar's fuel, like Karen's, is hatred. In Karen's case the cause of this generalized hatred is linked to her sexual abuse by an older schoolmate, referred to, in a conversation with a teacher, only as "the Revere boy" (88). Shar's no-less-generalized hatred is for the people who watch him race, but he also seems specifically to hate Karen, or perhaps more accurately himself, because his love for her threatens to destroy his self-containment. It is as if their mutual recognition of each other's self-obsession paradoxically glues them together as soul mates of the damned. Shar feels that Karen is "oddly like himself," while his own mask does "little more than mock his feelings" (118). And while she gives herself to him, her infrequent expressions of pleasure are "no more than a part of Shar, of what he created in her" (122). Where Karen seeks escape in him, Shar seeks escape *from* her: the representative of all the emotion that, he supposes, cripples his autonomy. Only on the track does he feel "safe from entanglements with anyone," "free of human bondage, of hatred, of jealousy, of anger, of lust, most of all, of love!" (123).

But all this seems far more figurative than literal. Shar's relationship with his manager, Max, reinforces this sense that Shar is more metaphorical than real, and more an artist than a racing driver. His unwillingness to articulate comes to seem merely an ironic reversal of the writer's gift. On a rare occasion when he speaks at length, he does so to describe what racing means to him. But his description might as well be of the kind of art that seeks private perfection. He tells Max that he took his first car "to the limit," "until the rear hub wanted to come off." Starting young, he has got through a succession of cars with the speed that Oates evidently turned out novel manuscripts even in her days as an undergraduate at Syracuse.[14] Shar's loudest cry, occurring just before a verbal attack on Karen, is also his most drunken, desperate, and defiant:

> I wasn't seventeen when I begun it and I'm still alive now—still alive now, and how many of them are dead! Poor goddam bastards! I force them—force them—Cars or people or myself, all the way out, to the limit, as far as it can go without killing me. I force it! What the hell is it any other way? Are you alive any other way? I know how much the car can take, but not what I can take. I never yet found my limit. (148)

The racing aesthetic sounds very much like the writing aesthetic that pushes the novelist to "the invisible point at which control" turns "into chaos" (261). Max despairs at Shar's monomania. "The whole world is shrunk down to fit him—he carries it around in his head!" he tells Karen. "And this is true for you as well!" (180). Max sees in Karen, then, much the same as he sees in Shar. On one side of the double-headed coin, there is Karen "staring at herself," and whether "murmuring to God, evoking Christ" or muttering love to Shar, "in fact talking only to this reflection" (189). On the other side, there is Shar racing frenziedly around a track. "I've been so many times around a circle," he complains, "I'm sick to death of it" (190).

In the end, the two characters meet opposing fates as if the struggle has not really been between two people but between self-destruction and survival. As in Oates's best-known early story, "Where Are You Going, Where Have You Been?" in her 1970 collection *Wheel of Love*—conceived, in her words, as "an allegory of the fatal attractions of death" for an innocent girl mistaking death "for erotic romance"—the lovers suggest an internal struggle. In that story, a mysterious drifter named Arnold Friend entices a girl called Connie to take a ride in his car to her probable death.[15]

What seems to matter there, as here, is control, especially self-control. Karen's contempt for others derives in part from her "thrill of horror" that she can deceive them so easily, "that they should assume, however briefly, that a human being" stands before them, when really most of her emotional responses are contrived (188). Shar, too, has been "proud of his self-control," his "lack of emotions, his failure to involve himself seriously with anyone." This is why he feels that Karen has destroyed his vision of himself. Yet Karen treats his suicide (bizarrely, unless one is of the school of Marcus Aurelius or Albert Camus) not as tragic but as his way of reasserting self-control. The whole love affair has been a nightmare of lost control, she thinks, so she has reasserted her autonomy by destroying Shar's final overtures of devotion, telling him he makes her "sick" (257). While she can get well only by destroying their love, he kills that love by killing himself. Since the whole thing has been more bad dream than reality, his smashing the car into a track wall reads less like a literal death than an attempt to wake from the nightmare. And if he merely obliterates himself, the novel's logic suggests that even this is preferable to a dream crowded with hateful strangers. Karen herself has had nightmares of staring into an empty hole only to find herself "looking into a darkness filled with shape," and she has decided how much easier it would be "to look into a darkness that meant nothing than into a darkness that was really an open, straining mouth" (261). It is therefore unsurprising that she sees Shar's life as an accident, but his death as triumphantly planned. "He made his death for himself!" she says. "He was a man!" (271).

The novel ends on equilibrium between the life force and the death force, and between meaning and meaninglessness. Shar asserts self-control through self-destruction (in, appropriately, an "Independence Day race" [25]) because he believes he can "never escape himself." "Communion," in both racing and in his passion for Karen, is forever "blocked" (262). Meanwhile Karen's survival brings with it suggestions that she will struggle to escape self-absorption. "If there was pain," she has decided earlier, "she would feel it" (161). Since pity withers the heart, she has determined to "pity no one," least of all herself, whom "she must forget" (162). After Shar's death, she sees that she can transform her self-pity into empathy. "When it came time to retrieve her life," she reflects, "she would grope and come back with someone else's life" (304). Her refusal to pity may lead her to take on Shar's masculine hardness rather than see his wasted life and pointless death as so nearly paralleling her own fate. But, as Schopenhauer reminds us, if art and suicide are psychologically linked in that through them we can be "freed from ourselves," then the first—when it involves looking outward at other lives—can prevent the second. Shar's moment of enlightenment signals this. Having resolved to die, he finally escapes his self-absorption, suddenly feeling "a peculiar tenderness" for his racing team (260).

Similarly, Karen's decision to focus on others is a form of self-negation to cure her self-obsession. Kneeling in church and nominally reconciled with her family, she remains determine not to "lose control" since, much like Shar's hated spectators, her family and perhaps even a "perverse part of herself" are surely "waiting for this" (312). But at least she, too, senses some enlightenment. "Be as bitter as you like," she imagines her father telling her. "But still you are alive and that is a miracle" (314). As Ellen Friedman puts it, while

Karen is back where she started, she seems "grateful to be a survivor." "It is insane to look for meaning in life, and it is insane not to," her thoughts continue. "What am I to do?" (315). To ask a question (and a pragmatic one) at least allows for the possibility of answers. If Karen's quest for meaning remains unresolved in *With Shuddering Fall*, what had yet to be articulated in the Oatesian universe is that any answer to such a query depends upon the kinds of meanings sought.[16]

There are other aspects to the novel that do allow it to be read as social critique. Shar's death is wrongly seen by the white spectators as occurring as the result of a duel with a black driver, Vanilla Jones. This sparks a race riot that pulls the latter part of the novel away from Karen and Shar's claustrophobic love tussle. But I agree with Pamela Smiley that *With Shuddering Fall* reads as something other than "a realistic portrait of American life." Rather, it calls to mind a comment that Ted Hughes made about Sylvia Plath. "Every work of art," he said, "stems from a wound in the soul of the artist. When a person is hurt, his immune system comes into operation and the self-healing process takes place, mental and physical. Art is a psychological component of the auto-immune system that gives expression to the healing process." Karen and Shar seem to represent nothing so much as a dialogue between two versions of a wounded being. As Oates would later write in *New Heaven, New Earth*, the artist might be wise to look through the window rather than to face the mirror. But evidently it took time to turn from one to the other. While it may be the case that the demands of self-creation and social effort remain incommensurable, Karen sets herself the task of developing, in Rorty's phrase for his utopian goal of human solidarity, "the imaginative ability to see strange people as fellow sufferers."[17] The best case to be made for *With Shuddering Fall* itself as a novel of social effort lies in Karen's decision to "come back with someone else's life." The best case for seeing it as a quest for private perfection is that for most of the novel we seem to witness a "communion of pain" that is as much an enclosed circle as Shar's race track or Karen and Shar's passion (247).

"The great American adventure has always been one of social ascension," Oates observed in 1996. "Only the writer who has risen economically in America (in contrast to one born with money and privilege) can understand the fascinating, ever-dramatic class war in its infinite variety. This is the very material of the modern novel."[18] Like many of her subsequent works, Oates's second novel, *A Garden of Earthly Delights*, depicts precisely such a journey of social ascension. Structurally and thematically reminiscent of *East of Eden* as a family saga of generations and revenge, the migrant Walpole family from which the novel's main protagonist, Clara, comes exist among a bunch of itinerant fruit pickers who might have been plucked from *The Grapes of Wrath*. Clara's parents subsist in rural America after the Great Depression, bemused by the disparity between their stubborn dreams and the cultural and economic reality, and for the first of its three parts the novel is social realism. But again a drama of community ultimately gives way, in its primary focus, to a drama of the self. For all the young novelist's desire to write about America, once Oates has laid the parameters of the Walpole's social world, and (since Clara enters a world of wealth and privilege) perhaps outstripped the limits of her own social experience, introspection takes over.

Part 1 deals with Clara's childhood and adolescence amid the vivid setting of the migrant workers' lives, and most of this first section is firmly grounded in a detailed social and historical context. Clara and her father, Carleton, are portrayed as representative individuals of the era. Aspects of this are gender-defined. Clara is the novel's central character, yet, as Brenda Daly and other critics have noted, the three sections bear the names, respectively, of her father, her lover Lowry, and her son Swan. But it is also very much a novel about class. In a male-dominated, wealth-driven, family-focused world, she is not just female, but impoverished, homeless, and orphaned. "You are all—white trash," her teacher has told her. "What are you going to do?" (49). Just as Karen has ended *With Shuddering Fall* with the question, "What am I to do?" so Clara spends her life attempting to answer the teacher's question. "I want you, I want something," she tells Lowry. "I don't know what it is but I want it" (107). Her first inkling about how to get what she wants—which turns out to be to grab for herself and later for Swan the wealth denied her parents—comes from a passing friendship with a girl named Rosalie, who shows her how to steal. Having watched Rosalie rob from a shop, Clara takes an American flag from outside a house. Two Methodist ladies recruiting from the migrant's camp are impressed because they think her flag represents her interest in America. But to Clara it stands "for something simple" (80). Witness to the extremes of poverty, she intends to do whatever necessary to secure that better life.

Even in part 1, however, the beginnings of a drama of the self are evident in Carleton, Clara's father. Her mother, Pearl, dies in a later childbirth, and Carleton struggles to provide for his family while filled with some "inexpressible anger" that he cannot exorcise (4). His bitterness smothers his sense of the reality of the world around him. Economically and socially marginalized, he nevertheless believes that "everything—everyone—the whole world—was joined in him, only in him" (126). He sees the other laborers at the camp as "trash" (57) and believes that he alone can "rise up out of that mud and leave them far behind" (62). Much like Karen Herz and her father, Clara and her father fall out over her relationship with an older man. Where Shar beats up Herz, here the drunken Carleton's violence provokes Clara's elopement. Driving hundreds of miles in search of her, he slides toward despair, delirium, and eventually death.

If Carleton's journey suggests his daughter's own dreamlike, later life, the novel's social realism itself begins to mutate when Clara flees with Lowry, sheds her former identity, and then takes up with Curt Revere, a wealthy landowner. As Walter Sullivan notes, "it is only after she is translated from poverty to ease and security, first as the mistress, later as the wife of a rich man that the novel begins to falter."[19] On the one hand, she fulfills her dream by becoming Revere's mistress and eventual wife. On the other hand, her relationships with Lowry and then Revere, together with Swan's subsequent alienation from his mother, stepfather, and everyone else, are as abstractly drawn as were aspects of the previous novel. Like Karen's flight from her father, Clara's flight from hers seems to involve a flight from real life. Again not unlike Arnold Friend with Connie in "Where Have You Been, Where Are You Going?" Lowry attracts Clara with his energy and air of "knowing secrets but not telling them." She sees him as a man who has "somewhere to get to," whereas she has nowhere to go and can think of nothing except what she is leaving behind. She admires the fact that, unlike the family she once had, he does not live in a world "controlled by someone else" (139). But like Shar and like Arnold, Lowry hardly seems real. In fact, for all his energy, most of the details we discover about him involve some form of negation. "I don't live anywhere," he tells her (140). "I don't stay in one place long, and nobody comes with me" (141). He sets her up in a rented room in a town called Tintern, near which he says he was born, but mysteriously disappears, only to reappear "out of nowhere" when he wants to talk. His favorite word is "nothing," and he has "the look of a young man with no youth" (143). Nor is he very forthcoming about his job, though, like Shar's, it involves driving. "Driving is part of my job," he says mysteriously. "I always like to drive." "There's all this energy stored up that I got to use up. Every place is the same but you got to keep going" (135).

Just as readers may begin to harbor suspicions that Lowry is less than real, so, too, does Clara. The feeling seems mutual. "There might have been a gap in the air where she sat," she thinks, as if he "did not need to avoid looking at her because he was not even aware she was still with him" (134). Even as the detailed Steinbeckian setting dissolves, so Lowry comes to seem more and more like another version of the unfocused Universal Will: the ignition for Clara's own ambition, but with no say in how she should go about satiating it. In contrast to her, Lowry has no goal. "The absence of any goal and of any limit is essential to the Will," wrote Schopenhauer, "for it is an endless striving."[20] "I never look for anything," says the ever-restless Lowry. "What is there to look for?" (135). What he does do is become a guardian who allows her consciousness to evolve, not offering positive advice—other than that she should not "make any mistakes" (147)—but at least encouraging her to discover her own way forward. "Where are we going?" she asks. "You have to make up your mind what to do," he replies (134). When he is not acting like her conscience, he sounds like her muse, explaining his lack of sexual interest in her (a single, crucial incident aside) in terms of her having the wrong voice. "What I want is a voice," he tells her. "When I find her I'll know it, and you're not the one" (141). Clara takes to mouthing Lowry's words as if she is using him to discover her own. "You are just a child," he tells her. "You are just a child," she mouths after him (136). She spends their time together formulating her ambition. "I want lots of things an' I'm goin' to get them," she tells him. "If nobody gives me what I want, I'll steal it" (137). While it is "clear what not to do," it is not clear "what she should do" (147).

But out of this vacuum, Clara learns that she must make an art of her identity, an art of her life. Whatever he is—Schopenhauerean Will, her muse, the devil she gives her soul to—again, there is more than a hint here that this novel is as much about a young artist exploring her artistic direction as about Clara's rise to wealth: her artistic self-creation. Clara's relationship with Lowry, however we translate it, seems an external manifestation of an internal dialogue. Existing as he does "like a dream person," a kind of silence into which she can spill her thoughts, he seems to represent nothing more than her relationship with her own imagination (181).

Clara's relationship with Lowry is not only echoed in her relationship with Revere, but eventually characterizes her son's mind, too. The focus on distorted inner worlds actually renders that outer world unconvincing, and the novel slips away from anything more than a semblance of the social realism with which it began. Waller suggests that "the 'real' events by which Oates's characters are motivated lie deep within the Protean chaos of the personality" so we are "directed back into the depths of their own inner worlds."[21] In Clara's case, the novel's rendering of sociohistorical context gives way almost completely to that inner life. Forever wondering "at the deep vast depths of herself," her dreamlike vision—or Oates's—permeates every crevice of the rest of the novel, regardless of which character's mind we are in (250). Where Lowry has focused Clara's energies, Revere becomes the dupe whose resources will fund her ambition. She knows what she wants now, and intends to get it.

On the level of external events, the solid realism of part 1 now melts into melodrama. Lowry finally makes love to Clara and immediately decides to go to Mexico, unwittingly leaving her pregnant. Aged sixteen, she rapidly seduces Revere, and since he thinks he is the father of her child he sets her up in a remote farmhouse. But we remain in much the same emotional and psychological territory as we have seen with Lowry. Revere may represent tangible wealth, but he is as unreal to us as to Clara. When told he is at a wedding she is attending on his farm, she looks but does "not see anyone" (167). The months of her pregnancy are "a kind of dream" and she can never afterward "remember how she had passed all that time" (224). Indeed, an air of the dream has largely taken over. Clara becomes Revere's mistress, but she sees him about as often as she saw Lowry. Her house is as abstractly drawn as it is geographically remote. Revere, as his name heavy-handedly signals, is literally her dream come true. But he is still a dream. She has "only to close her eyes to see not Revere but any man, a man, an idea of a man itself come to take care of her as she had supposed someone must, somehow" (226).

There is no more emotional intimacy between Clara and Revere than between Clara and Lowry or between any other two people in the novel. Like Lowry, Revere is "a stranger," and she and her eventual husband merely "act out roles" (227). He gives her a picture of a house that means more to her than her actual home. She can "be moved by such things but not by reality," which simply stretches about her "without meaning" (229). In a sense, Clara has allowed herself to become a work of art to Revere, who likes "to frame her face in his hands" (227), but seems "always to see another Clara, not Clara herself" (231). By this stage of the novel, as Clara says of the death of a friend, everything is "unreal, faintly incredible" (252). Stuck in her house with her growing son, time passes, but it is just "seasons blending into one another or days turning into night, nothing that got you anywhere" (261). Lowry reappears after a stint in World War II, a marriage breakup, and after "driving a long time," but Clara rejects his offer to go with him to British Columbia (236). "With you everything is just what comes into your head," she tells him. "It comes out of somewhere like a dream" (276). The interests of their son create an ironic yet insuperable barrier between them, but Lowry, ever the instigator of activity, stays long enough to sow, this time, the seeds that will grow into the denouement. "You ever killed anything?" he asks Swan. "I can see in your face you killed something already and you're going to kill lots of things" (281).

In the final section, Lowry's assertion that Swan is a killer proves true when Swan causes the death of Revere's thirteen-year-old son, Robert, in a hunting accident. Yet another alienated figure, Swan sees nothing ahead in life except a struggle with Revere's surviving legitimate sons. The only way out of it, he thinks, is death or madness. Where Shar had racing, Swan's particular treadmill is reading, something pressed on him by his barely literate mother. He rebels by refusing to go to college. Reading and thinking, he decides, are dangerous because they give too *much* meaning to the world. He also blames reading for setting him apart from his classmates, who seem to him to "swirl about in their own trivial little world" of "friendships and hatreds" (397). He hates his mother's materialistic values and wants "nothing so much as to destroy" not just all that Clara has won for him but "everything, the entire world" (418). Clara, after all, in turning her life into art, has turned her son into art, too. "I don't know who made me the person I am," he exclaims, "but I have this strange idea it's someone who's watching me right now." "I don't want to be a character in a story," he says. "I don't want to be like someone in a movie. I don't want to be born and die and have everyone watching—reading along. Everything decided ahead of time—" (433). But of course, the game is up. A novel that began as social realism has become a novel in which even the offspring of Clara and Lowry sees that theirs has merely been the affair between the artist and her muse. This novel, like Oates's first, is ultimately a kind of burning, introspective prayer. After her relationship with Shar, Karen ended up, for a time at least, in a mental hospital; Clara's relationship with Lowry sparks events that leave her the youngest resident of a nursing home. Each woman's ecstatic, visionary experience has been as assuredly destroyed.

Like *With Shuddering Fall*, then, *A Garden of Earthly Delights* exhibits this tussle between art as private perfection and art as social effort. The impulse to explore issues of identity and perception is harnessed to a socioeconomic framework that convinces so far and no further. In the end, Karen and Shar, and Clara, Lowry, Swan, and Revere seem all too plainly the dimensions of a single mind contemplating a world of mirrors. It is not that *A Garden of Earthly Delights* fails to reflect genuine economic struggle: Clara is undoubtedly an American type and her tale a post-depression-era American story. But what starts out in *Grapes of Wrath* territory migrates to a dreamland. While *The Grapes of Wrath* is most memorable for the family's odyssey, the family's cruel circumstances, the courage of Ma Joad, and Tom Joad's speech of solidarity with working people, *A Garden of Earthly Delights* leaves no such comparable memories. Its depiction of the historical moment is subsumed, much of the time, by its depiction of the narrow inner worlds of a group of people alienated from each other and from themselves, rather than convincingly connected by their social context.

Of course, this may be in itself social realism. But it would seem to have more to do with the author's focus, which is so often here on the relations of inner and outer worlds, rather than on the dynamics of an American era. We learn a lot about these characters' thoughts about themselves, but much less, after part 1, about their specific times or the stream of history through which they vainly wade. What really seems of interest to the young author is the drama of the self in its relation—or more often nonrelation—to other people, whom it creates rather than observes. Carleton, Clara, Lowry, Revere, and Swan, whether seen through their own eyes or those of others, exist like shadowy figures who, despite the novel's undeniable trajectory of social ascension, take part in a strange, private reverie.

Oates's next two novels, *Expensive People* and *them*, each provide rich landscapes for discussion, though for very different reasons. *Expensive People* is highly experimental and highly unsuccessful, while *them* is surely the best of her early novels. But in terms of novel writing as an "evolving of consciousness," what now seems most revealing is that each contains a self-reflexive musing on the purpose of the journey Oates had set out on. *Expensive People* may be an artistic failure, but it is valuable in helping us understand that journey. "Messes are made by people who want but don't know what they want," says the narrator, Richard Everett.[22] Sometimes for this reason "messes" can also reveal things hidden in neater work. As Oates has said of Lawrence's poetry, such unevenness is "for people who want to experience the poetic process as well as the product; who want the worst as well as the best." For the less-impressive work is often crucial to the production of the significant art, and some writers, as Oates elsewhere suggests, may need to "write many books in order to achieve a few lasting ones." For instance, *them*, despite taking up some similar themes to her first three novels, is Oates's first widely acknowledged success and the first time she began to harness her opposing artistic impulses to powerful effect. Oates the exemplar of private perfection successfully merges, in *them*, with Oates the fellow citizen. Her pondering of artistic purpose there may even urge us, depending upon the background of a given reader, to take up the position Rorty assigns to the "liberal ironist" and "to extend our sense of 'we' to people whom we have previously thought of as 'they.'"[23]

But first we have *Expensive People*. Sympathetic critics have tended to gloss over *Expensive People*'s indifferent quality with hyperbole. Greg Johnson writes of "a startling leap into the postmodern era" and of "the brilliant invention of a narrator who is both intelligent and mentally disturbed." Eileen Bender mentions "verbal trickery and conceits exploding in a barrage of puns and arch allusions." The theme of gluttony, she suggests, "has interesting academic dimensions," and this "work of waggery" is after all Oates's "most academic work of fiction." Joanne Creighton calls it a "successful experiment in the satiric mode." The nearest a sympathetic critic gets to negative criticism is Gary Waller, for whom "some of the jokes don't work too well." "We laugh as we laugh at Barth or Barthelme, because there is nothing else to be done." In contrast, Walter Sullivan is bluntly dismissive. "Whatever the theme was meant to be," he writes, "it might have served very well for a short story, but it is not substantial enough to sustain a book."[24]

Despite Sullivan's skepticism, the novel does have a theme: rebellion. It seems designed to cajole the writer out of lethargic conformity and in search of new directions. Yet quite what those directions will be is unclear. *Expensive People* "isn't well-rounded or hemmed-in by fate in the shape of novelistic architecture," says the narrator. "It certainly isn't well-planned. It has no conclusion but just dribbles off, in much the same way as it begins. This is life. My memoir is not a confession and it is not fiction to make money; it is simply . . . I am not sure what it is. Until I write it all out I won't even know what I think about it" (4). While Richard's hesitancy is Oates's conscious ploy, authorial hesitancy nevertheless seems an issue. The novel constantly shadows Lawrence's remark that writers shed their sickness in their books, or to use Tennyson's phrase that Richard quotes but fortunately fails to pursue, "we poets are vessels to produce poetry and other excrement" (79). Vomiting, as much as gorging, is the novel's main motif. *Expensive People* may be dressed as a critique of suburbia, but it reads like a projection of the novelist's story-so-far: a disgorging of anguish even as it explores the relationship between literature and life. Richard plans suicide (by overeating) "immediately after this memoir is finished" so that he "won't be around to throw a damp blanket into the cogs of any critical/scholarly machinery and ruin anyone's theories" (82). It is a death he equates with that of his novelist mother, Nada Romanov (or Nothing Novel).

Again, this is not to deny the novel's social dimension. In her 1990 afterword, Oates explains how she conceived of *Expensive People* as the second in a trilogy that included *A Garden of Earthly Delights* and *them,* examining "American culture, American values, American dreams," but she also hints at another, more personal story (239). "The 'I' of my protagonist Richard," she writes, "became so readily the 'eye' of the novelist that, at times, the barrier between us dissolved completely." Albeit exaggerated, Richard's morbid thoughts do seem closely akin to his author's. Novelists, she writes, are haunted by "a terror of dying before the work is completed, the interior vision made exterior" (240). Once it is done, they can think, "*Here it is. Now I can die*" (241).[25] *Expensive People* weaves between revelation and concealment. "The interior vision made exterior" perhaps, but also the exterior vision made interior. "An 'eye' enraptured by the very jumble and clamor of America," it is equally, Oates admits, an "eye" contemplating her "romance with novel-writing itself" (242). Richard is the first of the idiosyncratic, sometimes aberrant narrators Oates will use in several later novels, even as his voice signals Oates's gathering dissatisfaction with straightforward realism. In my view, it is because *Expensive People* explores the meaning and purpose of novel writing, rather than because it is in any way "brilliant" or "startling," that the novel is significant to her developing career.

Expensive People seems consciously constructed as a classic "anxiety of influence" novel: a son who describes himself as a writer tells how he came to kill his novelist mother. From the outset, Richard makes self-conscious references to illustrious precursors. Bubbling with literary allusion and parody, in the second chapter he mentions Flaubert, Chaucer, Shakespeare, and Stendhal, and elsewhere writers from Dickens and Tolstoy to Proust and Mailer. As for literary strategies, Richard himself is reminiscent of numerous aberrant precursors from Poe's narrators to Dostoyevsky's Underground Man to Plath's Esther Greenwood to Salinger's Holden Caulfield. Like *The Bell-Jar* and *The Catcher in the Rye*, both of which Richard mentions, he depicts alienated youth beset by the "phoniness" of an adult world (60). The studied artlessness of his "hostility toward you, my readers" is straight out of Dostoyevsky (81). "I am a sick man," begins the Underground Man. "I am an angry man. I am an unattractive man."[26] "I am a child-murderer," begins Richard. Unlike his readers, whom he assumes to be "normal" (3), he is an alienated, abnormal figure, "a Minor Character" at odds with the surface world (209).

Given Johnson's biographical information about Oates, it seems clear that the novel is partly about the links between writing, identity, and eating disorders. But, to borrow a phrase from Kim Chernin's *The Hungry Self*, it also reads like "an underlying developmental crisis" about its author's direction as a novelist.[27] What seems at issue is how to turn literary influence into a worthwhile literature of one's own. "Now you are wondering," says the overweight Richard, who constantly equates reading and writing with the intake and expulsion of food, "what good did it do me to read a great deal?" "Ancient, Medieval, Neoclassic, Romantic, Victorian, Modern, Avant-Garde—everything, what good did it do? Not much. My feverish mind, sievelike and pulsating constantly, loses most of what it takes in just as my stomach once lost most of its intake. I am a mess and messes don't take well to culture" (80). "What more could she want?" he exclaims, spewing up his angst over his ambition to escape his novelist mother. "I had even pushed myself beyond what I could do, and still it wasn't enough for her—I wasn't enough for her—and what else could I do?" (99). Tearing up Nada's papers, wrecking her office, spilling her ink, he vomits up "the most vile streams of fluid that had ever graced any Record Room in history" (100). Obese as he is (or believes himself to be), and gorged with reading, his sentences gargle the twin themes of writing and eating. "This chapter," he writes, "must at one time or another throw up its hands in defeat ('throw up' is a deliberate pun, part of a pattern of puns, my dear squeamish readers!)" (82).

Nada, as Oates's early novels lead us to expect, is partly a projection of Richard's mind, a "dream-self," even as she is—in his view—a "real, unhappy, selfish, miserable, and rather banal person" (83). Two Nadas exist: "the one who was free and who abandoned me often, and the other who has become fixed irreparably in my brain, an embryonic creature of my own making, my extravagant and deranged imagination" (90). A literary bulimic, like Juvenal she too vomits "much of what she took in so eagerly" (176). Loving and hating her, above all Richard seeks to escape her power. Nada's brain, says Richard, is "stuffed with books. What was 'only real' couldn't be very important, and I have to confess to feeling this way myself. I have caught her solipsism from her, the way I used to catch colds and flu from her" (76–77).

Once again, as Dike notes of early novels, there is that "strange, alien" quality about the characters and setting and so about the book itself, a quality that, pervasive from novel to novel, has to be put down to the young novelist's perspective, rather than a symptom of her disturbed narrator. Daly sees Nada Romanov as a projection of Oates's "anxiety" that "she is failing as a mother/author," and certainly there is scope for reading *Expensive People* in terms of gender-based anxiety. Since Oates situates the antagonism as a son's rebellion against his novelist mother, one could see this as a deliberate reversal of the real source of uncertainty. Deeply immersed in the writings of male precursors, Oates needed to carve her own course.

In these terms, Richard's anxieties regarding his reading and his "mother" figure might be seen as disguised versions of Sandra Gilbert and Susan Gubar's set of key questions for women writers. "What does it mean," they ask, "to be a woman writer in a culture whose fundamental definitions of literary authority are . . . both overtly and covertly patriarchal?" "If the Queen's looking glass speaks with the King's voice, how do its perpetual kingly admonitions affect the Queen's voice? Since his is the chief voice she hears, does the Queen try to sound like the King, imitating his tone, his inflections, his phrasing, his point of view? Or does she 'talk back' to him in her own vocabulary, her own timbre, insisting on her own viewpoint?" Either way, just as Oates's subsequent story collection *Marriages and Infidelities* (1972) involved rewrites of stories by Chekhov, Henry James, and Joyce, so *Expensive People* is indicative of her work of this period in its search for tone, direction, and focus.[28]

To the extent that *Expensive People* is Oates's first, if rather awkward, foray into the realms of metafiction, its uncertainties stretch to the ontological. It draws specific attention to the problematic relationship between inner and outer worlds evident in *With Shuddering Fall* and *A Garden of Earthly Delights*. Toward the end, doubt is even cast on whether Richard is his mother's murderer after all. When he goes with his father to the scene of the shooting, he can find no trace of the buried rifle. "Hallucinations are as vivid as reality," says his psychiatrist, Dr. Saskatoon. But the gun's absence and Mr. Everett's remarriage and general attitude after Nada's death toward his "neurotic little nut" of a son suggest the father may have been involved (234). The question, perhaps, is whether the actual circumstances of the murder really matter to the novelist or reader. For in the long run, Oates's depiction of the angst-ridden alienation of a suburbanite seems more interesting, and convincing, as a reflection on the possible avenues down which its author might pursue a literary career. While this is a novel about killing a novelist, Nada is also

Richard's muse. Self-destruction proves no more an option than postmodernist metafiction. "The mind's dissection of itself" had somehow to blend with Oates's equally strong desire to reflect the broader social tensions and preoccupations of her era.[29] Her contemplation of the relationship between art and life had its focus not only in her desire to reflect her own intellectual and emotional disposition but in the fate of people whose lives fell short of the coherence of realism even as they remained outside postmodernist self-consciousness. In *Expensive People*, Oates does at least overtly begin to explore her options, and she will exercise these options to greater effect through her next novel.

With *them*, her first foray into inner-city America, Oates was fulfilling her stated objective of critiquing "American culture, American values, American dreams." Her first four novels now covered postwar American culture from blue-collar to white-collar, from rural to suburban to urban. Moreover, *them* would prove to be her most acclaimed such critique up to that time. The novel also suggests a greater awareness of this tension between the impulse to record social forces and identities within specific contexts and the impulse toward introspection. Like *Expensive People*, its metafictional aspects have to do with Oates's contemplation of the function of literature beyond self-dreaming and self-definition. The links between *them* and *Madame Bovary* and *The Red and the Black* were part of her ongoing dialogue with past forms in light of present contexts. The respective dramas of Julien Sorel's and Emma Bovary's twentieth-century American counterparts, Jules and Maureen Wendall, rework novelistic traditions even as they dramatize the social pressures that fanned the flames of the Detroit riots. But where Jules's creative drive has purely to do with self-definition, Maureen engages her teacher, named Joyce Carol Oates, in a dialogue about art's wider social function.

The author's note provides an early sign that Oates was starting to intervene in social debate by way of radical empiricism. "This is a work of history in fictional form," she writes; "that is, in personal perspective, which is the only kind of history that exists." There are "certain similarities" between her and Maureen. The work is "psychological therapy" in temporarily blocking out Oates's "own reality." Yet the Wendalls' world is "remote" from her (11). So we are invited to read *them* as both a plunge inward and an escape from the author's personal life. All four characters create their partners in the mirrors of their own minds. But as the novel's working title "Love and Money" suggests, Jules's and Maureen's love affairs, like Clara's marriage to Revere, involve economic desire. Their fantasies are born of social deprivation even as their lover's fantasies involve romantic yearnings to escape material contentment.

Oates's aestheticism is evident throughout Jules Wendall's story, even as the economic thrust of his story is made clear. Much like Stendhal's Julien, Jules projects his life as a narrative in which, as Stendhal says of Julien, he moves "like a playwright to his own story." The core of that story is his fantasy-led passion for Nadine Greene, niece of his wealthy but soon-murdered mentor, Bernard Geffen. His infatuation with Nadine is as much a mixture of materialism and idealism as Gatsby's with Daisy Buchanan. The image Oates gives us of Jules driving "a truck filled with flowers around the unflowery streets of Detroit" and "rehearsing Jules Wendall, her lover," captures both his abstract imaginings and his concrete economic imperative. The aroma of his dreams smothers the stench of his surroundings. Only occasionally, "beneath the frothy odor of the flowers," does he catch a whiff of "the foul, dark joke of a world in which he had lived all his life and might never escape."[30] A symbol of all that is denied him, Nadine mirrors back his desire. Like the young Clara, everything is "above him, all of America," so "why not try for it all?"—"make a million dollars before the age of thirty and marry this girl, Nadine Greene" (281). But her name warns of the empty center of his jealous desire, and sure enough, physical reality soon impinges on his fantasy. Their romantic escape to Texas reaches its nadir when he gets diarrhoea. "*This is Jules in Texas,*" he tells himself, in a weakened attempt to reinvigorate himself as the hero of his narrative (306). But Nadine deserts him, and he ends up taking part in government experiments that damage his health. Sick and in jail after a car crash resulting from the driver's attempt to molest him, he seems about to become, like his uncle Brock, one of those men who "just can't get back on their feet" (342).

He and Nadine rediscover each other and renew their relationship, but their love is mutually constructed out of abstractions. "A man's love creates a woman's," she tells him. "You've made me the way I am" (373). Consummation, when it finally occurs, seems unreal. Supposedly experiencing "the deepest, essential Nadine," Jules struggles "to penetrate her to the very kernel of her being," but she seems "to slip from him." While the real seems unreal, the fantasy becomes a reality that drives Nadine mad enough to shoot and wound him (and so mirror Julien Sorel's shooting of Madame de Renal). "You don't believe in me, you don't believe that I'm real," she has told him, "even my body is something you made up" (391). Like Julien, Jules remains perpetually engrossed in the fictional narrative he is making of real life. "Jules risking this, Jules leaping to that, Jules plunging in," he is "the hero of countless stories." The "conclusion of one story" fades "into the beginning of another, all of it imagined" through "endless chapters" as he pursues a woman herself "under an enchantment like his own" (393). His love is both real and unreal, connected with the environment and society, yet borne of self-absorption.

For Bloom, Oates has affinities with Maureen, but "more clearly resembles Jules," a kind of artist-of-life who suggests "a weird version of the portrait of the artist as a young man."[31] But whereas Jules's self-absorption seems all too similar to Karen's, Shar's, Clara's, and Swan's, Maureen offers something new. Indeed, it is through Maureen that Oates's Nietzschean aestheticism more obviously signals that it will ultimately translate into fully-fledged pragmatism. The concept of the artist in us all is Nietzschean, but the potential for this to have positive and practical social consequences in a melioristic universe is Jamesian, and it is Maureen who represents Oates's attempt to move to an articulate moral position in her art. More effectively and endearingly than the obnoxious Richard Everett, Maureen actually questions these links between art and the facts of her life. Alone among these early Oates characters, she is self-conscious enough to view her position in society, as it were, from outside the literary legacy Oates had inherited. As with Karen and Clara, domestic violence triggers her escape, but in Maureen's case that escape will involve rather more awareness of her wider social context. Recovering from being beaten up by her stepfather, Howard, for prostitution and faced in Loretta with a mother who sees her own life as "a joke" (322), Maureen realizes she must "escape the doom of being *Maureen Wendall*" (338). Like the young Oates, brutal reality drives her to seek sustenance in literature, but in Maureen's case nothing she finds seems relevant to the life she is forced to live.

Her hostility to the "Joyce Carol Oates" who is her teacher focuses on a class on *Madame Bovary*. She writes to this Oates, attacking the false values of her teaching of literature. "The books you taught us," she charges, "are mainly lies" (329). "The happiness in the room for you was in the book and not in us" (331). Maureen's challenges to Oates are versions of the questions George Steiner asks in *Language and Silence*. "To teach literature as if it were some kind of urbane trade, of professional routine, is to do worse than teach badly," he writes. "To teach it as if the critical text were more important, more profitable, than the poem, as if the examination syllabus mattered more than the adventure of private discovery, of passionate digression, is worst of all." Steiner quotes Kafka's famous letter asking, "If the book we are reading does not wake us, as with a fist hammering on our skull, why then do we read it? So that it shall make us happy? Good God, we would also be happy if we had no books, and such books as make us happy we could, if need be, write ourselves." "Students of English Literature," ends Steiner, "must ask those who teach them, as they must ask themselves, whether they know, and not in their minds alone, what Kafka meant."[32] The links between Kafka's letter and Maureen's challenge to Oates is on the question of the *uses* of literature. Oates sees herself in Emma, says Maureen; whereas, for Maureen, none of it seems to matter. "Why did you think that book about Madame Bovary was so important?" she asks. "All those books? Why did you tell us they were more important than life? They are not more important than my life" (333).

The character's challenge to the novelist has to do not just with the relationship between the novel form and the readers whose lives are supposedly reflected, but is also part of a rereading of canonical literature that marks much of Oates's work early in her career. Here, specifically, Oates seems to be commenting on the traditions of realism from which she would increasingly stray before returning to revised forms of them in the 1980s. When Walter Sullivan complains that personality in Oates's novels is "not an organic development from stage to stage, but a random shifting from one manifestation of character and being to the next," he is judging the novels in terms of precisely that kind of traditional realism that *them* challenges. The fictional Oates flunks Maureen for "*lack of coherence and development*," in other words for being unable to live up to the skills privileged by realism (335). In contrast, Maureen, like Richard in *Expensive People,* points out that lives are *not* coherent, and often lack development. Like Loretta's and Jules's they may instead be a long, tedious joke. "You failed me," writes Maureen. "You gave me an F" (337). But in what sense has the teacher failed the pupil, or the writer the reader? The challenge Oates presents herself is how to make her fiction reflect the complexities of lived human experience, given that "coherence and development"—whether in a realist novel, a biography, or a critical commentary—is inevitably what Milan Kundera would call "an intelligible lie" masking "the unintelligible truth."[33] "Literature gives form to life" is the answer that the fictional Oates gives to Maureen (338). We know from Jules's vision of himself as a hero—as well as from Julien, or Emma, or Don Quixote, for that matter—that this is true. But life also shapes literature, and its evolution. The fictional

Oates fails Maureen by stressing merely coherence and development, which Maureen sees as yet another lie. "There is no form" to her life, she says. Of this, she concludes, Oates knows nothing. "You write books," says Maureen. "What do you know?" (341). What, in other words, is the value of your art?

Roughly correspondent to Richard Rorty's description of two incommensurable kinds of art—the struggle against social injustice versus the devotion to private projects of self-creation—Oates's first four novels, then, combine social critiques with introspective and/or abstract dialogues about the self and the purpose of art. But Maureen's explicit challenges to her teacher/author, together with Karen's decision in *With Shuddering Fall* to escape self-pity and seek out fellow sufferers, signaled Oates's determination to harmonize those two impulses and to link self-creation, and creativity more generally, with social responsibility. This, too, finds its echo in Rorty. With *them,* the drama of other and self, of you and I, has already become the wider social drama of them and us. For Rorty, "the right way to take the slogan 'We have obligations to human beings simply as such' is as a means of reminding ourselves to keep trying to expand our sense of 'us' as far as we can." "We should stay on the look out for marginalized people," he argues, "people whom we still instinctively think of as 'they,' rather than 'us.' We should try to notice our similarities with them."[34] In the long run, Oates's artistic project would successfully wed a private vision with the projected vision of American types. But while her novels were raising the questions, she still had to find *how* best to relate her work to a wider community while retaining that risky aesthetic of pushing (as Shar would have it, of racing) the limits of her psyche. Asking the questions was one thing; finding the answers was quite another. We know, in retrospect, that Oates experienced a gathering mental crisis between *them* and *Wonderland,* culminating soon after the latter's publication. Given that knowledge, the tussle between introspective inquiry and social critique seems all the more evident in reading *Wonderland.*

The title *Wonderland* suggests both tendencies. Oates described it, in her 1992 afterword, as referring to both America and the human brain as regions of wonders. "And 'wonders' can be both dream and nightmare." In this case, *nightmare* appears the more apt word. For Oates herself, as for some of her critics, *Wonderland* seems to have been a desperately claustrophobic experience reminiscent of *"the ball of air circling itself"* of the novel's epigraphic poem. "We are led to value the highest that which cost us the most," Oates begins her afterword, and describes this "bizarre and obsessive" novel as her "most painful in conception and execution." "The runaway Shelley, wasted and ungendered and sickly yellow" at the end, is, like Richard Everett, "an exaggerated self-portrait."[35] "Her novels are fiercely claustrophobic and you experience them like a privileged sickness," writes Calvin Bedient. Gordon Taylor suggests that *Wonderland* stands "at the center of the record of her imaginative life, a pressure gauge of an accumulating artistic past, her explosive prolificness in reality an implosive intensification." That the wonderland of the brain was indeed at this time a personal, and painful, issue seems borne out by Oates's guarded comments years later in "*Wonderland* Revisited." "Perhaps," she writes, "I should mention parenthetically that my interest in neurology . . . was the consequence of an apparent medical condition, which necessitated one or more trips to a neurologist in Windsor." The condition, however, "turned out to be, not physical, or in any case not seriously physical," but a "confluence of symptoms" brought on by what we now call "stress." In artistic terms, this stress perhaps had to do with pushing the limits of a certain kind of cerebral exploration. "Any study of the human brain leads one again and again to the most despairing, unanswerable questions," she said at the time, " . . . there is no way out of the physical fact of the brain, no way *out* of this confinement."[36] *Wonderland* provides the first suggestion of an impasse in her intellectual inquiry that by the end of the 1970s had produced a dramatic shift of emphasis. She would come to believe that abstract inquiry into the nature of identity is an intellectual dead end. This novel would prove to be one of the last manifestations of Oates's authorial self—rather than characters within a novel—tackling unanswerable and therefore debilitating philosophical and/or neurological questions. If the social commentary of *them* has an introspective side, *Wonderland* really *is* about the mind's self-dissection, even as it is a novel about America.

Like almost all her novels, *Wonderland* was "political in genesis," writes Oates, and "could not have been conceived, still less written, at any other time than in post-1967 America." But even if we are meant to read it as a critique of American society, Oates presents us with an odder set of characters than ever, moving through an even stranger landscape. Far from the hints of Steinbeck in *A Garden of Earthly Delights* or the allusions to Stendhal and Flaubert in *them*, *Wonderland* is nearer Carson McCullers or Flannery O'Connor. The American society it depicts is alien indeed, and the gaze inward compels far more than the social critique. A novel, in Oates's own words, of "deep verticality and inwardness," and with epigraphs from Borges and from Yeats ("knowledge increases unreality"), it challenges any kind of straightforward notions of "seeing" the outer world. "Any resemblance to reality," warns the author's note, "is accidental and should be resisted." As Taylor points out, Jesse's life story is picked up in approximately the year Oates was born and ends near "the present moment for the novelist herself as she completes the book." "It is as if entering the histories of her characters at that point and in the way she does were a way of re-entering and retracing herself," he writes. It thus suggests "both her commitment to reality and her journey through the looking glass." This story of "a boy of working class background," as Johnson summarizes it, who driven "by the need to exert control over his own destiny" subsequently "becomes a brain surgeon," clearly burns on the fuel of Oates's own life.[37] In detail, it is as different again from each previous novel as each is different from the others. But the underlying pattern is familiar. An act of violence propels the protagonist away from home and on the run to discover a life. The protagonist becomes attached to one or more abstract, dreamlike figures who help propel the journey to some form of denouement.

At the start of *Wonderland*, Jesse Harte's father, Willard, shoots Jesse's mother and siblings, leads the unwitting Jesse to the body-strewn house, then wounds Jesse as he makes his escape. Willard is shot dead by the police, and Jesse lives with Grandpa Vogel before being adopted by the peculiar Dr. Karl Pedersen, then mentored by Dr. Benjamin Cady, and finally, mentored yet again, by Dr. Roderick Perrault, while becoming first a medical student and then a neurosurgeon. On the way, he encounters two other bizarre figures, Talbot Waller Monk and Reva Denk, and marries Cady's daughter, Helene. A fugitive from childhood and memory, he winds up searching for his runaway second daughter, Shelley, who has eloped to Canada to live with a dropout named Noel. From its opening in 1939 to its ending in 1971, the events dance across the scaffolding of midcentury America, from Willard Harte's loss of his gas station because of the Great Depression, through World War II, Korea, the Cold War, and Vietnam. But Jesse's survival and aspiration, as with all Oates's previous protagonists, involves a strong sense of self-alienation and a refusal to accept the outer world as altogether real. Just as his reluctance to reflect echoes comments that Oates has made throughout her career about amnesia as self-survival, so his relationships with others seem as much self-projections as he and they seem projections of their author. "One of life's minor satisfactions," writes Oates in "In Traction," a story from *The Assignation*, "is forgetting." "Amnesia is the great solace," she writes about her sense of threatened identity on visiting a maximum-security prison, "the most available form of self-protection." As Taylor observes, "one survives inward as much as forward in the novel," and, as Johnson points out, that survival has a great deal to do with Jesse's ability "to avoid contemplation, to escape memory" and to recoil "from his own unfathomable self."[38] There is a strong sense, however, that everybody Jesse encounters is just as hung-up as he is on issues of personality and on the mysterious relationship between mind and world. As a result, there is rarely a feeling in the novel, however Jesse recoils from that "unfathomable self," that any such release is achieved. Rather, the faster he runs, the harder he pushes himself; the greater a status he achieves, the more enigmatic that reality becomes.

Jesse's relationship with Dr. Pedersen is a case in point. Pedersen may be, as Joanne Creighton argues, "a grotesque parody of the American spirit," but he is also a figure barely sustainable in the realist world with which the novel begins. The drift away from the carefully defined Lockport setting of the first two chapters occurs early in chapter 3 when Jesse arrives at his grandfather's farm as if "in a dream."[39] Adopted by Pedersen, he enters a distinctly odd world. Pedersen is himself a physical oddity, with the kind of proportions usually found only in fairground mirrors. A "tall, fat man" with "an immense torso," he has a "large and pale and moony" face that seems to "give off a subdued, clammy light" (80). His short feet and pudgy hands are offset by enormous thighs, knees that seem to strain his trousers to the point of ripping, and ankles "the size of an ordinary man's knees" (81). This Dickensian caricature, who knows of Jesse because he has kept a newspaper cutting of the murders, makes Jesse the subject of his overbearing fascination. Much as Karen asked of herself and Clara was asked by her teacher, Pedersen asks Jesse how he proposes "to confront the riddle of existence" and organize his own life. "By going as far as I can go," Jesse explains, "as far as . . . my abilities will take me" (87). Pedersen is to Jesse what Shar is to Karen and Lowry to Clara: the driving force, the Schopenhauerean Will. He is the "voice" that propels Jesse onward, but away from society. Once ensconced with the Pedersen family, Jesse finds he has Pedersen's voice in his head whether Pedersen is there or not. He starts to apply himself to his studies and feels as if "he had never attended school before; he had never taken it seriously before" (14). As for Swan, so for Jesse: the voices of other teenagers seem "sounds rather than words, like music too trivial for Jesse to bother with." His contemporaries seem like "tall, scrawny children," while he is an adult. Something in him yearns for their childishness, but then he remembers "who he must become" and looks at them as if "grown safely free of their spurts of friendship and their spiteful little feuds" (114). All this is a fairly transparent disguise of the same story we have had more than once before, the artist in pursuit of the meaning of her enterprise, and verging on pure solipsism. Other people are "not very real," and there is no time for Jesse "to think of them with reality." Only Pedersen's voice is "close, intimate." Following him everywhere, it prods him on, gives him courage, chides him when he is lazy, and is always quizzing him, "bringing him up short by saying *What have you just read?*" and "*You have so much more work to do*" (115). Clearly, then, Pedersen's is an internal—or internalized—voice, the voice of ambition from which Jesse cannot escape.

Pedersen himself, for all his fairground-mirror dimensions, has a distinctly Oatesian energy and ambition. He is a physician who, stripped of the medical metaphor, reads like authorial self-parody. "A diagnostician by instinct," he cannot explain his talent except as a "unique gift" that has never let him down (82). Interested "not in establishing a reputation" but in just doing his work, he argues that "it is only truth that matters." The human destiny is "to pursue the infinite, to create maps and boundaries and lines of latitude and longitude with which to explain reality" (124). When Pedersen says, "I am only to sink into my deepest self until the truth comes to me," his quasi-mystical aesthetic is essentially that of Oates's Emersonian self-reliance or Jamesian radical empiricism. "My thoughts arrange themselves," says Pedersen of his assessment of patients' symptoms, and "somehow the truth comes to me. It comes into my waking mind and I understand" (122). Jesse is as much his patient—or specimen—as his disciple. "It seems you are becoming yourself," Pedersen tells him (19). If book 1 of *Wonderland* seems above all to be about Pedersen's igniting of Jesse's ambition and self-creation out of a painful past, that ambition reads much like a novelist's. The fact of that ambition seems to outstrip the subject matter through which that ambition manifests itself. The book becomes about itself. Jesse's relationship with Pedersen ends after Jesse, witnessing the plight of Pedersen's wife and children, sees just how monstrous Pedersen actually is—which is perhaps to say how domineering and destructive the insatiable Will can be. As Jesse comes to know him, it becomes clear that Pedersen's confidence and energy has evolved into "a patriarchal greed and tyranny," in Johnson's words, "raised to a level of grotesque insanity."[40] An apparent mentor, he turns out to be a demonic control freak. "I know how to interpret reality for you," he tells his daughter, Hilda. "You must allow me to interpret everything for you" (139). Mary Pedersen reveals the extent of her husband's depravity when Jesse helps her attempt to escape, telling him of Pedersen's perversions and cruelties and belief that a "patient's life is *his*" (186).

This is not to say that the break with Pedersen prevents *Wonderland* from coiling inward. Oates continues to scribble her depiction of the wonderland of the brain across her depiction of the wonderland of American culture. Jesse traverses the American 1950s and 1960s, but his relationships after Pedersen amount to studies of the nature of personality. "Reality is constantly turning into something else," wrote Oates of Dostoyevsky, early in her career, as if contemplating the way in which her own early novels evolve.[41] In book 2, Jesse studies medicine at the University of Michigan. He takes his mother's maiden name, becoming Jesse Vogel, but continues to resist the distractions of other people and avoid self-reflection. Like that key figure from Oates's later writing, Marya Knauer, he is always in a hurry, always with work to do, so has little time for others. A relationship with a nurse named Anne-Marie Seton dares him to think that maybe he is "really a normal young man. Not isolated" (210), but even though he thinks they will marry, he still fails to recall her face when she is away, envisaging "her presence, but only as an abstraction" (211). One reason this relationship fails is because Jesse is befriended by another strange being who seems as much an internal voice as Pedersen. Talbot Monk, also known as Trick, appears from nowhere, describes himself as "essentially a silent person," but proceeds to tell Jesse that marriage with Anne-Marie will not happen and to draw Jesse into confessing his deepest desire (226). "I want to perform miracles—I want to make miraculous things ordinary again," Jesse tells him. But "I'd like to be a presence that is invisible, impersonal. I won't want any personality involved" (226–27). Jesse's ambition, once again, seems all too obviously the ambition of a writer—an invisible writer—with his patients, like readers, "impersonal and without private history" that he knows of, people for whom he will feel "just this abstract love" (227).

Trick Monk is a Dostoyevskian double, a kind of Minnesotan Svidrigailov who turns out to be every bit as horrendous as Pedersen. He would "like to be a great gynecologist," to "take loving, gentle smears" to examine "in the solitude of a laboratory" (228). Just as Pedersen dreams of invading the minds of others, so Trick talks of impregnating women with words. "Discharging in your beloved's body, discharging in her brain with a few delicate words— which is more rewarding, after all?" (229). Meanwhile he not only predicts the demise of Jesse's relationship with Anne-Marie but befriends Jesse despite the latter's initial repulsion and encourages his interest in Helene Cady (Helene's father, a Nobel prize–winning neurochemist, has fascinated Jesse by lecturing that "the world is our construction" and that "even our most precise laboratory findings" will always fail "to reveal the relations of the senses to the outside world" [21]). Like Shar, Lowry, and Arnold Friend, Trick is both otherworldly and a kind of mirror image of the main protagonist. The writer of a sequence of poems ("Poems Without People"—"because the only person in them is myself and I don't count" [276]), he tells Jesse and Helene that he is really "about the size of the jack of hearts seen sideways" (273). He seems little more than one of the pack of cards that, like the fantasy figures in *Alice in Wonderland,* populate Jesse's overwrought mind. When Jesse rediscovers him while searching for Shelley, Trick has rejected the physical world and become a counterculture poet-guru to the young. Spaced out on drugs and babbling nonsense, Trick proves useless to Jesse's quest, falling into a state of semiconsciousness that leaves Jesse realizing that he is "alone" in the room (486).

Helene, too, once Jesse marries her, becomes very much part of this claustrophobically internalized world, as does his would-be mistress, Reva Denk, even while both, like Trick, have problematic relationships with their own and others' bodies. As alienated from others and from her physical self as most early Oates characters, Helene feels that her father and husband have "no real consciousness of her except as a point of contact, an object" (285). Jesse's desire for children horrifies her because she wants a man to "exist in part of her mind, but chastely." She fears her body, feels she only inhabits it "like a tenant," and is even "a little ashamed of being female" (288–89). When she does become pregnant, a gynecological examination exacerbates her self-revulsion. However nightmarish the wonderland of the brain, the physical world is depicted as just as terrible, regardless of whether we see it through Helene or Jesse. In particular, the novel emphasizes a horror of blood, of flesh, and especially of obesity. From the hefty Pedersens and their gargantuan meals to Jesse's work in the emergency ward, it is crammed with suffering corporeality. Pregnant women show up at the hospital having tried "to dislodge the flesh inside their wombs, feverish with the need to scrape themselves out" (137). Another time there is "a huge fat man" billowing with "flesh, flab, blubber," his "wobbling chest smeared with vomit and blood" (321).

Wonderland offers ample evidence as to why Oates, at this stage of her career, was so drawn to the world of books and why she so often allowed her characters to sink into a world of dreams. In turning to Reva Denk, another dream-like, semifantasy figure, Jesse attempts just this. But while, like Trick Monk, she appears mysteriously, she later reappears, pregnant by another man, to request an abortion. The dream woman is revealed to be no less physical than the patients whose bodies Jesse patches nightly in the emergency ward. He drives out West to elope with her, rather than give her an abortion. But once she agrees, he retreats to a motel room and, before returning East alone, mutilates himself with a razor blade, and watches himself in a mirror, fascinated by the blood dripping from a dozen nicks. For Jesse, as for Helene, the realities of the body are very different from the safety of fantasy. Nevertheless, the fantasy woman consumes his thoughts even years later, and his dreams of her create "a kind of storm in him" that he associates with "the demands of his body" (422).

Jesse's final mentor, neurologist Dr. Perrault, is another exaggerated self-projection in a novel where self-projection reigns supreme. No less a control freak than Pedersen, he takes it as a personal affront when one patient's symptoms turn out not to be of neurological origin but the result of lung cancer. Nor are Perrault's pronouncements calculated to brighten the proceedings. "Life is pain," he explains. "Pain is life" (336). Jesse's life has almost come full circle. He imagines "the waves in his own brain subsiding" to Perrault's "greater pattern" (335). By this stage, Jesse has decided he has no interest in a personality of his own, but merely wants to survive. This is just as well because the novel circles in to center on a conversation at Perrault's dinner table where Perrault asserts that the notion of personality is nothing more than "a conscious system of language. And when the language deteriorates, as it must, the personality vanishes and we have only the brute matter left—the brain and its electrical impulses" (359). For Perrault, the mental world is physical, and personality is a myth "expressed in certain language patterns we recognize because we are accustomed to them" (360). Jesse does not dispute Perrault's claims, although Helene does, and while Jesse feels "a strange thrill of certainty" in what Perrault says, the general tone of the conversation suggests Helene's misgivings to be well founded. When she says that Perrault's views are "terrible," Jesse's response—"the truth can't be terrible"—not only involves a mutual ego rubbing between the men but reveals that Jesse has not really escaped Pedersen's influence so much as embarked on becoming a version of him (361). "Truth," Pedersen has told him, "is to be honored wherever it is found" (124). But Perrault's and Jesse's feelings of superiority remind us that personality is more than a system of language. The mind, as Perrault has equally asserted, cannot be separated from the body. His later jealousy over Jesse's success, and the fact that he dies while angry with a student, confirm that he is as much a victim of visceral feeling as anyone. Just as Pedersen seems to have worked his way into Jesse's brain, so Perrault lingers on in his protégé's thoughts for years afterwards, almost more real in his mind that he ever was in body.

Wonderland's exploration of inner and outer worlds culminates in book 3, "Dreaming America." Jesse's search for Shelley at least returns us to a recognizable, referential depiction of 1960s counterculture, as well as yoking together the dichotomy of American culture/human brain through Shelley and Jesse's memories of the death of President Kennedy. But Shelley's boyfriend, Noel, has the same preoccupations as just about every other character. He advises her to "dream back right over" her father and "erase" him, even though her physical suffering is all too evident (409). When Jesse finds them in Toronto, he learns that she has taken a VD test and that "the world could get at his daughter through the orifices of her body" (469). Shelley and Noel deny physicality. "There's nobody here," she whispers. "I don't exist and you can't get me" (504). Noel may be a version of Pedersen and Perrault—"I ground her down to nothing and freed her!" he says. "She didn't even know her name when I was through!"—but Jesse, too, is now a would-be controller attempting to force his daughter home, just as Pedersen retrieved his wife from Jesse (506). He remains a sympathetic character, but the demarcations between caring and control are no more obvious by the end than are the lines between reality and fantasy, mind and body, or past and present. In *Wonderland*, much that is solid melts into air. Conversely, much that seems intangible—memory, desire, *personality*—turns out solid. One form of action can become its opposite. Protection can become domination. Altruism can become egotism.[42] But from almost beginning to end, for all the novel's postwar scaffolding, the mental-physical preoccupations hold sway.

So while, as with *With Shuddering Fall* and *A Garden of Earthly Delights*, by the time you exit this feverish novel it is possible to argue that it has after all been a troubling dream about America, again something else competes with this social critique. Pedersens' rapacious consumerism and the male will-to-power in Pedersen, Trick Monk, Perrault, and Jesse himself at the expense of Mary Pedersen, Helene, and Shelley take place within a recognizable American setting and era. But that backdrop exists as if across a crowded room, all but hidden by obsessive figures involved in a clamorous debate about the nature of personality. Oates's comments on other writers in *New Heaven, New*

Earth, then, seem most apt in terms of her own early novels. They stand "between two worlds"—the material and the mental. They may show more concern with economic hardship than the novels of Henry James or Virginia Woolf, but their abstract qualities at times suggest a "near hallucinatory obsession with psychic experience." If their stimulus is the window onto America, it is also the mirror into the self. "Inner and outer reality are confused," Oates will say of Lawrence's "controlling aesthetics." But this is so of her own early novels, as indeed of her early poetry. For this sense that "each of us can only be one," but that on the other hand, through that we can "know all" (as Schopenhauer puts it), that the inmost becomes the outmost, was as much the early Oates's dominant aesthetic as it was Schopenhauer's or Emerson's or Lawrence's.[43]

Oates's critiques of American society in her work of this period involved just as much an "experiment of the mind's dissection of itself, and its dissociation from the body" as any to be found in Henry James and Woolf. For to investigate the foreign/intimate nature of other people, from the perspective of pragmatic self-reliance, is simultaneously to investigate the foreign/intimate nature of the self, and Oates evidently needed to try to fathom that "self" in order to pursue her wider investigation. No matter what the truth is of that assertion, Oates also says in *New Heaven, New Earth* that, with tremendous will, one can "break free" of any such tendency to solipsism. Indeed, to do so may be a necessity, given the risks to the writer of an aesthetic based on "controlled hysteria."[44] If we are all in some ways artists involved in the continual creation of our own lives, then we are equally free to reject contemplation in favor of active engagement. It was this escape from the dead end of self-analysis, this recognition of the possibilities for artistic engagement, this rediscovery of the outer world by achieving ironic distance from the pursuit of unanswerable neurological questions, that would become a key subject matter of Oates's novels through the rest of the decade.

> For many years I endured a long maniacal struggle that I thought was myself vs. the world
> ... but was really myself vs. myself.
> —JOYCE CAROL OATES TO GAIL GODWIN, 18 September 1972

2 ABSTRACTION INTO ACTION

ALL THE WHILE that the young novelist was pushing at the limits of "artistic" consciousness and the mysteries of personality and identity in her early novels, she was not only producing poetry and essays but also becoming a prolific master of the short story. As Johnson, Sreelakshmi, Loeb, and others show in their studies of the short fiction, Oates has often used the story form to work through preoccupations treated rather differently in the novels. Johnson's much-echoed view is that "Oates has clearly found in the short story a genre particularly genial to the protean and relentlessly experimental nature of her creative impulse." Sometimes stories will parallel themes and characters in novels; other times they will express more clearly the kind of agenda Oates has set herself. In her first collection, *By the Northgate* (1963), the racing driver Shell in "Edge of the World" more than a little anticipates Shar Rule. Moreover, in his ill-fated determination to go "far away" from a community he considers the edge of the world if he "just knew which way to go," he is a prototype for many of the other restless, would-be escapees who populate Oates's novels. But if Shell has about him something of Karen and Shar, Clara and Lowry, Jesse and Shelley, what seems problematic in the novels—the dissolution of social realism into abstract introspection—is not an issue in the stories. Gritty realism—where that is Oates's mode—is after all easier to sustain for the length of a story. Even in the early collections—*Upon the Sweeping Flood* (1966) and *By the Northgate*—the stories are largely as assured and integrated as they are rewarding. It is perhaps true to say, therefore, that Oates came into her own as a story writer far sooner than she did as a novelist.

Most critical attention has focused on Oates's next three collections, *The Wheel of Love* (1970), *Marriages and Infidelities* (1972), and *The Goddess and*

Other Women (1974). The first of these includes some of Oates's best-known stories, not only "Where Are You Going, Where Have You Been?" but also "Unmailed, Unwritten Letters," and "How I Contemplated the World from the Detroit House of Correction and Began My Life Over Again." The second contains Oates's much-discussed rewrites of "The Metamorphosis," "The Lady with the Pet Dog," "The Turn of the Screw," and "The Dead." The third, as Johnson notes, "is Oates's most overtly feminist collection," written as it was "during the intense years of first-wave feminism."[1]

In terms of the novels, it is noteworthy that both sides of Oates's evolving consciousness are represented in these early collections. The social concerns evident in "The Edge of the World" and "How I Contemplated the World"—and given a more feminist perspective in *The Goddess and Other Women* stories like "Small Avalanches"—are matched by her search for artistic direction in her rewrites of the Kafka, Chekhov, James, and Joyce stories. But it is *Night-Side* (1977), published the year before the last of this next group of novels (and after four further collections, *The Hungry Ghosts* [1974], *The Poisoned Kiss* [1975], *The Seduction* [1975], and *Crossing the Border* [1976]), that contains a story most revealing in terms of Oates's evolving consciousness. That story, "A Theory of Knowledge," which specifically dramatizes an attempt to reconcile the impulses toward social effort and private perfection, suggests how and why her early, realist novels gave way to the more complex narratives that prefigured *Bellefleur*. "A Theory of Knowledge" is about the seductive nature of self-absorption and the temptation to retreat from the outer world in favor of introspective contemplation. But ultimately it is about the struggle to balance the pursuit of knowledge for its own sake with active and useful involvement in the social sphere. Its protagonist, long-retired Professor Reuben Weber, has devoted a lifetime to abstract reflection, but finally forgoes self-imposed isolation to provide practical help to another human being and so symbolically rejoin society. In this, the story is a microcosm of Oates's evolving novelistic concerns.

As Harry Berman notes in an excellent essay on "A Theory of Knowledge," Weber's life has some parallels with that of Charles Sanders Peirce, whom William James (himself cast as a character in the title story) credited with being a founder of pragmatism. Like Peirce, Weber has not only spent the latter part of his life in philosophical contemplation and increasing isolation, but he has failed to complete the one, substantial book that would articulate his "theory of knowledge" and so perhaps justify his life.[2] In old age, he dwells bitterly on his sense of betrayal both by others and by Time. "I had anticipated in the fifties the methodology of pragmatism," he tells himself, if not "that despicable, misleading term," but "they could not forgive me that I valued Truth over social pieties and religious nonsense."[3] Certainly aspects of pragmatism pervade Weber's thought. He claims to have spent a lifetime "trying to cut through obscurity, murkiness, the self-indulgent metaphysics of the past" (352). "Is not belief 'that upon which a man is prepared to act?'" he asks (356). But having retreated into philosophical abstraction and essentially rejected the outer world, he still believes that nominalism (the denial that abstract entities really exist; the denial, for instance, that Truth, rather than being a linguistic convention, exists to be discovered) "has poisoned all of western thinking" (353). Withdrawing from the outside world, he has stuck to his doomed goal of articulating "his system" (355). He knows no one in the neighborhood and barely bothers to go into Rockland, the suitably named nearby town, considering other people's affairs insignificant. Almost no one comes to interrupt Weber, and it has been years "since he really talked with anyone" (354).

As one might expect, then, despite his latent pragmatism, most of what Weber has up to now believed is diametrically opposed to the views of "the outrageously popular William James" (354), whom, despite James's kind letters to him, Weber has dismissed along with that "scatterbrain" Emerson (360). Philosophy, he believes, must be "purified," kept aloof of "the historical world altogether. And the church in any form" (356). A lover of humanity in the abstract, but with no time for individuals, Weber cares more about the "acceptance of his ideas"—his systematic rebuttal of neonominalism—than about anyone or anything else (358). Increasingly isolated and unable to publish, he has consequently given his life up to "fifty-five years of brooding" and used his energies negatively. In full, Weber's self-imposed isolation has let him persuade himself that somehow, despite his inability to participate positively in a social realm, his life has been a "triumph" (363).

But "A Theory of Knowledge" is also, in Berman's phrase, a story of "generativity versus self-absorption." Weber is converted from abstraction into action when a dark-eyed gypsy boy wanders over from a nearby encampment and interrupts his contemplation. He becomes aware of the boy watching him one day while he is outside reading. Weber tolerates his presence, but Weber's daughter, despite the boy's bruises—suggestive of violent treatment in the encampment—discourages her father from taking a greater interest. Nevertheless, Weber insists on keeping a window open at night to hear the boy's "isolated, piercing cry," writes to the authorities about him, and, receiving no response, finally takes it upon himself to go to the encampment, where he finds and frees the boy (367). In opting to act in the world and address the needs of another individual, Weber has become a true pragmatist. In Berman's words, "the evolution of generativity" in Weber is "from self-aggrandizing production of a comprehensive, abstract, intellectual project to self-less, particular, concrete caring actions." Berman's summing-up of the story also nicely distills this major preoccupation in Oates's novels of these years. "Generativity projects that focus exclusively on the expansion of the self," he writes, need to be coupled with generativity projects "whose main focus is intimate caring and concern for the welfare of particular others."[4]

Weber's ideas may be patently the opposite not only of Jamesian pragmatism but of just about everything Oates's novels eventually espouse, but it is clear from her comments inside and outside her fiction that she understands, from within, this desire to withdraw from social life into introspection. Even before this moment of redemption, Weber is a sympathetic character. He takes an interest in the boy from the start, and while his self-absorption delays action, it does allow him to reassess the balance of his life. Walter Clemons captured this split in Oates between private perfection and social commitment when commenting on an interview with her prior to the publication of *Do with Me What You Will* and *New Heaven, New Earth*. Oates had told him that *Wonderland* was "painful to write," partly because she "couldn't resolve the moral questions it raised." "As she talks," he wrote, "one realizes that the 'moral failure' that is worrying her is one that has tormented writers before her, most notably Tolstoy: what use is art if it doesn't help people live better?" "With *Wonderland*," Oates tells him, "I came to the end of a phase in my life, though I didn't know it. I want to move toward a more articulate moral position, not just dramatizing nightmarish problems but trying to show possible ways of transcending them." "A Theory of Knowledge," then, reflects something of the process that Oates's own writing of novels would undergo between *Do with Me What You Will*, written during the time of her "mystical vision," and *Son of the Morning*. The logic of *Wonderland*, Johnson notes, is that "if all human and social reality originates in the brain's own impulses, then the demons Jesse has spent so much time evading actually lie within himself." If so, then Oates's own demons—her "long maniacal struggle," as she put it in a 1972 letter to Gail Godwin, "that I thought was myself vs. the world"—originated, as she now realized, in her own mind. Three of these next four novels certainly show characters acting out dramas of this sort. What had changed, however, was that "myself vs. myself" had become the novels' actual subject matter, rather than merely an unexamined quality found in them.[5] Oates began to make practical use of her abstract introspection in order to provide a worthwhile critique of America. In particular, she began implicitly to suggest not only the shapes that self-absorption and introspection could take, but also ways to overcome them.

Where the themes, if not the form, of *Do with Me What You Will* (1973) seem drawn from the same well as *Wonderland*, the diverse subject matter of *The Assassins: A Book of Hours* (1975), *Childwold* (1976), and *Son of the Morning* (1978) only disguises their formal and thematic similarities. All four novels free up chronology and viewpoint to produce something reminiscent of the "dizzying jumble of colors" that is the Bartletts' weed- and flower-strewn farmhouse in *Childwold*.[6] All four novels still seem at least as haunted by their own coming-into-being as they are sustained attempts to achieve ironic distance from that process. But they do suggest a more purposeful assessment, rather than simply reflection of, the characters' "nightmarish problems." Each focuses on loss and its consequences. *Do with Me What You Will* is about loss of certainty. *The Assassins* is about grief. *Childwold* is about loss of youth. *Son of the Morning* is about spiritual loss. But each is also really about the loss of the "I"—in Nathan Vickery's case, described as the literal loss of an eye—and the discovery of a very different sense of human experience in which self and other can merge.

Representing (as Lawrence had it of the dual "rhythm of American art-activity") a "sloughing of the old consciousness" and "the forming of a new consciousness," this period shows Oates working toward some of her most innovative novels, the foremost of which, *Bellefleur*, was already gestating. As such it is Oates's equivalent of Faulkner's moment of freedom: the day he shut a door between himself "and all publishers' addresses and book lists," said to himself, "Now I can write," and leaped from conventional novels like *Soldier's Pay* to *The Sound and the Fury*. Unlike Faulkner with his third novel, *Sartoris*, Oates was finding publication easy and had won the National Book Award for *them*. But she felt more concerned with her "actual work," she wrote in her journal, than with what she saw as her declining "public reputation." While her most experimental work would come just after this period, these particular novels were crucial to that subsequent work coming into being and reflect her most significant moment, perhaps, of personal, intellectual, and emotional enlightenment.[7]

Critics have noted significant changes between Oates's earliest works and *Do with Me What You Will*. For Calvin Bedient, the "defeatism under which the earlier novels groaned" has begun to dissipate. "Oates's world is scarcely less raw and terrible than before," he writes, but "the lighting has changed, and what was hell has become a heroic arena." No longer so nightmarish or nihilistic, "it is now freely Nietzschean, elatedly frictional." For other critics, this change has a specifically feminist emphasis. Eileen Teper Bender calls *Do with Me What You Will* Oates's "first extended feminist critique." Brenda Daly sees in it a rejection of the "father-author" model of authorship (Howe) in favor of individual "self-authoring" (Jack and Elena).[8] Indeed, if the idea of authorship, and of evolving concepts of authorship, was always near the surface in previous novels, in *Do with Me What You Will* these perennial preoccupations break through and disrupt the hitherto comparatively smooth surface—the realist "coherence and development"—of Oates's fiction. What *Do with Me What You Will* lacks in terms of inherited order it makes up for in raw energy, as if splashing and crashing around in an effort to disturb the becalmed waters of conventional perception.

Bedient's reference to Nietzsche is wholly appropriate to negotiating *Do with Me What You Will*. Nietzsche's first book, *The Birth of Tragedy*, describes two cultural forces, which he designates the Apollonian and the Dionysian. The Apollonian is a form-giving force that seeks "to grant repose to individual beings by drawing boundaries around them." The Dionysian is the form-destroying force. It is the equivalent of "direct and unmediated participation in reality," and its immediacy, argues Nietzsche, is unbearable. But life is an unending struggle between the two. The Apollonian provides the "illusions without which we cannot go on living," while the Dionysian undermines the Apollonian tendency to "freeze all form into Egyptian rigidity and coldness."[9] Oates's adaptation of this is to talk of the "two contradictory forces in American culture" as Love and Law. These forces, she is quoted as saying on the flyleaf to the first edition, are "the tension between two American 'pathways' "— that of "spontaneous emotion" and that of tradition. "In the synthesis of these two apparently contradictory forces," she says, "lies the inevitable transformation of our culture." These oppositions hint at the tension between delirium and detachment, between introspection and social observation, and between an invigorating yet alarming chaos and an ordering, yet deadening, coherence.

But as "pathways" they also seem to stand here for something else. While

Love seems to represent the spontaneity that facilitates rebellion and innovation, the Law, as Mary Ann Wilson describes it, seems to stand for "the more traditional narrative techniques of [Oates's] earliest novels."[10] These forces of Love and Law, then, are not just private vision versus public order, but also the struggle against the fictional coherence of tradition and the creation of new realities by way of a new language. Because of this, *Do with Me What You Will* throws out at the reader a "ceaseless swirl of consciousness" and seems to levitate somewhere above its purported subject matter.[11] In doing so, it begins to move Oates's art into new realms.

Dionysius outwits Apollo at almost every turn in this novel, and readers are mostly put in the position of trying to impose their own Apollonian forms of illusory order. While the novel is nominally held together by a table of contents that parodies both the realist novel and legal proceedings, the subtitles—and the novel's overall form—dissolve precisely the order and coherence that Howe and the realist novel represent. While the novel divides into three parts and a "Summing Up," the unevenly distributed subtitles cut against such easy coherence. "Twenty-eight Years, Two Months, Twenty-Six Days" is the subtitle of part 1; "Miscellaneous Facts, Events, Fantasies, Evidence Admissable and Inadmissable" is the subtitle of part 2. Part 3 is simply subtitled, "Crime," while the summing up has no subtitle at all. Equally, the novel does have a plot, or at least a basic narrative development, but to capture that plot in the process of reading is like trying to hold a ship's wheel steady in the midst of a storm. The narrative is thrown in all directions by the fluid rendering of the characters' lived experiences. Although we could be forgiven for missing this point on a first reading, the novel, as several critics have noted, is built by the two main characters, Jack Morrissey and Elena Howe, telling each other their versions of how they came to be together. "The first book [part] of the novel relates the history of Elena up to the moment that she meets Jack" is how Ellen Friedman summarizes it. The second part "relates the history of Jack up to the moment he meets Elena."[12] The third part and summing up then follow their story through.

At the age of seven, Elena has been abducted by her father, and then abandoned by him. She is rediscovered by her cold-hearted mother, Ardis, before being married off at the age of seventeen to Marvin Howe, a lawyer, who is as wealthy and powerful as he is domineering and unloving. Twenty-eight years old and—as stipulated in Howe's forty-five-clause marriage contract—childless, Elena meets Jack, who is himself married to a woman named Rachel.

However, Jack is younger than Howe, and, while hardly idealistic, has been involved in civil rights cases in the South. Ardis's original marriage target for her daughter had been Ardis's employer, Sadoff. So Howe, in marrying Elena, has saved her from marriage to Ardis. And, earlier, Howe had saved Jack's father, Joseph, from a murder charge by getting a nonguilty verdict by reason of insanity—a success that involved Jack's participation as a teenage defense witness. Elena and Jack begin an affair that presumably leads to divorce and probable remarriage, official or otherwise, prior to their narration of the novel. (We can assume this because, while the contextual narrative ends with their respective partners' discoveries of the affair and the couple' breakaway, the final two lines—"*Did you forget everything else? Almost everything*"—continue the pattern of inserted, italicized dialogue that constitute Jack and Elena's retrospective discussion of events (561). Although Jack, too, is now a lawyer, he and Elena basically stand for Love, while Howe stands for the Law. In turn, the couple and the cuckold represent the Dionysian and Apollonian forces.

Do with Me What You Will is too experimental to engage us on the level of character and too disorientating to remain in the mind in the kind of detail a great novel can. Yet it is strangely memorable as a reading experience that challenges the expectations we might bring to a work that gestures, however nominally, toward realism. Encouraged to approach the novel from an Apollonian perspective—seeking order, in other words, or trying to impose it, like Howe—we find ourselves constantly tossed back toward the Dionysian and all the chaotic emotions of the lovers. As Marilyn Wesley points out, Howe "is the fictive embodiment of patriarchal power," but unlike *Wonderland*'s Pedersen, who so dominates his section of that previous novel, what we remember most of Howe is how he loses control of events and how his imposition of meaning is overturned.[13] It is as if the novel's "swirl of consciousness" engulfs his discourse and shows it to be a flimsy construct unable to withstand the oceanic unruliness of Love.

Howe is a projection of the novelist-as-realist, his forte being the construction and maintenance of fictional coherence. He knows that he creates intelligible lies that function as instruments for mastering unintelligible truths. "There is no reality in the mind that can be measured," he says; "everything is states of consciousness" (176). He knows that his are the skills of artifice, that the conventions of Law are, like the rules of realist-novel writing, a means to an end, and that that end is coherence even if the coherence is a lie. Like Pedersen, he is patently an artist, an actor, a purveyor of fiction to get at a "truth."

In his case, it is the courtroom that serves as his canvas, his theater, his novel; it is a symbolic—if pragmatic—arena that bears only the most schematic resemblance to the experience of real life. Just as an artist imposes a necessarily distorting vision, so Howe, in the courtroom, suspends the complexities of the world beyond that setting.

Both in terms of what Howe says and what others say about him, Oates makes his role as would-be omniscient author explicit. "Sometimes it's as if I were high above," says Howe, "able to see for myself the magical curve of the earth, which no one else has ever seen. And I see it all—I see everything." As with Pedersen, the all-consuming Howe may well be meant to be an American type, but his vocabulary here is less that of a high-powered lawyer than that of a novelist for whom control of material is all important. His description of the point at which he gains control of a trial might as well be the novelist's description of the point at which a novel takes off. "Then I know what will happen: exactly how the future will turn out," he says. "The present divides itself routinely and tamely into days, court sessions, recesses and breaks and weekends," but "a point has been passed. So I can see into the future." From that point on, he says, "I know how deeply I have pushed myself into the imaginations of other people, how powerfully I have guided their wills. It only remains for enough days to pass in order for the fact of my victory to be realized—in what is called 'real life'" (120). A workaholic, he never sleeps "more than a few hours a night, any night," because he has "so much to figure out." "Some of it I do in my dreams—but the rest I have to do at my desk—I need to get a pencil in my hand, I need to pick up a pencil in my fingers. So I can't waste time in bed, I have to get up. It seems to be getting more obvious as I grow older—the pattern of sleep, and waking, of dreaming about work and then waking, suddenly, when the dream has fulfilled its function and I need now to think logically, cunningly." In this way, he believes that he lives "a multitude of lives," burrowing "more deeply into certain people" than they do "into their own souls" (121).

But far from his being omniscient, Howe's Apollonian rage for order is swamped by the Dionysian narrators, Jack and Elena. In previous novels, Oates used the craft of fiction, in Bender's phrase, as "a metaphor for the self-struggle for identity and control." In *Do with Me What You Will*, as less dramatically in *them*, Oates celebrates our self-authoring capacity. In Howe, Daly argues persuasively, "the novel parodies, and transforms, this notion of godlike author/ing." "The novel actually offers two models of the novelist," she suggests. But it is the democratic ability of characters, or individuals, to "grow and develop" that allows them to "acquire their own capacity for self-authoring" against the imposed "father-author model."[14] What Daly expresses in broadly feminist terms is also very much the approach of a novelist-as-pragmatist. All that Howe champions—imposed structure, stasis, solidity—gives way to the pragmatist values of growth and development, fluidity and motion.

The realist novelist of courtrooms is doomed once his strategies are exposed, and Jack, at his father's trial, sees through Howe. No longer the author controlling his clients/characters, Howe becomes a character in his former client's narrative, his devices laid bare. "In real life a man like Howe would not speak so dramatically and so confidently to those twelve people," thinks Jack, "and in real life they would shy away from him, knowing themselves unworthy of his attention or distrusting it, fearing it" (201). Once Jack realizes that Howe conducts the trial "like a television play," he sees how inadequate it is to the lived reality of Jack's and others' lives. "It was not difficult if you understood the plot," he reflects, and "the main character, 'Morrissey,' whom Howe was explaining" (201–2). The more believable Howe's narrative becomes, the less believable is "the plot the prosecution had explained" (202). As the courtroom's realist novelist, Howe provides the kind of coherence and development that Maureen Wendall's teacher required of her. Jack feels that Howe has coaxed him into semifictional replies that nevertheless provide answers for all the trial's "jumbled and conflicting and puzzling questions." "Once you knew the main character, once you knew why the plot went the way it had, it was all very simple" (211). The very things that make it seem real reveal the artifice. The notion of the Law as fiction—like Shar's racing, Clara's ambition, Richard's bulimia, Maureen's challenge to her teacher, and Jesse's self-creations—again allows Oates to use ostensible social commentary to reflect on the direction of her art. This time, however, the realist artist is not just displaced from the narrative center, but effectively drowned out by new voices and a new form.

The innovative, multidimensional aspect of *Do with Me What You Will*, then, is thematic as well as formal, and linked to the novel as social critique. Oates, suggests Mary Ann Wilson, "experiments with multiple points of view and sudden time shifts" to try to give aesthetic form to the novel's "redemptive vision." Wilson sees Jack's hippie client, Mered Dawe, as "the voice of the future" because he "adds a mystical dimension" that sparks "Jack's latent optimism and hope for America." This claims a lot for a figure characterized, as Wilson admits, by "fanatical ravings" and eventual insanity—a character drawn, as Bedient notes, in so "perfunctory" a manner.[15] But Dawe, together with the novel's experimental form and tonal shift, does anticipate the values of the better-realized Stephen Petrie of *The Assassins*. Seeing "heavenly, cosmic love" as "the basic force of the universe" that includes everything from "the kingdom of physical presences" to "works of art," Dawe is clearly a Love representative (330). And formally, the ordered fictions of the Law are overwhelmed by the chaotic fictions of Love. Fluidity and provisionality wash away rigidity and certainty. In turn, the accounts of events as told to each other by Jack and Elena dissolve the fictitious coherence that Howe tries to assert via the Law and emphasize the troubling fictions even of that supposedly most authentic of experiences, Love.

For Jack and Elena's relationship is hardly simple, and its complexity lies, in particular, in Oates's deconstruction of what a supposedly coherent self actually amounts to, and therefore what we mean when, for instance, we talk of loving someone. "We're our own ideas," says Elena's mother, Ardis, who is conspicuous for constantly changing her identity. "We make ourselves up." (74). The truth of her remark is everywhere evident in the lovers' thoughts about one another. Thinking of Jack, Elena feels that were he actually there "his voice would profane itself, saying all the degrading ordinary things again, in his ordinary voice," and "the dazzling certainty of her love would die as if pounded into mute flesh again by a man's body" (389). She believes there are two versions of herself, providing "a perfect reflection as in a mirror: the Elena lying beside him, the Elena in his brain" (346). The less she says, the more he makes up about her. But it is the same for Jack, too, or so she imagines. "*He wants my husband's wife,*" she thinks, "*not me*" (390). In turn, Jack shares with Howe a sense of the artifice of even the most supposedly authentic experiences. Just as trials seem like everybody "acting out their parts" as if in "a bad television show," so Love seems partly artifice and partly arbitrary (256). Like Jules Wendall, Jack builds a narrative fiction—"the Word Machine"—to explain his behavior. "*In a former life, Jack had loved and married a woman who had given birth to a child, his child (who was Robert); and the woman (who was Elena) had died or somehow disappeared. Had died, that was best. Was dead. . . . Yes, permanently dead, dead for the remainder of the narrative*" (505).

Both lovers, then, are acutely aware of the artifice they build around the brute fact of that other "pathway," "spontaneous emotion—in this case Love." But in particular, they are chronically uncertain of the status of their own, let alone each other's, selves. Provisionality and contingency, rather than order and coherence, may rule in spontaneous emotion, but just as too much order can deaden, so too little is unbearable, and even lovers must make up stories to impose meanings on their emotions. Love is a story just as much as Law. Set up as something authentic in face of the imposed order of Law, it turns out to be in some ways inauthentic. Meanwhile Law, set up as something concrete against the fancy and fantasies of emotions, turns out to be itself a fictional construct, a creation demanding that those involved in its proceedings take on fantasy roles as illusory as those adopted by romantic lovers.

Like *them* and *Wonderland,* the title *Do with Me What You Will* itself merges the inward and outward vision, but it also stresses provisionality and open-endedness over stasis and certainty. As a translation of the legal term *nolo contendere*—to throw oneself at the mercy of the court—it seems very specific (350). But more generally, the phrase reiterates Oates's preoccupation with the subjectivity and indeterminacy of identity. Both the *Me* and the *You* of *Do with Me What You Will* could refer to any of the characters, just as it could refer to the relationship between the novel and its reader. In Love, as in Law, it implies, we designate roles for others that may have little to do with their inner sense of self. "Believe anything you want about me," Jack tells Elena (428–29). The moment of greatest communion, in all these early novels, serves only to reinforce the sense of individual isolation. In reading novels (at least in reading Oates's novels from this point in her career onward) we are all co-creators, just as we are self-creators in life itself. If we recognize this freedom, we recognize that we do with ourselves what we will. Me and You turn out, like the Law or Love, to be other examples of how language can imprison or free us, depending upon whether we live within another's discourse or discover our own.

Something, then, had changed in Oates's novel writing by the time of *Do with Me What You Will.* Where *Wonderland*'s claustrophobic structure mimics the structure of the brain itself, confronting the reader with "inwardly tightening circles of mental experiences" that move toward "a terminus in Jesse's baffled brain," *Do with Me What You Will* swirls expansively.[16] Yet both novels, in their different ways, are attempts to shift linguistic practices and so shake off the blinkers of conventional perception. Oates was straining the novel form to accommodate her changing vision. Coherent, progressive narrative and clear-cut distinctions between inner and outer worlds—between "us" and "them" and "me" and "you"—were proving too restrictive to explain the interrelations of her characters. In the pivotal period leading up to *Bellefleur,* Oates's novels offered an increasing sense of fluidity and sometimes opacity, as she stretched the form to accommodate her evolving consciousness, delving further into issues of the self so as finally to break free of them. This helps explain the shape of novels like *The Assassins, Childwold,* and *Son of the Morning.* It also explains why her subsequent novels would move, for a while at least, further from "coherence and development" and deeper into this "ceaseless swirl."

At the same time, however, it shows Oates trying to break free of her old forms and to turn the introspection toward a more pragmatic, social end. Asked in more recent years what she meant by morality in art, she defined it as "what is life enhancing."[17] In this sense, *Do with Me What You Will,* despite the triumph of adulterous love over institutional marriage, was her most "moral" novel to date. Jack and Elena escape Howe's tyranny. That work provided something of a sea change after the bleak conclusions of all the novels up to and including *Wonderland,* novels in which, as Bender puts it, "her characters achieve a measure of control, but always with destructive outcomes."[18] Like the latter, its social commentary seems sometimes smothered by a preoccupation with the complexities of introspection and identity. But its epigraph, from Henry James, explicitly argues in favor of facing up to the complexities of life, rather than retreating into self-pity or abstraction. "The world as it stands is no illusion, no phantasm, no evil dream of a night," wrote James. "We wake up to it again for ever and ever; we can neither forget it nor deny it nor dispense with it." That epigraph could hardly be more different from the claustrophobic poem that fronts *Wonderland.* It seems that Oates was now ready to take up her self-challenge from *New Heaven, New Earth* and to forego mental self-dissection in favor of rediscovering the world, or had written *Do with Me What You Will* with that eventual goal consciously or subconsciously in mind.

Samuel Coale writes with some justification that "when consciousness consumes itself and the palpable physical world is swallowed up within the bloated blur of that babbling consciousness as in *The Assassins* and *Angel of Light,*" Oates's novels "become monotonous, tedious and inert." In contrast, "when she has a firmer grasp on some wider reality," as in *The Son of the Morning,* "her novels succeed." Even sympathetic critics almost unanimously condemn *The Assassins.* Johnson echoes Coale in concluding that the novel lacks "dramatic tension and dynamic momentum," is "inert on the page," and "goes hopelessly awry." While Creighton calls it "intricate and thematically complex," it is also "not as illuminating as a reader would wish." Few critics find much good to say about any one of the three characters who try in different ways to survive the sudden death of Senator Andrew Petrie.

The book is in three parts. The first third is from the viewpoint of Andrew's cartoonist brother, Hugh, whose narrative, for Creighton, contributes "in large measure to the book's tedium." Waller calls Hugh a "despicable and weak character whose parasitism and paranoia become increasingly vicious." So self-absorbed and self-indulgent and self-pitying is his monologue, suggests Johnson, that "for most readers the suicide attempt by this hate-filled, deranged man cannot come soon enough." The second third of the book is narrated from the viewpoint of Andrew's widow, Yvonne, who despite the positive role accorded her by Brenda Daly—one of the few critics who argues that *The Assassins* even "deserves attention"—receives scant interest from other quarters. The book's final portion belongs to another brother, Stephen, described by both Creighton and Johnson as "ineffectual."[19] But it is as well here to remember William James's view that what matters is to concentrate on the general flow (in this case of a career), rather than the limitations of an isolated product. For *The Assassins*, like *Expensive People*, is an important marker of where Oates was going. Had she not written it, perhaps more successful novels like *Son of the Morning* and *Bellefleur* might never have assumed their distinctive shape. Most crucially, *The Assassins* is the first clear articulation of the shift from self-absorption to selfless action that shapes both "A Theory of Knowledge" and really the rest of Oates's novel-writing career.

While *The Assassins* has all the signs of being a process of experimental thought, it remains a necessary doodle on the margins of Oates's career. Its three voices portray a movement from almost total solipsism (Hugh), through a problematic relationship between the inner and outer world (Yvonne), to transcendence of ego (Stephen). The poisonous Hugh at least touches on the relationship between creative output and the social world. Goya, too, says Hugh, "discovered his genius the day he dared to give up pleasing others."[20] There are signs, starting with *The Assassins*, that Oates decided to do much the same, and so discover her own genius. To do this, however, she had to go back to the drawing board, to rub out and redesign the novel form as practised by her precursors to suit her evolving vision. Having begun with the working title *Death Festival*, *The Assassins* might as easily have been called *As I Lay Dead*. With its competing voices all coming to terms with the senator's death, it owes much to Faulkner's innovations in *The Sound and the Fury* and *As I Lay Dying*. Following on from *Do with Me What You Will*, it is even more relentless in its disruption of chronological time. "Why insist upon chronological experience?" says Hugh (148). Scenes and memories, dreams and actualities, all intermingle. Characters can be in three places at once, the mind can detach from the body. The novel is Pollockesque in its swirls and coils. Each character has a different vision and stance on Andrew. But since "all experience is a process," to cite William James, "no point of view can be the *last* one. Every one is insufficient and off its balance, and responsible to later points of view than itself."[21] Only Stephen, despite or perhaps because he lacks the destructive egocentric dynamism of a Shar or a Lowry, is in a position to have any kind of final word, because his survival—and health—has depended on precisely his provisional, almost "self"-less viewpoint. An observer and listener, he alone proves adaptable, synthesizing the inward/outward paradox, and comfortable with the ambiguities involved.

Hugh's is undoubtedly the least engaging of the three viewpoints. But the problem with his monologue is length and repetition, rather than that it is "hate-filled." As with *Expensive People,* we can echo Oates's words on Lawrence's poems: such sections of her work are for readers who want process as well as product, the worst along with the best. Hugh's section suffers, if anything, from being too accurate a rendition of self-absorption. It is allowed to become not merely a portrayal of "the artist at [her] drawing board," but the artist actually doodling around the implications of her art (86). For while the novel transcends Hugh's caricaturing and caricatured perspective, he is still a distorted exaggeration of the artist: a caricature of a caricaturist caricaturing himself, doodling faces or versions of his own name, just as Oates, at this stage of her career, habitually did in the margins of manuscripts. Hugh's doodles are verbal "whimsicality," an "overflow of imaginative energy." He is "the Artist following the thread of a queer private dream, unafraid of the labyrinthine risks" (159). "I am in a tiny place without walls," he says. "It is stifling here—but the walls are gone" (3). In retrospect, we know that he is on a life-support machine. But he is also the artist trapped in his own mind, contemplating the limitations of his craft. "Art demands structures," he says. "Chaos may be entertained—often is—may be entertained and courted," but there is a need for conventions, for order, even as the artist desires to stretch the boundaries in keeping with changing human experience (185). For Hugh, art alone seems to ensure order. "The quick-darting movements of my pen had kept Chaos at bay for years," he says. But now Chaos has begun "to seep forward, inward." The "brute ferocity of life," once "muzzled," has begun "to jabber and squeal with delight" (100). He is a carnivalesque self-portrait of the artist as neurotic, "grappling with and embracing phantoms, whispering to himself, pleading and cajoling with himself, -self, -self, to the exclusion of the world," and producing only a "series of portraits of -self" (73). Not really Hugh against the world, but Hugh against Hugh, he is the most self-absorbed of characters in early novels, which, on some level, are all a "series of portraits of -self." Only his work, he complains, "carries me out of myself," only "my *art*" (74). The rest is frustration, anger, self-directed hostility that purports to be hostility toward others. Not really "myself vs. the world," as Oates wrote in that letter to Gail Godwin, but "myself vs. myself."

Yet while Hugh is "an exaggerated self-portrait" of the introspection that would seem to have been one of Oates's initial aesthetic impulses, he differs from earlier such characters in that he seems consciously created that way. For the first time, the ironic distance is evident both in the novel's actual structure—in the way it leaves Hugh's viewpoint behind—and in what others say about him. "You don't care about the real world," he is told by his neighbor, Eva; "you don't even notice it—you're always sketching or doodling or seeing things in your mind" (62). He is patently a man who believes that "we experience nothing but what we already are."[22] The very length of his soliloquy reflects his self-absorption. He is a Francis Bacon portrait, his grotesque innards visible through his screaming mouth. He is the artist as self-pitying freak, but still the artist, aiming for invisibility, so that "no one knew him, but he knew everyone" (132). So his drama turns out to be the drama of art in relation to "the external world" (139). And it is that world, ultimately, that *The Assassins* is about. For all his self-absorption, Hugh sees himself as "a lover in search of a beloved" (192). But his real emotion is grief, so love and loss fuse in the idea of marrying his brother's widow, Yvonne, even though she seems barely to exist for him beyond his own mind. "There is no woman—there is no sister-in-law—the widow is an illusion," he tells himself, "an image your mind has seized upon" (195).

Yvonne herself lies somewhere between Hugh's solipsism and Stephen's transcendence of ego. For Brenda Daly she is the novel's heroine, a key figure in Oates's changing perspective on issues of gender, "a (woman) writer whose own artistic hallucinations have the power to free her from masculine projections." Through close analysis of Yvonne's main hallucination—that she is shot by strangers, and hacked up with an axe—Daly argues that "her figurative dismemberment transforms the homosocial center of *The Assassins*." "While the Petrie men look to Yvonne for salvation," says Daly, "Yvonne's salvation can be found in her own imagination."[23] On the other hand, Yvonne's alienation and cynicism are such that she is never able to contribute anything healthy or positive to the situation. There is nothing remotely communal about her attitudes toward others, whether men or women. Her escape from self-absorption is merely into self-negation and alienation, rather than transcendence. Her features do not "represent her" but mask her so she can "hide" deep inside, while her voice performs. She witnesses "her own behavior from a distance," and the world is full of strangers, "irrelevant and apart from her." Socially, her only "strong cerebral pleasure" has to do with her need to control others' "interpretation of her, the image they carried away in their imaginations." This ability confirms "her cynicism, her detachment, her pure and undefiled identity" (298). This jaundiced perspective has much to do with her situation as a wife and then widow in a patriarchal family. She "knows a great deal," but has no power to act on it because her identity has for so long been as her husband's adjunct (232). Andrew's death has therefore metaphorically killed her as well. She is, thinks Stephen at the funeral, seeing her "bright hard glassy defiant stare," "already dead" (44). She and her husband have lacked emotional commitment, a love of others, or, as Oates talks of it elsewhere, a "reverence for life."[24] She may discover emotional detachment, but it isolates rather than frees her, and her cynicism is as repellent as Hugh's self-pity.

If Daly's reading of Yvonne's "death"-scene as heroic and symbolic is accurate, however, then the dismemberment of self that it signifies places Yvonne one step nearer the transcendence of ego demonstrated by the novel's final voice, that of Stephen Petrie. For it is Stephen, despite critics' general dismissal of him as "ineffectual," who turns out to be the best placed of all to understand what Andrew calls "the intoxication of the world as it spins" (555). During the course of the novel, Stephen is transformed, rather than petrified. He is neither cynical, angry, nor self-pitying. Rather, he is adaptable and aware that "one must always respect the magical rites by which others live" (455). Most of his time is spent focusing on others' behavior. The first we see of him he is springing forward "to help" Yvonne (443). Instinctive and energetic, he does so not for personal gratification, but as an impartial observer and listener. He is as capable of self-torture as Hugh or Yvonne, but—to paraphrase Oates's words in a 1975 interview—he does not get depressed or feel emotions like other people do. He seems to have worked his way through all that.[25] His family are always a temptation for drawing him "into the net of those old, dismaying emotions" (457). But although he has found a balance that enables him to help his family, he yet feels "almost euphoric with freedom" on leaving them (451).

In the end, Stephen's self-negation brings about a new form of life, rather than the living death it brings Hugh and Yvonne. In the funeral limousine, three years after walking out of his father's house, his transformation is complete. His empathy contrasts with Hugh's solipsistic chatter, the "sort of emotion" Stephen rejected years ago (457). *"Don't do this to us and yourself,"* he tells Hugh (462). Just as he sees through Hugh and Yvonne, so Stephen sees that Andrew's public service has been a version of self-aggrandizement and therefore as self-centered as Hugh's turmoil. Where Andrew has viewed "the average human being" as "a cripple, a wreck, a parody," Stephen's viewpoint is Whitmanesque in its inclusiveness and sense of self-dispersion (471). He imagines himself "as one of thousands out on the street today. Miracles, all of them; but not distinguishable from one another." He blends with them, falls "in step with them unconsciously" (472), and senses "the harmony of the street, the harmony of the world," "warring rhythms" that are "nevertheless contained in one pulse" (473).

As with Yvonne, the parallels with Oates's sense of "generalized emotional detachment" in the mid-1970s are obvious.[26] But Stephen seems closest to what Oates believed at the time she had worked through to. He shares with Oates a fascination with the out-of-body experience of reading. "In the midst of staring at one of the illustrations that always attracted him," he can "find himself suddenly and unaccountably in another part of the house, suspended weightless in his own room." In the alternative world of reading and writing, the novelist escapes her own body and enters others. Writing and reading become the same activity. Stephen's privacy and contemplation lead him from *Through the Looking Glass* (and his childhood fascination with Alice, "arms outstretched, leaning forward into a mirror that dissolved in order to allow her entry") to books about America (489). The inward act of reading leads him outward, "transported" elsewhere (490). Finally, Oates links Stephen directly to her own revelation—during her "mystical vision"—that the "self" is really a "column of light" in which "the 'I,'" "deluded as to its sovereignty," is really "many," rather than "one."[27] Stephen believes, for instance, that he is "many creatures struggling for dominance inside the same envelope of flesh." He alone, of the Petries, discovers his intimate connection with the rest of humanity as "not a jumble of pieces making war upon one another, but a single whole" (494). Unlike Oates's demonic earlier figures, his ability to "slip into the consciousness" of others, "to suffer with them," is not domineering or self-promoting, but selfless and benign (515).

By the time of *The Assassins*, then, Oates had transformed her introspective tendencies into a sense of inclusiveness. Denying the unitary self, she was paradoxically free to explore her own psyche in an "impersonal" way. The melding of author and character evident all the way from Karen to Jesse had found a more specific thematic purpose. Instead of these author-figures being distractions that competed with the social critiques the novels were intended to provide, "myself versus myself" had become a conscious part of the subject matter. The merging of character and author—of the introspective and the social—had now evolved far beyond being simply introspective slippage that revealed the writer's obsessive ambition in relation to her craft. Stephen is comfortable with himself because he concentrates on interconnectedness, even though this results from an awareness of solitude. To use Schopenhauer's terminology, Stephen sees that "at bottom it is *one* being that perceives itself," in that "we are inseparably joined together as parts of one whole." He alone of the Petries sees that self-awareness leads to awareness of others. The world is a window *because* we mirror one another.[28]

"No one knows anyone else," says Hugh, "it's an utterly boring platitude" (536), but the very fact that Stephen intuits both Andrew's and Hugh's plight defeats Hugh's logic: "I know why you're here, you ghoul," says Hugh. "You can smell the stink of my decay." No one *knows* anyone else, but one can intuit the minds of others from seeing the links between what they say and what they do and from examining one's own emotions. The truth of this is evident in the success of the novel form. For while Hugh's self-absorption incarcerates him, he is right that *"the Artist,"* in art if not life, *"is free,"* and for Oates we are all artists (537). What limits more productive forms of creativity are the battles—in the form of doubt, paranoia, bitterness (grappling with phantoms, as Hugh puts it)—that we have with ourselves. Stephen, then, who does not entirely believe in his own existence, is the novel's hero because he frees himself of that self-absorption. By the end, he is roaming America, touching others' lives, visiting friends who remember him while he is there and forget him when he goes. He is perpetually in motion in his unending willingness to accommodate diverse viewpoints. Oates had begun to come into her own, and for the next few novels she would explore ever more diverse and wild territories, slipping like Stephen in and out of all variety of American eras and American minds. A necessary prerequisite for that exploration, as *Childwold* testifies, would be formal experimentation in terms of the relations between the self and others, inner and outer worlds, mirrors and windows: what might be meant by "myself versus the world" or "myself versus myself" had implications for the formal conventions of the novel as a tool for probing social issues.

Childwold, equally marked by this characteristically pragmatic preoccupation with the permeable nature of our inner and outer worlds, provides another, again more convincing, merging of the pursuit of private perfection with the act of citizenship. For John Dewey, to cite one pragmatist, what traditional philosophical discourse divided into humanity and world, "inner *and* outer, self *and* not-self, subject *and* object, individual *and* social, private *and* public," are really "parties in life-transactions. The philosophical 'problem' of trying to get them together is artificial." In turn, *Childwold* folds a drama of the self into a social critique, but the blend is now the very essence of the novel's structure. A number of critics have tried to separate the "voices" of *Childwold*. Waller talks of "the diseased world of Kasch's mind." "All the major characters have their narrative voice," he says, even if there are "confusions and overlapping of minds and feelings, wordless collisions of incommunicable realities and perspectives." Creighton wishes "for more guidance in evaluation of character and action" and "greater clarity of presentation." Bender suggests that "Laney, Oates's youthful alter ego, will write her own story"; she notes that "appropriately" the last words are not those of "the fabulator, Kasch, or any of the novel's allusive literary voices, but a child's words."[29] But statements of this kind seem a little like trying to separate the ingredients of a cake after it has been baked. Such conjectures seek "coherence" of a novel whose narrative "voices" are inseparable, and that seeks to challenge the very conventions by which we "read" the world.

As Daly writes, in *Childwold* "voices flow into each other like a river." Distinctions between first- and third-person narrative are deliberately confused to the point where they cannot be satisfactorily disentangled. We simply cannot know where one voice ends and another begins because both Kasch and Laney are capable of appropriating the other's voice. "In the process of reading the novel," Daly continues, "it isn't always possible to separate his voice from hers, her memories from his, their experiences from those of their families." To seek coherence somehow beyond the language of the novel is to succumb to the illusion of a pure story behind the pattern of words, like seeing, say, a coherent, "realist" image behind a painting by Mark Rothko. As Rorty says of language, "truth cannot be out there—cannot exist independently of the human mind—because sentences cannot so exist, or be out there."[30] So, with *Childwold*, its patterns of language are not a scrambling of an otherwise viewable, coherent story, but the essence of that story, and amount to a new idiom, a new way of seeing, and of creating meaning. Where Bender suggests that Laney will one day "write her own story," it might as easily be observed that *Childwold* could *be* Laney's story, and Kasch merely Laney's intuitive projection of herself into Kasch's mind. The logic of the novel's composition dictates that either or neither character could be the narrator. The only certainty is that the words of Oates, Kasch, and Laney are the tracks of the author's consciousness in composing the novel, thereafter to be creatively revised by a given reader.

To see *Childwold* in the context of Oates's stream of novels clarifies what she was up to in experimenting with the construction and dismantling of meaning. Greg Johnson says of *Son of the Morning* that Oates's "long meditation on the novel had led her toward an innovative structure" that combined first- and third-person narrative. "The third-person narrative is framed by brief, interpolated monologues by Nathan himself, all addressed to an inscrutable God and suggesting that the novel is Nathan's own attempt to make sense of his experience."[31] But something of the same "innovative structure" equally accounts for the indeterminacy of *Childwold*. To try to make sense—as opposed to "make" sense—out of the confusion of voices and chronology may be beside the point. Given Oates's position on the unity of inner and outer worlds, in the three novels *Do with Me What You Will*, *Childwold*, and *Son of the Morning*, order, as we have come to expect it, disappears, but, within the apparent disarray, the twin impulses of self-contemplation and social commentary remain. On a first reading, *Childwold* seems, indeed, opaque. Kasch's inner world merges with the social lives of the people he hopes to help, just as Laney's inner world merges with Kasch's imaginings.

Mixed irretrievably into this jumble are glimmers of a historically situated world, a social context of violence, exploitation and economic imperatives that we almost feel we could separate from the medley of voices. But Oates has irrevocably wedded the two; for the first time, the introspective reflection and social critique are inextricably intertwined. Like a stereogram or three-dimensional artwork (if one can conceive of three dimensions purely within the realm of thought), the novel entices us to see depth, and even individuality, where in truth there is only language. Unlike the practitioners of nineteenth-century realism, who sought to sustain that illusion of depth, the Oates of *Childwold*, like her modernist precursors, foregrounds language as the creator of that illusion. But like James, Rorty, and other pragmatists, part of her agenda is to lay bare the illusory nature of the rock-bottom, isolated self. This involves showing how individual selves, along with concepts like "meaning" and "truth," are wedded to social activity, rather than definable in and of themselves.

The blending of Oates's, Kasch's, and Laney's voices into a linguistic soup continuously unsettles our attempts to interpret *Childwold* and ensures that each reader is always creatively involved in "writing" the novel into "meaning." The novel seems to be about Kasch's love for Laney and about the writer's relationship with her childhood and youth. But Kasch, for all his Thoreauvian self-exploration, is also a wealthy heir to a family of exploiters, and his object of affection—his Lolita-like "angel" Evangeline Bartlett, or Laney—is a poor farm girl. The novel, on this level, depicts a world of violent, frustrated men, like Vale, the war veteran-turned-murderer; Earl, Laney's stepfather, and her father, Lyle, whose death one New Year's Day in "a pile-up on the highway" probably results from alcohol-fueled frustrations (42). Sensitive though Kasch is in contrast to these men, we still have to confront him, on a literal reading, as a voyeuristic pervert who commits statutory rape. But the novel's social realism—to the extent that we read any of Kasch's activities as physical or accept his or Laney's social (as opposed to merely textual) existence—is one aspect of a novel that attempts to fuse not just disparate worlds but disparate perceptions of the same phenomena.

Oates's comments from the time confirm this dual vision. On the one hand, she said to Robert Phillips, "it always surprises me that other people find the novel admirable because, to me, it seems very private." But she rejected Phillips's suggestion that her novels, especially *Childwold*, were becoming "more subjective and less concerned with the outward details of this world." For Oates, the novel's tension is precisely between two opposing ideas, "the image-centered structure of poetry and the narrative-centered and linear structure of the interplay of persons that constitutes a novel. In other words, poetry focuses upon the image, the particular thing, or emotion, or feeling; while prose fiction focuses upon motion through time and space." These "two impulses"—given Oates's comments in her Plath essay on the tendencies of lyric poetry toward "self-analysis" and of the writing of novels toward greater social commitment—are other names for the world as mirror versus the world as window.[32]

The novel has two epigraphs, one from Emerson, the other from William James. The Emerson epigraph can be taken to represent the inward-looking, "poetic" story. Kasch focuses on an image, symbolized by Laney, that will save or damn him. "*Every man's condition is a solution in hieroglyphic to those inquiries he would put,*" runs part of the epigraph. The inquiry Kasch puts to himself is essentially whether to die or to seek salvation by way of this symbolic union that will, he hopes, bring about his self-recovery. The novel begins not with narrative, but with an actual object that has symbolic potential. "The moon is a stone. The moon is nothing but rock. You must think of it that way, but without weight, weighing nothing: that way you can't think of God" (3). The moon, Kasch must continually remind himself, is not a symbol, invested with meaning, but a material object. The world, too, must be seen for what it is, and not superimposed with superstitions. By implication, too, *Childwold* itself is an object, a collection of words without meaning unless actually read. The moon, however, *is* a symbol, regardless of how we try, intellectually, to dispel that notion. For as soon as Kasch contemplates the moon, he gives it meaning even in the act of denying it. He indirectly equates it with Laney, whom he has equally invested with a meaning that has all but destroyed him. "The moon is a stone, the moon has no meaning, the light that falls across your legs has no meaning" (4). Since "the human self is created by the use of a vocabulary, rather than being adequately or inadequately expressed in a vocabulary," consciousness of oneself and of other selves or objects in relation to oneself really means the ability to create meanings.[33] At every turn, we are all artists of our own experiences. Oates creates Kasch and Laney creating one another; Kasch gives meaning to the moon; the reader—or reading—gives meaning to the novel.

Oates's aestheticism leads her to posit a world without God, without meaning, but with *meanings*. That "the world has no meaning" is something she felt "sadly resigned to" as far back as 1970. "But the world has meanings, many individual and alarming and graspable meanings, and the adventure of human beings consists in seeking out these meanings."[34] The moon (or a book or person) may not intrinsically have meaning, but certainly has meanings for us, both as individuals and collectively, when we "read" it. Meanings belong not to the object itself, but depend upon human interpretation. Therefore the human subject can shape these meanings and is in turn shaped by them. Kasch has returned to Yewville after twenty years, rather as Thoreau retreated to Walden Woods. Citing the second chapter of *Walden*, he aims to find out "where I lived, and what I lived for." Unlike Thoreau, however, he seeks companionship, and the girl he finds (the "you" of *Yew*ville) is Laney—the moon as symbol and the moon as stone. "Hello," he calls out like a representative for every human being alive, "are you anyone I know? Do you need help? Are you a form of myself?" (20). On the one hand, she is the moon as symbol: her delicate beauty is, for Kasch, the transience of youth. She is memory invested with all the symbolism that romantics reserve for the moon. "In the uncertain moonlight," her skin is "like pale china, translucent china," like Kasch's "grandmother's white chinaware," which, "held to the light," reveals "its fragile nature." On the other hand, she is the moon as stone: beyond her "angel's face" she is an ordinary person who reeks of "cheap red wine," wears smeared lipstick, has protruding collarbones, and is covered in mosquito bites (29).

Childwold up to this point, then, is an unsettling experience. A reworking of *Lolita*, critics often note, its ostensible subject is an older man's relationship with a young girl.[35] Yet just as Laney is no angel, so Kasch is less threatening and more interesting than the stereotype that a lesser writer might have drawn, perhaps because he so often seems merely a projection of Oates's own reflections on her youth, symbolized by Laney. His interest in her, for instance, is constantly linked with the loss of his own "boyhood": "My boyhood, myself: gone" (127). Now Kasch/Oates is "an adult," muses the narrative voice, "But where is she? Where is the girl?" (20). While this could be Kasch asking where Laney is, he likely would have no need to ask, given that he has found her, so it sounds more like Oates asking after her past self. As in previous novels, we can interpret *Childwold* in terms of the "private" story that Oates hints at. On this level, it is the author contemplating the distance and loss involved in growing up and away from the world of childhood.

This confusion of stories, however, is the essence of the novel's attempt to render how we actually relate to and interpret the outer world. Oates is and is not Kasch, chasing Laney, chasing youth, chasing childwold. Ev-*angel*-ine is at once Kasch's angel and Oates's *memory-lane,* and it is this yearning for the insubstantial dream of the past that is perhaps the novel's real love affair. "How real the world strikes us, the world of the present moment, the world of daylight!" reflects Kasch at a moment when he seems indistinguishable from his author. "Yet once the world slips into the past tense, once it shifts into 'history,' it is revealed to have been insubstantial; illusory; deceptive." "A certain force, perhaps no more than linguistic habit, connects me with the Fitz John of those years." When Kasch asks, "what force connects the two of us?" he is referring to his past self, not to Laney (128). Oates, on this level, has simply disguised (and complicated) the story by portraying Kasch, one of her two alter egos in the novel, as a man.

What Oates has said of Henry James, she might have said of herself. "His main characters are artists, and the art they make is their own lives."[36] Kasch writes books, but he is also an artist in his relationship with Laney. "I will transform her. I will invent her," he says. "I will write about her with devotion, abstracting from her certain qualities I find poignant and eliminating others I find vulgar." In this, he parallels Oates in her reshaping of her own past—and of course the reader in remolding Oates's novel. In Oates's view, in reading, as in love or any other human interaction, we mirror our own desires. "One leaps at life. One invents wildly" (111). There is no escaping at least an aspect of this in everything we do, and for the writer that means primarily writing. Every book is a love affair. Every love affair is a book, a narrative, a mirroring of desires and needs in another who, in their own way and for their own reasons, either does or does not reciprocate. The novel's indeterminate structure, the impossibility of determining who is "I" and who is "You," expresses this human situation. For Kasch, who sounds very William Jamesian here, "human life," as it is really experienced, "is far too muddled, too complex, too meandering. There is no single moment of comprehension, no key to one's relationship with anyone at all." "The authentic life," he says in sentiments Oates often echoes, is "the interior life." "Our outward gestures are misleading," and to accept them as the "real" would be a "false unity" and "a lie" (138). Life is certainly not a series of gig lamps symmetrically arranged, here. But nor is it quite the luminous halo that Virginia Woolf suggested modern fiction should try to depict. For even the modernists asserted differentiation between selves, however bizarre their characters' internal worlds became.

Oates/Kasch/Laney, then, are all part of the swirl of consciousness. To ask whether the passages in which Laney is referred to as "you" are from Laney's viewpoint or from Kasch's is less pertinent than to ask why we refer to ourselves as "you" and not to others as "I." The answer would have to be tradition, convention, "linguistic habit," certainly not logic. In *Childwold*, such differentiations are treated, Lorna Sage points out, as "open illusions."[37] If a passage nominally given to Kasch can suggest Oates or Laney, so Kasch and Oates can at times be inextricably synthesized in Laney. "You lie in bed a while, not knowing what you are listening for—the creak of a tree limb against the roof, the hollow, bell-like sound of the wind in the old silo, maybe Butch barking downstairs, or the side door being slammed shut," thinks Laney. "But no: no. Those sounds are there, in Childwold, but you are no longer there to hear them" (237). While at first glance this reads as Laney describing her own mind, it could as easily be seen as Kasch describing Laney's mind, Kasch projecting his own mind in terms of Laney, Oates describing her own memories of childhood by way of Kasch describing Laney's, and so on without resolution. The narrative voice asserts innocence and experience in equal measure, as if Oates as Kasch could become Oates as Laney within the space of a few sentences. "Should it surprise me to realize that I have written so much, that I have published these books . . . ?" asks the voice. "It should. For my mind is deliriously empty now. I am new, I am trembling with newness, I am like a child, I am innocent of past accomplishments as well as past sins, there is no connection, no attachment" (253). In *Childwold*, author-character distance and character-character distance finally collapse because the conventions that separate one voice from another are acknowledged *as* conventions. Ultimately, one being perceives itself. Kasch, Laney, Oates, and the reader are all linked, and Kasch/Laney/Oates is speaking of us all when (s)he says; "I am the author of myself" (253).

So much for "the experiment of the mind's dissection of itself." Oates was also interested in how a novelist might combine the search for private perfection with the desire to provide social critiques. *Childwold*, Oates has said, "represents, in a kind of diffracted way, a complete world made of money and imagination, a blending together of different times."[38] There is a whole other story in *Childwold*, and it is predicated on a recognizable world of economic imperatives. On this level, *Childwold* is social commentary firmly rooted in the context of a rural America some of whose inhabitants remain haunted by memories of the Great Depression at home and the fallout of wars abroad. "We are not the readers but the very personages of the world drama," runs the William James epigraph. Impossible as it is for the author or reader to get "outside" the novel's voices, the James epigraph also points beyond self-contemplation to the world of social involvement. Kasch's fate results, if we now switch focus and read the novel's social story, from his inability to adapt to that outer world. The novel's introspective story is primarily driven by philosophical reflection. In the novel's social story, Oates emphasizes the intimate connection between self and past, or family "history"—the continuity, economics, family life of the "real" world—and positions her art within the traditions of the realist novel. While the realism of *With Shuddering Fall* and *The Garden of Earthly Delights* belied a rather different story beneath the surface, *Childwold*'s "poetic" prose belies the novel's realist aspects. For the novel is a great deal interested in that social realm that Kasch and the Bartletts inhabit.

Kasch, seen in this light, is a more sympathetic version of the solipsistic Hugh Petrie, and fated to end in a similar coma. He is a tragicomic misfit trying to recover something in order to find a way forward. This is Kasch the "Pervert. But lonely: lonely" (15); "Kasch groveling in Kasch, no lover but Kasch."

Kasch, "[w]anting only a voyeur's pleasure," "Kasch the poet, Kasch the pervert," is a sad loner "in the forty-first year of his life" (22–23). He has wealth and an education. Laney has neither. Their differing needs relate to their economic and social situations. Their relationship is entwined with Arlene's awareness of her daughter growing away from her, from Childwold, and the family life that has been intimate and geographically close since immigration two generations before. Laney, like Oates, is a third-generation immigrant, with the chance to rise economically and intellectually out of the frustrated lives of her parents and grandparents, but into a situation her mother cannot "understand" or "share" (89). Their economic decline coincides with Laney's opportunity. Kasch provides her with access to money and an education, and his intellectual and emotional interest in her obviously contrasts with the indifference of the working men who otherwise surround her.

Nowhere is the latter kind of man better exemplified than in Laney's uncle, Vale, Laney's first savior (from drowning when she was three), just before he went to Vietnam. Vale, of course, is just the man to be sent to war, a man at the mercy of his historical context and the forces that twist him, both physically and mentally, out of any redeemable shape. His war has ended with an airlift from Hué City, "wire strung throughout his body, holding him together" (25). "They killed him," reflects Laney. "He disappeared, someone else was shipped back, Vale died, Vale had been smashed, his face wasn't put together right, the two halves did not fit" (29). With his misaligned face, he is another kind of misfit. Much like a mirror image of Yvonne Petrie, the discrepancy between the way others see him and the way he sees himself has left him cynical, and so as good as dead. Living in the seedy De Sales hotel, he is awakened by a row between alcoholics that results in a man having his throat slit. He attempts to arrest his own slide into criminality by enroling in a GI education program, but ends up taking a teenage couple for a ride, and later, after the couple have been shot, he is stopped by police investigating the matter. Oates thus embeds Vale in the context of his war experience, and the Bartletts in general in a historical as well as immediate cultural context. Vale's ancestral counterpart, for example, is Lenny, who, fated to die in World War I, just as Vale is effectively killed by his military experience decades later, still haunts the family's older members. The theme of personal loss, of loss of a past self, becomes the theme of family loss: the continuities and losses of a family's history. The Bartlett family are therefore representative of a specific American era.

In such ways, *Childwold* dramatizes the clash between the world of the imagination and the world of economic survival. Even while Kasch's inner world is about his "falling under an enchantment" (48), Earl is beating up Arlene because of some man "fooling around at the bar" and Laney is waiting with a gun for Earl to return (52). The scene foreshadows the collision that will result in Earl's death and Kasch's crippling, the precise moment of collision between inner and outer dramas. Nor is Kasch's love for Laney divorced from the social world that Oates depicts. His desires are fired, rather than dampened, by his knowledge that the Bartletts are "white trash" and the successors of the poor farmers exploited by his lumber baron ancestors (126). So while the novel is a portrait of love and knowledge, every aspect of it is also, ultimately, about power, economics, class, and exploitation in a particular region of America. Kasch may be Kafkaesque in his self-examination, but as other critics have noted, he is also Cash. He desires Laney as once his forebears desired the land her family farmed. He wants to own her as if she were herself a run-down farm. Taken as a whole, then, *Childwold*'s inward and outward stories, far from jarring, as in some of the early novels, create the novel's tension and interest. Moreover, they anticipate the emphasis on boundary-dissolving fluidity that will characterize Oates's mature work—in her stories, poetry, and plays as well as her novels—even when at first glance those later novels will look much like the traditional realism with which she began her career.

The end of *Childwold* brings us back to the beginning. Kasch withdraws into books and make-believe. He has invested Laney, and then Arlene, with unrealizable symbolic weight, as well as exaggerated his own power and importance, and is destroyed by reality. While it is a given of Oates's worldview that meaning is created by the human mind in interaction with others, this does not mean a modernist retreat from history, but a new way *into* history and into the novel as social commentary. It also means that "to think well," as Kasch reminds himself through Pascal, "is the principle of morality" (14). In shaping the world and so our lives, we help shape the lives of others, and Oates continually illustrates the consequences of excessive introspection. The plight of the bookish Kasch, who feels he may have been wrong to develop his "gift for words at any cost," may have echoed Oates's own (183). But *Childwold* is also a very public novel about America in the post-Vietnam era. It looks out the window as well as into the mirror, even if the viewer is by no means certain whether the others whom one looks out on are anything more than versions of oneself. In sum, it was perhaps the first of Oates's novels clearly to articulate her pragmatist outlook. John McDermott notes that William James became convinced early in his life "of the diaphanous and utterly fragile character of the classically alleged, rock-bottom personal self." For James, "we are actually multiple selves," and he was nagged by the fundamental question of "whether we have any control over the making of our own self." While all Oates's early novels explore this question, *Childwold* actually merges form and theme to illustrate the "fragile character" of the self, even as it explores the extent to which we have control over its creation. *Childwold* "marks a shift," argues Daly, "to a more subversive—that is, to a feminist—aesthetic practice; it subverts hierarchies of gender and class." But it also marks an art deeply embedded with the key beliefs of classical American philosophy, reinvigorated, as is the nature of pragmatism, to suit contemporary concerns.[39]

As with *Childwold*, *Son of the Morning* involves its protagonist's attempt to discover a new vision of himself and his world. While there are echoes of *The Assassins*, in which a man arranges his own assassination, another attempts suicide, and a woman imagines her own dismemberment, Nathan Vickery's physical self-mutilation is self-punishment, but not suicidal. Rather, it is—symbolically at least—an attempt to destroy one part of his vision and so save himself. For Nathan, as for the author, *Son of the Morning* marks the attempted destruction of a self-limiting perspective. His loss of an eye (a motif of impeded/altered vision, repeated over and over, if less catastrophically, in subsequent novels) surely symbolizes the loss of the "I" that Oates saw as so crucial a recognition early in the 1970s. This is not to contend that this process necessarily took place for Oates without struggle or with total ironic distance from Nathan's predicament. Like so many of the earlier novels, *Son of the Morning* is more nightmare than transcendence, and it ends with no great revelation beyond the successful destruction of an old self. But in a way, there is affirmation in the fact that, followed as it is by the very different *Bellefleur*, it signals the end of the first part of her writing career. If ever a novel were to be designed to wake its reader—and perhaps author—like a fist hammering their skull, this one would be it. But it is made very clear that, to remember Oates's comments earlier in the decade, *Son of the Morning* is not merely the "dramatization of nightmarish problems" but a study of someone trying to transcend them. Nathan's great fear may be the loss of his preaching talent, and preachers and writers may be kindred wordsmiths. Yet the fist that hammers the skull is unquestionably the protagonist's own. He alone thrusts the knife into his own eyeball, and he alone must, and does, find a healthier perspective by coming to terms with the limits of his ability to find answers to the questions he has for so long posed.

Of course, links between a character and an author should always be regarded as tenuous. "It is just as impossible to forge an identity between myself, my own 'I,' and that 'I' that is the subject of my stories," writes Mikhail Bakhtin, "as it is to lift myself up by my own hair." But Oates's whole aesthetic is built on the idea of fusion between her own emotional experiences and her intuitive and observational assumptions about American types. Nathan Vickery is another such fusion. The novel, she told Robert Phillips, was "painfully autobiographical in part; but only in part." It reads, if only in part, like a private, unanswered prayer that echoes Oates's own fascination, exaggerated here into religious fanaticism, with an individual's search for transcendent meaning. The novel's "ideal reader," she said, is "God," adding, "Everyone else, myself included, is secondary."[40] But just as traditional beliefs held little water in Oates's previous novel, so, here, quite who or what "God" is constitutes one of the main deliberations.

Like *The Assassins* and *Childwold*, *Son of the Morning* is essentially about loss and the doomed search to rediscover that sense of a significant other. Once again that "You" seems to be no more than a projection of the "Seeker."[41] The great battles in Oates's novels of this period are always to do with the protagonist's relationship with self—himself or herself. *Son of the Morning* is equally about a search for direction, depicting, as with "A Theory of Knowledge," what Erik Erikson would term a generativity crisis, whereby "a man looks at what he has generated, or helped to generate, and finds it good or wanting." Indeed, the reader is positively encouraged, as Sharon Dean shows in an acutely perceptive essay, to recognize that the pain of the prophet is also "the pain of the artist."[42] What "torments" Nathan Vickery—or William Japhet, as he becomes—is "that the composition of this prayer is such a painful, such a relentless undertaking, for I who compose it must also live by means of it, sucking and gasping for breath" (329). He exhausts himself trying to grasp the paradoxical relationship between "a geographer's idea of the earth set out clearly and neatly in the pages of a book" and "an irrefutably real earth" that carries us "hurtling through space" (154).

But at the same time, as Samuel Coale notes, compared with *The Assassins*, *Son of the Morning* has a stronger grasp on that broader reality. It depicts a realistically observed social world that, like the social world we glimpse in *Childwold*, seems for the most part to take place in rural upstate New York, although its world of home-grown cults is Anyplace, USA. Nathan's tortured mind is as convincing a rendition of self-taught religious leadership as William Styron's 1967 novel, *The Confessions of Nat Turner*, and provides further extraordinary insight into the thinking of a Nat Turner or, say, David Koresh. Like Turner's enslavement, the brutality of Nathan's world (beginning with the fact that he is born of a gang rape) is very much a factor in his subsequent story. Nathan is on a spiritual roller coaster, but he is also fatherless, virtually motherless, since he is brought up by relatives, and eventually becomes a tax write-off for a corrupt clergyman, the Reverend Beloff. Since the brute fact of that outer world is there in the circumstances of his conception, his mother Elsa's suffering ties Nathan irrevocably to the real world and leads him, via his grandparents, to create a heroic narrative to explain his birth and mold his life. As with Jules's narrative in *them* and Vale's in *Childwold*, Nathan's solipsistic drama clearly grows out of cultural and social forces.

Also like *Childwold*, *Son of the Morning* deliberately problematizes the narrative viewpoint. At issue again is the question of what Oates had come to see as the illusion of the self as unitary coupled with the paradox of, simultaneously, having a sense of isolation. Oates, in Dean's words, shows us "the prophet/artist praying, creating," even as we witness "the reality of that which is created—the new Bible put down in Nathan/William's words" in the hope of giving "some form of reality to the self that he was." In this way "Oates becomes herself the playful author manipulating and knowing that she manipulates throughout all of her imagining, knowing that Nathan/William is only words, but that she, too, as author is made up of the words that define her." Nathan's "impossible imagining," Dean sees, "is also the plight of the literary artist forced to deal in words that cannot mirror reality but only reflect a portion of the reality the writer may wish to present at the moment."[43] In simplistic terms, the novel's narrator is Nathan himself. But Nathan, quite aside from renaming himself, presents that self in both the third person and the first person. The supposed recipient of the narrative, or prayer, is "You," whom Nathan interprets as God, but whose complex, illusory nature is very much the novelist's concern.

As with *Childwold*, the most useful way to understand the novel may be to avoid asking who or what the "I" or the "You" is—whether it be Oates, the reader, God, Oates's creation Nathan, or William, his recreated "self"—and to see the novel as a challenge to linguistic convention. By this stage of Oates's career, the drama of self and the social dimension had neatly melded into both the novel's form and its subject matter. For instance, the novel's key moment is Nathan's act of corrective surgery on a faulty vision. Occurring at the end of book 2, it ostensibly takes place because he sees himself as guilty of lust for the Reverend Beloff's daughter, Leonie. But both on the level of Nathan's own story and in terms of the novel as part of Oates's own evolution of consciousness, it has profound symbolic significance. The self-mutilation occurs not simply because Nathan considers his desires sinful, but because they cause him to agonize over his links with the outer world. "He puzzled over the situation for days at a time," he explains. "Why must a man be attracted to a woman, or to any manifestations of the world at all," for "the exterior, physical manifestation of another human being is the least significant part of that human being" (174).

Like Oates, Nathan comes to believe that an individual's inner world is vastly more significant than any outer manifestation. From start to finish, the human eye is a key instrument in his thinking. In the opening pages, he contemplates "the improbable precision of the eye: the perfection of the iris, the pupil, the mirroring brain" (4). But the senses can also deceive, as can a certain perspective on the distinctions we make between ourselves and other people. Nathan realizes that in order to attain a more authentic version of human consciousness, one aspect of his vision has to be eradicated. That aspect, he believes, has to do with the traditional sense of the individual self as separable from others, and therefore able to desire, or hate, or in any other way compete with or treat others as if they were either an opponent or a partner. And since this had become the logical conclusion of Oates's own evolving consciousness up to this point, the novel's characterization and narrative technique reflect this merging of two "selves," character and author. "We are all one," Nathan tells his followers. "If I narrow my eyes just a little I can see through the eyes of my brothers and sisters—I can see through their eyes *almost* as easily as through my own. In Christ there is no male or female, there is only Christ" (203). His vision of spiritual genderlessness connects with his view that "the physical aspect" of a person's being is "inconsequential." "The soul," he says, possesses "no sexual differentiation" (174).

Again like Oates, Nathan has a mystical experience. This temporarily blinds him in his other eye, but ultimately leaves him with a clearer perspective on his role in life. Just as Oates had seen the human body as a "column of light," so Nathan experiences "the Spirit of Absolute illumination: the Many-in-One" (258). Recovering from his injuries well enough to continue his ministry, Nathan forms a movement called the Seekers. Like Stephen Petrie, he devotes his work to preaching and healing that is self-less, rather than self-aggrandizing. At such moments, he feels his personal vision "obliterated," as if he is somehow "in complete union with the other's soul." Like a man with a flashlight in a cave, he feels "able to penetrate the darkness surrounding the other person, and to discern the cause of sickness" (174). In such a way, he feels able to escape himself and actively help others. "The only reality," he therefore reaffirms, is "interior and invisible" (175). The senses—particularly the sense of sight—lie.

Nathan's new perspective on the permeable barriers between the self and others finally leads him to forsake his ministry and rename himself William Japhet. Crucially, he ends the novel without the large answers he has been seeking. But he is not defeated, merely transformed. In a word, he has achieved ataraxia, an idea that his grandfather, Thaddeus, got from reading Epicurus. Nathan, in other words, can look back on his former self, even observe that self in photographs and the newspapers, but the wisdom he has achieved has to do with perspective, rather than new-found answers. "The torment of his former life, the relative aimlessness and insecurity, the frequent half-wishes for death," he comes to realize, "had been caused all along by this poisoned spirit, which he had sheltered without knowing it; which perhaps he had even defended in his stubborn pride in his own self-reliance. Now all that was changed" (287). His stance is literally philosophical, and, as Epicurus advised, "there is nothing nobler than to apply oneself to philosophy and there is no greater goal for mankind than the attainment of ataraxia—tranquillity, equanimity, the repose of one's soul" (48). The "riddle" of self and other in which he nearly drowned has been discarded like a waterlogged coat, as has the quest for ultimate meaning. He is left content to enjoy life's motion, rather than to seek metaphysical answers.

Nathan's prayer, then, and Oates's novel, reveal a further turn in the evolution of a consciousness. Nathan, like Stephen Petrie, rather than Shar or Pedersen or Howe, is a harmonizing figure. He succeeds in assimilating "everything completely in himself" and so obliterating "false barriers between one form and another." In his particular language, he has experienced "grace as the cessation of all duality." He comes to realize that the "You" he has sought is within him, and he is now ready to "gaze out upon the multitudes" and explain that "wisdom" (323). He still suffers solitude and loneliness, but the Nathan Vickery he knew himself as is "extinguished" (329). Rather like the old

Joyce Carol Oates, his public image passes away from the person himself into the public domain. In Nathan's words, he "passes from my consideration, belonging to You and not to me" (329). In his final lines, there is a recognition that certain kinds of intellectual exploration—of consciousness, the brain, perception, about ultimate meaning—always lead, to quote Oates's comment to Joe Bellamy at the time of *Wonderland*, "to the most despairing, unanswerable questions." "Repeatedly," as Oates wrote in the afterword to *The Poisoned Kiss*, "one is brought back to the paradox that one can experience the world only through the self—through the mind—but one cannot know, really, what the 'self' is."[44] So far as her art was concerned, then, the quest for certainty that pragmatists criticize in traditional philosophy, not least when based on false dualities, seemed now to be over.

Son of the Morning therefore both replays old themes and manages to take a new, ironic stance on them. The old, intense introspection and barely disguised authorial ambition are still factors in the narrative. "You must keep to the path," Nathan tells himself. "And never doubt!" (144). But there is also an acceptance of limitation and of the writer's nature. "I am discovering," says Nathan, "that my prayer is my life: my self. To break it off would be to break off my own being" (283). "Myself versus myself" had, by *Son of the Morning* at least, become "myself about myself," or even ourselves about ourselves. With hindsight, we can also look at *Son of the Morning* as a stage in Oates's career where she was ready to move beyond the repeated patterns of these early novels and to recast her creative agenda.

Oates's decision to go with the flow rather than continue with teleological inquiry brought her all the more firmly in line with the values of pragmatism. "What Nathan/William names himself to be in the process of writing is ultimately insignificant," concludes Dean. "So are all religious documents and all products of the artist. This is not a view that should lead to despair, for there is value in striving, in setting down a reality that may be seen dualistically and that is in a state of flux." Dean makes no mention of pragmatism, but what she describes is clearly a pragmatic vision. Just as Jamesian pluralism underpins the fluidity of *Childwold* (as Ellen Friedman notes), so too does Dewey's stress (in John Stuhr's words) on the "precarious, changing, unsettled" nature of "the unity of experienc*ing* subject and experienc*ed* object." And Dean's conclusions show how *Son of the Morning* echoes the founding pragmatists' perspective that (again in Stuhr's words) "there are no final ends *for* experience (as traditional teleological philosophies and religions hold), but only ends in view (and means to them) *within* experience." Nathan may have God in mind, but for Oates this is *literally* so: what Nathan calls "God" is shown to be as much his own self-projection as Nathan himself is in fact a projection of Oates, who in turn, as "author," becomes the reader's projection while reading the novel. From a pragmatist's viewpoint, this is in keeping with the novel's focus on the religious quality of creative experience. For, by Dewey's distinction, this means any "activity pursued in behalf of an ideal end against obstacles and in spite of threats of personal loss because of conviction of its general and enduring value." Religion and art both provide a focus and purpose in life: holding the landscape together like the metaphorical pottery in Wallace Stevens's "Anecdote of a Jar" or Lily Briscoe's paintbrush in *To the Lighthouse*. The value of creating and reading, Dean interprets Oates as saying, is that "writing creates the reality in a more permanent way even as that reality is in a state of constant flux depending on reader response." Books paradoxically capture and contain the world only because they continue, in our experiences of reading them, to "live."[45]

This brings us to Oates's next works. For after two short novels, *Cybele* and *Unholy Loves*, she did indeed produce something very different. Between *With Shuddering Fall* and *Son of the Morning*, she had driven herself into what Dewey terms "the cul-de-sac of the theory of knowledge" and followed it to its logical end.[46] To paraphrase Nathan, the composition of that "long, torturous prayer" had been "exhausting," yet she could not "give it up." She wanted "to *know*" (283). To break out of this cycle yet remain socially engaged, without retreating into traditional realism, modernism, or game-playing postmodernist metafiction, required an art that would take into account all that had gone before. The works that resulted remain among the most unusual American novels of the twentieth century.

Much in the Alice books has to do with the mind's disintegration in the face of unanswerable questions, but Alice, the "prime" heroine, is strengthened by her experience. Indeed, how comforting and exhilarating the conclusion of Wonderland, when the emboldened Alice defies her elders by demanding: "Who cares for you? You're nothing but a pack of cards!" Immediately the dream creatures are routed, the fantasy nightmare ends.

—JOYCE CAROL OATES, *(Woman) Writer*

3 REWRITING THE NOVEL

BELLEFLEUR (1980), A BLOODSMOOR ROMANCE (1982), and *Mysteries of Winterthurn* (1984) provide the long-sought artistic release from the emotional and intellectual coiling of the four novels discussed in the preceding chapter. *Wonderland* and *Son of the Morning* seemed to bind those spirals ever tighter, even as *Do with Me What You Will* and *Childwold* struggled to loosen the bonds of conventional novelistic discourse. These next three novels simply sideline the issues by changing the agenda. They mark the point at which Oates suddenly seemed far more interested in looking outward at American history and culture than any deeper into the kind of philosophical abstractions that compete for attention in her earlier novels. Oates's partly retrospective 1982 poetry collection, *Invisible Woman,* illustrates her sense of taking stock, just as further evidence for this new agenda can be found in Oates's essays of this period, in *Contraries* (1981) and *The Profane Art* (1983). While the organization and omissions of *Invisible Woman* illustrate something of Oates's shifting perspective, the essay volumes allow us to witness the author continuing to reflect on writers past and present as well as expressing her changing perspective on the motives and mysteries of the artistic impulse.

To take the poetry first, quite aside from the omission of any poems from her first volume, *Anonymous Sins,* few of her past poems made it into the selection. Those that did were largely from her most recent previous volume. Only one comes from *Love and Its Derangements* (1970), two from *Angel Fire* (1973), three from *Fabulous Beasts* (1975), whereas seven are taken from *Women Whose Lives Are Food, Men Whose Lives Are Money* (1978). Her choice of later, rather than early, poetry may not be surprising, but it does fit with the sense of an evolving consciousness established from her novels of this period.

As with *Anonymous Sins,* to read back over these earlier volumes is to witness an impulse toward introspection that, if not overwhelming, at least strikingly contrasts with her later poetry. Tending to dwell on the inner/outer patterns of relationships, they do so in ways that reinforce the sense of introspection. "The Grave Dwellers" in *Love and Its Derangements,* for instance, depicts the lovers inhabiting a space more claustrophobic than cozy. Living "in a box" that they

>   maneuver
> from a set of walls
> to another set of walls—
> no space in between

they see themselves as symbols of themselves,

>   inspired
> to an infinite love
> in a series of boxes.

Even in the more hopefully entitled "Loving," we have again an image of alienation from the outer world. This time the lovers have an invisible "balloon of skin" around them that isolates them like a single mind in a single body. Other poems focus on the human body as a form of imprisonment. In "Giving Oneself a Form Again," the poet feels her "ribs are stuck too close together," and her "body has always been too close." The mysteries she explores are not those of the world at large but of the world "too close up." If many of the poems are about the poet compelled to a desired but sometimes terrifying unity with her lover, that compulsion toward oneness becomes truly hellish where the individual is the object of unwanted attention. The title poem depicts male admirers trying to drag her "by the hair, away," wanting "to sink into" her "as into an enemy / with a sister's face." The poem ends with her turning outward and witnessing her body,

> at its fate tugged by the moon
> all the inches of its skin
> rubbed raw with the skin
> of men.

The American landscape only comes into the collection late on, when, in "Jigsaw Puzzle," a woman's body is likened to "a topographical map, / with proper directions of North and South." This is followed by "American Expressway," a poem that startles because suddenly we are not inside a human body and mind but watching the Detroit rush hour, although even that is described as a column reassembling itself "like a backbone / of detachable vertebrae." The one poem selected from *Love and Its Derangements* for *Invisible Woman*—the last, "How Gentle"—is typical of the 1970 volume except for its tender, celebratory tone. "I am illuminated / in and out of love's breathing love," writes the poet. "I am loved," she concludes. "The noon slides gently / suddenly upon us to wake us."[1]

All in all, then, *Love and Its Derangements* contains personal, introspective poems, with only scant glimpses of a wider social world, and that usually seen in alienated terms. The general tone and mood reinforces our sense of the undercurrent of the early novels, where the dramas of the self convince far more than the social dramas that the novels purport to be about. Throughout the collection, the focus tends to be either on the mind and the internal organs or close-up depictions of the body: knuckles, backbones, skin, [eye]lashes, eyes, flesh, skulls, lungs, hips, hands, forearms, bones (all words used in a single poem, "Sleeping Together"). If there is a completeness about the collection, it is the completeness of a private world in which two people become one, but also in which the poet—or speaker—translates that other into a version of herself. Much the same mood prevails in Oates's 1973 volume, *Angel Fire*, where in poems like "Contrary Motions" the outer landscape and the intimacy of bodies merge in a confusion of imagery. Along Lake Erie, "ice like teeth," when loosened, melts back to droplets of "harmless saliva." The sense of imprisonment in the self is as tangible as it is in so many of the early novels. "Insomnia," for instance, sees the poet "stare upon the self that is me / imprisoned in a box of four stark walls." The blood/body obsessions of *Wonderland* reprise in "Bloodstains," a poem about "bloodstained women growing fiercely / up out of girls" that continues:

> so damp with blood
> we fear
> the muzzles of dogs will dip
> into us.

Angel Fire itself ends with a version of the poem used as the epigraph to *Wonderland* and ascribed to Trick Monk, "Iris into Eye." From title to final lines (despite the adding of the word *sacred* to the penultimate line of the version in *Angel Fire*) this is one of the most claustrophobic of all Oates's early poems, just as *Wonderland* is among the most claustrophobic of her novels. Oates's early aesthetic is nowhere better captured than by those final lines:

> I make my way up through marrow
> through my own heavy blood
> my eyes eager as thumbs
> entering my own history like a tear
> balanced sacred on the outermost edge
> of the eyelid.[2]

But to turn to *Fabulous Beasts, Women Whose Lives Are Food, Men Whose Lives Are Money,* and then to the new poems in *Invisible Woman* is generally to follow a bend into a much broader, more varied poetic landscape. If introspective tendencies remain, they are at least balanced by outward-looking observation. One thing that comes to the fore in *Fabulous Beasts* is immediately recognizable American landscapes, as in poems like "An American Tradition," "What Has Not Been Lost in the Deserts of North America?" "Approaching the Speed of Light," "A Vision," and "Flight." Moreover, this new external immediacy goes hand in hand with a reduction in the sense of the significance—or at least the self-examination—of the individual speaker, who tends to observe what is outside, rather than what is within. Negation of the self, then, seems to coincide with a new situating of the self. Such poems, including one of Oates's better-known, "Dreaming America," reveal a degree of social observation not only light years from the introspection of early volumes but also anticipatory of the dominant tone and subject matter of much of her poetry from then onward. Where the early poetry, if it referred to the landscape at all, typically depicted it in terms of the body, or else to describe the body, *Fabulous Beasts* expresses its altogether more social themes and observations with reference to news headlines and Exxon signs, K-Mart and coast guards, highways and helicopters. *"Where did the country go?"* cry the travelers soaring along the highway past *Sunoco, Texaco,* and *Gulf* signs in "Dreaming America": "Where did the country go?—ask the strangers. / The teenagers never ask."[3]

That the social observer has largely taken over from the self-analyst by the time of *Women Whose Lives Are Food, Men Whose Lives Are Money* and *Invisible Woman* is suggested in the collections' titles, as in the titles of many of the poems. In *Women Whose Lives Are Food,* "Former Movie Queen, Dying of Cancer, Watches an Old Movie of Hers at a Film Festival in San Francisco" gives some idea of the sudden breadth of these poems. It anticipates Oates's later novel, *Blonde*, in which the plight of womanhood is contextualized into a meditation on American fame. Similarly, "Happy Birthday," "Public Outcry," "American Independence," and "Gala Power Blackout in New York City, July '77" in their titles alone signal the predominance of social subject matter. If (as Oates writes in "Lovers Asleep") there is still "the impulse of the abyss" and images (as in "The Lovers") of lovers "locked in love" as if it were a soft prison, and "tortured by Furies / of thought," there is also ample room for a panoramic vision of America. In "Holy Saturday," she depicts the Universal Will holding sway throughout the metropolis. "Intoxicated with pride," Schopenhauer himself is "flown about / in a Detroit police helicopter," witnessing proof of his theories. "Here—and here—and here also! And *here*," he shouts above the busy streets. The emphasis is on the artist-philosopher as witness, watching and recording because (she writes in "After Sunset")

> wave upon wave
> so much is breaking
> so much is happening
>
> for centuries, here,
> so much has happened
> unrecorded
> irretrievable

Haunted by time and death, the poet in "There Are Those Who Die" sends messages "shredded and rainstained / held trembling in someone's hand," and even Love has its public setting when, in "Enigma,"

> In public places they kissed.
> Audiences sprang into being
> to define their love.

All in all it is a social America we witness in *Women Whose Lives Are Food*: poetry as an act of citizenship. Similarly in *Invisible Woman*, "The Stone Orchard," which addresses the corrosiveness of bitterness, and "*F—*," which suggests that if you stare long enough at an ugly American industrial landscape "it becomes beautiful," are reports from the front line of American life. To echo Wendell Berry, they are intricate acts of patriotism. The poet's private life and emotions are secondary to her role as witness.[4]

Turning now to her essays, as ever the literary commentary ranges widely, from *King Lear* to *The Brothers Karamazov*, *Wuthering Heights* to *The Adven-*

tures of Augie March. But one particularly interesting essay in terms of the writer's evolving consciousness is "Notes on Failure" in *The Profane Art*. This is not least because all four novels looked at in the preceding chapter are about degrees of failure from which protagonists glean some kind of new awareness or level of maturity. "It seems reasonable to believe that failure may be a truth, or at any rate a negotiable fact," writes Oates in that essay, "while success is a temporary illusion of some intoxicating sort, a bubble soon to be pricked, a flower whose petals will quickly drop." Nevertheless, she argues, "the spectre of failure haunts us less than the spectre of failing," because a battle lost is "necessarily lost to time: and won or lost, it belongs to another person." The battle in the process of being lost, in contrast, is "the unspeakable predicament."[5]

If *Do with Me What You Will* is slanted rather differently, certainly the three novels immediately prior to *Bellefleur* depict not only battles lost—Stephen's inability to help his family, Kasch's loss of love and youth, Nathan's loss of his ministry—but battles that Stephen, Kasch, and Nathan come to terms with losing. In particular, all three accept loss of certainty. They embrace provisionality and limitation. "Maturing," Oates has said, "is about learning your limitations." Through failure, then, each "matures": they grow beyond the predicaments that have haunted them or that haunt those around them. But in doing so, Stephen and Nathan, at least, turn supposed failure—which after all can be a matter of viewpoint—into a form of success. "Though most of us inhabit degrees of failure or the anticipation of it," writes Oates in *The Profane Art*, "very few persons are willing to acknowledge the fact, out of a vague but surely correct sense that it is not altogether American to do so." In other words, far from countenancing resignation, Oates's art of this period counsels that the healthy vision involves the ability to switch perspectives.[6]

In line with this newly pragmatic argument—itself a new, more ironic and detached perspective than would seem to have shaped her early novels—the subtext of *Contraries*, too, is very much a rejection of rigidity in all its forms. "Without contraries is no progression," runs the epigraph from Blake's *Marriage of Heaven and Hell*. In essay after essay, Oates goes on to advocate such qualities as fluidity, incompleteness, contradiction, spontaneity, plurality, and imperfection, and to query the overriding validity too often accorded structure, completeness, unity, and so-called perfection. Citing Blake's contraries as "the Eternal delight that rests in motion, in strife, in passion," she agrees that energy "is the *only life*." What troubles and stimulates us about certain works of art, she argues, is that they are "riddling and incomplete." And the kind of art she champions here is that which is "genuinely spontaneous," that "seems to be in the process of being born as we attend." "The creation of small, tidy, 'perfect' works of art is by no means as tempting to the serious novelist as critics might like to think," she writes. Indeed, it may be "that great works of art are necessarily flawed or incomplete because they represent, to the artist, one of the central mysteries of life—that which cannot be resolved, but which *must* be explored."

While the values that Oates is upholding are plainly in line with American pragmatism, so too is another argument she makes in *Contraries:* that art has a moral role. She describes *A Picture of Dorian Gray* (despite Wilde's insouciance about assuring us that all art is "quite useless") as "a highly serious meditation upon the moral role of the artist." She says of *King Lear* that "part of the play's terrible pessimism" is due to Shakespeare's implication that the enlightened person must withdraw from the political and social world if he hopes to maintain "a measure of transcendence, or true 'selfness.'" Psychologically plausible as this may be, writes Oates, it "represents, in art, an intolerable paradox." The artist "cannot surrender the world to those who demand it," but must, she implies, strive to create art of some use.[7]

This brings us full circle back to *Bellefleur* and its companion novels in what, along with *My Heart Laid Bare* (1998) and the still-unpublished *The Crosswicks Horror,* had been intended as part of an eventual quintet. Unlike *Angel of Light* (1981), which appeared "out of sequence," these four novels all explore the genres and social mores of the American nineteenth century.[8] But as critics have noted, they also strongly resemble one another, not only in their historical engagement but also in their feminist revisionism. To cite first Ellen Friedman and then Eileen Bender, while it is true that labeling Oates's novels under any single issue is "too constraining," it is equally true that *Bloodsmoor,* if not *Bellefleur,* is Oates's "first explicitly feminist novel," and that much of her subsequent work expresses feminist perspectives. Perhaps for the first time she began to do what Charlene Haddock Seigfried has urged of feminists: to use pragmatism as "a helpful ally" and to revise it—as it was always meant to be revised—to suit specific needs. Marilyn Wesley suggests this in her discussion of Oates's use of Jamesian conversion theories. "What matters," she says, is "Oates's adaption of James's theory to her own revolutionary intention." But Oates's pragmatism seems so much part of her overall vision that once she incorporated feminist issues, the natural parallels between the two movements came together. "The difference pragmatism makes," as Cornel West puts it, "is always the difference people make with it."[9]

In reading these and later novels, readers retain the option of considering the more personal side of Oates's art. "By the end of 1977," writes Greg Johnson, Oates had "begun to recognize that her generalized emotional detachment of the past five years, her introversion and invisibility, had led not to liberation but to painful isolation. She had reached a turning point that, within a few months, would prompt her adventurous plunge into a new creative and personal life." "I *want* to be open to wounding," wrote Oates that same year, "otherwise I won't be living." The achievement of a "premature 'detachment'" around "1972 or thereabouts," which "seemed to me marvelous at the time," in the end "wasn't marvelous at all."[10] But while these biographical concerns—so often connected with Oates's preoccupation with her artistic identity—seem of interest with regard to her early work, where they may have distorted her social subject matter, from *Bellefleur* onward they feel less relevant. Excessive abstraction and introspection fade from view. The anxious, breathless psyche one might associate with Nathan's "torturous prayer" gives way to a more relaxed, ironic art. The "cul-de-sac of the theory of knowledge," the desire "to *know*" the answers to unanswerable questions, is all but abandoned in favor of tackling more practical problems. Once her novels had brought her to the Duchampian conclusion that there was "no solution" because there was "no problem," once, like Alice in Wonderland, she had called the bluff on metaphysical questions and said, "Who cares for you? You're nothing but a pack of cards!" the dream creatures were routed and the fantasy nightmare ended.[11] In effect, Oates changed her focus, changed her language, and so changed the form of her novels. Having flirted with meaninglessness, she came back triumphantly with an art that, albeit constructed ironically around older forms, she had cast in an image unquestionably her own.

She had emerged, to use Rorty's phrase, as a "liberal ironist." Rorty describes such an ironist as someone who has "radical and continuing doubts about the final vocabulary she currently uses," who "realizes that arguments phrased in her present vocabulary can neither underwrite nor dissolve these doubts," and who refuses to think that "her vocabulary is closer to reality than others."[12] All these next novels have been widely described as postmodernist novels that ironize past forms. They all clearly rework conventional genres, structures, and language systems, and in doing so remind us that to change— and continue to *challenge*—one's language system is to render one's values fluid, provisional, revisable. In this sense, Oates's novels from *Bellefleur* onward are pragmatic in the full sense; they bear witness to and intervene in contemporary cultural debate in ways that can actually be of practical use to those who read them. They may as ever stem from that impulse to private reverie, but they are more significantly designed to provoke the reader into ongoing reflection, rather than to substitute new dogmas for old.

All these novels reflect a new approach that Oates articulated in 1975, about the time she conceived of the quintet. Her journal entries suggest she no longer saw the novelist as a monomaniacal driver (or demon-driven lawyer) racing headlong on a potentially fatal journey against fierce competition and self-created obstacles. Instead, in characteristically pragmatic terms, she saw "the novel as discovery." The novelist is "an observer of facts," who "must guard against the demonic idea of imagining that he possesses or even can possess ultimate truth." Like "an ideal scientist," he strives to discover "what he does not yet know," rather than "to impose a pre-imagined dogma upon reality." Given such musings, it seems no coincidence that Oates's comment that "writing a novel is an experience that evolves" also came in 1975. Just as a novel's "subject is always the evolving of consciousness," so Oates's journals and manuscripts—perhaps even more than the essays, since they are unpolished—show that process in action. "The person who completes a novel is not the same person who began it," continues the novelist-as-scientist entry. "As soon as the novelist stops observing, however, he becomes something else—an evangelist, a politician." "Absolute truth is a chimera that draws us all but that will destroy us should we ever succumb. Art especially is destroyed. Or, rather: set aside. When one believes he has the *Truth*, he is no longer an artist." The change in outlook and practice brought a change in tone and subject matter. Preoccupation with neurological and metaphysical issues gave way to recognition that in great works "we *know* less than we did when we began" and end "unsettled by mystery." *Bellefleur, Bloodsmoor,* and *Winterthurn* brought this maturing perspective on the writer's role to fruition.[13]

As one might expect of a novelist keenly attuned to philosophical discussion, this change in her novels seems to respond to our wider cultural dilemmas. In *The Passion of the Western Mind*, Richard Tarnas likens our modern sense of our "profoundly unintelligible situation" to Gregory Bateson's famous concept of the psychiatric "double-bind." In Tarnas's view, this double-bind has been understood since at least the time of Pascal, who commented on being "terrified by the eternal silence of these infinite spaces." "Our psychological and spiritual predispositions are absurdly at variance with the world revealed by our scientific method," writes Tarnas. "We seem to receive two messages from our existential situation: on the one hand, strive, give oneself to the quest for meaning and spiritual fulfillment; but on the other hand, know that the universe, of whose substance we are derived, is entirely indifferent to that quest, soulless in character, and nullifying in its effects. We are at once aroused and crushed."

If the thoughts of Pascal remain a constant presence in Oates's worldview, the more claustrophobic corners of her earlier novels echo Tarnas's description of much twentieth-century philosophy. With some exceptions, he suggests, it has by and large resembled "nothing so much as a severe obsessive-compulsive sitting on his bed repeatedly tying and untying his shoes because he never quite gets it right." Meanwhile, "Socrates and Hegel and Aquinas are already high up on the mountain of their hike, breathing the bracing alpine air, seeing new and unexpected vistas." Characters like Jules, Jesse, and Kasch, striving vainly "for meaning and spiritual fulfillment," reflect Kant's famous articulation of the discrepancy between our sense of internal significance yet external insignificance. None of them is more "aroused and crushed," or more terrified by eternal silence than that "Seeker" Nathan Vickery. Such dilemmas seem, equally, to parallel Oates's own intellectual quest.[14] In contrast, *Bellefleur*, like the transformation of Mahaleel in its opening scene from a storm-drenched, "skeletal" creature into a "puffed and silky" wondercat with a "plumelike tail" and "whiskers that fairly bristled with life," is the equivalent of those obsessive-compulsives getting outside themselves and climbing to view unexpected vistas.[15] The drive to create becomes not a claustrophobic, inescapable hell of endless yearning and empty "fulfillment," but its own reward. If this is partly Schopenhauerean pessimism routed by Nietzschean celebration, at the same time, Oates's pragmatist and feminist pluralism ensures that the novels read as deliberate contributions to social debate.

Bellefleur! Beautiful flower. Fresh air. In novelistic terms, *Bellefleur* is marked by a shift in tone, in scope, in language. As Oates says of Mann's *Doctor Faustus*, so it is true of *Bellefleur* that analysis "must distort the novel's complexities and subtleties." To try to disentangle its many elements or schematize it into some kind of thematic unity would misrepresent it. As Brenda Daly observes, "whatever theoretical unity one posits, the novel's plenitude of 'meanings' always escapes such formulations." Bender notes that Emmanuel Bellefleur, the seemingly ageless family cartographer, fails in his attempts to chart the domain of the (actually white) "Noir Vulture" because of the ever-changing landscape, where even the mountains are "different from year to year" (332). For Bender, Emmanuel is "an artistic alter ego, whose efforts to fix the contours of reality are forever foredoomed." Readers, too, of course, become cartographers if they try to map and so stabilize the plot of a novel that, as Bender says, is like life, "risky, marginal, unpredictable, unmappable." Only when we realize the impossibility of achieving this—only when we seek meanings rather than The Meaning—can we relax and enjoy the flow. Like the description it contains of a movie projector, *Bellefleur* is a novel of "reflections darting through reflections," of "faces swimming out of the movie projector's ghostly light, or taking shape out of the dark still water." There is "not a single current, a single substance," but "currents entwined with currents, many waters, many spirits," and (implicitly like life) aspects of the novel are better experienced than analyzed (315). The quest for certainty, for absolute knowledge, is the very thing the novel works to defy. As Bender says, then, *Bellefleur* requires "an experimental *reader*." It challenges our very notions of what it means to read, even as it challenges any quest for truth somehow beyond the language systems we employ as the weapons of our pursuit. People make truths through language, and *Bellefleur* is above all, as Oates says, a "massive, joyful experiment done with words." Perhaps, as Oates's fellow novelist John Gardner wrote, "the artifice undermines emotional power" and sometimes "makes the book cartoonish." Perhaps admiration for the novel is tempered by the fact that "it too noticeably labors after greatness." But for all that, Gardner considered it "simply brilliant." With *Bellefleur,* Oates sails off the edge of the hitherto known parameters of the novelistic world.[16]

Bellefleur does resemble aspects of other novels. As a family saga, it owes something to *Buddenbrooks*. It is reminiscent of E. L. Doctorow's groundbreaking 1975 novel *Ragtime* in its treatment of history as interweaving, postmodernist narrative, melding historical data with fiction and fantasy. Its Gothic mélange of overwrought emotions, fierce weather, and wanton cruelty calls to mind *Wuthering Heights,* as do its wild family tree of recycled names and its challenges to novelistic conventions.[17] But its total effect is very different from any of these. In its treatment of historical time in relation to the decline of a prominent family, it is altogether wilder and less easy to grasp than *Buddenbrooks,* while *Ragtime* is a sturdy hut beside a smooth, secluded pond compared with Oates's exotic, multiturreted achievement on the stormy shores of Lake Noir. Where in *Wuthering Heights* a horror of childbirth is implicit, in *Bellefleur* the carnage of Leah's delivery results in a monstrous double child. After "the stench of blood in the room, and the first sight of the infant's head between Leah's smeared thighs" (102), "one and a half" babies are born: "a single melon-sized head, two scrawny shoulders, and at the torso something hideous," resembling "part of another embryo" (104). This is Germaine's Siamese brother, unceremoniously severed to allow Germaine to become "normal." But no one tone dominates. Germaine's androgynous origins are presumably symbolic, and the novel abounds with (in a phrase from Oates's journals, cited by Johnson) "exuberant shameless playfulness." "Intensely personal" as it may be on some unfathomable level, it is primarily (writes Johnson) "a sprawling examination of American history and culture." A meditation on early nineteenth-century American history that, in Oates's words, is "absolutely faithful to its source," *Bellefleur* illustrates the inextricable enmeshment of fact, anecdote, and imagination that constitutes our inherently unstable and semi-illusory images of history and lineage.[18]

The tangled links between the so-called real world, the world of history, and the world of the imagination begin in the dizzyingly rich language of the opening pages. Mahalaleel the wondercat enters Bellefleur Manor, and *Bellefleur* the novel, in an eighteen-line first sentence on a night "stirred by innumerable frenzied winds, like spirits contending with one another." Then in the next sentence—this one of eleven lines—information about Bellefleur Manor itself situates the novel in American history. Built by Raphael Bellefleur, grandson of Jean-Pierre Bellefleur, a fugitive from France, it is known locally as Bellefleur Castle. Raphael and his heirs dislike that name because it calls to mind the "rotting graveyard Europe" (3). "We are all Americans now," says Raphael. "We have no choice" (4). So the novel's opening melds the world of the imagination with a solidly historical, cultural, and geographical setting as substantial as the manor itself. Bellefleur Manor and *Bellefleur* the novel each lay claim to solidity and insubstantiality. "*Bellefleur* is a region, a state of the soul, and it does exist," writes Oates in the author's note, "and there, sacrosanct, its laws are utterly logical." Bellefleur Manor is at once a stone building and an imaginary space, and *Bellefleur* the novel, too, is both a solid object and a mindgame. Yet "states of mind," as Oates writes elsewhere, "are real enough—emotions, moods, shifting obsessions, beliefs—though immeasurable."[19]

Like American history itself, *Bellefleur* is built out of the twin elements of imagination and factual data. Its subject matter is the false dichotomy between art and life, dramatized in terms of the contradictions of the culture. Even as it exposes itself as artifice, it reflects a culture that claims to be a place of freedom, democracy, and equality, where individuals—and individual families—are ironically therefore able to exploit the natural and human resources and build a wholly unequal society from their accumulated wealth. The manor has taken "a small army of skilled workmen more than seven years to complete" (4). Raphael has done it partly for his wife, Margaret, but "partly as a step in his campaign for political power" (3). His dislike of the word *castle,* then—though Bellefleur Manor boasts "battlemented towers and walls" and an "English Gothic" design—has little to do with Raphael despising Old World values. He does not want to be reminded that, in all but name, he is perpetuating the social architecture of Europe.

Bellefleur Manor is a version of *Bellefleur* the novel. All books, as mere language, are less substantial than "real life," words being, as Doctorow has put it, "things that are almost not there."[20] But as solid objects, books are *more* real than what, individually or collectively, we imagine of our pasts or futures. Bellefleur Manor is therefore described in all its concreteness even as it appears dreamlike. Horse-drawn wagons haul "tons of sand" from the pits at Silver Lake, "for the mixing of mortar." There are "oriel windows and immense archways of limestone," "heavy, imported slate" on the roof, and "the heavy, even funereal effect of the walls and columns." Yet from across Lake Noir— "the dark, chaotic, unfathomable pool of time" through which we view the past and future (3)—the manor looks "airy and insubstantial as a rainbow's quivering colors" (4). Concreteness and illusion; history and imagination; dream and reality all contend at the start of *Bellefleur.* The winds that coincide with Mahalaleel's arrival are presented as if ushering in the voices and ghosts of the family's history. The young Raphael hears "disembodied cries, blown like mere leaves (8)." Vernon has had his ears pinched and lips kissed by spirits in the woods that afternoon, and he hears voices in the winds.

Mahalaleel has the same double qualities as the manor. Imagined by Christabel as "a ghost trying to get in" (11), like the manor, which is "pink-gray" from a distance (4), he appears "one color, a frosty, pinkish-gray" from afar, but close-up he is a shade of bronze. As the morning sunshine penetrates his "fine, delicate" cat's ears, he seems "eerily transparent," but from another angle, with his long, thick tail and outsized feet he looks "dense with muscle." Just as Leah sees him as "an omen of great good fortune," yet soon her smooth skin is scratched into "hairlike ridges of coagulated blood" (16), so Mahalaleel is both solid yet not quite "*believable*" (17).

The descriptions of Bellefleur Manor and Mahalaleel set the novel's tone. A colossal monument to the powers of the imagination, it mixes outlandish fantasy with historical fact. For all the Gothic pyrotechnics—the half-imaginary cats and castles, the sixth senses, the metamorphoses of humans into dogs and owls, Hepatica's marriage to a black bear named Fox—for all the hyperbole and the slippages of time (and for all the long, entangled sentences), embedded in *Bellefleur* are a clear-cut social context and a commentary on an era of American history in the Northeast of the mid-nineteenth century. The mythic manor is built on the edge of a black lake, which, while at times it seems to represent the past, elsewhere suggests the darker underside of this grand façade. In Hiram's nocturnal adventure onto the lake, he sees a figure beneath the surface whose feet are attached to Hiram's and whose head hangs hidden in the depths.

> The figure was motionless, as if paralyzed or frozen in place. And a few feet away another figure stood, upside down, shadowy as the first, unmoving. And there was another ... somewhat smaller of stature, a child or a woman ... and still another ... and as Hiram's eyes adjusted to the gloom [here, even his clouded eye possessed a penetrating vision] he saw to his astonishment that there was a considerable crowd of reversed figures, some of them moving but most fixed in place, their feet against the thin crust of ice, their heads nearly lost in shadow. He wanted to cry aloud in terror; for who were they, these upside-down silent people, these doomed people, these strangers! *Who on earth were they and why did they dwell in the Bellefleurs' private lake?* (527)

These "doomed people," existing in the shadow of the manor, have been exploited and finally submerged in that "unfathomable pool of time." They represent the dark underside of American history. In particular, there are the fruit pickers employed in the Nautauga Valley. The Bellefleurs' response to talk of a strike is first to have a young leader "badly beaten, blinded in one eye" (26). Jean-Pierre II then follows this up by slashing "the throats of not only Sam and his Lieutenants, and the dozen or so men who most vehemently supported him, but some eight other people" (421). The Bellefleur business enterprises include controlling the Walpoles and Wendalls of American society—Oates's latter-day workers, depicted in *A Garden of Earthly Delights* and *them*. They also include the kind of raping of the American landscape perpetrated by the ancestors of Fitz John Kasch. "Next year should be the most exciting year yet," says Louis, "with the White Sulphur Springs hotel, and the coach line, and if that scheme for a railroad actually goes through, or even some halfway decent roads—why, we'll be able to clear half the timber in the mountains, clear it and get it to market" (73). Like *Childwold*, *Bellefleur* is partly a social critique of power and exploitation, and Bellefleur Manor, built on that dawning century's burgeoning capitalism, concretely part of American social history.

But *Bellefleur* is also, as Gardner notes, a "religious" novel, if "not in any conventional sense" (to use Oates's caveat). Perhaps closest to the authorial vision is Vernon's oscillation between Henotheism and Pantheism. Oates has talked of believing in a "higher humanism, perhaps a kind of Pantheism," that includes "all substance in the universe" and recognizes creativity as a natural part of experience (whether manifested in "art" or, less obviously, in the pursuit of medicine, law, racing, and even in psychopathic delusions).[21] What matters, thinks Vernon, is "not the *content* of one's belief but its *depth*." "Since his God encompassed and swallowed up everything, every particle of matter—the filigree of synapses in that masterwork of cunning, the human brain; the speckled boxlike armor of the trunkfish; the screech of planing mills, Germaine's happy smile, his mother's tearful farewell, the splendor of Mount Blanc and the rank gloomy silence of Noir Swamp—since his God was identical with His creation, there could be nothing left over, no room for laborious theorizing. The pulses sang as pulses have always sung *Here I am, I am right here, I exist, and the spirit of all creation through me,* and the wise man, and certainly the poet, echoes this song" (302).

Little interests Oates more than "that masterwork of cunning, the human brain," since from this stems everything. But where *Wonderland* coiled in on itself and, like *The Assassins* and *Son of the Morning*, dwelled on self-mutilation, *Bellefleur* is triumphantly effervescent in language and range. Where these earlier novels spiraled inward again and again on unanswerable questions, *Bellefleur* illustrates, as Oates perhaps first sought to illustrate in *Do with Me What You Will*, what the human brain *can* do, what ebullient worlds of imagination "that masterwork of cunning" can conjure up. Mingling the "imaginary" and the "real," the novel exuberantly celebrates the imagination as the instigator and medium of all social and historical commentary, however firmly grounded in substantiated facts. It asserts connectedness, the melding of inner and outer worlds that renders distinctions between self-conscious art and socially committed art no longer necessary.

So while *Bellefleur* is once again a meditation on the writing self, its tone and approach is very different, even while, seen in retrospect, the worrying at conventional linguistic practices that was so evident in Oates's novels of the 1970s was clearly leading to some such artistic leap. Its religious element is part and parcel of its celebration of creativity. But it really is *celebration* here, rather than the oppressive depictions of vain spiritual searching in *Wonderland* or *Son of the Morning*. Despite the veneer of Vernon's half-insane religiosity and nineteenth-century rhetoric, his poetic aesthetic is surely close to Oates's. For Vernon, poetry is "God dictating." It is the language of "one soul addressing another." Poetry is both "a perpetual mystery" and "a way of coming home" (154). "The poet knows that he is water poured into water, he *knows* that he is finite and mortal and may drown at any time, in God, and that it's a risk to summon forth God's voice," says Vernon. But the poet "must take the chance of drowning in God—or whatever it is—I mean the poetry, the voice" (156). Rambler and babbler though he is, Vernon's religious rhetoric is merely a metaphor for the unknowable. The point is the immersion, with the risk that immersion will result in permanent submersion—in drowning. For what most informs the novel is the fact of creativity as a mystical experience that takes a person not only into themselves but also into an intuitive exploration of others by way of a demonstrable assumption of a oneness in human emotional and intellectual experience.

Bellefleur's religious dimension, therefore, is mysticism without expectation of ultimate understanding. In its emphasis on the flow rather than teleological inquiry it is pure pragmatism. It accepts the unknowable in direct contrast to Nathan Vickery's doomed quest "to *know*." Meanings exist in experiences. Existence is a mystery without final explanation, not least because (to use Kurt Gödel's theorem of incompleteness cited in Oates's worksheets for *What I Lived For*) "the full validity of any system, including a scientific one, cannot be demonstrated within that system itself."[22] Bromwell, chatting to his baby sister, points to the sky: "Cassicopeia, Canis Major, Andromeda. And there is Sirius. (And the baby would repeat, almost accurately, *Sirius*.) But only in our language, Germaine. And only in our galaxy. And only from this position in our galaxy. Do you understand? Yes? No? Of course you don't understand because no one does" (223). Our words shape a world, but in doing so they delude us into believing in shapes that seem the way they are only from our perspective and experience. "I shall repeat a hundred times," writes Nietzsche, "we really ought to free ourselves from the seduction of words!" Or, as Wallace Stevens puts it, through language we presume to conquer the night, and portion out the sea, yet we know that we are the makers of the songs we sing. "The world divides up," John Searle reminds us, "the way we divide it."[23] Its mystery, Oates's Bromwell is told by one of his teachers, "is its comprehensibility" (224). We comprehend the mystery, but are mystified at how we can comprehend the world, and even aware that our comprehension may in certain ways be itself a fiction. This, as Tarnas would have it, is Bateson's double-bind applied to the larger modern condition.

With *Bellefleur,* then, the "obsessive-compulsive" route, which distorted the inner and outer realities of so many of Oates's earlier characters, is rejected in favor of playful rather than tortured uncertainty. If anything, the stress is on balance, fusion. Even as it celebrates the imagination, it is a novel about science and facts. Inner and outer times are in dialogue. "Time is a child playing a game of draughts," runs the Heraclitus epigraph; "the kingship is in the hands of a child." Unlike the chronological time of *Buddenbrooks,* the whimsical time of *Bellefleur* is what Portuguese novelist José Saramago would call "poetic time." It is "at once linear and labyrinthine, uncertain and inconstant; a time with its own laws, a flood of words carrying a duration which in turn brings an ebb and flow." The clocks of the inner and outer worlds, as Oates elsewhere quotes Kafka, are "not in unison." "The inner one runs at a devilish or demoniac or in any case inhuman pace," while "the outer one limps along at its usual speed." Samuel hides in the Turquoise Room for eleven hours, but believes it has only been "an hour or so," and then that time is "different there" (203). He disappears for days, claiming he has just been reading. *"Time is clocks, not a clock,"* he realizes. *"You can't do more than try to contain it, like carrying water in a sieve"* (86). He enters the Turquoise Room to experience the "drowning of the ego" that Oates talks of in relation to Kafka and his identification "with the ahistorical, the timeless, the spiritual."[24]

While in the Turquoise Room, Samuel experiences a mirror that becomes a window so that "beyond the filmy glass surface," the room is "only dimly reflected" and his own image "as transparent as a jellyfish's." Like Hiram with the lake, he sees "in the mirror a mist-shrouded group of people," but in his case "all of them black" (200). Specifically, they are linked with three of John Brown's army of former slaves, given shelter in Bellefleur Manor's most elegant room as a sarcastic gesture by Samuel's father, Raphael. But more generally, the presences that haunt the Turquoise Room—the Room of Contamination—also haunt the American mind. Oates now uses a leitmotif of the early novels —all that mirror-gazing solipsism—to portray history as a melding of our imaginations with verifiable facts. She historicizes what up to now has seemed like ahistorical self-analysis. To look inward at the mirrored self becomes to look outward through the window at society, at history, at America. The "dark eyes" that mock Samuel through the mirror are simultaneously the eyes of the African woman who seduces him, and Oates's own dark eyes on America (201).

Bellefleur is not by mere coincidence, then, Oates's first novel to focus on documented history rather than the era of her own or her parents' lives. The escape into the imagination is also an immersion in history. *Bellefleur* at first seems to be a word-castle divorced from "reality," but turns out to be faithful to historical documentation. For the first time, Oates uproots a suspicion planted by some earlier novels that her art would never quite manage satisfactorily to wed private angst with public commitment. For *Bellefleur* succeeds in being both about the timeless world of the imagination and itself a tangible part of a real world: a commentary on American history and a musing on the aesthetic impulse. In the end, Oates does not take Samuel's path, as some of her earlier novels suggested she might, and disappear into the misty mirror of her own mind. The pure poet, Vernon, is beaten, tied up, and drowned. Rather, like Raphael, Oates is aware of the novel as itself as tangible a construction as the manor, a real thing in a real world. Raphael would like "to withdraw from the world for a spell, in order to properly mourn the loss of his son," but finds himself unable to do so. "For wasn't the world always there, always in turmoil, no matter that one closed one's eyes to it?" He rejects the tendency of others "to place the castle out of time, and to give it an otherworldly, an almost legendary aura." Raphael, after all, owns the estate. "*He* knew all the blunders and heartbreaking miscalculations that had gone into its creation, *he* alone was responsible for its upkeep. Like the God of creation he could not reasonably take solace in his creation, for wasn't it—after all—*his*?" (318). Such sentiments echo Oates's use of Henry James's comment in the epigraph to *Do with Me What You Will*: " . . . the world as it stands is no illusion." *Bellefleur*, too, is no illusion. It may be "a region, a state of the soul," but it "does exist."

As the novel closes, Bellefleur Manor is destroyed. Raphael's descendant Gideon flies his plane, packed with explosives, into it. Like so many of Oates's protagonists, he destroys himself, too. But it is not his death, it is the manor—the work of art—that we most remember. We finally see Bellefleur Manor from above and so can survey it as a whole. It looks, of course, remarkably like the architecture of the novel. "How oddly it had been constructed," thinks Gideon, "with its innumerable walls and towers and turrets and minarets, like a castle composed in a feverish sleep, when the imagination leapt over itself, mad to outdo itself, growing ever more frantic and greedy" (553). The manor may be obliterated in the explosion, but the destruction of Bellefleur Manor reminds us of the comparatively indestructible nature of *Bellefleur* the novel. The imagination transformed into narrative art is far less transient than the physical present. Since the artist turns imagination into tangible form, the artist has the luxury of destroying what is imagined. As Bromwell would have it of life, so it *is* of art. There is no death within the world of the novel since even destruction can be part of the creation. The imagination *is* life. The days Oates spent writing the book no longer exist, but the novel itself is on innumerable bookshelves. And in it the imagination has been preserved and sanctified. Something ephemeral has been made solid, and, because reproducible, protected against time's attrition. Such is the beautiful paradox of art: and art, as much as history (itself, we know, a form of art) is *Bellefleur*'s subject, "standing between two worlds—one the visible, material, "real" world, the other a world no less real, but not physically demonstrable."

Oates's use of Heraclitus as the epigraph to *Bellefleur* thus seems particularly apt. Bertrand Russell wrote of Heraclitus that "the facts of science, as they appeared to him, fed the flame of his soul, and in its light, he saw into the depths of the world by the reflection of his own dancing, swiftly penetrating fire. In such a nature we can see the true union of the mystic and the man of science—the highest eminence, I think, that it is possible to achieve in the world of thought." "Wisdom is one thing," wrote Heraclitus. "It is to know the thought by which all things are steered through all things." Such phrases echo the experience of reading *Bellefleur,* where Oates achieves the task, as she saw it in *New Heaven, New Earth,* of the artist-as-mystic: to explain "why the two worlds (the 'physical' and the 'spiritual') are not two at all, but one."[25]

Several critics illustrate how these characteristics of *Bellefleur* can be read in feminist terms. Marilyn Wesley, for instance, shows that it is "concerned with the repression of a feminist unconscious." When Gideon destroys the house and all the family except Germaine (whom he has sent to visit Aunt Mathilde), this, she suggests, "symbolizes the dissolution of a philosophy of competitive power largely perpetuated by gender ideology within the family." Wesley, too, sees the ending as positive; while "*a family is obliterated,*" the "ideal family" stays "paradoxically intact" since the final chapter "recounts the beginning of the recovery of the Bellefleurs after an earlier massacre." Similarly, Daly uses Julia Kristeva's ideas to illustrate that *Bellefleur* implicitly urges against ego-centered, male-style romanticism in favor of a communal approach, not least to the concept of authorship. "The depressed romanticism of Leah and Gideon," she writes, reveals its destructive results in, for instance, Gideon's abuse of Little Goldie and Leah's exploitation of her children. Neither can become master of the manor or author of the novel. "Who, then, is the 'author' of Bellefleur/Bellefleur?" asks Daly, herself answering, " 'We' are." "If we imagine Germaine as the novel's narrator, she is 'our' creation. She cannot exist without a community of readers," so "as readers we become co-narrators." Perry Nodelman, too, uses Kristeva's terms in seeing Bellefleur's innovations as a "feminine form of experimentation" that, in transcending "the limitations of both conventional and conventionally innovative forms of fiction" has "liberating potential for both women and men."[26]

These interpretations illustrate in turn that Oates's feminist perspective is also very much a pragmatist one. Wesley's focus on Bellefleur's critique of patriarchal values and Daly's stress on the novel as communal art mesh with its emphasis on fluidity, pluralism, multiplicity, experimentation, and metamorphosis, rather than structure, duality, linearity, convention, and stability. True as it is that definitions of feminism resist a single formulation, the same is so of pragmatism as a movement. But for Charlene Seigfried, while "none of the founding pragmatists made women's experiences central to their own discourse," "they did explicitly, frequently and consistently encourage their students to develop their own experimental basis for reflection." They did privilege individual experience over authoritative discourse, and they did, for the most part, create a philosophy that exhibited "a recognizably feminine style." Seigfried singles out William James in that while his writings are "among the least feminist of all the classical American philosophers," they are nevertheless arguably the most conventionally feminine. Images of fluidity and merging abound; boundaries are permeable." By "the 'feminine' in James," Seigfried means his emphasis on "the chthonic, the liquid, the vague, the inconstant, the chaotic," in other words, the very qualities that characterize Bellefleur. (Nodelman, for example, quotes not only Kristeva's definitions of feminism as championing the "exploded, plural, fluid" but also Hélène Cixous's emphasis on "luminous torrents.") So Oates managed to synthesize pragmatism and feminism. That male and female readers agree on the quality of Bellefleur—described by Joanne Creighton as "the most impressive of these reworkings of nineteenth-century genres," and, as already noted, by Gardner as "simply brilliant"—testifies to just how well this experimental, reader-centered novel works.[27]

In A Bloodsmoor Romance and Mysteries of Winterthurn, Oates's feminist deconstructions of nineteenth-century genres and values are more explicit, yet several critics seem less sure that the experiments succeed. Responses to *A Bloodsmoor Romance,* in particular, and in contrast to responses to *Bellefleur,* have tended to divide along gender lines. "Female critics generally praise the narrator's 'feminine' voice," writes Daly, "whereas most male critics consistently criticize it." Elaine Showalter sees it as closing on "a triumphant note of feminist vision." Eileen Bender calls it "a rich feminist parody." But among male critics, even Oates's biographer qualifies his praise, designating it "a demanding, often eccentric book that, as Joyce [Carol Oates] had perceived, would appeal primarily to a small readership with academic interests in social and literary history." *Mysteries of Winterthurn* has brought out no less polarized but perhaps less gender-split responses. For Daly, it is a feminist murder mystery with a discoverable solution, whereas for Linda Wagner-Martin it is "a completely inexplicable novel" in which none of the mysteries are "explained in any way." For Allen Shepherd, it seems designed to *be* inexplicable in conventional terms. It ends, for its protagonist Xavier Kilgarvan and for the reader, not in "clarity, but mystery itself." Oates, Shepherd adds, "is intent on confounding the reader's expectations in the effort to reinstate 'mystery' as a kind of philosophical category."[28]

Shepherd's perspective makes some sense after *Son of the Morning* and *Bellefleur.* Whatever answers we find are unlikely to resemble the stable solutions that the detective genre traditionally encourages. Oates's novels, by this stage, were hardly designed to fulfil any reader's quest for certainty. Her philosophical pragmatism had led her to refute anything that smacked of Absolute Truth, Firm Category, or Ultimate Meaning. Instead, what mattered was the extent to which her characters and novels could defy labeling, usurp or revise genres, stereotypes, or any other compartmentalizing, and so revise readers' perspectives. Seen this way, Oates's explicit revisionism in these two novels can be interpreted in ways that allow us to honor their pragmatic, unfinalized spirit.

Freedoms of all kinds are at the thematic heart of *A Bloodsmoor Romance.* In particular, the novel is about women's struggles to free themselves from patriarchal discourses that seek to dictate social and gender categories and curb individual female self-definition. Set between the autumn of 1879 and New Year's Eve 1899, it uses the structure of Louisa May Alcott's *Little Women,* as Showalter shows, "to explore the widest possible range of female relationships" as they work within or free themselves from the restrictions and stereotypes endemic to nineteenth-century culture.[29] That changing a language system is central to this is implicit in Oates's comments earlier in the 1970s. "A new morality is emerging in America," she wrote in 1974, "the experiencing of life as meaningful in itself without divisions into 'good' or 'bad,' 'beautiful' or 'ugly,' 'moral' or 'immoral.'"[30] It is to escape the oppressive categories created by language that the female members of the Zinn family flee their prescribed fate as a collective, inferior group in a patriarchal culture. The mother, four Zinn sisters, and Deirdre, an adopted orphan, have two particular authoritative discourses to escape. One is that of the narrator. The other is that of their inventor-father, John Quincy Zinn, whose initial qualities unravel to reveal a worldview that has monstrous consequences.

"The narrator," says Oates, is "the very voice of the era; the 'good' 'prim' 'admonishing' 'ladylike' voice of repression most, or all, women have internalized since girlhood. (A variant of Woolf's 'angel in the house.') To outwit, escape, extinguish this crippling narrator is the sisters' only hope. And they succeed!"[31] In other words, in order to find their individual freedom, each of the Zinn sisters has to defy the very language of nineteenth-century American patriarchal culture. Presumably accurate with details, the narrator's language and judgments ensure our sense of ironic distance. "Knowing well the prospects that lie ahead, for each of the sisters," the narrator wishes she could "guide their destinies in happier directions."[32] For the narrator, this is a tragedy of waywardness, but from a contemporary perspective it is a triumph of emancipation. Daly provides a convincing argument that this narrative "voice" is in fact part of "the novel's challenge to the romantic concept of a unique or individual narrative voice." For Daly, it is Deirdre, the spiritualist manipulator of voices, who orchestrates the narrative. Because "Deirdre has considerable skill in channeling voices," suggests Daly, "it is reasonable to assume that she acts as the narrator," parodying and satirizing her own story as well as that of the sisters. Deirdre uses the narrative voice to parody "feminine language" in general, and the author-narrator of *Jane Eyre* in particular. But in the end, even she has to come to terms with "the limits of the imperial 'I.'" This isolated orphan spirited away by a black balloon finds reconciliation both with her adoptive sisters and with her true mother, Edwina Kiddemaster. Sharing her newly inherited wealth with her sisters, she is finally able to reunite the Zinn women and give them all "the economic freedom to pursue romances with a decidedly feminist slant."[33]

Daly's interpretation of the narrative voice helps pinpoint the relationship between that voice and the other ultimately destructive figure for the girls, their father. If the narrative voice is ironic and involves transition from isolated individualism to the communal, John Quincy Zinn's perspective tends to label others—particularly women—rather than see them as individuals free to define themselves. In some ways, Zinn seems at first to be the artist as inventor, "the novelist as empiricist," humbly "striving for what he does not yet know." Oates wrote in her worksheets that, like Benjamin Franklin, he has a "sense of a divine mission. The 'perfecting' of America," which manifests itself through "inventions to ease the drudgery of life" and "to perfect mankind's spiritual harmony." But what Oates also shows Zinn to be, therefore, is the male version of "the very voice of the era." He "represents the overwhelming force of good-which-denies-evil (i.e., 'reality') which his daughters must resist," writes Oates. They love him yet break with him "because his vision of the universe is so aggressively benign."[34] That they must indeed escape him becomes even clearer when he accepts government sponsorship to make a state-of-the-art execution apparatus. Believing that if execution is necessary it should be as humane as possible, he designs an electric bed, summarily rejected by Congress as not "flashy" enough (422).

Showalter, arguing that Oates "deepens and extends" Alcott's "critique of Emersonian and patriarchal genius, satirizing its pretensions and dangers," notes that Zinn is "an ineffectual but dictatorial father, a Transcendentalist sage and inventor, who eventually produces both the electric chair and the atomic bomb." "The end of masculine technological genius is destruction," she writes. "The man of science, consumed by envy of the reproductive powers of women and nature, tries to appropriate them, but instead of creating life, can only invent more efficient and terrific forms of death."[35] Where Deirdre can mimic voices and so show how language shapes the reality of a culture or an era, Zinn's vocabulary of benevolent certainty lacks any such ironic distance. Where Deirdre's provisional vocabulary lets her consciousness evolve, Zinn's consciousness is static, and hence ultimately destructive of himself and others.

Above all, the daughters must escape forms of categorizing that, while expressed benignly, are in fact as suffocating as whalebone corsets. Zinn is a scientist, and they of all nineteenth-century men, argues Cynthia Eagle Russett, tended to define women in ways detrimental to female individualism. Like other disciplines of nineteenth-century intellectual endeavor, says Russett, science "can be seen as a weapon used by men to rationalize the perpetuation of traditional sex roles and men's continued dominance of women." But "the unanimity and strength of the scientific consensus" stands out when contrasted with the many men in other intellectual fields (such as John Stuart Mill, Thomas Higginson, Wendell Phillips, Frederick Douglass) who felt secure enough to "encourage women to fuller participation in society." Russett argues that the reason for this consensus lay in contemporary scientific theory and practice, in particular the habit of categorizing. "Refusal to view women as individuals was the common intellectual stance of antifeminists, not something peculiar to the scientific community," says Russett. "Yet the normal practice of science itself strongly reinforced this stance. Scientists classify and categorize and generalize, and this often means that the scientist's vision is fixed on the larger collectivity rather than on the single individual." Therefore scientists of the time tended to focus on a sort of "composite Woman." Assuming that the sexes should be classified separately, they became committed to group homogeneity, wherein all women shared a basic femininity and all men a basic masculinity. The scientists therefore felt justified in focusing "not on an individual particularity, but on the properties shared by the group." In addition, pessimism about human potential teamed with Darwinian notions to commit the scientists to describing gender differences in hierarchical terms. Russett, arguing that "the open espousal of a hierarchical order is . . . part of the same intellectual universe that was so absorbing the meaning of evolution for human nature and society," notes, "Under any circumstances it would have been extremely difficult for nineteenth-century scientists to arrive at more favorable conclusions about women." Quite aside from long habits of upbringing, there was fear of anarchic flux. "Sharing with other men the apprehension created by women's determined assault on the enclaves of masculine privilege, scientists had a particular need to reaffirm their ontological stature."[36]

Bloodsmoor's six main women—Mrs. Prudence Zinn, her daughters, and Deirdre—symbolize various paths by which individual women could escape that tyranny of collective categorization. Until her final emancipation, Prudence Zinn is a living warning to her daughters to avoid her fate. She has existed in servitude to a patriarchal husband and to the admonishing voice of the era. In her youth she displayed as much of a sense of individualism as her daughters now have, but has since calcified into a petty narrowness reminiscent of Austen's Mrs. Bennet or Mann's Tony Buddenbrook, wholly given over to the mores and hierarchies of the prevailing order. Because of his "ancestral name" she is pleased that the baron is Philippa's suitor (36), and she is anxious "that her Kiddemaster cousins should be marrying off *their* daughters with such ease" (37). But later it turns out that the energetic young Prudence Kiddemaster's spirit had been broken through "the repetition of pregnancies, miscarriages, labors, births and occasional deaths" too "morbid" for inclusion in the narrative (167). Mrs. Zinn finally becomes a suffragette in widowhood, but the bulk of her life has been one of subjection.

Her first two daughters are the rebel and the conformist. Constance Philippa is literally freed from her body, metamorphosizing into a man called Philippe Fox and eloping with Delphine Martineau. In effect, she is a version of what the Victorians called a "hoyden," a boisterous, "mannish, strong-minded woman," as Deborah Gorham puts it in her study of Victorian feminine stereotypes. But she is one who in this case leaps triumphantly beyond the borders of "acceptable" behavior to leave behind the category "woman" altogether. The conventional and obedient Octavia, in contrast, chooses to be her "husband's belovèd help-meet," but manages to widow herself in one of his hood-and-noose sex games (369). She is the equivalent of the Victorian ideal of, in Gorham's words, "the good daughter, gentle, loving, self-sacrificing and innocent." But she, too, ultimately finds a more equal relationship with Sean McInnes. The third daughter, Malvinia, is an egotistical beauty whose "shortness of breath" results from her adherence to nineteenth-century clothing etiquette (60). The equivalent of what Gorham terms "the bad daughter"—"vulgar, self-seeking, lazy and sexually impure"—she too strikes out on her own, as an actress whose excessive physicality and sexuality leads her to opt for a celibate relationship with the Reverend Kennicott. The youngest daughter, Samantha, searches for intellectual freedom. She works for her father and believes in his utopian vision. But not only is she scarred in one of his experiments, she also receives scant recognition for her work, and in the end elopes to escape the fate of an arranged marriage. She finally denounces her father for submitting to Congress's demands for the execution instrument. "I was his first human experiment," she says, "and shall not have been his last" (418). Returning to scientific research, she contrasts with her father, as Showalter notes, by using technology "to make life more pleasant," inventing "the disposable diaper and the washing machine."[37]

The narrator states that these four girls so violate "the customs of propriety, good sense, and daughterly obligation, as to be lost—indeed, *damn'd*—forever." That they "plunge into the wide world" only to "find their divers ways back home," she describes as "a triumphant affirmation of God's grace" (521). Despite such moralizing commentary (or perhaps Deirdre's ironic gloss) the triumphs belong to the daughters and help to topple the dominance of patriarchy. Zinn's death at the final moment of the century is appropriate. Not only has he helped prolong a status quo the daughters fight against, but his Perpetual Motion Machine turns out to be connected with "*atom-expansion, or detonation*" (607). When the crucial information is destroyed in a fire even as Zinn dies, Deirdre is exhilarated at having possibly spared humanity "the madman's dream" (614).

No less than *Bellefleur*, *Bloodsmoor* dismantles novelistic conventions born of the language of a past culture in order to rewrite and revise cultural presuppositions that might still linger. Russett writes of how a youthful William James provided hints of a changing perspective. She talks of the young James's encounter with a severe epileptic during a visit to a French insane asylum in 1872. James described how the youth "sat there like a sort of Egyptian mummy, moving nothing but his black eyes and looking absolutely non-human." Terrified, James's response was "*That shape am I,* I felt potentially. Nothing that I possess can defend me against that fate, if the hour for it should strike for me as it struck for him." Russett notes that James, who rebelled against the dogma and determinism, if not the inherent sexism, of the science he studied, shows an instinctive identification with the youth, presaging his later writings. In contrast, "in the eyes of the scientists whose dogma James rejected," "the same epileptic youth could have a very different significance." Far from feeling a "temptation to empathy," he would probably have been viewed as "a visible reminder that in the Great Chain of Being the scientist himself stood at least one link away from the ape." Russett's point is that "in their more refined way, women served the same need. Far more numerous than idiots and more proximate than savages, women objectified a phase of evolution which men had transcended. They testified in their very otherness to masculine excellence."[38] As far as *Bloodsmoor* is concerned, Zinn's apparent benignity still consigns his wife and daughters to live as members of a category, rather than as individuals, or would have done had they not, with the coming of Deirdre, each in their way managed to rebel. In doing so, they helped usher in the modern world.

So as in *Bellefleur,* in *Bloodsmoor* Oates's pragmatism finds a natural meeting place with her overt feminism. Unlike the self-satisfied Zinn, whose certainty of belief leads to negative consequences, the dissatisfied rebel, Deirdre of the Shadows, embodies the new century's spirit of innovation, revolution, and emancipation. Where Zinn at first seems benign yet turns out to preside over malignant effects, Deirdre starts out "bitter" and "haunted" and only gradually learns how to put her talents to constructive social use (302). At first she is driven by resentment intuitively connected with the denied rights she glimpses in the inexplicable hatred apparently felt for her by Edwina Kiddemaster (who turns out to be her mother). "How bitter it is, her heart!" she thinks, as it had been at sixteen so it is "still, at the sober age of thirty-one" (384). But while Deirdre begins the novel very much like the artist who, convinced she is born damned, "must struggle through life to achieve redemption," her ultimate rejection of this introspective solitude in favor of communal creativity parallels the journey toward artistic maturity traceable through the first half of Oates's career.[39] She begins her evolution after her kidnapping by the black balloon. The abduction can be read as a form of self-destruction (*"You shall all sail away into the sky,"* promises Father Darien, *"in time"* [327]), but it also frees her to assume a new identity and become a medium. At her lowest ebb, the inner voices become "a vale of temptation," but they also help her fight against her own bitter heart. *"Do not surrender to the wicked spirits. Love thy enemies, Deirdre, love thy sisters,"* the voice of Mrs. Bonner tells her (328). *"You will not drown yourself in the well—nor will you wade and swim out into the river, to a clownish muddy death. Rouse yourself from your dream; get to your feet; clear your head of evil thoughts"* (329).

Deirdre transforms her suicidal urges into a form of art useful to others. In particular, she helps the ghost of Florette, a sexually abused adolescent, who seems "a *stranger,* yet a *sister*" (494). She then uses her experience of persuading Florette to end her ghostly search for vengeance, and so her suffering, in her final speech to her sisters. She remembers her own sense of "revulsion for one's very *being,*" and thinking back realizes how her "*own* penury of spirit gave substance to these fancies," or how she "too energetically seized upon some small provocation" to feed her bitterness (577). Deirdre has grown to recognize that "myself vs. the world" has really been "myself vs. myself." But, unlike the young author who created Karen Herz and Clara Walpole, the Oates of *Bloodsmoor* now had time and the perspective of maturity between her and the pain of the young girl. Deirdre's befriending of Florette, in turn, anticipates the subject matter of Oates's several novellas and short novels in the 1990s, such as *First Love* and *Man Crazy,* that depict the traumas and survival of just such girls.

Like so many of Oates's novels, *Bloodsmoor* thus contains a meditation on the direction of her art even as, like *Bellefleur,* it seeks to stretch the parameters of the novel form. Commentators have sometimes noted Oates's tendency to wear her ambitions on her sleeve. Gardner's sense that *Bellefleur* "too noticeably labors after greatness," echoed Benjamin De Mott's earlier suggestion that "knowingness" casts "a shadow everywhere" in her work by way of "needlessly pretentious titles and epigraphs" and in "displays of self-reference." *Bloodsmoor*, in turn, is an almost perverse demonstration of the scope of Oates's ambition, and sometimes the novelist's story seems entirely coincidental with Deirdre's. Deirdre, we are told, rarely speaks "about so external, and so materialistic, an issue as her career, let alone her income," but might concur, silently, with Madame Blavatsky's "fervent belief" that she is "undervalued," despite the attentions she receives "and the incontestable mystery of her powers" (339). Clearly, as Showalter notes, Deirdre "represents the novelist and Oates herself," and at times her career resembles nothing so much as a hard-working writer on a book tour with Blavatsky as an ever-faithful agent and "champion" (338).

But if that self-referential side remains an element of Oates's art, another of De Mott's criticisms seems, by the time of *Bloodsmoor,* wholly untrue. "She continues to appear as an *un*developing talent," he wrote in 1969, "a writer making no apparent advance toward reflective intelligence." In keeping with the new tone in *Bellefleur,* the self-references of *Bloodsmoor* appear as ironic self-mockery and are offset by Deirdre's eventual ability to gain a more balanced perspective. It is precisely this reflective intelligence that becomes so evident in Oates's novels of maturity. She would continue to wed her own emotional life with ostensibly diverse American individuals, but self-reference diminishes. *Bloodsmoor* is primarily an outward-looking rather than introspective novel, dramatizing (in a phrase Oates used years earlier) "the revolt against science and scientism that characterizes much of twentieth-century literature," originating "in nineteenth-century dissatisfaction with the utopian vision of man as essentially rational."[40] Zinn is the utopian rationalist, while Deirdre, the intermediary "between the *visible* and *invisible* worlds," is at once a nineteenth-century woman, escaping rational, male structures, and the Oatesian mystic (343).

The narrator ends by misrepresenting the opening stanzas of Longfellow's "A Psalm of Life." Standing alone, the stanzas might seem to focus on an expectation of an afterlife. "Life is real! Life is earnest!" she quotes.

> And the grave is not its goal;
> "Dust thou art, to dust returnest,"
> Was not spoken of the soul.

But the real story of the novel—and of the Longfellow poem, subtitled "what the heart of the young man said to the psalmist"—is about *this* life. It "grieves" *Bloodsmoor's* narrator to say that the young will read the lines as "a *riddle*" rather than "a gladsome *certitude*" (615). Life, she suggests, is "real" because the soul survives death. But clearly life, as Oates portrays it, is about riddles, rather than certitude, with irony, rather than literalism, her dominant tone. Given *Bloodsmoor's* feminist thrust, the rest of the poem reinforces this irony. "Art is long, and Time is fleeting," read the unquoted lines:

> Lives of great men all remind us
> We can make our lives sublime.
> And departing leave behind us
> Footprints in the sands of time.[41]

Oates would soon return to a more accessible and contemporary exploration of American fates. But first she had to demonstrate once and for all the nature of that futile, destructive desire to solve insoluble mysteries, to grasp precisely the "certitude"—the "chimera" of "absolute Truth"—that the narrator, ironically or otherwise, appears to assume. Acceptance that "the world has no meaning" would leave Oates all the more space to explore "the many individual and alarming and graspable meanings" it *is* the human adventure to discover.

The ironic, revisionist tone of *Bellefleur* and *Bloodsmoor* continues in *Mysteries of Winterthurn*. The ironist, wrote Søren Kierkegaard, "must always be understood at a distance." In other words, to borrow Allan Megill's advice on approaching the work of Jacques Derrida, "we ought not to view the ironist from three inches away. We must not allow ourselves to be too caught up in the individual brushstrokes." Rather, we should step back and view "the effect of the canvas as a whole." To take on the role of detective and solve the mysteries in *Winterthurn* is an ever-present temptation since a convention of art—and especially of the detective genre—is to provide keys for the reader to "unlock" the work. But in *Winterthurn* we are in the world of Franz Kafka, or perhaps even (suggests Linda Wagner-Martin) Thomas Pynchon, not Poe or Conan Doyle. As Sharon Dean argues, comparing Nathan Vickery's doomed pursuit of knowledge with the plight of Kafka's heroes, Oates, like Kafka, knows that what she writes can never achieve "a stable reality," and certainly never "capture that part of experience that is beyond the invented language of the mind." *Winterthurn* reflects this as much as *Son of the Morning*. For Wagner-Martin, the reason why the novel is "completely inexplicable" is because Oates offers "so few clues that her fiction becomes a great wry mystery." Oates "gives the reader the most rational of frameworks: 'Editor's notes,' 'Postscripts,' 'Epilogues,' and the detective-tradition itself." Such organization "suggests ends and reliable conclusions (the three-part, separate mystery structure)," all held together by "a sane narrative voice that describes a seemingly sane detective figure." But none of this leads us anywhere. Similarly, Shepherd sees the novel as offering "a proliferation of radically ambiguous, undecidable stories, and as they accumulate, a subversive proposition: that perhaps what we really want is not the solution but just this teasing postponement, this slightly dizzying frustration; not clarity, but mystery itself."[42]

Whether or not that is what we want, it is surely what we get. *Winterthurn* is in every sense an ironic novel, and if *Bellefleur*, as Bender suggests, needs an experimental reader, *Winterthurn* needs an ironic one. If we read the novel in literal terms, we assume that since it purports to be a mystery novel it has mysteries to solve, and that the novel's violence is actual physical crime. We assume that "murder" means murder, "crime" means crime, and "mystery" means mystery. But as with the previous two novels, *Winterthurn,* above all, ironizes the genre it purports to adopt—a fact made fairly explicit by the parodic use of double titles for all three stories—so we cannot approach it as we would a conventional detective novel without ourselves becoming versions of Xavier Kilgarvan or his fictional precursor, Joseph K. Any attempt to solve/interpret the mystery/novel in straightforward terms, to prove the novel's meaning or the identity of the various murderers, automatically places the interpreter in the role of detective and requires the use of a detective's vocabulary. Kilgarvan may well be a defective detective, but, since the whole vocabulary that creates the notion of detection in the first place is in fact called into question, the novel has to do with a whole wordview/worldview, rather than with the shortcomings of a single man.

Equally, while several critics have shown the extent to which Oates's critique of the detective genre again involves a specifically feminist form of revisionism, such interpretations tend to overlook the novel's fluidity and ambiguity and so resurrect the very discourse Oates ironizes. "In the manner of classic detectives," writes Lorna Sage, "Xavier persists in imagining the likely culprit as male, solitary, vilely ingenious: in short some kind of rival individualist. Whereas he might read a different message in the words of his elusive love, his cousin, Perdita." For Daly, "critics who do not become Oates's accomplices in this feminist project—especially those who fail to identify Perdita either as the murderer of her minister-husband or as the Editor of her detective-husband's most famous cases—often charge the author with the failure to edit her writing." But, in turn, to seek such cast-iron answers to the various mysteries, including the narrator's identity, is to cut against Daly's own surely accurate view of *Bellefleur:* that "whatever theoretical unity one posits, the novel's plenitude of 'meanings' always escapes such formulations." Seeing the identities of all these narrators as "puzzles for readers to solve," Daly concludes that we must engage in "a feminist questioning of conventional authority" if we are "finally to 'solve' the murder mystery, as well as the mystery of the narrative voice."[43] Questioning conventional authority does seem to be very much the point, but this is precisely why any quest for a conventional, "provable," authoritative interpretation of *Winterthurn* seems suspect.

Mystery in Oates's novels is a positive category to be celebrated, rather than demystified into what may be a spurious certainty. Rather, as Wagner-Martin and Shepherd note, *Winterthurn* has the same (pragmatic) emphasis as *Bellefleur,* an emphasis (remembering Charlene Seigfried's description of the "feminine" in James) on "the chthonic, the liquid, the vague, the inconstant, the chaotic." Perhaps Perdita can indeed be seen as a murderess and her husband's editor. But to argue this is already to see that Perdita or Xavier are somehow "real" personalities, rather than literary devices that Oates employs to make her playfully serious points about the nature of literary detection or of reading and interpretation. The first preface, for instance, suggests that the so-called "mysteries" might as easily be called metaphors. Citing Thomas De Quincy, the editor draws parallels between the purported subject matter and the act of reading about it: "Is not Murder an art-form?" the editor asks. "And does any art-form require justification?"[44] Murder and art are thus immediately equated as acts-in-the-world, and interpretation or explanation are just as immediately challenged. The reader, therefore, who sets out in pursuit of solutions, who wants "to *know,"* sets out with much the same attitude as the young Xavier or that proactive solution seeker, Joseph K, or even the youthful novelist, Joyce Carol Oates.

Mysteries of Winterthurn, read in this way, is a Kafkaesque labyrinth, and to claim to "solve" it is to be like Kafka's heroes, whose attempts to "win" ensure their doom. If we go back to Oates's pivotal essay collection, *New Heaven, New Earth,* we find a revealing essay entitled "Kafka's Paradise," in which Oates interprets Kafka in terms of his interest in Taoism. Kafka's heroes, she argues, are their own enemies. The more they "strive for victory, the more violently their intellects demand explanations, the more inevitable their doom." The quest they engage in is the quest they create. "While Joseph K. and K. struggle to achieve an impossible goal—the self-defining autonomy of the self—Kafka directs us toward the realization that their struggles are pointless, for the salvation they crave is already in their possession." Kafka's heroes suffer as a result of their own definitions. They create their own problems: "life is a paradox only when it is defined as such." Turn back to *Winterthurn* and it is clear that Xavier, too, is determined to discover answers to questions he himself has posed. "Therefore the attempt to achieve victory of any kind—even victory over one's own impulses—even victory over the flow of time—is the tragic revision of paradise into hell, a misreading of the 'parable' for the 'reality.'" We are meant to see Kafka's heroes, Oates argues, as models of how the intellect can be the enemy. "It is in Taoism," she asserts, "that we come across the very spirit of Kafka himself; the awareness of a dominion of absolutely impersonal and incomprehensible Being over the efforts of individuals to influence it, or even to influence their own lives." To read the novel literally, therefore—to read "murder" as murder and "mystery" as mystery—may be to read "the 'parable' for the 'reality.'" As the editor suggests in the first preface, murder can mean "*soul-murder,*" or self-murder (4). This is very much Oates's focus in "Kafka's Paradise." "To make war against one's own self is suicidal," she explains. "At the very least, it is ludicrous." Moreover, she provides a direct link between Kafka's world and the world of detective fiction that Kafka's own novels also parody. "Kafka said, in explanation of his dislike for detective fiction," she writes, "that in real life mystery isn't hidden in the background." On the contrary, "every-day is the greatest detective story ever written."[45]

As in her Kafka essay and elsewhere, so in *Winterthurn* Oates makes it plain that she believes that many of our battles are with ourselves. ("We do battle," as she puts it in *The Edge of Impossibility,* "but battle with a shadow"). To have any hope of remedying this, we need to create ironic distance from our own individual and collective behavior. Reading the novel this way, it becomes clear that Xavier, who matures from adolescence in the first story, through to early middle age by the third, discovers that detection is a metaphor for a self-created way of living. He starts out seeing too literally, pledged as a conventional detective "to seek out the cause of death in terms of its *literal agent.*" He discovers that the nature of the world is, in the words of Dr. Holyrod Wilts, "quite otherwise" (460). But while, as the *K* of Kilgarvan suggests, he is Kafkaesque, he does not, like Joseph K., condemn himself. Instead, he comes to see that he is complicit in the events he examines and so able to become his own savior. As Daly points out, "his brilliance leads not to personal triumph but to a recognition of the limits of his authority." Each solution presents the dilemma that "he will at the same time betray those he loves by exposing their complicity in crime."[46]

Xavier comes to see that the worldview he has for so long held cannot help him deal with the mysteries he encounters. Justice is not always done. Mysteries are not always solvable, and solutions, where available, are not necessarily desirable. The epigraph (Samuel Johnson's famous dictum that "when a man knows he is to be hanged in a fortnight, it concentrates his mind wonderfully") suggests that the fact of death should focus our minds on how to live. The dogged pursuit of insoluble mystery leads nowhere or is self-destructive. Rather, Xavier gains a new perspective by way of a new language. *Winterthurn*, like *Bloodsmoor*, turns out to be fundamentally concerned with renewal and reinvention, not only for individuals but ultimately for a whole culture whose idiom has become so habitual as to allow us to mistake "the 'parable' for the 'reality.' "

In the first story, "The Virgin in the Rose-Bower; or The Tragedy of Glen Mawr Manor" (the title is taken from a trompe l'oeil painting), the adolescent Xavier is himself virginal in his naivety about the nature of mystery. His "tricked eye" is his conventional view of the art of detection—a false way of seeing that, like the paintings, gives an "air of the *artificially lifelike*." In the opening pages, we learn that the first "mystery" is "old, much-analyzed, yet still tantalizing," and that while "it would seem at first blush to declare itself a classic of the *locked-room* variety" (3), it owes its true fame to having been "*never satisfactorily resolved*" (4). Given Oates's philosophical preoccupations through so much of her early career, it seems that Xavier is intent on solving the insoluble. Once again, quoting Shepherd, we are in the realm of " 'mystery' as a kind of philosophical category." Xavier has as much hope of solving these "crimes"—ostensibly multiple murders in Glen Mawr Manor—as we have of solving the mysteries of metaphysics. This is because his pursuit of "Truth" has to do with a language system that has created the notion of detection, rather than anything necessarily inherent in the world beyond language. Our focus, then, might best be on words like *murder* and *mystery* as properties of language, rather than essences somehow beyond the novel's pages. They function here as metaphors for the way we live and for our pursuit of meanings.

Xavier, of course, cannot entertain such a notion. Murder, he thinks, can be "exposed, and explained, and 'solved.' " What lies "in the beclouded realm of the *mysterious*" can be "transposed, by the rigorous logic of detection, into the *comprehensible*" (99). He believes in a logical world in which "what appears to the untutored eye as Chaos may be read, by the proper intelligence, and by the proper faith, as Order" (99–100). Unable to "remember *forward*" to the disappointments that will come, he looks to a time when "all that is now baffling, vexing, and mysterious, could be read as History!" (100). His naïve vision is based on the paradox that the world is God-centered but also mind-centered, the logic of which suggests that God is in the mind. The vision is enticing—as deceptive visions must be—but is no less a trompe l'oeil for that, any more than language, while it shapes reality, is itself "real." ("Logic, and its translation into a rigorous grammatical form," he later says, can afford the doomed a "semblance of *control*" [257].) In the end, Xavier's investigation does "yield fruit," but he burns the solution (151). The pursuit of solutions may itself be a defective vision of the world.

The novel's scope broadens in the second story, "Devil's Half Acre; or The Mystery of the Cruel Suitor," and Xavier, now aged twenty-eight, moves toward a mature vision. His suspect for the murders of a series of factory girls is a Hamletian figure, Valentine Westergaard, dressed in theatrical black after his sister's death. Valentine's attitude is that of Hamlet to Rosencrantz and Guildenstern. Xavier would pluck out the heart of his mystery as if he were easier to be played on than a pipe. He fails, of course, but defective visions, we learn in this second story, are not merely some internal, precious form of artistic game playing. Set against the theatrical cat-and-mouse tussle between Valentine and Xavier, and within the entertainment genre of detective fiction, Oates inserts the real historical phenomena of bigotry, racism, and lynch mobs. The "real" world invades the story in the shape of the Jewish scapegoat, Isaac Rosenwald. Blindness to the realities of other people is not just self-destructive but the root cause of many historical and contemporary atrocities. As Georgina Kilgarvan, writing as the Dickinsonian poetess "Iphigenia," puts it in a poem used for the epigraph to chapter 1,

> If I—am You—
> Shall You—be me?
> If You—scorn I—
> Where then—We—
> Be—?

This echoes James, Dewey, and Rorty, as well as fellow pragmatist Jane Addams's argument that "much of the insensibility and hardness of the world" is due "to the lack of imagination which prevents a realization of the experiences of other people."[47] The crimes that Xavier explores partly stem from the treatment of others as somehow unreal or inferior because they are different from the perceiver. We superimpose visions on circumstances and events, and with concrete, sometimes lethal, results. Xavier ends this second story pursuing and catching his own brothers, who are Westergaard's accomplices. He is one step nearer his final suspect, who, in the third story, turns out to be himself. He begins to see that, since amateur detection is a human activity, what is at issue is not so much how you choose to perceive the world but that you recognize your own nature and gain ironic distance from your own activity.

In the third and final tale, "The Bloodstained Bridal-Gown; or Xavier Kilgarvan's Last Case," the forty-year-old Xavier is called back to Winterthurn to solve the triple ax murders of Perdita's minister-husband, the Reverend Harmon Bunting, the minister's mother, Mrs. Letitia Bunting, and his mistress, Mrs. Amanda Poindexter, in the Grace Episcopal Rectory. Without any satisfactory solution to the mystery even by the end, Xavier marries Perdita and abandons "the accursed art of crime detection" as "suited uniquely for *bachelors*" (482). Again, this can be read metaphorically. Xavier implicitly weds himself to society, discarding the role of solitary pursuing hero. He lives up to his Emersonian motto, "I make my circumstance," by redefining his agenda (389). His pursuit of two improbably named suspects, Jabez Dovekie and Amanda's husband, Ellery Poindexter, he comes to recognize, is both a pursuit of death (Dovekie being a former iceman) and a pursuit of himself. This final story critiques not only Xavier's defective detective perspective but also the detective genre in general, including the *"tidiness of the conclusion"* (353). "The mystery or detective novel," says the narrator, "upholds the principle, *in defiance of contemporary sentiment,* that infinite Mystery, beyond that of the finite, may yield to human ratiocination: that truth will 'out': that happiness is possible once Evil is banished: and that God, though, it seems, withdrawn at the present time from both Nature and History, is yet a living presence in the world,—an unblinking eye that sees all, absorbs all, comprehends all, each and every baffling *clue,* and binds all multifariousness together, in a divine unity" (353–54). But the mysteries of Winterthurn illustrate progressively not only how untrue that vision is but also how dangerous, destructive, and self-defeating it can become if you try to apply it to actual life. Xavier's initial response to the appalling things he witnesses—and to the fact that even if he discovers the truth justice may not be done—is to exchange optimism for Timonian pessimism. Like Oates with her "premature detachment" in the

1970s, he retreats inward, believing that he has "seen everything the world might offer, at least by way of evil," and that "normal" preoccupations are "forbidden him" (395). He grows cold, and chills those who come near him. Regarding the case itself, there is "little *mystery*" at all (402). He has himself become the mystery (pursuing a solution to ax murders—or X murders). Living off death, the detective, as his brother Bradford says, is "drawn to corpses, that he might feast and glut himself" (404). It is simply that the mystery and the investigated death (by the argument of Oates's Kafka essay) are his own.

Ultimately, then, Xavier comes to stand for us all and detection becomes a metaphor for other forms of human activity, including writing, reading, and interpreting. Xavier himself sees that "all the academic disciplines" are "paradigms of the detective's search for Truth: that life itself might be imagined as a pursuit,—a hunt—an impassioned quest, as to the nature of one's 'baptism'" (206). Combating one's nature is futile. Nevertheless, detection can give coherence and meaning to life, so long as one gains ironic distance from the activity and realizes that some mysteries are beyond us or have no certain answer. The reader may be a detective, then, but so is the writer. On some days, Xavier is "provoked to near-frenzy, by a contemplation of Time, that he must work more quickly, to assemble a great mass of data, a veritable miniature galaxy, it seemed, proving Poindexter's guilt." On other days he feels "near-paralyzed by the terrifying thought that, even as his pulses beat, *Time beat*, and though he labor at his task ten, or twelve, or fifteen, or eighteen,—or, indeed, twenty-four—hours a day, he could never hope to catch the phantom Poindexter; or even, for a scant minute, to still that dread passage of time" (435). "Probably, we are all more like our 'past' selves than we might wish," Oates has said. "Like those proverbial identical twins, separated at birth, who turn out to mimic each other in all sorts of trivial, ancillary ways that suggest an almost sinister genetic determinism—a challenge to those of us who not only 'believe' in free will, but need to believe in it." We cannot escape our own genetic disposition, perhaps, but we can develop a reflective "attitude" toward our experiences and activities—creative, critical, social, emotional, intellectual—and so steer them to productive ends.[48] Just as, in chasing Poindexter, Xavier chases himself, so all our pursuits are, to some degree, phantasms of our own mind. We cannot necessarily stop the pursuing, but we can develop a perspective on the nature of the pursuit. Poindexter tells Xavier how God appeared to him in childhood and let him know that "Heaven will never be any closer than it is, at the present moment" (444). This is the nub of Oates's pragmatism. Heaven is in the writing. Paradise is in the pursuit, in the doing, the being, not in the result, the "solution." Ambition is in the act, not the result. The novel's "evolving of consciousness" is the story of how a detective (Xavier, Oates, the reader) can at least become aware of the nature of detection, of the human need to *know*. But the joy must be in the needing, not always in the knowing.

Toward the end, Xavier follows Poindexter into the "labyrinthine passageways" of the ironically named Hotel Paradise, a brothel of tortured women (456). Here he meets Dr. Wilts, who treats the men and women for their sexual diseases and who reaffirms the power of death, that "wondrous force" whose strength "fills all of the universe, and all of Time: while on the other side, in feeble 'opposition' to it, we have a frail organism, indeed,—the *human body*." The mystery and miracle of life is survival itself. The doctor, detective, and novelist are all in the limited game of trying to heal wounds, restoring the temporality of "health" to an individual or community (460). When, finally, Poindexter attacks Xavier and suffocates on his own fury, there is no mystery, and Xavier feels no joy but looks as if he has lost "his closest friend—or his very brother!" (469). He shuns the year's Christmas festivities and tells his host's servants to say he is "departed—or dead." If he tries to sleep, his brain works "all the more frenetically," as it has habitually "in the past several months," but now without focus. "I am indeed a mirror suspended above an abyss," he thinks, "possessed of no content, and reflecting nothing save motion. And now, alas, that motion appears to have stilled" (471). He is the novelist not just at the end of this novel but at the end of a particular evolutionary stage of individual consciousness, left "perusing his coded notes" and "the several labyrinthine charts, graphs, and maps he had so meticulously devised,—in another phase of his life, it seemed" (471). On New Year's Eve he consigns all his notes to the fire, and, after twenty weeks of convalescence, his suicidal urge dissipates and he discovers some words of Thoreau's that echo Kafka's comments quoted by Oates in "Kafka's Paradise": "Talk of mysteries!—Think of our life in nature,—daily to be shown matter, to come into contact with it,—rocks, trees, wind on our cheeks! the *solid* earth! the *actual* world!" (476). Mystery is here. Mystery is in everyday life, in the solid world. Xavier feels he has failed as a detective, but another way he can view it is to see that the fault lies not in him but in the vocabulary of detection. "No one," he decides, "can return to the art of crime detection who has once been broken." In this lies his "salvation" (477). Mystery, after all, is not hidden in some plot. "On the contrary! It stares one in the face. It's what is obvious. So we do not see it. Everyday is the greatest detective story ever written."

Mysteries of Winterthurn continually inserts ironic distance between the author and her art and between readers and their interpretations. Just as we as readers cannot help but mold the novel into meaning, even if we can at the same time witness that act with a smile at our own collusion, so the novelist-as-detective pursues her narrative as part of her "painstaking labor, the daily and hourly 'grind' " (354). Novelist and reader remain "detectives" despite self-awareness about our meaning-making natures. We retain the same instinctive drive toward a conclusion or solution that is not—when we really look at it—wholly desired. As Shepherd suggests, this is the novel's "subversive proposition"—that what we really seek is "teasing postponement." The solution to a mystery leaves the novelist/reader aimless, and with no option but to pursue another case, or novel. "I yearn," says Oates, "for that deep plunge."[49]

But with *Winterthurn* the "evolving of consciousness" reached a specific, hard-earned conclusion that would shape Oates's subsequent career. From now on, the "plunge" would not be as purely instinctive as such a word suggests. Xavier opts to pursue only *solvable* mysteries. "Mystery, satisfactorily *solved*," says the narrator, "yields immense pleasure," but "the Mystery which cannot be solved, which defiantly resists all analysis, yields immense displeasure," and even "physical sickness, and dread,—*a vertigo of the soul*" (391). Xavier leaves Winterthurn, and Oates leaves behind the pivotal moment of her career. In retrospect, the *Bellefleur* period can be seen as a manifestation of Oates coming to terms with aspects of her own nature and artistic motivation, and in doing so altering both the style and tone of her novel writing. She had finally worked through "that region (in the detective's imagination at least) that could not be comprehended, or 'solved' " (392). *"The place of my birth,"* Xavier often broods, is also *"the place of my damnation"* (391). "Virtually anywhere else," he thinks, "his enviable powers of ratiocination, detection, and intuition rarely failed him" (391). For Oates this would mean the social situations of a contemporary America.

The turning point that *Winterthurn* suggests perhaps explains why the fourth and fifth novels of the conceived quintet, while drafted in the 1980s, did not quickly follow as published novels. *My Heart Laid Bare* (1998) was heavily revised and published at least a decade after Oates first drafted it. But in its historical setting, its emphasis on identity, metamorphosis, revisionism, and reinvention, it continues with many of the issues already explored in the preceding three novels. Once again, it is a work built on a "play of ironic seriousness," a novel about a historical period—the end of the nineteenth and the early years of the twentieth century, but one that displays a late-twentieth-century aesthetic-consciousness. "The art of fiction takes many guises," writes Oates in *(Woman) Writer*, "just as telling the truth requires many forms." But if there are limits to how long we need to dwell on the unfathomable mysteries of human personality, *My Heart Laid Bare* seems to reach them. The novel lays bare no one's heart, of course; certainly not that of the probable (third-person) narrator Abraham Licht, and even less so the heart of Joyce Carol Oates. Rather, "laying bare the heart," to take a definition attributed to Licht in Oates's worksheets, is "that which must [and perhaps can] never be done." The characters are playactors, con artists, emotional and intellectual entrepreneurs forever donning new disguises. It is a deliberately depthless novel, a poststructuralist labyrinth of "truths" built and destroyed by their own system that continually reasserts the fact that we are dealing with the illusory nature of language. It reminds us that we can never, at bottom, have *the* Abraham Licht, any more than, "beneath" him, we can find Joyce Carol Oates or "beneath" her "carapace of fame" find Joyce Smith or the Joyce originally named by Frederic and Carolina Oates in 1938. If it lays bare anything, it is only Oates's obsession with, in Johnson's words, "the riddling nature of human identity." Yet at the heart of this identity is the inevitability of disguise: from others, and from ourselves, and in terms of the coherence that masks a fluid and unfathomable world. To use lines from Wallace Stevens, *My Heart Laid Bare* confronts these "ghostlier demarcations, keener sounds" both "of ourselves, and of our origins."[50]

Like *Bellefleur, Bloodsmoor,* and *Winterthurn, My Heart Laid Bare* is a kind of antinovel, systematically undermining the very constructions of coherently illusory "characters" that are the staple of the realist novel. If Perdita and Xavier seem explicit narrative constructs rather than "life-like" in the realist sense, this is even more so of the cast of *My Heart Laid Bare*. All that is revealed is the fact of masks. If it is confession, it is the confession of disguise. If it is about identity, it is only to assert the elusiveness of identity. Abraham Licht's name is incorporated into many of his pseudonyms, from Dr. A. Washburn Frelicht and Mr. Lichtman to Dr. Moses Liebknecht and the Reverend Blichtman. What the young novelist anxiously sought to conceal—her own existence, her own *story*—the mature novelist celebrates and manipulates. The author's position so flimsily camouflaged in early novels is now a teasing, elusive proposition. The authorial face disguised by the racing driver's helmet, the neurosurgeon's face mask, the lawyer's smile, is now deliberately laid bare, only to prove the impossibility of such an act. The authorial "I" is concealed in the various names of Abraham L-*ich*-t and his offspring. (Hence, when his son, Harwood, disguised as Harmon, meets his murder victim, Roland Shrikesdale, himself disguised as Robert Smith, we have a composite of Oates's own pseudonym, Rosamond Smith.) For ultimate revelation is logically impossible: each revelation leads only down the unending hall of mirrors and windows of any person's, let alone any writer's, consciousness. Personality becomes a mere rearrangement of signs, with no final revelation.

My Heart Laid Bare deliberately distances the reader. Reviewing it, Joanne Creighton felt that "sometimes its contrivance and two-dimensional charlatans fail to compel."[51] To talk of them as "two-dimensional" is to evoke E. M. Forster's famous distinction between flat and round characters. But both metaphors are illusory—mere words to describe a particular arrangement of other words. It seems apt to describe them as two-dimensional, but just as apt to describe them as so multidimensional that they become dimensionless. Try to view them as individual "beings" that we can believe in, and Creighton is right: they totally fail to compel. We see no characters, but only "characters," a parade of disguises that renders any sense of "self" no more than an acknowledged illusion of an illusion. Where, in Oates's later "realist" novels, Marya Knauer or Corky Corcoran provide versions of the traditional illusion, in *My Heart Laid Bare*, whenever such selves seem to appear they are quickly reveiled by, or revealed as, further disguises. Licht's most gruesome and—one would think, were he a realist or even modernist character—"upsetting" discovery is his literal uncovering of Harwood's body parts sent to him sealed in tins "stamped with the familiar heraldry Fortnum's." "With shaking hands, yet with that stoic fortitude that has characterized his entire life and career," he pries a tin open "to discover—dear God!—*a bloodless-white naked human foot with misshapen toes and nails ridged with grime, attached to the remains of an ankle.*" But it is more than Licht's "stoic fortitude" that prevents any sense of intimacy. All we learn from the narrator—who might well (or might as well) be Licht himself, writing in both the third and the first person—is that he "would one day note in his memoir" that he was "luckless." Why? Because had he "begun the unwrapping with the hat-box package containing Harwood's head" he "*would have immediately comprehended the horror of the situation and would have been spared proceeding further*").[52]

When we are not distanced from the characters, we are so close up that they seem no less strange. The "animal loathing" that Licht's black son, Elisha (here disguised as the "Negro revolutionary" Prince Elihu) feels toward a group of prominent white men from whom he seeks funding for the World Negro Betterment and Liberation Union is an exacerbated version of this strategy (474–75). In a Swiftian passage, he sees these white men (among them Pierpoint Morgan and John D. Rockefeller) as grotesque and repellent. The "very pigment of their skin" curdles in "sickly hues, ranging from ashen-white (the ninety-year-old cadaverous Rockefeller) to a mottled beefy red (the fat-bellied bishop)," and their skins are "curiously and morbidly" blemished with "moles, warts, broken capillaries, liver spots and discolorations inscribed deep in the flesh, like rot" (477–78). They are like the Brobdingnagian Maids of Honor who, seen close up by Gulliver, have coarse skin "with a mole here and there broad as a trencher, and hairs hanging from it thicker than pack-threads."[53]

Throughout *My Heart Laid Bare,* alienation prevails over engagement, so that, even when the issue is not disguise, the human form is rendered so unfamiliar as to once again reinstate ordinary life as the greatest of mysteries. To some extent, this is the logical extension of a tendency evident through much of the first half of Oates's career. It takes to the limit the alien and alienated quality of many earlier characters There is—in this sense only—family resemblance between the Lichts and the Walpoles, Wendalls, and Pedersens. But in this much later novel, such effects are more purposeful. In the words of Darian, the only one of Licht's children who does not playact (because he is a pianist so his art is his disguise), *My Heart Laid Bare,* like *Bellefleur* above all the others, seeks "to alter the sound of American music" (452).

For all its antinovel aspects, *My Heart Laid Bare* equally resembles the *Bellefleur* group of novels in being a critique of a nineteenth-century, male-oriented, competitive mindset. Licht, a representative turn-of-the-century entrepreneur, is both a con artist who devotes his life to deception and "an angry man" convinced that everyone else is "the enemy" he must outwit (252). Commenting on the novel, Oates has clarified the historical critique. "The Game is a strategy of manipulating other people," she has explained, "as if they were your enemy." "The younger Licht children repudiate this philosophy," based as it is on the kind of social Darwinism so "eagerly embraced" in the 1890s.[54] She does at times elusively entwine herself with her scurrilous antihero. (Both author and protagonist, for instance, resist identification by asserting numerous identities.) But where the novelist seeks to create something edifying and affirmative, Licht is a kind of devilish, inverse pragmatist seeking purely selfish ends. The game each plays may be a manipulation strategy or a matter of survival, and one of its hazards, as a Licht daughter, Millicent, comes to see, may be "that one may imagine too much. Or too little." (357).

But there is even the possibility that whatever is true of it is mostly a matter of our own creation or that, as Katrina says, "there is no Game, there is only life itself" (93). Either way, for Oates and Licht, as for Schopenhauer, Nietzsche, and James, life is fundamentally about questions rather than answers: pursuit rather than arrival. Definitions—no less than success, ease, fulfillment—are empty categories in any long-term sense. From such a perspective, all forms of stasis or category are life denying. Our beliefs, like our labels, whether we turn them to selfish advance or communal betterment, "are really rules for actions." "'God,' 'Matter,' 'Reason,' 'The Absolute,' 'Energy,' are so many solving names," writes James. "You can rest when you have them. You are at the end of your metaphysical quest." "But if you follow the pragmatic method, you cannot look on any such word as closing your quest." It is less a solution "than a program for more work" and "an indication of the ways in which existing realities may be changed."[55]

Bellefleur, Bloodsmoor, Winterthurn, and *My Heart Laid Bare* all reassess, in their differing ways, Oates's career as a novelist. All emphasize reinvention and renewal and suggest Oates moving beyond mere personal ambition and into her mature vision. Where *Bellefleur* stretched the novel form beyond previous boundaries, *Bloodsmoor,* most explicitly of the four novels, channeled Oates's burgeoning pragmatism into primarily feminist aims. *Winterthurn* then reasserted that psychological exploration does indeed *have* limits. Each novel also stresses that "the composing of fiction" in fact "*is* experience": that we are all, to reprise David Bromwich's phrase, Novelists of Everyday Life. They reveal the artist seeking out intellectual limits and finding a way forward within those limits. If, for Kant, the starry heavens destroy human importance, while one's sense of one's inner world "possessing true infinitude" raises one's "value infinitely," for Oates (as perhaps for us all) the mysteries within seem no more fathomable than the universe. Such novels leave us "unsettled by mystery," but relieved, perhaps, to discover that mysteries, in particular the mysteries of "the phantasmagoria of personality," are part of the point. Some such mysteries, unfathomable and insoluble, are, Oates decided implicitly by returning to realism from *Solstice* all the way through to *The Tattooed Girl, Rape: A Love Story, The Falls,* and beyond, best left alone.

Despite the fact that *My Heart Laid Bare* came out later, then, this period was the watershed. This was, if not the escape from self, the letting go. This was where Oates finally and fully articulated a perspective gained through continuous exploration. She could now go back—evidently needed to go back—and rewrite herself and her experiences in historical context. Having explored, revised, and rewritten just about every major genre of the American novel, she was able to turn around and explore her background directly. To borrow a phrase from contemporary astronomy that she uses in *Foxfire*, the second half of her career would be Look Back Time.

> Please do not misunderstand, esteemed ladies and gentlemen:
> I am not bitter.
> I had to find a way out of the cage or die.
> So I became one of you. As you see.
> —JOYCE CAROL OATES, "A Report to the Academy"

4 LOOK BACK TIME

TOWARD THE END of Tolstoy's "The Death of Ivan Illych," Illych has a sudden revelation, as if he has sunk "through a hole and there at the bottom was a light." His self-justification has prevented him seeing anything but good about his way of life. But he has finally been forced to reconsider his priorities. It occurs as it "sometimes happened to him in a railway carriage, when he had thought he was going forwards whereas he was actually going backwards, and all of a sudden became aware of his real direction."[1] This recognition of the illusory nature of a dogged ambition to secure a half-imagined future is central to Oates's novels from *Marya: A Life* (1986), through *You Must Remember This* (1987) and *American Appetites* (1989), to *Because It Is Bitter, and Because It Is My Heart* (1990). Donald Dike's 1974 observation, we remember, was that Oates's major characters were typically "fugitives, real or imaginary." "While running away, running from, may seem to imply running towards," wrote Dike, Oates in fact put the greater emphasis on "escape (or departure), as opposed to quest (or approach)." This in turn led to a sense of "blind, haphazard, undirected motion" in her fiction. A little later, in 1980, Ellen Friedman said of Oates's work that with it "American fiction has abandoned its raft, its forest, its whaling ship—what Poirier has termed its 'world elsewhere'—to reenter time and history." When you look at the ostensible subject matter of even Oates's earliest novels, this seems true enough. But clearly, as Dike showed, the urge to flee social restrictions—if only that world elsewhere could still be found—absolutely did inform those novels. It informs the novels of the second half of Oates's career, too. But suddenly the contexts seem so much more convincingly drawn, the issues so much more sharply realized, and the fact of Oates's own ironic distance from her characters' confusions beyond challenge.

If there was ever truth in De Mott's view that Oates's early novels suggested an "*undeveloping talent*" lacking in intellectual distance, or Susan Cornillon's uncertainty early in the 1970s over whether Oates separated "her own attitudes" from those of her characters, by now such criticisms belonged to the distant past. In Oates's later novels, you may still often feel the same sense of flight, but Oates was now very deliberately homing in on her own and her characters' pasts, so that forward motion turned out to be backward motion, and escape a returning home. Where in earlier novels characters like Karen, Jules, and Jesse run from their past, in these later novels characters like Marya, Ian, and Iris grow aware that what they run toward may not in fact be desirable, while what they have sought so hard to escape they long to recover. Quod petiit, spernit; repetit, quod nuper omisit. "That which one sought one spurns; what one has lost one seeks."[2]

Quite aside from the novels, the late 1980s into the 1990s was, for Oates, also a period of discovery and rediscovery through other genres. This included a renewed interest in playwriting, an area Oates had hitherto entered only sporadically, for instance with *Ontological Proof of My Existence* (1970), *Miracle Play* (1974), and the 1980 version of her novella, *The Triumph of the Spider Monkey* (1976).[3] In this, and in her essays, poetry, and stories, it is clear that she had become a wide-ranging commentator on her culture, far more given now to the notion of active participation than even disguised introspection. In 1987 she published the book-length essay *On Boxing* as a result of research done for *You Must Remember This,* and in 1988 a new essay collection, *(Woman) Writer.* The next year saw another poetry volume, *Time Traveler,* and in 1991 came *Twelve Plays.* At the same time, Oates was continuing to publish numerous stories, many of them collected in book form—for instance in *Raven's Wing* (1986), *The Assignation* (1988), and *Heat* (1991). As if that were not enough, this same period saw the first appearance of the novels she had begun writing under the pseudonym Rosamond Smith, starting with *Lives of the Twins* in 1987.

Just as *On Boxing* was something of a departure for an author mostly given to writing essays on literary subjects, so *(Woman) Writer* differs from Oates's previous collections in combining her usual literary essays with several on other topics. The first section, "Does the Writer Exist?" contains many significant statements about the way she now saw her role as a writer, an issue that clearly continued to exercise her. But that her sense of that role had altered over the years is in itself amply illustrated by the inclusion, in another section, of essays about Mike Tyson, and in yet another section essays on painters (Annie Johnson, Winslow Homer, and George Bellows), Budapest, the Gorbachevs, and even the Ferrari Testarossa. In her poetry, too, the difference between Oates's early volumes and the topics and approaches of *The Time Traveler*, or indeed the 1996 volume, *Tenderness*, is no less striking than between the earlier and later essays. Indeed, the links between all her writings of this period, including drama—not only *Twelve Plays*, but the subsequent volumes, *The Perfectionist and Other Plays* (1995) and *New Plays* (1998)—are more compelling than any links between the early and later essays and the earlier and later poetry.

All her work from now on exudes a sense of a writer extraordinarily involved in and open to the variety of American lives and determined not just to record or reflect upon but to embrace the polyphony of her times. It practices and speaks for possibility, fluidity: creativity in its broadest senses, a leaping at life even as it critiques the various ways in which we can opt out—or betray ourselves and those around us—to the detriment of our own humanity. Moreover, Oates's genre hopping is not just a question of using several forms of artistic expression but itself a statement of open-ended opportunities. She had begun not only to switch genres but to merge them. *The Time Traveler* includes poems that reflect the subjects of current and future novels, others that grow out of contemplation of subject matter also discussed in essays (including poems inspired by Winslow Homer and Edward Hopper paintings), and another entitled "Playlet for Voices." The plays, meanwhile, include not only subjects increasingly important in her fiction—notably race and feminism—but also collage plays made up of monologues, some of which appear elsewhere (in *Invisible Woman, The Time Traveler, The Assignation,* and *Heat*) as either poems or stories. Even *Black Water* is rewritten as drama in *New Plays*. While some of Oates's early poetry can be described as obsessively introspective, it would be hard to find poems in these later collections that would stand such a label. Rather, they embrace all manner of form and subject. Their tone ranges between elegiac and ironic, humorous and gently satiric, and the poet's own voice is mostly dispersed into the voices of widely different American individuals. "As for me—I turn the mirrors to the wall," she writes in "A Winter Suite," "and walk wherever I wish / unobserved." The worldview on offer is less entranced by the mystery of what is within the observer than by the fascinating nature of those people and things she witnesses. "Why is so much in life taken for granted," she asks in "Love Letter, with Static Interference from Einstein's Brain," "when it so transparently partakes of the miraculous?"[4]

Similarly in her plays, Oates's keen eye for the clichés of human behavior is as accurate as the satire is sympathetic. The limitations of Frank and Emily Gulick (whom Oates asks us to see as indeterminate and without "unusual distinction" rather than as individuals or even "representative" characters) are all too clear in *Tone Clusters*. They stutter to answer the faceless, authoritative voice that interrogates them with a range of social, political, philosophical, and metaphysical questions. But their hesitancy, prejudice, vanity, ignorance, and inconsistency make them all the more recognizable as versions of everyone. Not unlike *Mysteries of Winterthurn*, *Tone Clusters* ostensibly involves the reader, along with the Gulicks, in trying to solve the mystery of a girl's death and the implied involvement of the couple's son. But again, that mystery is less significant as far as the themes of the play are concerned than its depiction of the human condition and our contradictory desires at times to seek knowledge and at other times to seek refuge in ignorance or amnesia. "It is subsequently ironic to me," writes Oates in the afterword to *Twelve Plays*, "that *Tone Clusters*, which exists in my imagination as a purely experimental work about the fracturing of reality in an electronic age, is always, for others, 'about' a crime." In her view, "the horror of the piece arises from its revelation that we reside in ignorance, not only of most of the information available to us, but of our own lives, our own motives." If this is another statement of the need to accept that there are limits to what we can know, it is also a statement in line with the Jamesian notion that we can never be detached observers, but are the very personages of the world's drama.

Indeed, this would seem to be one of the attractions of theater for Oates. "Stories are being told not by us but by way of us," she writes in the afterword. "'Drama' is our formal acknowledgment of this paradox, which underscores our common humanity." So while *Tone Clusters* is "about the absolute mystery—the *not knowing*—at the core of our human experience," other plays in these two collections are very much about the practicalities of how we actually involve ourselves with the people and issues around us. For example, *The Eclipse* is about the uneasy relationship between a "prominent feminist" and the mother who sacrificed her own ambitions to help her daughter succeed. *How Do You Like Your Meat?* is about white, middle-class Americans' mistrust of immigrants from other ethnic backgrounds. *Greensleeves* is about AIDS. *Friday Night* is about parochial youths discussing European and American history. (The verdict of one on the Holocaust is that, "It's hard to feel sorry for people, they don't watch out more for themselves, y'know.") *I Stand Before You Naked*, *Bluebeard's Last Wife*, and *I'm Waiting* address feminist issues. *Imperial*

Presidency is about the relationship between the theater of politics and ordinary American lives.[5]

In *The Perfectionist and Other Plays*, too, several plays, including *Negative, The Rehearsal*, and *Black*, explore issues of racial or gender identity, or both, and stereotypes, while others examine the links between historical events and ordinary suburban lives *(Gulf War)* or the balance between social interaction and personal ambition *(The Perfectionist)*. While this later collection includes one very early play, *Ontological Proof of My Existence*, most are from the early 1990s, and on the rare occasions that authorial self-reference exists it is glancing and playful or self-deprecatory. For instance, *The Interview* satirizes the mismatch, during the kind of celebrity interview Oates herself is constantly asked to do, between a distinguished, elderly man known only as "The Immortal" and a thirty-something interviewer. During the course of the play, it turns out that the so-called immortal is the wrong person, that the interviewer hears only his own ideas, and that he and "the immortal" have such wholly different perspectives on the experience that it might almost as well have never taken place. Similarly, in a nightmarish play called *The Psychic* in *Twelve Plays* (nightmarish because the psychic cannot switch off) we are told, in what is surely a satiric self-portrait, that "most folks think they know what a psychic looks like—some frazzle-haired skinny gal with pop eyes, clothes smelling of cats."[6]

The context of the novels published between 1986 and 1990, then, in terms of Oates's other writing, is one of altered tone and shifted focus, characterized by the embracing of ever-wider subject matter and styles. While Oates continued to experiment in these other genres, her novels abruptly switched back to realism, but, partly for that reason, those from *Marya* onward represent, as Greg Johnson says, Oates's "major artistic turning point." For one thing, she now showed a sudden willingness to reexamine the path of a career very like her own and to confront the environments that either made her or that she had become part of. The novels' new, direct style suggested something akin to the pragmatist ideal of direct action over abstract contemplation and of creating easily accessible art of broader social use. "It was not until I wrote the sentence 'Marya, this is going to cut your life in two' on the novel's final page," wrote Oates in *(Woman) Writer*, that "I fully understood Marya's story" and was then able "to recast it as a single work of prose fiction."

In fact, having already used the analogy of a new start in the titles *Winterthurn* and *Solstice*, Oates was beginning again in more fundamental terms.

Solstice, a short novel about, among other things, a woman's struggle to find a new life for herself after a terminated pregnancy, is the first to signal this return to realism. While Tolstoy's "The Death of Ivan Illych" reflected an intellectual crisis, this turning point—or *returning* point—for Oates seems, at least, to have marked a period of clearer reflection after the rollercoaster experimentation of her previous novels. "After great pain, a formal feeling comes—" is the Dickinson poem she chose as an epigraph for *Solstice*. Dickinson's final stanza runs:

> This is the Hour of Lead—
> Remembered, if outlived,
> As Freezing persons, recollect the Snow—
> First—Chill—then Stupor—then the letting go.

If Oates really had seen her career, in part even, as an attempt "over the years, to draw out the poison drop by drop," in the hope of moving, as she writes in *on Boxing*, "through pain to triumph," then this is an apt epigraph indeed. Tolstoy's comment that Illych "sank through a hole and there at the bottom was a light" stands good for several characters from Xavier Kilgarvan onward, but few before.[7]

The novels also continue Oates's new-found feminist emphasis. As Linda Wagner-Martin writes, "Oates's poignant cry for women to have control of their bodies and their lives shapes both *Marya* and *You Must Remember This*." Where, as Wesley puts it, "most of Oates's early critics labeled her as decidedly anti-feminist or at best moderately feminist," this is no longer the case. Friedman is far from alone in arguing that Oates's fiction from the 1980s on has seen "a shift in consciousness" regarding women and their place in society. If the *Bellefleur* grouping was the first clear manifestation of this, *Solstice* provided "an unprecedented move" in that Oates defined "two women not in relation to men and not even in relation to society, but purely and simply in relation to one another." It would be misleading, however, to suggest a total switch from Oates the nonfeminist to Oates first-and-foremost-a-feminist, and so pluck her from one category and place her in another. Wagner-Martin sees the feminist themes in *Marya* and *You Must Remember This*, but also comments that Oates's thirty-five-year career up to there had "engendered a tapestry of criticism about the absence of feminist themes in her writing." Then suddenly critics again took up "their pastime of making Joyce Carol Oates into a feminist writer." No doubt, as John Mulryan puts it, "gender is as inescapable for critics as for the authors they study," but these later novels seem, to me, clearly to explore not just the perils, pitfalls, and possibilities of being a woman in a male-dominated world but also nongender specific behavior.[8] As Friedman writes, for all her range of female characters we need not constrain Oates with any single category, however "generously defined." Along with Marya, Enid, Sigrid, and Iris, these four novels also have, in Sylvester, Felix, Ian, and Jinx, male characters just as caught up in the complexities of late-twentieth-century American life. Moreover, while gender helps shape each life, so, too, do such factors as race, region, social class, family circumstance, life experience, and genetic disposition. Marya's "attempt to find her mother," points out Wagner-Martin, can be read "as less a matriarchal connection" than as "a humane one": "She acts against the betrayer, the parent who happens to be mother rather than father." Similarly in *American Appetites*, "gender is less important than morality. Men and women alike break codes of marriage and friendship and professional loyalty."[9] As Friedman suggests, "Oates's focus on women is a natural outgrowth of her particular vision of America." While Oates's feminism fed into her identity as a novelist, her pragmatism ensured that she would continue to resist, in interviews as in her art, the labels and categories that "can be restrictive" for her as a writer "for whom gender is not a pressing issue in every work."[10]

Connected with this is Oates's now leaving behind the search for neurological/metaphysical explanations. Turning away from this philosophical quest for certitude meant rejecting other forms of certitude as well. Instead, Oates's novels focused on the practical task of exploring where, in all kinds of individual American lives, positive change might be possible. Paramount was the pragmatic belief in using—in art and life—one's insights as instruments for action and being ever willing to revise those insights, rather than be constrained by a single perspective. Oates's comment that *Son of the Morning* is a prayer that "begins with wide ambitions," "ends very, very humbly," and is "painfully autobiographical in part" could stand for an important but sometimes debilitating tendency throughout her early career.[11] By now she had come to the same open-ended conclusion so vividly expressed by James: "objective evidence and certitude are doubtless very fine ideals to play with, but where on this moonlit and dream-visited planet are they found?" The specific perspective she had adopted was to focus her energies on a melioristic art that acted as a witness to culture and presented possibilities for improvement; that took up Dewey's call to become an organ for clarifying people's ideas about contemporary social and moral conflicts. "Intellectual advance occurs in two ways," writes Dewey. "At times increase of knowledge is organized about old conceptions, while these are expanded, elaborated and refined, but not seriously revised, much less abandoned. At other times, the increase of knowledge demands qualitative rather than quantitative change; alteration, not addition." People's "minds grow cold to their former intellectual concerns; ideas that were burning fade; interests that were urgent seem remote." "Former problems may not have been solved" but "they no longer press for solution."[12]

Dewey's words virtually describe the change between the novels of the early and latter part of Oates's career. Her dominating interest, to use further Dewey definitions, became "the *use* of knowledge; the conditions under which and ways in which it may be most organically and effectively employed to direct conduct." Knowledge, seen in this light, really becomes significant only when the test of it becomes "the ability to bring about certain changes. Knowing, for experimental sciences, means a certain kind of intelligently conducted doing; it ceases to be contemplative and becomes in a true sense practical."[13] From this perspective, it makes perfect sense that, after the You/I musings of *Childwold*, and *Son of the Morning* and the intense experimentation of the *Bellefleur* period, Oates should have returned to a recognizably "realist" world and the more immediate everyday experiences of her American contemporaries.

One aspect of this involved reflecting on the hitherto unacknowledged tensions of her path so far. Oates chose to return to the background she once sought to escape and to recreate the girl in herself she once tried to destroy. Where once she was disinclined "to discuss her family background, especially with her affluent suburban friends," *Marya* and *You Must Remember This* are respective tributes to her mother and father. "I joined my mother and me together," she has said of *Marya*. "The novel is very much about mothers and absent mothers and a daughter who won't admit that her mother is absent from her life." With *You Must Remember This*, Oates tried to synthesize her father's and her own "'visions' of an era now vanished." If maturity is learning your limitations, it is also about recognizing, as Linda tries to explain to that "boy" Biff, in *Death of a Salesman*, that one day you'll knock on the parental door and "there'll be strange people" there. Oates's return to realism was therefore a return home in emotional as well as artistic terms.[14] It was not, however—as her continued radical experimentation in poetry, stories, and plays testifies—simply a retreat into an old literary formula but, as Joseph Dewey suggests, a kind of "new realism," taking an ironic, revisionist stance toward the form in question.[15]

Despite the drive toward a conclusion, these novels display (in contrast to the disruptive treatment of time in, say, *Childwold* or *Bellefleur*) a pragmatist preference for motion over stasis. The race toward misty notions of fulfillment is countered by awareness that running is better than arriving: the protagonists chase desires that they are not always glad to achieve. Each is, or becomes, symbolically posthumous, a comment perhaps on Oates's sense that her contemplation of "the 'I,' which doesn't exist," yet "is everything," had run its course.[16] Monica lives a postabortion life. Marya loses her sense of self. Enid survives a suicide attempt. Felix is finished as a boxer. Glynnis lives on only in the memory of Ian, who himself feels strangely posthumous. Jinx destroys his basketball career; and Iris lives on, after Jinx's murder of Red Garlock and death in Vietnam, in an empty marriage. If *Winterthurn* and *Solstice* represent a turning point, these four novels suggest the need for a new lease on life beyond dead perspectives.

Marya: A Life is about a woman who, despite an impoverished, difficult background, succeeds in a male-dominated environment. Looked after by her aunt Wilma after her mother has abandoned her, sexually molested over several years by her cousin Lee and bullied and abused by classmates, she retreats from her physical self and pursues intellectual ambition at the expense of personal relationships. In terms of that rise from relative poverty to a career as a writer and academic, Marya's story makes the novel something of a *Künstlerroman* that analyzes a career trajectory similar to Oates's own. "Whether Marya Knauer's story is in any way my own 'story,' it became my story during the writing of the novel," writes Oates. "It is my hope that, however obliquely and indirectly, it will strike chords in readers who, like Marya, choose finally not to accept the terms of their own betrayal."[17] Oates's ambiguity here is part and parcel of the ambiguity of a novel the complexity of which, like so much of her later work, belies its seemingly straightforward narrative.

Male and female critics, for instance, have tended to read the novel very differently. For Bernard Levin, "Marya has made her own life, denying to all others both credit and blame." Her "solipsism" leads her to pass through life "unseeing" and essentially "damned." In contrast, Marilyn Wesley argues that "Oates expresses the possibility of female development of consciousness beyond the confines of male imagination." But there is also some disagreement among feminist critics as to quite how Marya's story should be read. For Elaine Showalter, Marya becomes Oates's "most compelling heroine," a "brilliant writer who has been hurt by both women and men." Yet for Ellen Friedman, Marya, "though extraordinarily intelligent, is not heroic."[18] Indeed, even the word *intelligent* needs some scrutiny. For most of the novel, Marya's intelligence is theoretical, abstract, academic, perhaps, but certainly not social. She constantly fails to *act* intelligently or with empathy for those around her, male or female. If anything, she suppresses her social and emotional intelligence until the very end. While there is something heroic about anyone who overcomes adverse circumstances to succeed on a chosen path, her truly heroic, truly wise act is her ability to recognize her own self-betrayal and to look back, and go back, to rediscover what she has all but lost. The novel's epigraph, William James's famous statement, "my first act of freedom will be to believe in freedom"—has an obvious relevance to Marya's escape from circumstances that might have defeated her. But, as Wagner-Martin notes, she remains mentally trapped. She needs not just to believe in freedom but to reinterpret what that freedom might constitute. In this sense, the novel sustains both Showalter's and Friedman's views, and even Levin's. Over the novel's course, Marya acts both intelligently and foolishly. But in her ability finally to alter her perspective, she finds her familial and presumably eventual social and personal redemption.[19]

Joanne Creighton echoes the view that Marya has suppressed her social intelligence. Creighton contends that Marya rejects "the inner world of emotion, softness, and femaleness, for the outer, analytical, hard, masculine world of success." Similarly, Eileen Bender sees the novel as an "angry protest against the mutilation suffered by women in the academy." But it is also true to say that Marya's story has something to tell us about what the neglect of roots and relationships in pursuit of ambition can do to anyone, man or woman. Marya may well, as Wagner-Martin argues, typify "Oates's fragile, damaged characters" and go through her "countless debilitating relationships with men" (and women) as a result of her early traumas, but it is not impossible for Marya's story, as Oates puts it without reference to gender, to "strike chords" in male readers who, prior to or as a result of reading the novel, "choose finally not to accept the terms of their own betrayal." Self-betrayal, as Oates would continue to illustrate, is open to us all. Moreover, either Marya's damaged perspective is partly to blame for her poor relationships or she simply meets bad people. So to argue simultaneously that she is "damaged" and that she is "used and reused, both sexually and professionally," is to verge on contradiction.[20] Either her damaged state of mind leads to further damaged relationships or she has a healthy state of mind but the incredible bad luck to meet only rotten individuals. The former is surely the more convincing: Marya's poor relationships have as much to do with her own perspective as with those she meets. While we are encouraged to identify with her, we also grow aware of how and why Marya's worldview betrays her until finally she, too, recognizes this and, like any other intelligent pragmatist, seeks to revise it.

Marya, like Oates, comes from the same kind of poor rural background as such predecessors as Karen, Clara, and Laney. But while Clara's adulthood becomes melodrama and Karen's and Laney's are theoretical, Oates knows not only where Marya has been but also where she has reached as an adult and at what emotional cost. Marya's ambition partly stems from her struggle to escape a sense of "self-disgust" resulting from the sexual abuse by Lee. But she is also "terrified of examining her face too closely in the mirror" in case she sees her mother's "slack-lidded wink" and "glassy stare." She therefore approaches her own "Life" in diametric opposition to what she sees as her mother's apology of a "life." A child of the Great Depression, she believes that her early experiences have created her "stoniness of soul." To this extent, *Marya* is a realist novel in the Lukácian sense that "the individual and the sociohistorical are inseparably connected in regard to both characterization and action."[21] Her determination to escape through study is specifically a reaction to all of this. But, like Pip's in *Great Expectations,* Marya's attitude is deeply flawed. Her expectations are "wispy, murky, indefinable," and ultimately illusory, and pursued at the expense of personal relationships. Her cultivation of the art of being *"not there"* results in a self-absorption and self-negation that is social suicide (24). By the end of the novel, her second act of freedom will be to release herself from the protective mechanisms that have become counterproductive and hindered important aspects of her life.

Marya's story is built like a path of stepping stones across the people who influence, admire, love, use, or try to befriend her. Marya does go through "debilitating relationships with men," but not all her relationships with men are debilitating, any more than her relationships with women prove enabling, and Marya's own adult perspective always has some influence on how these relationships turn out. Brandon P. Schwilk, for instance, is a bumbling teacher who cannot, in Marya's disdainful view, understand her mining community. "He thinks we matter," she muses, "doesn't he know us?" (49). Maybe Schwilk's shortcomings are all that Marya says they are, yet it is also the case that Schwilk's interest ignites her ambition. Spying on him with schoolmates by the canal, one of them pushes Marya downhill "with such helpless momentum" that Schwilk has to catch her (58). The physical metaphor echoes a mental fact. He arrests her near-plunge into obscurity.

It is Schwilk who, in class, introduces her to the ideas of William James, quoting James's example of a mountain climber who, faced with leaping across an abyss, will succeed only if he believes he will. Met with impassive stares, Schwilk tries to enlist support. "Marya understands the very *American-ness* of James's proposition," he says, "the melancholy of spirit must triumph over their own nature, for otherwise they will perish" (63). "How many mountain climbers made the jump?" mocks Marya, provoking "such peals of adolescent laughter" that she will "remember her triumph—for surely it *was* a triumph, in all its stillness—all her life" (64). Perhaps Marya, focusing on the concrete rather than abstract, makes a valid distinction between theory and reality, but Oates's use of a James quotation as the novel's epigraph surely signals that Schwilk *has* influenced Marya. "Stillness" is not the answer; what matters are the leaps of faith that carry us to new perspectives. The "pathetic," "loathed" Schwilk eventually resigns, but donates his salary to a poetry prize that is first won by Marya (67). If she does indeed transform her mother's resignation about her life into a Life, it is because she rejects "Old World obstinacy and self-defeat" in favor of the New World myth of reinvention and self-fulfillment—"the *will to believe*"—introduced to her by the beleaguered Schwilk (64).[22]

Nor is Marya's friendship with Father Shearing purely debilitating. Shearing's cancer transforms him from a "lithe" and "audacious" young man into a dying invalid (80). Where the Schwilk episode is about the place of art and learning in blue-collar life, Marya's conversations with Shearing are about the quest for meanings. She challenges his religious beliefs as improbable, and he points out the unlikely nature of the atom. Marya picks up his wristwatch. Unlike matters of faith, she says, echoing her challenge to Schwilk, the watch is real. Shearing asks if she can guess at the intricacies of the mechanisms just by looking at the outside. His faith contrasts with her self-loathing. She is "sick of envy of other people," even the dying priest, simply because they *are* other people. She detests her "silly spiritual pride" and "unspeakably disgusting body" (82). True, Shearing wills her this "man's watch," and so symbolically sets her on the path of "male"-style ambition (100). She is entering, not just literary competition, but the "man's" world—as she sees it—of ambition and intellect, and that age-old doomed race against time. "To write so well, to wield such a vocabulary; to *argue* so powerfully," she feels, is "an entirely masculine skill" (95). It is true, too, that Schwilk and Shearing are, in Wesley's words, the first in a line of "serial father figures" who help her "achieve mastery of written language" and so perhaps symbolize "the patriarchal possession of thought articulated through language."[23] But to feel such envy and self-disgust, to envy someone dying of cancer, illustrates just how warped Marya's perspective is at this point and how little empathy she feels. However understandable her bitterness, the one sure thing is that it will, and does, affect her present and future relationships.

A scholarship provides her with a way out of her community and into her solipsistic ambition. "I intend to begin a private life," she announces. "I've had enough of crowds!" (105). She embarks on a career that depends upon the praise of others—especially members of a male-dominated academy—and successful competition against her (again mostly male) peers. But her determination is a form of desperation, just as her self-absorption is a form of self-negation. To leave home means to go "where no one knew she was Marya Knauer," so she can therefore "give birth to herself." "If I fail," she thinks, "if I have to come back home—I'll kill myself" (107). The apparently sexual attack she suffers from some male contemporaries when her girlfriends leave her alone drinking with them on the eve of her departure confirms the male brutality of the community she is fleeing. It confirms her sense that she is going to have to encase herself in psychological armor against a hostile world. But it also displays her male and female contemporaries' sense that she feels both superior and hostile to them. It is a well-known observation in psychology that anticipation of hostility can, to use Daniel Goleman's description, provoke "the response it was meant to anticipate."[24]

Marya takes her "repugnance for any display of weakness" to university (114). Her "monastic isolation" is a mixture of self-communion and self-negation. Books allow her to check out of her own mind and, "with the stealth of the thief," cross "the landscape of another's" (134). Her relationship with literature becomes more important than her relationships in everyday life. She proves George Steiner's hypothesis that "our emotion in the written word" might blunt "our sense of present realness and need."[25] "A writer's authentic self," she thinks, lies "in his writing and not in his life." It is "the landscape of the imagination" that is "really real." "Mere life" is "the husk, the actor's performance, negligible in the long run" (135). She becomes a monomaniac, and the novel's narrative drive becomes the drive of her ambition against diminishing time. *"Every moment not consciously devoted to her work"* is "a blunder. As if you can kill time, Thoreau said, without injuring Eternity" (154). Amid her wide reading—Schopenhauer, Marx, Euripides, More, Hobbes—is, naturally, Dickens. She is chasing her great expectations without "the faintest idea" of what it will lead to or leave behind (309).

Marya's man's watch weighs heavily indeed. Hard as she is on herself, she is harder on others. She despises what she sees as the mediocrity of a popular professor, "an ebullient balding popinjay who lectured from old notes in a florid and self-dramatizing style, presenting ideas in a mélange clearly thrown together from others' books and articles" (156). She sees this "satyrish middle-aged man" as "a totally mediocre personality in every way," whom she would like to see dead. Yet, like Schwilk, he sees something in Marya that she cannot see herself. "You seem like rather a grim young woman," he tells her, "you never smile—you look so *preoccupied*" (157). She is certainly "grim" and certainly "preoccupied." Ambition, to use a phrase of Jiddu Krishnamurti's, has her "by the throat."[26] Her verdict on the professor may be accurate, but so is his on her. She is preoccupied with excellence at the expense of human warmth. She is, as he says, "unforgiving" (158). "'Truth,'" as Pedersen would say, "is to be honored wherever it is found."

Marya's refusal to acknowledge the need for relationships, or to give as well as get, explains much about her failure to retain her one significant female friend in college, Imogene Skillman. Imogene is assured, outgoing, dominant, forthright, whereas Marya is held together by her inner world. "You're alone and you don't mind, that's *just* like you," says Imogene. "You have a whole other life, a sort of secret life, don't you" (147). Marya hardly has time for something so "ephemeral" as friendship. Like the other scholarship students, she is "frightened, driven." She feels that "great handfuls of her life" are "being stolen" (148). Friendship is "a puzzle that demands too much of the imagination" (151). Like most of these acquaintances, Imogene has a lot more time for Marya than Marya has for others or for herself, and she worries about Marya's health. "My health isn't any use to me," replies Marya, "if I don't get anything accomplished. If I fail" (155). Achievement, then, is everything, not because Marya is egotistical, but because her self-worth depends on her work, without which she is nothing. Perhaps it is so, as several critics argue, that Marya's "betrayal" has to do with her acceptance of male values, but if so then this is also a comment on how ambitious men, too, can live lives of self-deception. Marya is simply, and desperately, unhappy. Her self-hatred is evident in her drawings of "glowering, defiantly ugly" faces that turn out "to be forms of her own" (168). Not only is she destroying her health, she is also as disliked as she wants to be. Imogene tells Marya of her sorority sisters' view of her. "They'd never seen such eyes as yours—taking them all in and condemning them! *Those* assholes!" (169). Marya's harshness is evident, too, when Imogene gets her a date. "Is this idiot really going to kiss me?" she wonders (171). Imogene notes

Marya's "jealousy" and "morbid possessiveness" and of the way she sits "in judgment" of Imogene's parents, of her "poor father trying so hard to be *nice*." Imogene's mother's query to Imogene as to whether Marya is one of her "strays and misfits" suggests that Imogene might be befriending her because no one else will do so (180). Imogene's interest in other people is a total contrast to Marya's solipsism, and the root of Marya's jealousy is that Imogene enjoys—and really does have—a Life.

Finally, as if, like Clara Walpole, to get some of that life for herself, the kleptomaniac Marya steals Imogene's earrings and has her own ears pierced, bypassing the procedure of temporarily substituting a gold stud because she has no "time to waste" (181). Her ears become as infected as her outlook. Like Xavier Kilgarvan, the terms she has set for her own success have turned out to be self-defeating. She has become her own opponent, just as Xavier sought to resolve a mystery of which he himself was the core. Like Xavier's, Marya's worldview disintegrates as she begins to realize the suicidal nature of her ruthless ambition. Self-protection has become self-absorption, tilting into self-pity. Increasing success is matched by increasing unhappiness. As Showalter says, "every intellectual advance intensifies Marya's sense of estrangement."[27] But there are constant clues for Marya that, in battling her own shadow-self she is blinding herself to a wider world. "Professors in the humanities," she muses, spend "their lives rigorously analyzing texts, classical or otherwise," but display "a curious reluctance to examine the 'text'" of "their own lives. Perhaps the irony of the situation might be explored" (242). Marya, who takes herself so seriously, is oblivious to the fact that had she followed her own hunch and explored how "professors in the humanities" live their lives, she might have started with herself.

Her subsequent interactions with her janitor, Sylvester, and her colleague, Gregory Hemstock—encounters framed by her two lovers, Maximilian Fein and Eric Nichols—reveal her ever-darkening self-image and eventual enlightenment. In different ways, they each reveal aspects of Marya to herself that, by her final decision to rediscover her roots and her mother, she implicitly accepts. The self-absorbed Maximilian has driven himself to the top of a profession he does not really believe in. "Marya," he says, "has a future awaiting her," but it looks much like the hellish present he inhabits (196). Marya hero worships him as a representative of the world she has aspired to. But their mutual attraction is a kinship of the damned. Like Andrew Petrie, Maximilian's inner life has atrophied as a result of his public self. He suffers from a periodic descent into "a species of hell contained within the perimeters of his skull—or, if you like, his soul" (202). To use a later phrase of Marya's, he is dying *"from within"* (273). "Hell," he tells her, "is ourselves" (203).

Maximilian lays a trap to prove their kinship. Where once she saw herself as stealing through other people's minds in books, she now steals through his house, taking an offprint of an essay because "no one would ever notice" (197). "A kind of bride" with "a future awaiting her," she ventures further (at one point disturbing the Feins' cat, Deuteronomy, the book containing the Ten Commandments) as if into the hell of her role model's brain. In the Feins' bedroom, she finds a note anticipating her trespass. "I know you," Maximilian has written. "I seem to have recognized you from the first—do not be frightened, my dear (do not be less brazen) if I shortly make my claim upon you" (201). He knows she is a thief, happy to steal from him, and to steal him from his wife (named Else—as in Someone Else: not a person Marya therefore need take much note of). He also knows how little self-regard she has. "You're a hard young woman, aren't you?" he says, "hard on yourself." "Apart from you," she replies, "there is nothing." Her ambition—which is like Maximilian's and like, say, Jesse Harte's—fills emptiness. She is "fired to work, *work,* to keep from despair" (214), to lose herself in something, "it scarcely mattered what" (223). Her "inviolable—autonomous—entirely self-sufficient" state is a version of hell as oneself (207). Maximilian, for all his faults, is the one to tell her to "try to locate her mother" before "too much more time" elapses (209). Presumably he recognizes her misconception of time and achievement because, like Tolstoy's Illych, he has begun to see the true direction of the train he is sitting in. Before dying, appropriately, of a cerebral hemorrhage—an affliction that recalls the neurological stress so many early Oates characters succumbed to—he points out to her the questionable nature of her ambition (an ambition that, elsewhere, with an unconvincing stab at self-mockery she describes as "to be perfect" [203]). Art and scholarship, he warns, may really be mere "improvisation and illusion" that play at meaning to justify their "demands of time, spirit" (228). Like Maximillian and Illych, she is going in the opposite direction to the one she supposed. Racing away from one kind of self-negation, she is hurtling toward another.

The novel's great ironist is Sylvester, a black janitor at the university. Seen through Marya's eyes, Sylvester is entirely unsympathetic. Critics who mention him have tended to agree with Marya. Wesley's view of him is that "a female professor is an insult" to his "masculine privilege."[28] But the fact that

Marya views him unsympathetically—and even in veiled racist terms—is a more textually provable way of explaining his behavior. His disdain for her is matched only by her disdain for him (which is a notch up from her disdain for Schwilk, her contemporaries, the unnamed professor, and Imogene and her friends). "Sylvester was black," the chapter begins. "That was the first—but was it the most significant?—of the problems." Marya's physical disgust is palpable. "He panted, he sweated, his skin exuded a rich oily moisture" (233).

Harassed as he is, Sylvester finds time "to stare very hard at Marya, and to give the innocent words 'Professor Knauer' an exquisite sort of spin." "G'-Morning, Professor Knauer," he says, "his gaze dropping to her feet and rising, slowly, defiantly, to her face." "G'afternoon, professor." He has "a little catch in his throat as if he could hardly keep from laughing." Since she takes herself so seriously, "the irony in his greeting" and "the mockery in his heavy-lidded gaze" are devastating weapons. "Perhaps unconsciously," she has assumed irony to be "a prerogative of the learned segment of the white race," but she is mistaken yet again in "a year, generally, of mistaken assumptions." For an "assistant professor of English in a prestigious but rather small old New Hampshire College," she is remarkably ill-read in black American writing if she is unaware that irony is *the* mode of black discourse (234). This cannot, after all, be far off 1963 and James Baldwin's mockery in *The Fire Next Time* of white Americans' inability to understand the "ironic, authoritative and double-edged" nature of jazz and the blues. Sylvester, to use the term coined by Henry Louis Gates Jr. (later to review, favorably, *Because It Is Bitter, and Because It Is My Heart*) in his landmark study of African American culture and literature, is "Signifyin(g)," among the most common forms of which is "subtle and witty use of irony." Borrowing a phrase from Mikhail Bakhtin, Gates shows that the black tradition is "double-voiced," and constantly employs "the obscuring of apparent meaning" as a strategy of discourse.[29]

To Marya, Sylvester's actions are "strategies of harassment." But harassment or otherwise, to yank the venetian blind to the "top of the window" might also be to suggest she expand her perspective; to rearrange her things might be to suggest she rearrange her life. Marya is reluctant to explore possible answers to her question: "why *me* at this time in my life?" (235). Her magnanimous resolution not to take it as "a personal affront" if he smokes "to make his wretched job a little more agreeable" smacks of condescension (235–36). His "wretched job" is to clean her dirt. But really he *is* dirt to her, while she is an assistant professor at a prestigious college, who loves the fact that her name is "affixed to the front of the door" (236). He smells rank to her, while she *has* rank. But he sniffs out her pretensions. *She* has a class on Dickinson to teach, so no time to wonder why he has rearranged her things, as if to say: "I am Nobody / Who are You?" She, after all, has become Somebody, whereas he belongs to a class she has escaped. "Had she come so far (from Innisfail, from the Canal Road, from the tarpaper shanty of a house near Shaheen Falls)," she wonders, "to be persecuted by a stranger . . . ?" (237). Sylvester is nothing to her but a "filthy pig" (238). And as for his race, her metaphors betray her true attitude. "Racial prejudice was as much a fact of life back home, the separation of the races (economic, social, demographic) so taken for granted," that Marya has "long ago vowed to stand apart from it; which is to say, above it." She makes "the effort now to think of Sylvester not as a black man, but simply as a man; a working man with a very poor job; hostile toward others because he despised his own condition in life" (239). To stand "above" racial prejudice is to perpetuate the kind of hierarchical fallacies that sustain it. She will try "now" to see him as a man. Sylvester hardly needs more motivation. She has indeed come "a remarkable distance," but this need not be a positive phrase (261). All her actions assert hierarchy and separateness; all his assert equality and union. To read *Marya*, then, as a "protest against the mutilation suffered by women in the academy" may be entirely legitimate, but a black janitor, male or female, would surely offer quite another response.

Despite herself, Marya finally acknowledges their kinship, calling to him in the street while "caught up in an autumnal mood of gaiety and camaraderie." Sylvester, "his chin uplifted," passes by without a glance, while her companion stares at Marya as if to ask, "Who do you think *you* are" (240). But it is this semiconscious recognition that they are *both* from an underclass—that her professorial masquerade has led her to disown her background and previous identity—that suggests her possible redemption. Whatever else, her belated sense of comradeship with someone she has all but denied recognition to foreshadows her reunion with her mother. Marya's recognition, indeed, may also be the reader's. For a common strategy in Oates's fiction—especially her short fiction—is to get us to identify with a character and only then to reveal his or her shortcomings, and so perhaps our own. What Sally Robinson says of the same strategy in terms of Oates's story "Naked," for instance, could as well be said of *Marya*. This story from the 1991 collection, *Heat*, is about a suburban white woman mugged and stripped by black children who have come up from "the ragged edge of the old industrial city," an area she and her family had "rarely glimpsed except from the interstate expressway elevated over its ruins." Attempting to get home naked without being seen, she ends the story crouching in the dark outside her house, suddenly feeling that her family inside are mere strangers. In Robinson's view, Oates "subtly challenges the woman's secure conviction that she harbors no racist sentiments and, simultaneously, challenges her readers to place themselves in the woman's position." In "Naked," what we glimpse beneath her liberalism is "an absolute failure to see beyond a certain point of view—and, perhaps worse, a willed ignorance about the possibility that the 'Other' might *have* a point of view that could be trained on the self." For Robinson, this is an unsettling aspect of Oates's fiction, and, although Robinson does not use it as an example herself, *Marya*, especially in terms of Sylvester, would seem a case in point. The same strategy is evident in a number of Oates's plays, too, many of which—from the 1970s with *Miracle Play* to the 1990s with *Black* and *Negative*—focus far more sharply on race issues than do the majority of her novels.[30] Those novels that do—subsequent to *Marya*—such as *Because It Is Bitter* and *I'll Take You There*, reinforce the view that such issues are very much part of the Sylvester episode. In particular, *I'll Take You There* revisits and reworks the alienated-scholarship-girl scenario. But unlike *Marya*, it makes racial and religious prejudice central. Calling herself Anellia, the Jewish narrator escapes her bigoted sorority and embarks on an affair with Vernor Matheius, a black PhD student as desperately driven as Anellia herself.

If there is room for differing readings of Sylvester, this is certainly also the case with Marya's friendship with her work colleague Gregory Hemstock. Gregory may, for some readers, be another man who betrays Marya. But one can also read their friendship in a way that suggests he sees much the same as Schwilk, Imogene, Maximilian, and Sylvester. They go cycling, a "desperate little outing" while others decide who will receive tenure (267). As usual, Marya is thinking of herself and about how "even if she failed at this crucial point in her career (which is to say, her life)" at least she escaped Innisfail (261). Gregory sees her hardness. "*I* couldn't do the sort of things they're doing," says Marya of those deciding their fate. Gregory laughs, shudders, and eventually says, in a "subdued" voice, "Yes—you probably could" (262). The cycle ride ends when Marya takes her downhill plunge that she "can't stop except to die" (265). This is another physical image of a mental fact. Her self-absorbed and self-negating ambition amounts to a veiled suicide attempt. "I should have broken my neck," she says when she finally crashes. "It would have solved all my problems" (266).

Some critics see Gregory as a man who cannot handle a successful woman.

For Bender, he "sadistically leads Marya far beyond the limits of her physical endurance, and she takes a horrendous downhill fall." For Daly, "Marya wins the competition for a tenure-line position," so Gregory "punishes her by withdrawing his love."[31] Certainly Marya wonders if he "suggested the excursion merely to humiliate her" (255), and believes that beneath his "mild manner" lies "a deep anger" (269). But his disappearance from her life could also be explained by the fact he has lost the job. It seems as likely that Marya withdraws *her* love. She has, after all, beaten him to the post, and is interested primarily in men she sees as professionally superior. Indeed, Gregory's anger—if we accept her view that he might be trying to "humiliate" her—would seem to stem from his jealousy of her next would-be mentor and eventual lover, Eric Nichols, an editor who has been publishing her work in a magazine. Whatever else, in Marya's world, ambition precedes something so "ephemeral" as friendship.

Like Xavier Kilgarvan, Marya matures through the novel. She has latent Jamesian tendencies and is attracted to such tendencies in Eric Nichols—as perhaps she has been somewhere in the murky depths of Maximilian's cynicism. She views ambition as synonymous with motion. Stasis is death. Eric, too, needs "to keep in motion." "Energy is life, after all," thinks Marya. "Death would never grow inside them so long as they stayed in motion, swift and happy as a ray of light" (285). While Eric, in Nietzsche's phrase, may be "swift and happy as a ray of light," Marya decidedly is not. True to her thieving nature, she has taken up with another married man, and when he dies she will be jealous of his widow because she herself can "make no claim, legitimate or sentimental" on another dead mentor (287). Eric does, however, leave her a potential legacy. His work—and Marya's, once she leaves academia for a "real" world—puts her own troubles into perspective. Above all, he is engaged in trying actively to change aspects of the world for the better. As his assistant, she sees suffering in a wider context. Learning of torture in Uruguay and Brazil, of "killers-for-hire in the pay of their governments in the pay (not very directly) of the United States Government" and of "names begging to be remembered," she can hardly remain so solipsistic (270). When she bumps into Imogene again, her former friend remarks that Marya was "always so totally self-absorbed" (292). But where Imogene summarizes Marya's past, Eric offers a way forward. "There is blood on our hands," he says, "if we don't do all we can to help others, to be witnesses to their suffering" (382). Not only is this an articulation of the pragmatism of Oates's own later novels, but Eric's sudden death—through both a heart attack *and* a car crash, as if to underline the possibilities—reinforces the absurdity of self-absorption, given our transience as "fireflies, in the Void."[32]

Characteristically, Marya's first act of looking outward is in a sense to look inward. But it is also to look backward. Feeling that "these days" she is not "herself," she becomes intrigued by "the very question of 'self.'" Having formerly thought of Innisfail and "the profitless past" only in "weak moods," she now recognizes the hurt and grief that has driven her for so long and tries to contact her mother (184). Her story—her life—has been marred by a lack of self-knowledge revealed in her relationships with others. She finally sees that she has always "ignored all notions that did not correspond to her knowledge of herself," and been so self-absorbed as to be "incapable of serious grief" (294). With her new awareness, she returns home to a wedding, and for once has nowhere "to hurry to" (304). Yet the world she once escaped has been "so comically rearranged" that she cannot "locate herself in it" (306). The past is already "lost territory" (307). She has been not only battling herself but escaping a chimera. "For Christ's sake, Marya," she imagines Wilma saying, "why have you always taken yourself so seriously. . . ?" (310). She finally sees her story in perspective. Ambition and talent, even "success," can only bring fulfillment when individuals stop fighting themselves and turn that energy outward to honor the lives of others. Contrary to Creighton's view that "Oates's understanding of Marya perhaps exceeds the reader's," since "the novel trails off" with no "clear final portrait," we end up knowing Marya very well.[33] She has spent the first decades of her life wading through a mixture of pent-up grief, resentment, self-absorption and ambition, and is certainly guilty—as she comes to recognize—of having taken herself too seriously. But really she has defined her own self-defeating battle. What she has been running from ultimately exists only in her mind. What she has been racing toward she no longer desires.

Marya: A Life, then, may well be the story of a writer "hurt by both women and men," or a "protest against the mutilation suffered by women in the academy," but it is also about blinkered ambition, and a further reflection of Oates's own "evolving of consciousness." Prior to *Marya*, Oates had gone as far as she could, but away from her roots. For even though, looked at closely, novels from *The Assassins* to *Winterthurn* continually show that personal accomplishment can be a devil's pact, such novels were hardly designed to touch the minds and hearts of the world Oates had left behind. In contrast, the novels between

Marya and *Because It Is Bitter, and Because It Is My Heart* began to practice what Marya learns painfully and late. Oates's evolving vision therefore accounts for her sudden return to "realism." For art to have this social function of helping others understand their lives, it needs to communicate directly, as well as indirectly. A measure of the effectiveness of *Marya* is the fact that it manages to do both, setting out an apparently straightforward story, yet filled with subtleties beneath that apparently smooth surface that encourage the reader, as much as the central character, to reevaluate perspectives.

"From a pragmatic point of view," writes James, "the difference between living against a background of foreignness and one of intimacy means the difference between a general habit of wariness and one of trust. One might call it a social difference, for after all, the common *socius* of us all is the great universe whose children we are. If materialistic, we must be suspicious of this socius, cautious, tense, on guard. If spiritualistic, we may give way, embrace, and keep no ultimate fear." To the extent that Marya's provisional tragedy has been to live warily, against a background of foreignness rather than intimacy, her counterpart in *You Must Remember This* is less Enid Maria Stevick than Enid's uncle and lover, Felix, a former boxer with no one to fight but himself. If Felix provides the strongest link, however, the most striking difference between the two novels is the detail with which Oates here brings to life the American 1950s and the industrial setting of Port Oriskany. In *You Must Remember This*, "the individual and the socio-historical," to borrow Lukács's phrase about the merits of realism, are again "inseparably connected to both characterization and action," but this time "the characters' stories add up," as James Atlas suggests, to "the definitive history of an era." In again doubling back to the environment of her youth, Oates drove forward now with the novel as a vehicle not of "projected anxieties" (John Updike's phrase for some of her earlier work) but of social commentary informed by that journey out of solipsism.[34] Marya's drama of the self ends with her recognizing her need to look back over her life, and therefore cut that life "in two." *You Must Remember This* uses a wider lens. It follows the characters in their drive toward dubious or triumphant futures, but at the same time explores in detail the American era of Oates's youth. Like *Marya*, it is about desire, ambition and the way the world looks after certain kinds of fulfillment, but it integrates personal ambitions with cultural and national ambitions, and, unlike Oates's earliest novels, this interaction is sustained throughout.

While its title is a phrase from the sentimental song "As Time Goes By" that

Enid and Felix dance to in their preliminary erotic encounter, *You Must Remember This* itself ironizes the prevalent, romanticized image of 1950s America. It reverses the nostalgia for what Oates calls the fantasy "of a small-town simplistic past" in a "trouble-free stable world" by having the characters strive for an "ideal" future—a utopia often expressed as a death wish—in the face of their gritty, nightmarish present. The worksheets spell out Oates's intentions. Enid's brother, Warren, wants "to make pain, suffering, fear, vanish—to help as many people as possible to avoid what he has suffered." His utopia is "a vague glimmering city w/ many green parks, fountains, broad avenues," not unlike the governmental facade of Washington, D.C., where he ends up. Enid's ideal is the Green Island ("Green Island" is the title of part 1 and was originally planned for the novel as a whole), which represents "death; peace; solitude; ecstasy; silence." Felix wants "everything." "Greedy, manic, irresponsible, charming, perhaps somewhat psychopathic," "ultimately he too wants death."[35] But at every turn, *You Must Remember This* places these personal dramas in a wider commentary on postwar America since it is that meticulously realized setting that drives these fantasies of escape.

Described by Enid as "a cynical man," Felix's cynicism is as integrally connected to his war experiences as Warren's idealism is connected to his.[36] Warren's response to Korea involves heeding the words of an army chaplain that "we the living are the only link in the precious chain between the past and the future" (111). After the war, he turns to politics in support of Adlai Stevenson's vision of historical responsibility: the *"awesome mission"* of *"the leadership of the free world"* (107). Felix, in contrast, lives by the reactive perceptions of a boxer still in the ring, a soldier still at war. Always the fighter in midfight, always under fire, guard always up, he thinks first and foremost of what he can hit, how he can improvise, how he can feel good. "Fighting a fair fight in such circumstances" is "impossible," he says of his war experience. In the end "your soul goes numb" (391). He takes "his solace from speed, from the phenomenon of moving rapidly forward in space simultaneously with moving forward in time, all his concentration his very soul fierce and reduced" to what is "immediately in front of him" (397). All the Stevicks live near the lakeside factories, with "grit everywhere you couldn't help but breathe" and "poisons in the air you can't even detect" (11). But Felix is literally polluted by his environment and context. He stares "out of the window at the smog-heavy sky, traffic" and feels "his kinship with it." He belongs to the "foul, invigorating" stink of the city, and sometimes feels "his soul outside him in the very air" (160).

Similarly, Enid, her parents, Warren, and a younger sister, Geraldine, are representative individuals whose lives are bound up with the postwar period, the shadow of the Bomb, the mores of their community, and the frustrations of their class. Enid's suicide attempt described in the prologue is set in historical context at the start of part 1 with the references to news cuttings. For Enid, as for Marya, escape means self-negation. But where Marya saw escape in terms of ambition or death, Enid, who awaits *"a sign to release her into Death,"* sees escape in terms of death or sexual desire (3). Like Sylvia Plath, who attempted suicide the same year as Enid, 1953, Enid identifies with the Rosenbergs, who, as she sees it, will their own deaths. But while Enid, like Plath's Esther Greenwood, sees her own predicament in terms of "newspaper headlines concerning real atrocities" (to quote from *New Heaven, New Earth*), for Oates the Rosenberg trial reflects aspects of postwar America, including anti-Communist hysteria and the anti-Semitism of the pulp-press reaction to their deaths.

Oates's worksheets show how she planned Enid's parents Lyle and Hannah Stevick, too, in terms of this postwar context, including the differing degrees of their conformity to Roman Catholicism. After Enid's birth in 1938, Hannah —according to the worksheets—suffers "severe haemorrhaging," and "since the Church condemns birth control," sexual relations cease between her and Lyle. Resentful of the Church's attitude to contraception, Lyle objects "to being told about his life." Hannah, in contrast, "becomes increasingly religious as other elements/factors in her life, especially her personal, emotional life, atrophy." Her "hatred/anger/disappointment/ dismay/frustration" is projected outward as "intolerance of blacks/Negroes" and "support of McCarthy."[37] Oates's aims are clear. *You Must Remember This* has a solidity that wholly avoids the drift into dreamy abstraction that overtakes the initial specificity of setting in her early, realist novels. We are in the characters' minds, but also get a convincing, and constant, rendition of historical perspective. Also, while the characters exhibit plenty of introspection, the novel as a whole avoids the claustrophobia that colors works like *With Shuddering Fall, Expensive People,* and *Wonderland.*

Within this context, Felix's story follows Marya's in remaining a drama of self in which others—in this case Enid Stevick and Jo-Jo Pearl—play supporting roles. *On Boxing*, Oates's book-length essay that grew out of research for the novel, provides a commentary on Felix's relationship with these two younger people, each of whom, to borrow a phrase from Johnson, "participate in their own victimization."[38] Life, Oates writes, might be "a metaphor for boxing" in that it resembles "one of those bouts that go on and on" with nothing determined, just "you and your opponent so evenly matched it's impossible not to see that your opponent is you."[39] Felix, the former boxer, with his muddled sense of ambition and desire, keeps boxing without either a ring or an opponent. His love affair with Enid is a boxing bout, just as his coaching of the young boxer, Jo-Jo, is a form of love affair. His first flirtation with Enid is a sparring match on the lawn at a barbecue. He introduces her to the art of boxing, as he will later initiate her sexually. When she attempts suicide after their first sexual contact he feels "a blood bond" between them "as if between two men who'd fought each other to a draw" (168). For Felix, life *is* boxing. He has no idea why human beings are on earth except "maybe to fight" (176). When Enid asks *why* he fights, he says "Why fuck?—it feels good" (229). Part 2 of the novel, "Romance," in which Felix's discovery of Jo-Jo is described as "love at first sight," is as much about boxing-as-romance as about romance-as-boxing (230). Felix himself never articulates the links between his desires in boxing and his desire for Enid, but Jo-Jo falls "into place in Felix's life as Enid had fallen into place." It seems "crucial" that "they never meet" (219). For Felix, the speed bag is "an imagined opponent or a friend or a lover," someone he is "crazy to love, climb all over and beat into perfect submission" (233).

The death wish of Felix's relationship with Enid is matched by the death wish of boxing. Desire, whether sexual or careerist, gives life meaning. But it is also the pursuit of death. To this extent, boxing is not a sport at all but "life speeded up" (228). For the young, naïve Jo-Jo there is only ambition, and no sense at all of the posthumous life to be lived out once his all-consuming goals are achieved or discarded. If he gets to the top and becomes a world champion, then "everything in his life" will be "okay after all" (234). But the process of deterioration, the "hairline scars above his eyebrows, tiny half-moons in the flesh," the puffy nose from dropping his guard, is integral to the ambition (243). The very pursuit of success destroys him. "If boxing is a sport it is the most tragic of all sports because more than any human activity it consumes the very excellence it displays—its drama is this very consumption," writes Oates in *On Boxing*. "To expend oneself in fighting the greatest fight of one's life is to begin by necessity the downward turn that next time may be a plunge, an abrupt fall into the abyss."[40] Enid and Jo-Jo are thus described as being "like those saints, male and female, they'd learned about in confirmation class." Both present "their bodies to their torturers" (129). This is a large part of their appeal to the "psychopathic" side of Felix, who revels in torture, pain, and control. Both these young people come under his wing, and each in turn receives their knockout: death for Jo-Jo, an abortion for Enid. Just as the sex scenes between Felix and Enid reenact the force of a boxing bout, so the abortion is described in terms of a decisive blow. Enid, like Jo-Jo, undergoes "extreme physical trauma" (386) and might die on the table "without waking," bleeding to death "as surely as she deserved" (383).

Felix, too, seems, at least until the novel's end, doomed to continue his boxing-match life because he has "the psychology of the man born to fight, the man who knows nothing *but* fighting, no matter the suicidal nature of his calling." This involves the doom of the perpetual bouts, but also the "lying" that is part of the art: the systematic cultivation of "a double personality" in society and the ring, and "yet another split personality" in the ring "to thwart the Opponent's game plan vis-à-vis *him*."[41] But if anything, his particular tragedy is that life fails to provide him with the kind of killer punch that destroys Jo-Jo and ends that part of Enid's life. His own life has become a mental rather than a physical battle, and he is left "sparring with a partner he didn't know whose face he couldn't see clearly," even though it is his younger self. He discovers that his body is "not a boxer's body now but an ordinary man's body, leaden with fatigue, its youth gone" (407). The links between sexuality, love, and boxing remain entangled to the end. "No sport appears more powerfully homoerotic," writes Oates in *On Boxing*. "The confrontation in the ring—the disrobing—the sweaty heated combat that is part dance, courtship, coupling." "You got to get a hard-on," she quotes Bundini Brown, "and then you got to keep it. You want to be careful not to lose the hard-on, and cautious not to come."[42] Felix's affair with Enid and mentoring of Jo-Jo allow him to redream his youth. Sparring with Jo-Jo, he imagines "time looping luxuriantly back upon itself," so that he is "a kid twenty years old again dreaming all his life to come" (241). Jo-Jo and Enid's relationships with Felix also mirror each other in their denouement. Jo-Jo effectively dies for Felix. His devotion to his mentor leads him to lose control in his fight against Byron McCord and recklessly to continue. "Jo-Jo, don't!" shouts Felix, but Jo-Jo carries on to his death (233). Like Enid's "death," too, Jo-Jo's occurs in hospital. Appropriately, it is not the sexually dormant Lyle but Jo-Jo's father, Leroy, another former boxer, whose chatter on boxing is accompanied by vigorous rubbing of his crotch, who gives Felix the beating he knows he deserves.

So, while Enid will turn to art for sustenance and escape, it is Felix who, like Marya, seems in danger of eking out his life against a background of foreignness, rather than intimacy, habitual wariness, rather than trust. But like Marya, he may in the end be open to change. His refusal to name his assailant after Leroy has beaten him up could be no more than an attempt to rediscover the straightforward morality of the boxing ring. Before the end of the novel, he disappears into its shadows, apparently doomed to shadowbox his way through life. Going nowhere, building nothing, by the end he is exposed, shelterless. But if, as Victor Strandberg argues, "not thinking too much is his version of a bomb shelter," Felix shows signs of action based on reflection—for instance in offering Enid financial help with college and, as Strandberg notes, investing "only in legitimate enterprises."[43] He is perhaps realizing that the answer to the great mystery of "who you finally turn out to *be*" is bound up with what you *do*, and what you do has everything to do with how you think (401). When he beats up a pimp, he is beating up himself. When he boxes, he is boxing himself, and so boxing himself into a desperately limiting life. When he screws around, he is screwing himself. But what *is* there for the man who knows only fighting, however suicidal an activity it may be? What Felix has done, of course, is act out his life in terms of the dominant metaphor of boxing (just as Xavier's metaphor was detection), so the option he has, when he sees it, is of changing his metaphor, and so changing his life. Truth, after all, as Nietzsche defines it, and as Rorty seeks to show in pragmatic terms, is "a mobile army of metaphors." "Change the way we talk," says Rorty, "we change what we want to do and what we think we are."[44]

In the end, perhaps, Enid's parents provide the novel's true love story. After years of abstinence to avoid having more children, they finally return to lovemaking, and loyal Lyle prevails. His shelter may be illusory, but at least Lyle sees "the horrors of the world" and seeks to protect his family against them (401). Just as Felix's fate is open to interpretation, both by us and by himself, so too is the final sex scene. "I love you, Hannah," says Lyle. "I love you too," replies Hannah, her voice "nearly inaudible" (436). Where, for Wagner-Martin, this is Hannah "once again locked in the sex act," for William Heyen this is the triumph of love, and of Lyle, "that well-meaning and suffering and thoughtfully clumsy citizen," over the destructive passion of "that basically selfish, good-for-nothing" Felix. For Victor Strandberg, "the main event of the Epilogue is the resurgence of Eros—the origin of all family life—in the middle-aged parents." (He sees this as a feminist rewrite of the end of *Ulysses* in that, instead of Bloom driving Molly's lovers from her mind, Hannah routs Lyle's "fantasy lovers.")

Meanwhile, Joseph Dewey, in an equally convincing reading of the novel as a drama of "the tension that unfolds between fact and fiction," suspects a "savaging irony" at work in Oates's uncharacteristic parceling out of happy endings to all the characters in "a most Reaganesque finish." "Like some eccentric undertaker," he argues, "Oates ushers us past the embalmed, the soon-to-be-buried—if only to help us recognize the (extra)ordinary miracle of living." What we are meant to remember as time goes by is to "embrace flesh and spirit," not to deny life by entombing ourselves in bomb shelters or worlds of nostalgia and fantasy. Whichever kind of meaning a given reader creates, this focus on Hannah and Lyle still seems the perfect climax, with Enid, no less than Felix, already consumed into the novel several pages before. In fact Enid is so caught up in playing Mozart, one morning in May 1956, that nothing seems to intervene between the music as composed in 1770 and as now being played—"not the pianist, not the instrument itself" (424). Unlike in early Oates novels, the figure whom many readers would most readily see as Oates's nearest kin—described by Joseph Dewey as "Oates's dark-twin, her Angelface"—has been content to fade from, or into, the art. But it is a given of this novel, as of those that follow, that beneath this new realism's mirror-like surface, and beyond its neatly staked shorelines, lie depths and stretches of open-ended flux.[45]

The notion of being consumed into the work, so that the art becomes more significant than the physical self, is an idea most comprehensibly and influentially articulated by Schopenhauer. For Schopenhauer, the one great opportunity to escape our relentlessly driven natures is by losing ourselves in art, and particularly the art he considered purest: music. Through art "we surrender to pure, will-less knowing, we pass into a world from which everything that influences our will and agitates us so violently has passed away." But "the effect of music is so much more powerful and penetrating than that of the other arts, for they speak only of the shadow while music speaks of the essence." Indeed, Strandberg's essay on the philosophical contexts of *You Must Remember This* portrays the novel as a kind of philosophers' boxing match. "Lyle's salvation," he writes, "hangs on a precarious impasse of philosophical contraries, Schopenhauer versus Spinoza," while "Felix comes the closest of any characters to embodying the pure Schopenhauerean Will." Meanwhile, Warren's answer to "his soldier's career as a sort of irruption of the Schopenhauerean Will" seems "to combine Spinozan pantheism with the Saintliness of William James." Were it not for the epilogue, suggests Strandberg, "Oates's Schopenhauerean bias would be confirmed beyond a doubt." But, while Schopenhauer's tribute to the power of music is part of the final affirmation, in general the Stevicks rout "the sober philosophers." In doing so, they allow the comic spirit to surface, celebrating, in Oates's phrase about *Ulysses,* "the livingness of life, not its abstract qualities." "What matters most," observes Strandberg overall of this novel, "is the creation of values, sifted from that passing stream of life by the agency of memory."[46]

Strandberg does not say so (despite being the author of a book on William James), but these affirmations of action over abstraction and of sifting values from life's "passing stream" further signal Oates's pragmatism. If the "sober philosophers" are indeed routed, the intellectual tendencies upheld belong to classical American philosophy, revised by Oates's feminist sympathies. "Irresistibly contentious" as it is, it seems no coincidence that *You Must Remember This,* Oates's most complex and wide-ranging depiction of the era closest to her heart, is usually seen as one of her most memorable triumphs. Indeed, as with *Bellefleur,* the experience of reading it ultimately seems more important than "stabilizing" it through interpretation. It is simply Oates at her best, "a storm of experience," in John Updike's eloquent words of praise, "whose reality we cannot doubt, a fusion of fact and feeling, vision and circumstance which holds together, and holds us to it, through our terror and dismay."[47]

Like *You Must Remember This,* both *American Appetites* and *Because It Is Bitter, and Because It Is My Heart* explore the energy and motion that human beings are fated both to enjoy and endure. But unlike Enid, few of the characters in these two novels find art to be a tool with which to escape that Universal Will. For the most part, they cope instead by constructing narratives that allow them to explain their appetites to themselves and to others. In this they echo the activities of Oates's earliest characters, but now seen through the lens of Oates's artistic maturity. Back in 1966, she told Robert Phillips that her suburban friends, "who have everything they want," "are floating on top of a complex society that unfortunately keeps shifting and changing."[48] *American Appetites* and *Because it is Bitter* reflect this society, one from the viewpoint of restless suburbanites, the other from the viewpoint of those struggling to rise from the complexities of the society on which the suburbanites float. Two linking figures are Sigrid Hunt and Iris Courtney, each of whom makes her way from poverty into the professional classes. If it is true, as Oates claims, that the great American adventure is that of social ascension, then these two novels are as illustrative as any of how her mature work has sought to capture that class war in all its subtlety and variety. At the same time, the novels probe realism as a vehicle for that social commentary. The characters see their lives in terms of realist narratives. The theme of desire comes to seem integral to the narrative drive that keeps us reading, and living. Oates's new realism shows how we employ the fictions of realism even when we realize the illusory nature of closure and coherent identity. Beneath their realist façade, structure, stasis, hierarchy, and other forms of solidifying order are invariably seen as stifling, debilitating, and subject to dissolution by motion, action, and fluidity.

While both novels are infused with Oates's pragmatism, in *American Appetites* Schopenhauer remains an overt source of inspiration along with Nietzsche. In particular, Oates uses Schopenhauer for one of her epigraphs, but also one of his prevalent metaphors, that of hunger and appetite, to cohere the novel. *American Appetites,* Oates says, is "about the irony of a certain kind of success in corporate/academic upper middle class American circles not unlike the Princeton in which I've lived since 1978 as both a neutral observer and a passionate participant."[49] Like Marya and Felix, Ian and Glynnis McCullough are driven to feed their appetites, both professionally and sexually, but have already discovered "the irony of a certain kind of success." The well-heeled McCulloughs live in their glass house in leafy Hazelton-on-Hudson among like-minded friends, all of whom have for years led insular lives. Glynnis, a writer of cookery books, has alleviated the pressure of such domestic closure through illicit affairs within their social circle, but one evening wrongly accuses Ian of a relationship with Sigrid Hunt, an acquaintance from "a declassé area."[50] Her suspicions lead to a marital fracas that ends with Ian pushing his knife-wielding wife through a plate-glass window, causing a fatal head injury. Ian is eventually acquitted and marries Sigrid. He has achieved his unarticulated sexual desires just as he has through the years achieved fulfillment in his professional life. In each case, however, the satisfaction of the desire creates a new desire, because "in the end," as Nietzsche puts it, "one loves one's desire, and not what is desired." After all, says Schopenhauer, the "hungry Will" has to "consume itself, for besides the Will there is nothing else." "Hence the chase, the apprehension, the grieving."[51]

Glynnis's death and Ian's trial for manslaughter is Ian's equivalent of Ivan Illych's sudden awareness of the real direction of his life. In Marilyn Wesley's view, because "the novel concludes with another dinner party," "the only change is the woman who officiates it." But Ian himself has changed. He will blow his "brains out," just as his father did, "when the season turns" (337). He contemplates his father's detachment "in those final months," and feels a similar "despair" (339). To adapt an Oates comment on *Crime and Punishment,* "the redemption, the conclusion, are absolutely unconvincing," what matters are the transgressions that cause the narrative to unfold.[52] But the unconvincing nature of the ending—the ironic distance we feel, and Ian feels—is part of the point. If Joseph Dewey is right in assessing the "happy" ending of *You Must Remember This* as ironic, unlike with the Stevicks the irony is not lost on Ian. With the case closed, the glass case re-closes too, and Ian is physically re-encased by, but emotionally outside, his self-constructed prison. For Ian, the whole idea of appetite, of the drive toward satisfaction—a convention of realism—is shattered when Glynnis dies. If life is indeed motion, the fact that he finds himself in a "season of stasis" suggests he has reached something dangerously close to death (226).

As with Marya's ambition and Felix's sexual desire, however, even before this the results of Ian's drive toward closure have turned out to be anything but desirable. He has become an interpreted man, a man settled into an identity, a man who has seemingly solved that mystery of becoming but is now re-seeking that sense of fluidity, adventure, uncertainty, that actually constitutes life. His successful career has left him with the same hunger, but no focus, and his adulterous desires leave him in the same position as before but with a motherless daughter and a new and probably less suitable wife. His marriage to the Glynnis look-alike Sigrid (whose name is a distorted mirror image of Glynnis) suggests he is now fully conscious of the illusory nature of his realist world. In driving forward, he is really doubling back. Like Marya and Felix, he is seeking his own past. The rundown environment where Sigrid lives reminds him "of his boyhood neighborhood" (17). It is the obverse of the closed world he associates with the fulfillment of ambition. Her room seems "squalid and intensely romantic," like the one where he lived for "the most emotionally turbulent year of his life, in Ann Arbor, in 1959" (27). He constantly links the whole experience with a time of possibilities, when he could pretend to be "unnamed, a Kierkegaardian casualty of faith, an existential being-in-the-making" (116), rather than a successful, professional man whose life narrative has been closed off by a "heavily annotated calendar" (33). Finding himself at a point of closure, he starts a new narrative that is really a disguised repeat of his original story. He will discover that marriage to Sigrid merely perpetuates the grid he supposed he would escape. He thus exemplifies the contradictory human desire for narrative drive and the inevitable need for a closure that, when achieved even precisely as hoped for, proves undesirable. He leaves a world that is suffocating in its organized predictability, for one where everything appears open to possibilities, but the paradox is that he looks for, and finds, the same narrative patterns. Free will and determinism turn out to be almost the same thing.

So *American Appetites* critiques its own realist narrative at the same time that it explains the McCulloughs' upper-middle-class American lives. It is a set of narratives *about* narratives, and the desire for narratives. The brief prologue shows Glynnis and Ian as "young lovers" in Italy, seeing "inevitable" sights such as Michelangelo's "The Creation of the World." By the end of the day—a few lines later—they are "no longer hand in hand." One suggests food and the other supposes "that comes next" (1). The subsequent narrative is a succession of mini-stories that make—but ultimately unmake—the whole. Sigrid, the "non-Roman" from a declassé area, offers a story from beyond the McCulloughs' glassed-in world. Ian pursues the narrative to the ending he thinks he wants, and it becomes clear that his male friends might well have done the same (11). "My success is my problem," he says (7). The haven of the McCulloughs and their friends has become a prison. They have created a protective, sterile environment cut off from lower-class Americans. But sterility has two meanings. Glynnis's rage at Ian's supposed betrayal—otherwise inexplicable, given her promiscuity—has to do with her dread of death. Speculating on the number of sexual partners "a woman like that" might have, she accuses Ian of "bringing disease" into their lives, "for all I know bringing *death*—" (91). Ian has, she thinks, broken out of the "glass-encased" circle she sees as a sterile protection (71). But such closure is itself death, both in terms of circumscribing narrative drive and in the sterility it instils in people's lives. Their glass house may seem like an oxygen tent, but it is also a glass coffin.

Glynnis's dinner parties reveal that she shares her husband's paradoxical appetites. Near the end of Ian's (ironically) "surprise" birthday party, she feels "so melancholy," as "after the expenditure of love in passion" (62). The dinner parties provide her with the same narrative/closure pattern that shapes Ian's life and the whole novel. They offer that hope, expectancy, hunger, that appetite for life. But, as with Ian, the satiation of ambition proves undesirable, so the only thing to do is start a new dinner party, or affair, or novel. Apparently diverse personalities are essentially the same. As the Schopenhauer epigraph states: "Everything is entirely in Nature, and Nature is entire in everything. She has her center in every brute." We are all similar in this, even as we are often incomprehensible to one another. We are subject to the same urges, needs, desires, and the same melancholy if and when our desires are fulfilled. We simply differ in our metaphors. "The science of cuisine" that is Glynnis's lifeblood strikes Ian as "utterly trivial" (86). Like Glynnis and Ian asleep, we are each "the other's twin, though turned resolutely away from the other" (66). Perhaps it is true, as the second epigraph, from Chekhov, suggests, that "the center of gravity should be in two people." But in *American Appetites*, the two people can rarely understand the metaphor the other individual latches onto—dinner parties, squash, philanthropy, book writing, childbearing, adultery—to satiate the desires common to all.

Oates's exploration of narrative and closure, or motion and stasis, in *American Appetites* is captured by two phrases. One of them—John Dewey's remark that "complete adaption to environment means death" (117)—essentially sums up the success and insularity that will prove to be the McCulloughs' undoing. The other phrase is, naturally enough, the title itself. *American Appetites* is the name of Glynnis's posthumous cookery book. But food here is a metaphor for all forms of hunger. Life, the novel follows Schopenhauer in suggesting, is about hunger. Loss of appetite means loss of life. Hunger (as a character says in a passage that never makes it to the published novel) is synonymous with health. "How strange it is that we can speak of hunger without any object," says the unnamed voice. "In fact it's an assertion of health, to say that we have an appetite; that we're hungry; ready to eat; ravenously hungry etc. But it's improper, or at the very least awkward, to speak of desire with no object. 'I feel desire, I am ravenous with desire, will you satisfy my desire and interpret it/read it as "love."'[53] But appetite—especially sexual appetite—also destroys the marriage. Glynnis believes "that ambition was in fact hunger" (7). Yet as a friend, Meika, says, their hunger is thwarted by the contradictions of self-imposed closure. "You are terrified," she says, "of something happening to *you* outside the properly defined contexts of your lives" (295).

As with their lives, so with the realist conventions that Oates employs to tell their story. Narrative drive is a version of both hunger and ambition. We create narratives of our lives, and read, watch, and listen to narratives to supplement those lives. The desire for closure is a death wish, and the struggle against closure is against death. This is the paradox of all human desire. By the end, the only serious question left for Ian is suicide, the single way (so he supposes since, unlike Enid, Oates, and Schopenhauer, he does not consider art, even in its broadest terms, an option) of escaping predetermined fate. Only through death, he seems to think, can the individual terminate the life narrative, and therefore the fact of appetite, desire, will, at a chosen point. To the end, then, narrative closure is inseparable from social, personal, or psychological closure. "Success" is Ian's "problem" because to succeed, he discovers, can be to immerse oneself in a life without prospect: to arrive, and so have the rest of life determined. Success, if viewed as a form of closure or stasis, is a form of death. In *American Appetites*, the dis-closing of closure turns out to be perhaps the only hope for release. If there *are* other levels of existence, then Ian crosses from one level to another and becomes our unwilling pioneer. He might commit suicide, but then again he might not: he might simply live out his life ironically detached from the very drives that make him human. Alternatives are voiced, one of them by the McCulloughs' daughter, Bianca, who flees America and rejects a Western worldview in favor of Eastern mysticism. She denies the all-embracing Western emphasis on time and, hence, on narrative. For Bianca, "in a moment of time perfect enlightenment is obtained" (329). As Oates argued in *New Heaven, New Earth,* "it is not at all certain" that "what is necessary and immutable in human experience is the fact of time and space at all."[54]

So while *American Appetites* explores its own conventions, it also critiques the conventions of American society. The courthouse where Ian's trial takes place, like Hawthorne's Custom-House in *The Scarlet Letter*, seems to stand for the culture it serves. "Built in the heyday of Greek revival," it is superficially grand but "poorly lit and poorly ventilated." "Decades out of date, badly in need of renovation," it still exacts "from those who enter it a measure of frightened awe" as they approach "the faded, limp, yet still imperial American flag." It is "a self-referential little American world, staffed by females, ordained by males" (257). The America of *American Appetites* is no melting pot but a nation of sharply defined—and defended—cultural, social, and ethnic dividing lines. The McCulloughs believe in social compartmentalization. Ian's trip to Sigrid's apartment is an adventure, and when he goes looking for her, his view is that "if anything has happened" *this*, "not Hazelton-on-Hudson," is the place for a murder (76). But Ian's trip to Sigrid's apartment is not the only trip he makes to the "other side" of American life. In the fall of his acquittal, he voluntarily teaches remedial English in Newburgh as "a way of filling in the hours." Here his name means nothing, and "the color of his skin" marks him off from his black students (250). It is implicit that his experience frees him of some of this prejudice since his friends now seem "on the other side of a sort of barrier," a pane of glass that he does not want to break (243). One friend, Vaughan, who sees the enterprise as "naïve and dangerous," asks if Ian's students are "mainly black," or "drug addicts, and alcoholics, and parolees—" (273). The irony, of course, is that the only drug addicts, alcoholics, or parolees in the novel are in Hazelton-on-Hudson.

Like Marya, and like Enid and Felix, then, Ian's experiences lead him to outgrow his earlier self-deceptions and delusions. Ian, however, can only attain limited insight because, while he makes brave little adventures into the other side of American life, he remains essentially secure, if desperately restless to the point of being suicidal, in his limited world. The ending therefore focuses less on Ian than on the other voice—besides Bianca—that suggests an alternative perspective: that of Sigrid. In doing so, it offers further suggestions that Ian, or at best their marriage, may not survive. For Sigrid has her own "surely fascinating life's story, up to and beyond the point at which it intersected with the McCulloughs' tragedy" (339). None of the men at the table seem to want to hear that story, but rather than being offended, Sigrid is "quick, shrewd, inspired, leaning forward" to offer them more to satiate their insatiable appetites. The novel's final words are her question, "Won't you all have just a little more?" (340). And a little more is what we get: her story will be heard because in Oates's next novel, Sigrid, like the dressed-up adult ape in Oates's Kafka-inspired play and poem "A Report to an Academy," is effectively addressing the established classes of American society. "Please do not misunderstand me, esteemed ladies and gentlemen: I am not bitter," run the key lines. "I had to find a way out of the cage or die. / So I became one of you. As you see."[55] To all intents and purposes, this is also the story of Oates's next outlaw, Iris Courtney, in *Because It Is Bitter, and Because It Is My Heart*.

Where *American Appetites* critiques the irony of a successful life amid supposedly secure surroundings, *Because It Is Bitter* portrays the horrors of drowning in the "shifting and changing" realities beneath that artificial social coherence. Sigrid is a girl from the margins who insinuates herself into an upper-middle-class world. She remains, however, marginal to *American Appetites* until that very last moment. In contrast, Iris Courtney enacts the same drama by eventually marrying into another of Oates's liberal, academic families, the Savages, but the world she comes from is central to *Because It Is Bitter*. The "realism" of everyday life corresponds with the "realism" of the novel in being conscious artifice. "When you're standing on the bridge, which is solid and unmoving, watching water rush beneath your feet," reflects Jinx Fairchild, Iris's black, male counterpart, there is a "mysterious moment" when "the water becomes still and you're the one who is moving."[56] In another novel best understood in terms of movement and flux, the narrative drive and realist structure seem to float on ever-shifting ground with rhythms and repetitions more akin to the river than the decaying, concrete environment in which the Fairchilds and Courtneys live. For all its surface coherence, the novel is as much a masquerade as Iris's marriage to Alan Savage or her parents' assertion of the uniqueness of "The Incomparable Courtneys" (302).

"In a sense, all writing—all art—is 'postmodernist'; it's artificial," Oates wrote in a 1994 letter. "But some fiction makes a true effort to mirror a recognizable social world, while being firmly grounded in the subjective, spiritual existences of its characters, which may at times verge upon the surreal." *Because it Is Bitter* is infused with a postmodernist sensibility even as it fits the Lukàcsian ideal of historical realism. That its most eloquent praise should have come from Henry Louis Gates Jr. seems especially pertinent. Oates "sides with the outlaws" no less than her character, Iris (33), who by the end of the novel has taken over Jinx's role as (in the words of his brother, Sugar-Baby) a "performin' monkey" (191), and her novel is a "Signifyin(g)" of realist conventions. She uses realism as a tool for social commentary, but this "double-voiced" novel continually stresses the complexities beneath apparent coherence. As such, *Because It Is Bitter* gives credence to Oates's claim that her "'vision' has evolved over the years, and has become, if anything, more complex, ambiguous."[57] What is true of the novel is also true of the "realist" narratives of the characters' lives. Time is a sea in which a single enormous wave moves forward relentlessly, thinks Ian in *American Appetites,* "not bearing men and women along but simply passing through them" (174–75). The same surprise perspective meets the characters of *Because It Is Bitter.* Like Marya, Felix, Ian, and Tolstoy's Illych, they find that their drive toward a desired goal is really taking them in the reverse direction, merely masking their decay. The coherence they impose on their lives can suddenly seem to be stifling or disintegrating, but, either way, hardly providing them with the happiness they sought.

Another of Oates's attempts to capture something of "the true America, as opposed to the conscious, self-invented America," *Because It Is Bitter* deals with multiple aspects of that society, from the academic middle class to impoverished blacks and migrant Virginia hillbillies.[58] The race and class tensions and attractions in upstate New York become a microcosm of the country as a whole during the civil rights era. The white Courtneys and black Fairchilds offset but also mirror one another (as in turn they will reflect the Savages even as their poverty defines the Savages' wealth). Both fathers, Duke Courtney and Vernon Fairchild, are war veterans. Both mothers, Persia and Minnie, struggle to retain their family's precarious social status, yet Minnie seems ultimately set on following Persia into alcoholism. Each family strives to assert or retain a sense of identity to survive "the cruel face of the United States" as coherent units against the constant threat of dissolution (351).

To do so, however, "the incomparable Courtneys" constantly compare themselves with others, and not least the Fairchilds and Southern migrants like the Garlocks (302). The values they cling to in trying to control their fates—the Apollonian constructs with which they shape their identities—are those of hierarchy and category. Their sense of identity is synonymous with their attempts to grade others. Like the McCulloughs, Persia in particular tries to close herself off physically and mentally from those "below" her by differentiating between the clean and the unclean. "There's nothing so nice," she tells Iris, "as being *clean,* is there. *Clean* outside and in" (27). For Persia, the Garlocks epitomize dirt. When she first sees their "eyesore of a house," she is appalled by "the Garlock odor grimed into wood, wallpaper, the very foundations." The front room "has been made into a bedroom of sorts" (18). Red Garlock, supposedly "born dirty," is "not just dirty-minded and dirty-mouthed" but "truly dirty" (98). For the Courtneys to be "clean," not only must others be dirty but still others must do the cleaning; and those others are the Fairchilds. The night Jinx murders Red Garlock to protect Iris, he is cleaning the floor in Cheney's Variety. After the collapse of her employer, Dr. O'Shaughnessy, Minnie cleans at the Hotel Franklin. Sugar Baby opts for a life of petty crime to escape "janitor work or shoveling gravel or cleaning up white folks' shit at the hospital or some hotel uptown or hauling away their garbage" (192). Mrs. Rudiger's classroom seat plan is a microcosm of the Courtney's attempts to ensure physical and mental segregation. She positions children around the classroom by "good grades," "good 'citizenship'; cleanliness and clean habits; size, height, sex, race." But black boys "are inevitably toward the rear" and even "best-groomed Negro girls" never make it beyond the third row (32). Nowhere is the unofficially segregated world of 1950s America more apparent than at the Hammond horserace meetings, where the human races separate into customers and servers and "all the clubhouse patrons are white, all the waiters black" (71).

But while the Courtneys have the same desire to differentiate themselves as have the McCulloughs and the Savages, they lack the money. "The greatest realities," Oates has said, "are physical and economic: all the subtleties of life come afterward."[59] Rather than floating on top of this complex society like the Savages, the Courtneys are pulled down by economic problems into the shifting current beneath. The poorer they become, the faster they plunge. As they travel toward Lowertown, the poorer section of Hammond, "the buildings and houses and even the trees become shabbier" and there is "an increase in dark faces, an ebbing of white faces" (22). The worse the neighborhood, the closer it is to the chemical plants. Iris's school has "an asphalt playground crumbling at its edges, fenced off at the rear from hillocks of ashy chemical-stinking landfill" (30). Just as their differences from the Fairchilds are less clear cut than the Courtneys would wish, so they have more in common with the Garlocks than they pretend. Duke leaves Persia and eventually marries for money, as does Iris. The once-proud Persia succumbs to alcoholism and ends up sleeping off her drunkenness in the front room, where the unmade sofa leaves "that unmistakable smell, of a body in sleep," that once repelled her at the Garlock's house (41). Her facial mask becomes a "clownish streak of mascara" (207). She vomits continuously and "knows she's going to die" (218). As so often happens in those Oates plays of this period that deal with race, identity, and/or the veneer of civilized behavior (such as *Negative, Under/Ground, Here She Is!* and *Black*), the black/white, upper/lower, clean/unclean, rich/poor oppositional identity constructions collapse. Like Iris's multimirrored dressing table of "mirror images overlapping, mocking, challenging one another," Persia ends up mirroring and finally replacing Vesta Garlock, once her epitome of dirt, who, ironically, cleans up her act and escapes back to her native Virginia (90).

As Gates says, *Because It Is Bitter* "is less a novel about public history than one about private memory, the narratives by which we fashion our lives." But those narratives are shaped by the way the characters see and are seen by American society. The novel's core drama is not primarily a drama of self-identity so much as of American identities, and at its heart is the relationship between Iris and Jinx. Oates's worksheets show that it is meant to be emblematic of America's "tragic psychic split" during that era. Iris, she notes, "innocently recapitulates the tragedy of her nation." "Each is a projection of the other."[60] They reflect each other but their fates are socially determined by opportunities defined by race and economics. If Iris's "chronic sense of herself is that of a figure running just ahead of a wall of flame," Jinx's actions stem from similar desperation (275).

In the end, the white girl has an option not available to the black boy. But while Jinx's destruction is immediate and actual, Iris's is like a wasting illness, a survival that leaves her unrecognizable even to herself. Alan Savage redesigns her outwardly just as the white coaches have constructed Jinx to be the "performin' monkey" that Sugar-Baby has described him as. Both realize the culturally constructed nature of identity. But while Iris marries into a wealthy white family, Jinx slides into janitorial work. He might indeed have become the Sylvester of *Marya* (perhaps one day mocking Iris in her elevated social position) had he not opted for the army and Vietnam because "I WANT YOU makes you think *somebody* wants you at least," and that's "*something, ain't it?* Not just fucking *nothing?*" (350). Iris's choice, too, is effectively something over nothing. She consciously adopts the romantic/realist convention of marriage, single-mindedly pursuing this "happy ending" (described by Oates as "an 'ironic—'happy'—ending: a marriage, but not the passionately desired, and impossible, marriage") to escape her mother's failed constructions.[61] She sees that, since the truths and lies of life are so difficult to distinguish, she may as well play the game. She becomes fully aware that life—no less than art—is a world of "many-faceted, infinite" surfaces (281). Like Ian McCullough, then, she becomes aware of the fictitious aspects of her own reality. This radical doubt about language and identity has all but dissolved her sense of self, so she creates a new, conscious fiction to replace it.

Iris's marriage into the Savages in fact distills a main theme of both novels: the need for narrative realism and closure even as it is seen to be a construct. For Iris, as for Sigrid, this need is economic as well as psychological. She marries into the Savages fully aware that their world resembles a museum of antiquated notions. Their house has a "Victorian grandeur" (282), but seems, to Iris, as if "made of papier-mâché." It may look "*weighty,*" just as outdated beliefs from past centuries can still look to us, but "it's a dream castle," powerful enough, Iris thinks, for those living in it to come "to resemble it." The Savages live among illusory ideals and worldviews that nevertheless govern their identities and shape their actions. Their realism—which includes notions of racial and sexual hierarchy that those outside the Savages' belief system know to be fictitious—has become so habitual as to seem natural. "Since I've lived here most of my life," says Dr. Savage, "I'm not required to see it" (283). The house's interior—with its "French Empire table and chairs," Jacobean-style "English oak sideboard," and "Chinese carpet" (288)—is really a postmodernist pastiche of past ages. Even the food is a pastiche of past lives. The oyster stuffing recipe dates back "to George Washington's *mother*" (289).

In the end, then, Iris takes her own postmodernist stance and becomes a pastiche of the happy bride. A self-conscious realist, both in practical terms and in her awareness of the fiction of the coherence she has adopted, like a realist work she must ensure "that the life of Iris Courtney" as known to the Savages "is consistent, seamless" (338). She plays her role, but knows she is *"a sort of mirror or reflector for them, beaming back their happiness"* (312). She has had to become one of them or, like her mother, drown among the debris that floats beneath them. She stands in her "flawlessly white" wedding dress, an outlaw in the uniform of an in-law. She has "lost more weight" (386), and her hair is graying, but her near-rape by a gang who abducted her when she deliberately wandered into a black neighborhood is smoothed over like the "cosmetic dentistry" of "the chipped tooth, discreetly capped" (398). She receives a photograph of Jinx, and Jinx's inscription on the back, *"Honey—Think I'll 'pass'?"* (403), echoes her own question at the end: *"Do you think I'll look the part?"* (405). Both end as images in uniforms. Just as the murder of Red Garlock has been covered over and a gas station built on the vacant lot, so the questions raised are conventionally covered over by an ending that is no more than a gossamer veil. "The chipped tooth is perfectly disguised," her dress "a perfect fit," "a costume" for "the part" (405).

While Iris has to learn about the construction of identity, Jinx knows that his (black) identity is defined by white perceptions, and therefore that identity is "provisional, even nominal" (184). The first we see of him and Sugar-Baby (who turns to crime and is eventually murdered), they are performing "flawless dives" into Peach Tree Creek. But if the scene initially suggests images of, say, Thomas Eakins's pastoral painting *The Swimming Hole* or Rupert Brooke's poem "Peace," they are no "swimmers into cleanness leaping." Rather, Oates's river-jumping image is closer to George Bellows's painting, *Forty-Two Kids*, described by Edward Lucie-Smith as "an informal paraphrase" of *The Swimming Hole* in that Bellows replaced Eakins's pastoral idyll with ragged children diving against the dubious urban background of a wrecked jetty.[62] The creek picks up "sludge from the factories," along with "raw garbage and used condoms and sewage" (47–48). The Fairchild brothers can only plunge into filth and will themselves become waste products of American society. Assigned to the wrong side of the binary opposition of American postwar identity, Jinx knows early that we are not the selves that others see. His identity is forever bound up with white society's views of him and of his actions. At school, Mr. Hannah favors him only because the teacher is "a white man who favors certain selected Negroes—Negroes easy to like—as a means of demonstrating it isn't anything racial, certainly can't be racist, the way he dislikes the others" (126).

Basketball is Jinx's alternative world, the equivalent of the boxing ring for the boxer, art for the artist, alcohol for the alcoholic.

For Jinx, says Oates, "there are two worlds: the world of ordinary reality, and the court." So, too, for the artist: "what the writer wants, simply," writes Oates, "is 'a world to live in.'"[63] The basketball court is Jinx's clean, well-lighted, "own secret space" (173). But he is under no illusions that if he misses the foul shot the crowd will see him as "just another nigger-boy" (128). In the end, he destroys his probably doomed career himself by deliberately breaking his ankle in a fall, and becomes just that, a statistic in a brutally competitive world.

So Jinx has basketball, then nothing, while Iris turns herself into a work of art. Both see how identities are constructs. Both recognize "the extraordinary power of duplicity," yet for both, their bodies are to some extent their fate (156). The novel starts with a section called "The Body," which ostensibly refers to Red Garlock's corpse. But in fact Jinx's rise and fall is inextricable from his dark skin and athletic prowess, while Iris—who has said, "what good will beauty do me?" (268)—prostitutes that beauty to win marriage into a family who will see her as the work of art she becomes. "Impoverished people," writes Oates in *On Boxing*, "prostitute themselves in ways available to them." Both Iris and Jinx sell themselves to try to survive. Iris discovers her "white" destiny—her "white" wedding—while Jinx joins the army. Both end up in American uniforms appropriate to the roles open to them. Iris has a white wedding dress made for Alan's grandmother in 1904, while Jinx assumes the role of the black soldiers in the Civil War photograph Iris has shown him. As Iris knows with "a certitude beyond grief," Jinx is destined to die in Vietnam (403). Two people who might have suited each other stay apart and are subsumed into their representative cultural roles. The white girl is fitted snugly into a white wedding dress. The black boy is bundled into a body bag. Social hierarchies and injustices are vigorously reasserted, and fates confirmed. In broad terms, Iris and Jinx recapitulate "the tragedy of America's America": the tragedy of America's vision of itself, at least in racial terms, at least in the 1950s and 1960s. In Gates's words, Oates's "basic technique," certainly in these later novels of American social commentary, "is really quite simple: Find just where it hurts and then press, *hard*."[64]

Just as *American Appetites* has one character, Bianca, who is more a commentator than a participator, so *Because It Is Bitter* has Leslie Courtney. Iris's uncle is the novel's cultural witness. His quixotic goal to photograph every human being in Hammond is a version of Oates's own all-embracing aims. He charts Iris's growth and Persia's decline and is entrusted with Jinx's portrait. Unlike Persia, he has no more interest in his own mortality than in cleanliness. He serves wine in glasses "that probably aren't too clean" (55). He quits drinking after Persia's death, gets a better studio location, and is the only one who ends up unambiguously better off. His self-containment lets him avoid the pressures that contort the lives of Persia, Jinx, and Iris. While they make art of their lives, he makes art itself, of and for others. As a photographer, he has no allegiance to tribe or group or family. He photographs "human subjects with no particular reference to their race" (24). He has never taken self-portraits "because he was always embodied in the photographs he took of other people." He is "an absence," he says, "but there" (57). Where the bitter-hearted, self-consuming Iris is (to quote Gates on Oates) a "daemon from the lower depths" who infiltrates the upper-middle classes, Leslie is the compassionate cultural commentator—the artist or "writer as witness"—that Oates had become.[65]

Finally, the story of the Courtneys links with the novel as self-conscious realism. Just as Iris dons the uniform of the Savages, so Oates's narrative melds postmodernist doubt with the strengths of fabricated realist coherence. As Gates says, in *Because It Is Bitter* "the boundaries of character are so porous as to subsume everything else." When Iris/Oates says, "*Do* you think I look the part?" the italicized "*Do*" seems like the speaker's uncertainty. But it is also the kind of emphasis used when a question is repeated for an unthinking respondent. The answer should be "yes," but only if we see this realist format, no less than Iris's marriage, as a self-conscious construct by a novelist fully aware of the possibilities of the novel form far beyond the ostensible realism she uses here. The novel as realism mirrors the subtleties of the characters' struggles for coherence. *American Appetites* and *Because It Is Bitter* are as much about cultural realism as artistic realism. They critique the conventions even as they use them and so continue Oates's series of marriages and infidelities to the genres and conventions of the novel form. But, along with *Marya* and *You Must Remember This*, the subtleties that their accessibility belies reveal their pragmatic purpose. Oates by this stage of her career had no need to dwell introspectively on the complexities of identity. She had long ago solved for herself the mystery of who one becomes in terms of what one does, what use one makes of one's insights for the benefit of the wider community and its individual members. The novelist-as-pragmatist—perhaps the best description of Oates in the novels of her maturity—was now fully-fledged.

> *Time?—devours us*
> *in the name of wisdom*
> —JOYCE CAROL OATES, "George Bellows'
> 'Mrs. T. in Cream Silk, No. 1' (1919–23)"

5 DARK EYES ON AMERICA

TOGETHER WITH HER PLAYS, poetry, and essays, Oates's novels through the 1990s into the twenty-first century confirm her as one of our preeminent commentators on America. They provide a voice not so much for "projected anxieties" as for others who might have experienced—or be experiencing—something like the traumas of her own youth, but also for a far wider range of readers. She has written about male victims: Corky Corcoran in *What I Lived For* (1994), John Reddy Heart in *Broke Heart Blues* (1999), Vernor Matheius in *I'll Take You There* (2002). She has also written about both male and female victimizers: Quentin P. in *Zombie* (1995), Kathleen Hennessey in *The Rise of Life on Earth* (1991), victim-turned-victimizer Starr Bright in the Rosamond Smith novel *Starr Bright Will Be with You Soon* (1999). But many novels and novellas of this period—*Foxfire: Confessions of a Girl Gang* (1993), *First Love* (1996), *We Were the Mulvaneys* (1996), *Man Crazy* (1997), *Blonde* (2000), *Beasts* (2002), *I'll Take You There* (2002), *The Tattooed Girl* (2003), *Rape: A Love Story* (2003)—specifically focus on women as "victims/survivors."[1] The same can be said of many of her stories, not least two particularly devastating ones in *Faithless* (2001), both of which deal with the effects and aftereffects of divorce on children torn apart by the competing emotional claims of divorced parents. In "A Manhattan Romance," the narrator remembers the trauma she faced at the age of five when, "feverish with excitement," she went with her alcoholic father on what turned out to be their last "*Saturday adventure.*" It ends with him committing suicide in front of his little "*princess*" in a hotel room. "But don't tell me there isn't happiness," says the woman. "It exists. It's out there. You just have to find it, and you have to keep it, if you can. It won't last, but it's there." In "Murder-Two," a defence attorney, Marina Dyer, falls in love with Derek Peck Jr., her teenage client accused of murdering his mother, with whom he has lived alone since his father divorced her "same as divorcing *him*." Named after his father, "his precarious, adolescent sense of himself" is "seriously askew," and the assertion that "fifty-three percent of Derek's classmates, girls and boys," are also "from 'families of divorce'" reminds us that his situation is far from unusual.² Where once Oates wrote in "code," writes Greg Johnson, where she employed strategies of concealment or evasion, "intellectual and emotional distance from her own early traumas has freed her "to dramatize them more openly." Stories like "A Manhattan Romance" and "Murder-Two" show how powerfully she is able to capture the individual traumas enfolded within everyday American headlines. Direct as a fist in the face, there is more skill, power, and concentrated emotional impact in the twelve pages of "A Manhattan Romance" than in the whole of *Expensive People* and *Wonderland* put together.³

If anything, the pace of Oates's productivity has quickened, even as its range has widened. Every year there has been a new novel or novella and, at the very least, either a new collection of stories, an essay collection, another volume of plays, or a new Rosamond Smith novel. Whatever genre Oates works in now, the social, pragmatic dimension is invariably present. Her 1999 essay collection, *Where I've Been, and Where I'm Going,* provides an interesting contrast from early collections in that the essays, reviews, and general prose pieces are, while briefer, far more numerous than those in, say, *New Heaven, New Earth*. Whether collected or otherwise, there seems little subject matter she would not turn her hand to, from the death of Diana, Princess of Wales, to high-security prisons, from serial killers to September the eleventh, from Christina Rossetti to Raymond Chandler.

"The issue of art's purpose in the community" is rarely far from the surface, and Oates seems to have settled on a perspective—naturally a pragmatic, ever-shifting, paradoxical perspective—that best allows her to define and redefine herself and to enable her readers to do likewise with her work. "The artist," she writes in "Art and Ethics?—The (F)Utility of Art," is the perpetual antagonist of what is fixed and 'known'—what is 'moral,' 'ethical,' 'good.'" The artist, certainly the American artist, idiosyncratic and defiant, is "the voice of rebellion." "If we are told that art is only for the State, we rebel," writes Oates. "If we are told that art is useless, futile, we rebel; we are creatures of self-determination, yet creatures of our time, deeply connected with one another, nourished by one another, defined by one another, in ways impossible to enumerate." "The artist as perpetual antagonist," she concludes, "is supremely self-determined," "deeply bonded to his or her world, and in a meaningful relationship with a community—this is the artist's ethics, and the artist's aesthetics."[4]

This blending of ethics and aesthetics could hardly be a more eloquent definition of how Oates has merged the twin, apparently incommensurable impulses that set her off on her artistic journey. First there is "the creation of the aesthetic object," she writes in another essay. Then there is "the movement outward," "evoking in the audience or community a sympathetic response." But because art is a process for both writer and reader, one cannot simply extract, she says elsewhere, the "'theme,' 'vision,' 'worldview'" from the work "as if such were somehow distinct and separable from the experience of the art work itself." Rather there are responses—inevitably creative—that reveal art's ever-changing social 'use.' Oates's connections with theater in recent years have put this communal perspective in relief. "Doesn't it upset you to see your characters taken over by other people, out of your control?" she is asked. "But isn't that the point of writing for the theater?" she replies, adding (in the context of her afterword to *Twelve Plays*) that one might as well ask if a novelist minds strangers interpreting the novels.[5] If anything, Oates's most recent novels seem designed precisely to allow such creative responses to take place and so foster the utility of art.

Each of the novels under discussion in this chapter clarifies a range of issues connected with our contemporary mindset and the possibilities for cultural change; and each helps to define what we might mean by individual or cultural maturity. Three novels of the early to mid-1990s, *Black Water*, *Foxfire*, and *What I Lived For*, explore the question of individual and cultural maturity in the specific American social spheres of politics, high school, and business. Four later novels, *We Were the Mulvaneys*, *Broke Heart Blues*, *Blonde*, and her 2001 novel, *Middle Age: A Romance*, also seem preoccupied with defining mature perspectives and pinpointing the differences between those that enable and those that debilitate. *We Were the Mulvaneys* explores family life, *Broke Heart Blues* and *Middle Age: A Romance* look at localized nostalgia and myth making, and *Blonde* focuses on the quasi-religious cult of celebrity and of the female global icon. Overall, these seven novels show the range of Oates's subject matter to be perhaps beyond parallel in American writing—and that is in this genre alone. The review of *Because it is Bitter* by Henry Louis Gates Jr., which seems all the more significant for being a (black) (male) American's review of a (white) (woman) writer's novel about the tensions between the sexes and races in 1950s and 1960s America, suggests as much. Gates concluded by citing that half-joking comment, made early in Oates's career, that she hoped to do for late-twentieth-century America what Honoré de Balzac did for nineteenth-century France: "Over twenty years ago, Oates confessed to the ambition of putting the whole world in her fiction—an ambition she termed 'laughably Balzacian.' It may have seemed so to her. But no one is laughing now."[6]

One anonymous reviewer called *Black Water* "a flimsy gloss on Senator Ted Kennedy's Chappaquiddick scandal, and of dubious value," while Billy Abrahams, Oates's editor at Dutton, described it as "an amazing work of art, a master work." Editors may be drawn to hyperbole, but this short novel is far more than "a flimsy gloss" on an old scandal. If Gates is right in claiming that "a future archaeologist equipped only with [Oates's] *oeuvre* could easily piece together the whole of postwar America," *Black Water*'s 154 pages would be a good place to start.[7] Although the novel centers on so short a period of time, it nevertheless sketches some fundamental issues in late twentieth-century American society, and beyond. Its power rests partly on its suggestive allusions—most obviously to the 1968 Chappaquiddick crash that killed Mary Jo Kopechne and the presidential hopes of Senator Edward Kennedy—but also on its evocation of basic human desires and fears. "We live on speculative investments or on our prospects only," writes William James. "In this sense we at every moment can continue to believe in an existing *beyond*. It is only in special cases that our confident rush forward gets rebuked."[8] In *Black Water*, that breezy sprint is almost over as soon as it begins. Like cartoon characters running off a cliff or the spinning wheels of a car that has already left the road, we join Kelly—and in time even The Senator (throughout, Oates uses uppercase for both words)—over an abyss that stares up at us even as we continue the momentum of our drive toward an undesired conclusion.

On one level, Chappaquiddick was merely the specific catalyst for Oates's wider concerns. "The Kennedy-connection is not one I really want to do," she wrote in her worksheets. "All that interests me are the ideas, the issues—guilt/responsibility, denial/confession." But "the image of the drowning girl/trapped girl in the car, so many hours. This exerts a hypnotic appeal. This I suppose I really do want to write."[9] Where the novels from *Marya* to *Because It Is Bitter* explored the drive to fulfill "undesired" desires, *Black Water* is about the moment of death, which (in that Kelly Kelleher and the reader pursue the journey toward "fulfillment") is simultaneously desired, dreaded, and inevitable. Where previous novels explored the journey toward oblivion or enlightenment, here time is compressed to the moment of collision. *Black Water* is Oates's imagining of death itself—Kelly sees the black water as literally "her Death"—that seemingly impossible moment when the subject, of all people, will cease to exist.[10] "How crucial for us to rehearse the future, in words," thinks Kelly before the fatal drive. "Never to doubt that you will utter them" or "tell your story" (83–84). The novel plays to our nightmarish fascination with that final moment. Oates has said that its two-hour reading time corresponds with the time it takes for Kelly to die, but it is unclear at what point Kelly's awareness becomes the delirium of her dying brain. As Jean-Paul Sartre wrote of the Quentin Compson section of *The Sound and the Fury*, all we have is a view of what is behind us. Kelly's final "hours"—or moments—are mostly taken up with memories. "Since the hero's last thoughts coincide approximately with the bursting of his memory and its annihilation," asks Sartre, "who is remembering?"[11] The seeming paradox that holds us when we try to identify with the victims of fatal accidents is that the individual must experience something, but since experience is so quickly memory, the absence of memory is impossible to equate with the fact of experience.

The terrible irony is that Kelly retains hope, and her hope is our hope. "*You're not an optimist, you're dead*," she thinks (93). There is "blood in her eyes," which are "wide open staring and sightless." Her head is "pounding violently" where the bone is cracked, yet even in her delirium, where she believes that "through this fissure" the black water will "pour to extinguish her life," she thinks she can "find a way to escape" or the Senator "*will be back to help*" (74–75). Her hope is our hope not only as readers but also as human beings. We are prepared for her to die, whether or not we know of Chappaquiddick, because at the end of part 1 the water rushes in "to fill her lungs" (65). But we know for a more basic reason: the rush forward, the swallowing up of time, through ambition or anticipation or plain living, is the rush to death—the paradoxical desire to get to the undesired end. Her hopes are absurd, but we share them passionately, just as, in her delirium, she thinks she can sip the water rather than drown in it. For control is a theme, too. There is Kelly's control of herself, both physically in her tendency to anorexia and in her decision to go with the Senator, and there is the Senator's control of Kelly and—so he thinks—of the car. But this is a story about losing control in a doomed race against diminishing time. The Senator and Kelly race to reach the ominous ferry—which supposedly serves the mainland, but calls to mind the River Styx—even as the Senator and Ray Annick, Kelly's friend's lover, are well into middle-age and "determined to enjoy themselves" in the face of their decay (82).

The Senator's inability to control the car is put in relief by Oates's control not only of prose but also of space between prose. The blank moments between the rushed action are "patches of amnesia like white paint spilling into her brain" (10). Their stillness and silence accentuate the sense of rushing forward. They are like paparazzi flashes in a Paris tunnel, the sudden movement and stillness of successive camera shots, a constant reminder of the thinning line between consciousness and oblivion, and memory and denial, the areas of the past "partly obscured by pockets of amnesia."[12] Oates conveys character not just through description but through individual sentences. When at the party Kelly challenges the Senator's views, the Senator considers "this remark, thoughtfully" (101). The comma is part of the characterization. It tells us a great deal about his posturing, his professionalism, his condescension, his position with regard to Kelly, his attraction to her, his fake thoughtfulness and his genuine lust. It tells us he is thinking, but not merely about Kelly's remark. You know he has not read the article because of the way he insists that he has: "nodding emphatically saying yes he'd read her article on capital punishment in *Citizens' Inquiry*—he was certain he'd read it" (105).

Yet neither the twenty-six-year-old girl nor the fifty-something man is stereotyped. Elsewhere the "non-judgmental" Oates seems as transparent in her condemnations and opinions as ever. Kelly's views on Reagan and Bush Sr. as Republicans sound as if they echo Oates's own. "Those Reagan years, the dismal spiritual debasement, the hypocrisy, cruelty, lies uttered with a cosmetic smile," muses Kelly, "surely the American people would *see*" (106). But the novel as a whole is no shrill tract against hypocritical politicians or middle-aged, power-drunk cradle snatchers. It probes the motives that drive this middle-aged man and his, as far as the seduction is concerned, all-too-willing victim with care and consideration. Oates did evidently write the novel out of indignation against Kennedy's assertions that Chappaquiddick was a "tragic accident," but it depicts issues rather than presenting flat condemnations.[13]

Just as "Politics" is "the negotiating of power," so, too, is "Eros" (53). Kelly, no less than the Senator, has some power, though both think they have more control of the situation than is actually the case. This is not a straightforward story of a victim and victimizer. The Senator is "of a social background similar to that of the Kellehers" (57). Both are liberal do-gooders who feel ambivalent toward those they purport to help. Just as the Senator seems not unduly upset by repeated Republican successes, so Kelly views her voluntary work with the National Literacy Foundation of America, teaching "black adult illiterates to read primer texts," with some detachment (79). Her zeal for the job is mixed with "a Caucasian condescension" and a "visceral fear of physical threat" (80). She angrily rejects the selfishness of her father's conservative belief that "it *was* hopeless thus save your own white skin." Yet she feels "contempt for ignorant people not just blacks of course (though all her students were black) but whites, whatever: men and women whom the ruthless progress of civilization had left behind" (56). Nor is Kelly unaware or powerless in terms of where the situation with the Senator will lead. She sees it as an adventurous assertion of her own will. "Scorpio don't be shy, poor silly Scorpio your stars are WILDLY romantic now," thinks Kelly. "Demand YOUR wishes. YOUR desires for once" (54). She feels "that adrenaline-charge: as, on the beach, earlier that day, she'd felt the urgency of a man's desire, and vowed to herself, No I will *not*" (17). This is a thrilling opportunity, and her "seemingly impulsive decision to go with him" is not impulsive at all (54).

Just as Kelly is not merely a victim, so the Senator is no mere monster or caricature. His age, experience, and status are very different from hers, but his nature and needs are not. She wants to live to the full because she is young and excited by the glamour, while he, full of "impatient exuberance," wants to live while he still can (3). To Kelly he is "one of the immune," and has chosen *her*. "*He*, one of the powerful adults of the world, manly man, U.S. Senator, a famous face and a tangled history, empowered to not merely endure history but to guide it, control it, manipulate it to his own ends" (61). Two consecutive sentences, one long one short, define the Senator's driving forces.

> The Senator was what is known as an aggressive driver and his adversary was the road, the gathering dusk, the distance between himself and his destination, and the rapidly shrinking quantity of time he had to get to that destination, pressing down hard and petulant on the gas pedal bringing the car's speed up to forty miles an hour, and then hitting the brakes going into a turn, and then pressing down hard on the gas pedal again so that the car's tires protested faintly spinning before taking hold in the sandy glutinous soil, and then hitting the brakes again. The giddy-rocking motion of the car was like hiccups, or copulation. (16)

This is the Senator's whole life. Full of "reckless exuberance," he is egotistical, driven, ambitious, and doomed to chase an unreachable goal. He is racing toward oblivion, racing to catch the ferryman, racing against a "rapidly shrinking quantity of time," drunk, randy, and altogether heedless of any perspective beyond his boyish desire for self-gratification. In a sense he is another Felix Stevick, making the road "his adversary," when his only opponents are himself and "the gathering dusk." Unlike Felix, however, the Senator is a father, and a father-figure for Kelly, a man who will "come back to save her" (69). Like her actual father, he is a mixture of protectiveness and control. Artie Kelleher wants to "spare her hurt, harm, any sort of discomfort," but is angry that while "things are going boom . . . boom . . . boom . . . " in his business, he *"can't control"* his family life (23). Since birth, she has had an eye muscle imbalance, a "defect" known as *"strabismus"* (21), so Artie has had her " 'bad' eye" surgically corrected to ensure that "forever afterward the eye, the eyes, the girl, were, as all outer signs indicated, normal" (24).

In the end, *Black Water* is about not just control but self-control. But in being so, it is also about a national culture. Kelly and the Senator may be remarkably alike in their lonely desire to be loved, and the snatch of "Eleanor Rigby" on the car radio entirely appropriate. But the Senator's emotional immaturity—as opposed to Kelly's age-related immaturity—is culturally endorsed. *"The way you make your life, the love you put into it—that's God,"* says Kelly's much-loved, departed, and evidently pragmatic Grandpa Ross (73). It is not what you say or how you look, but how you act. *Black Water*'s ending provides a perspective on Kelly that the self-absorbed politician never considers: Kelly as a fragile human being, a child, a daughter, someone particularly vulnerable to a man in his position. She is "little 'Lizabeth," hoping to be rescued by her father, running "squealing in expectation in joy in her little white anklet socks raising her arms to be lifted high kicking in the air as the black water filled her lungs, and she died" (154). The Senator's failures of responsibility and of imagination become abundantly clear. His excuses to Ray—"the girl was drunk," he says, she "grabbed the wheel" (147)—jar because they are the only part of the novel that Kelly cannot know or even imagine. It is inconceivable that she—as opposed to Oates—would envisage such a betrayal by a man she thinks will save her. But, for that reason, the Senator's impoverished integrity is explicitly confirmed.

Brief as it is, *Black Water* deals with more aspects of American culture—including a detailed discussion of the relative merits of capital punishment—than a first reading suggests. It seems no coincidence, for example, that it anticipated the Clinton-Lewinsky case. "Of all the verbiage produced about l'affaire Lewinsky," wrote Andrew Sullivan at the height of the scandal, "the least persuasive argument is that it has nothing to do with the real America."

Sullivan's view was that most Americans were riveted by this story precisely because it was "about something real." For Sullivan, such scandals raise questions—about whether women are victims or victors "in the aftermath of the feminist revolution," about whether Americans have, or can afford not to have, "clear and coherent moral standards" in public and private life—that "go to the core of the country America is trying to be." "Other countries may be able to live with ignored hypocrisies or quickly ignored double standards," he wrote. But Americans, "blessed (or cursed) with the old puritanical desire to make their public life square with their private convictions, cannot live that way. They worry and pick at their moral and social wounds." The Senator is specifically a divorced liberal, and so not necessarily behaving hypocritically, yet he is clearly on morally dubious ground. For Sullivan, the Lewinsky case was fundamentally about the "war between the counter-culture of the 1960s and the counter-culture of the 1980s." In this struggle, the Right are as determined "to return America to the social and moral order of the past" as baby-boomer liberals are to expose "the hypocrisy of many conservatives, who have actually adopted many post-1960s social practices but refuse to admit it." In the middle stand the American people, "uneasy about the effects of the 1960s" but unwilling to see women back in the kitchen or to have adulterers "branded with the scarlet letter." Oates's strategy, as Gates said, is indeed simple. "Find just where it hurts and then press, *hard*." In *Black Water*, she distills the dilemma of what Sullivan calls "the semi-moral majority." The Senator and Kelly each behave in ways that dramatize the contradictions of their cultural context. *Black Water* captures the conflicts of turn-of-the-millennium America, torn between the straightjacketed, sexist hierarchies of its Puritan origins and the dangerous drift that self-determinist, laissez-faire morality seems to engender. "I have no message, no cause, no backs to scratch," said Oates early in her career. "If there are problems to solve, that is for others."[14] But those dark eyes are very clear about what they see, and what they see in *Black Water* are dark waters indeed.

When Oates commented that critics tend to be "very literal," she may have had in mind some of the responses to *Foxfire*. "My 'Huck Finn' I'd thought it playfully," she has written, "& now people tell me, assure me, it's filled with anger/rage." "*Foxfire*'s intentions are just a shade too conspicuous," writes D. J. Taylor, "its politics too obtrusive, and its readers—a point that nearly always has to be made with a book of this kind—a shade less imperceptive than Oates imagines." The novel is "so contrived and portentous," Michiko Kakutani assures us, "that her reader neither buys her simplistic message nor cares about her fictional creations." Lance Morrow takes a swipe at the novel in a *Time* essay entitled "Are Men Really That Bad?" In it, he suggests that men had become "the Germans of gender." Citing a comment from the novel that relations between the sexes are "a state of undeclared war," Morrow complains, "That's the tone exactly: Men are animals." "Every male who makes an appearance in Oates's 328 pages of female-empowerment myth is a slimy, sweating, smelly brute, a rapist, a feeler, a hitter, a fascist." Even Greg Johnson chimes in. "One of her weakest novels," he writes, "shrill and unconvincing in some of its passages." Yet many of these comments would seem to misjudge the ironic distance between the comic-strip idealism of the girl gang FOXFIRE (throughout, Oates uses uppercase for the gang name) and the mature perspective of Oates's alter-ego, Maddy Wirtz, the fifty-year-old narrator and one-time Foxfire chronicler. The "more complex, ambiguous; less thematic" vision of Oates's mature work is rendered here through a simplified, more direct style, and perhaps a number of critics have mistaken the style for the vision.[15]

Foxfire, suggests Oates, contains a "dialectic between romance and realism." It mimics the romantic discourse of immaturity—complete with a "mythic" heroine and men as comic-strip villains—and the complex realism of maturity that undermines the certainties of the idealistic girl gang.[16] The gang's youthful romanticism has been mistaken for Oates's final perspective, when the key to the novel is Maddy's double-voiced narration. Her strategy—and Oates's—is to present events through the eyes of the adolescent girls and her own younger self, and only then to pull back and present her mature perspective. "You can see how I am not a practiced writer," says Maddy, "not leading this material but led by it."[17] But this inexperienced writer turns out to be an experienced human being. While Foxfire as a gang "NEVER LOOKS BACK" (205), Maddy most assuredly does, and with a different perspective than she finds in her adolescent notebook, which contains, she discovers, "little evidence of adults" (208).

Maddy is now an astronomer's assistant. She is also, in all but name, a philosophical pragmatist in line with her novelist creator, whom she is, says Oates, "very much like."[18] "Human motives have come to interest me less, through the years, than human actions, *being,*" she writes. "The stars have no motives after all, even their death-plunges are pure, in the service of *being.*" Human motives differ little. What matters is what people *do.* Maddy's interest is in the subtleties and uncertainties of the relationship between word and action, indeed of perception and existence. As a student of the stars, she is aware that even they—so seemingly fixed and permanent—are not "even there." "The heavenly light you admire is fossil-light, it's the unfathomable distant past you gaze into, stars long extinct." Even time is more complex that we feel it to be. The sun "is eight minutes into the past," she notes. "*Look-back time* it's called." Maddy is only now able to assemble the Foxfire confessions because she has "the proper telescopic instrument for examining *look-back time*" (327). She has a perspective on events that at one time—like the reader in the process of reading—she could only view close up. This is why Maddy's age is revealed late in the novel. Oates once said of Saul Bellow's *Mr. Sammler's Planet* that the ending "forces us to immediately reread the entire novel, because we have been *altered in the process of reading it,* and are now, at its conclusion, ready to begin." The same can be said of *Foxfire.* Oates's strategy mimics life experience. As she did with Marya Knauer, the novelist encourages romantic identification with the girl gang. Only then does she undo us by drawing back to show the girls' actions from a broader perspective. In part the novel celebrates youthful idealism—and on this level Legs is a marvelous creation—but it becomes a critique of the pitfalls of simplistic visions. In other words, abstractions, once translated into actions, look very different. The practical effect of a belief, to use pragmatist terminology, is "its sole significance."[19] "Once you know to look with informed eyes," says Maddy, "you can never again see the WORLD like a palpable block or shape possessed of permanent dimensions, you can see only its swift shadowy MOTION" (221). Unlike the schematic vision of the gang members—immured forever in Maddy's memory of youth—Maddy's own vision has matured. The closer she came to adulthood, she says, the more aware she became of "an adult's increased sense of ambiguity, and irony, and self-doubt" and "the messier the entries in the notebook" (179).

Even the act of confession, then, is problematic, let alone the truth about whether "MEN ARE THE ENEMY" (246). "The *paradox of chronology* is hateful," admits Maddy, "because you are always obliged to seek out earlier causes than what's at hand" (196). The more straightforward Maddy tries to be, the more obvious the complexities of perception. The confession mode is self-consciously created as a simplistic construct rendered problematic by Maddy's complex awareness. Her essential lesson—learned and then taught—is that simple idealism turns out to have complex results. Foxfire's initial impulse is straightforward and entirely explicable. They live in a harsh world where many men systematically abuse women. From this initial perspective, Legs is certainly "heroic," but in the same way that Batman or Robin Hood are heroic. Like her mythic male counterparts, she embodies the idealistic impulse, the desire for JUSTICE against EVIL. The fact that injustice exists—in class, monetary, and gender terms—is not in question. But while, to paraphrase a Don Williams song, the likes of Robin Hood may remain alive in Hollywood, they are best left on the screen.

However straightforward the gang's motives, their actions have complex results. Legs's hero, Father Theriault, is wrong that "no individual can remedy injustice"; sometimes an individual *can* remedy injustice in immediate terms (202). But he is right that an individual cannot remedy injustice per se—cannot eradicate it from society—as Foxfire attempts. Legs can be a heroine to individuals—and Maddy, of course, admires her—but the naivety of her actions is underscored by the fact that nothing she does is enough, so the gang's activities escalate. Taking the law into their hands, they set fire to a house and tavern in which a male gang are raping a "dwarf woman" named Yetta (197). Presumably, the fire kills the victim as well as the victimizers. "The fox's fire burns," notes Brenda Daly; "in this instance, words of protest have proved to be useless."[20] But this seems an insufficient response to the novel's most disturbing episode. Set beside the graphic description of "the animal-men" entering the room, one by one to mount "the woman-that's-a-body," there is the fact that captors and captive are "never actually glimpsed" by Maddy, so she cannot verify the situation (196). Then there is the moral ambiguity of Legs's actions. Even if the men are as bad as the satanic cult who abuse Ingrid Boone in *Man Crazy*, Oates is hardly suggesting we burn the Enemy, and anyone else besides. The episode is one of many reminders that incidents in life, and appropriate responses, are rarely clear-cut.

Maddy revisits Rutherford Hayes Elementary School and discovers that things are even worse than in her day. The playground is littered with glass and debris and "everywhere on walls, sidewalks, even trees" are "ugly lurid words FUCK SHIT COCKSUCKER NIGGER and crude obscene drawings" that efface the "FOXFIRE proverbs and torches almost completely" (214). The anger that created Foxfire is the same anger vented by succeeding generations of children. But the words on the school wall shows that the comic-strip morality at the heart of any kind of doctrinaire tribalism can turn swiftly into bigotry. Sexism and racism both derive from the need to vent anger for personal experience onto a whole category of people. They turn something complex into something abstract. Maddy uses the analogy of the flattened corpse of a squirrel or rat, "its once-living body pounded into the pavement till at last it was pounded flat as a piece of cardboard." "That's how a thing starts out *real* then ends up just an *idea*," she says (215). Similarly, the gang's anger becomes dogma. Like Xavier Kilgarvan, Marya Knauer, and Felix Stevick, the Enemy they envisage is partly constructed in their minds. The gang's activities escalate from the humiliations of Lloyd Buttinger and Wimpy Wirtz to burning the house and tavern to "hooking" for money to beating of a man they think is Chick Mallick, the Florida Killer to kidnapping and shooting Whitney Kellogg (239). Legs's anger at her father eventually becomes anger at MEN, until the gang's charismatic leader hits on the "FINAL SOLUTION" (248). The idealistic heroines intent on righting the Enemy's wrongs have become thugs in their own right.

Lloyd Buttinger, who victimizes Rita in class, is portrayed—and remembered from Maddy's journal—as a pitiable, cruel, stupid man. But the same could be said of a Batman Baddy. They humiliate and probably destroy him, which is no less than a Batman Baddy deserves. But while the reader's sympathies are *meant* to be with the girl gang here, we might reflect, given Maddy's later questions about the fallibility of memory, that Buttinger's status as a villain rests on Maddy's juvenile perceptions, filtered through memory. Perverse behavior exists, but "you are always obliged to seek out earlier causes than what's at hand." Perhaps Buttinger was himself the butt of bullying, and so takes it out on WOMAN THE ENEMY. The point is that Oates creates him as a comic-strip villain, with no personal history, because that is the kind of figure Foxfire's collective imagination targets. The members of Foxfire are much more sympathetically drawn than are the Hell's Angels of *Man Crazy*, but their sorority mentality is certainly akin to the fraternity mentality of that particularly VILE GANG. In Oates's own experience, any such grouping, when shaped by notions of exclusivity, is a breeding ground for bigotry. Of her own sorority experience, she has spoken of "the racial and religious bigotry; the asininity of 'secret' ceremonies" and "the craven worship of conformity." Indeed, a more recent novel, *I'll Take You There*, preceded by a brief *New Yorker* essay, "Bound," explicitly draws on her experience of the bigotry of her particular "sacred sisterhood."[21] While in *Foxfire* the issues are implicit, the gang is a sorority in all but name. Each member wears a cross, each makes a pledge to *"consecrate"* themselves to their *"sisters,"* and never, among other things, *"to reveal FOXFIRE secrets"* (39–41). This is the stuff of Tom Sawyer's band of robbers, and Maddy's eventual expulsion and decision to reveal the gang's secret puts her in the position of Huck watching Tom's Phelps's Farm games. Maddy has traveled the river of time, and some of Foxfire's antics look childish indeed.

Even as they epitomize our impulse to create protective groups, they also exemplify the itch to exclude. *"This was a matter of life and death and at such extremities all women are sisters,"* says Maddy about Agnes's sister, beaten up by her husband (222). But evidently only if they are WHITE. Within a page, "a black girl named Irene, a friend of Legs' from work," is rejected because of race (223), as is another of Legs's BLACK friends, Marigold, from the correctional center. Legs and Maddy argue for the girls, but are outvoted. They have been defeated by their own paradoxical logic.

The kidnapping of Whitney Kellogg exposes Foxfire's faulty logic further. Sexual and racial bigotry is joined by class bigotry. "My theory is, a serious kidnapper must be a person of integrity," says Legs (252). But the theory is not much use in practice. The victim and his family refuse to be compliant abstractions. When Legs infiltrates their lives, she assumes them to be simply "rich man's wife, rich man's daughter. Class enemies" (263). She is not entirely wrong. Marianne's sheltered upbringing has left her naïve. Whitney is a sexist, anti-Semitic bigot who blames "Communists," "Socialists, pinkos, whatever ... " for "undermining" society, and believes that "that Jew-lover 'F.D.R.' " started it all (284). "And you, Veronica?" he says. "What do you hope to do?—I mean, between now and—getting married?" "Licking his pulpy lips" at the sight of Violet, he seems ripe for the slaughter (286). But while Legs has sought to meet him in order to "know the Enemy," she discovers not an abstract enemy but a human being: faults and virtues mix together (268). The bigot also turns out to be "truly *fatherly*" (282). "Both Margaret Sadovsky and Veronica Mason bite their lips in confused envy for of course *they're* fatherless" (283). "*I guess I like them, even him,*" says Violet, even though she knows "*he's evil 'cause of he's rich and a capitalist and exploiting and all that*" (287). In fact, Marianne and Margaret—as Legs is known to them—are like twins brought up on opposite sides of the track. They are doppelgängers whose "names sound alike" (174). They have simply had different experiences. As for Whitney, his bigotry derives from the same stereotyping as the gang members indulge in. The kidnapping itself turns out to be anything but abstract. He stubbornly refuses to play his part, and they have to "cart away his piss, his meagre watery shit" (302), "tug out the spittle-drenched gag," and endure "an odor as of rancid onions rising from his armpits" (305). This is a far cry, of course, from the simple rope binding that takes place in Gotham City or Sherwood Forest.

So realism defeats romance. Maddy's experience of being a gang member exhilarates her, but, even before the kidnapping, she has gradually detached herself. "FOXFIRE was my heart," she says, "and I have had to surrender my heart" (251). *"You saved my life,"* writes Maddy, of Legs, after the Chick Mallick episode, *"but I was afraid of you having seen you hit him the way you did."* It is, she observes, *"like Uncle Wimpy years ago. Except this time it's serious"* (253). Legitimate anger has escalated into violence and cruelty, laced with dogma and bigotry. It happens in terms of gender, race, and class, and all arises out of a sense of injustice, a bitterness as sympathetically portrayed as Marya's or Iris's. So emotional sympathy is tempered—for the mature Maddy, and for Oates—by intellectual realism. In the end, Legs is heroic in strictly mythical terms. With "almost the body of a young man," she is manlike, too, in her creation of the gang (191). She usurps the role of the mythic male hero to fight comic-strip baddies no less cartoonlike than the Joker and Penguin or King John and the Sheriff of Nottingham. Her cartoon enemies, like Buttinger and Wimpy (the name of Popeye's enemy, the curse of Olive Oyl) are not examples of Oates relegating men to "the Germans of gender." They are a reminder that Legs, so convincingly rendered as a "real" girl worthy of Maddy's love, has become a fantasy figure belonging to Maddy's nostalgic memories of the clear-cut emotions and responses of youth.

Foxfire's apparent simplicity, then, is deceptive. A mature work about maturity, it probably needs rereading, rather than just reading, and not least because it is about rereading primary experiences. Maddy's older perspective—necessarily withheld so that the reader sees the world through the girls' eyes—is crucial to its strategy. It celebrates youthful idealism even as it critiques the simplicity of outlook that characterizes immaturity (whatever the age). The final lines emphasize the elegiac, celebratory element. "Like a flame is real enough, isn't it, while it's burning?—even if there's a time it goes out?" (328). But it is this very perspective, this refusal to countenance any form of transcendent meaning, this awe at our evident insignificance both in the spatial reality of the universe and the temporal reality of humanity's tiny place in history, that accounts for Maddy's assessment. Actions rather than motives give shape and meaning, for good or bad, to the world. *Foxfire* shows how initial impulses toward justice can lead to bigotry and dogma if we lose sight of the subtleties of human relationships. But it explores these subtleties by dramatizing the simplistic perspective of the teenage gang. Far from being a straightforward, even angry, narrative, it is antisystem; antitheory; anticategory, and ultimately, like Maddy, for all its sympathies toward the girl gang, elegiac about the innocence of such concepts as those held by Foxfire. It sympathizes with the romance of Foxfire, but tempers this with realism about where such emotional responses lead.

"His joyless life is best symbolized by a clenched fist, never a relaxed open hand," writes Oates of Thomas Mann's doomed, solitary artist, Aschenbach, of *Death in Venice*. For all his upbeat manner and American "optimism," the same might be said of Corky Corcoran, the hero of *What I Lived For*. Corky's tailspin to destruction, part-willed, seemingly inevitable, is a parable of contemporary America.[22] "An American everyman" (in Johnson's phrase), Corky, for all his wealth and intelligence, lives a life of not-so-quiet desperation. Sexist, alcoholic, middle-aged, and too busy to pause and reflect on what he hopes to achieve, he is, to use Oates's description of the subject matter of our best literature, a "human soul caught in the stampede of time, unable to gauge the profundity of what passes over it."[23] He is admired by his "family especially the older ones" for how he has "raised himself up from practically nothing, how he'd made himself 'Corky Corcoran' the way you'd make yourself an athlete by training, endurance, sheer stubborn inviolable will."[24] Yet his inner world is so claustrophobic, cluttered, and frenzied, and his constant activity so intense, that it is something of a shock to be reminded, here and there, that he is a millionaire with a five-bedroom house. Like Xavier, Corky plays the role of an amateur detective—in his case, to try to discover who killed a girl named Marianne Plummer. But as with *Winterthurn* and *Tone Clusters*, the literal mystery is a side issue. What really interests us is the profound mystery of why Corky lives as he does. Where Thoreau sought "to spend one day as deliberately as nature," Corky lives his final days bobbing about alienated from his environment and as unable to control anything as a cork in an ocean.[25] The most haphazard of detectives, he has no real chance of discovering what, if any, solutions there are to the mysteries of life. His creed, if anything, is "complicate, complicate." Like Xavier, Marya, and Felix, he is his own opponent. Indeed, he is finally shot with his own gun. "Suicide can be murder," he says. "If you're forced into it. Like murder, sometimes, is suicide. Asking for it" (361). His death, like his father's it turns out, is self-willed, not just because he throws himself into the path of the bullets that his step-daughter, Thalia, fires at Corky's political associate Vic Slattery but because the way he has lived his life is a slow suicide.

Corky does have an opponent in addition to himself: Time. "*Never race a train,*" he has been told (9). So he races against time, and can never catch up— until finally he discovers that time has been racing *at* him, and hits him full on. In this, he resembles not only Ivan Illych but also the Senator, and *What I Lived*

For is *Black Water* writ large. The tragicomic irony of Corky's story is that, for all his frenzied activity, he is always late. "A man in a hurry, a man with appointments," he can never catch up with himself (145). The frenetic pace of his cluttered, racing mind is wholly in contrast to Thoreau's deliberate musings, as set out in the second chapter of *Walden*, "Where I Lived, and What I Lived For." Rather, Corky's story is the territory of John Updike's *Rabbit at Rest* or even Arthur Miller's *Death of a Salesman,* both of which are works Oates wrote essays on in the 1990s, collected in *Where I've Been, and Where I'm Going*. Indeed, Corky's inner turmoil perhaps resembles no one's so much as that of that archetypal male American of an earlier era, described by Oates as "our quintessential American tragic hero, our domestic Lear, spiraling toward suicide as toward an act of selfless grace."[26] Of course, there are some crucial differences, one of which is that Corky is rich. Yet like Willy Loman, he is morally and spiritually impoverished, and like Willy (and so many Oates heroes and heroines), he is the egotistical hero of his own narrative. "Corky's stories have one thing in common, of course: Corky's at the center. He's the hero, or he's the jerk you have to love. He's the victim, or the worm-that-turns, or the guy-who-loses-his-temper, or the dumb-fuck who wins in the end. He's the sneaky counter-puncher. He's the mastermind. He's the man with the aces, the royal flush. He's—who? *Corky Corcoran!*" (68).

Where Willy Loman famously has to break his neck "to see a star in this yard," Corky gazes wistfully at the sky, which seems so clear and blue compared with the polluted frenzy of his crowded hours.[27] "Strange how by day sometimes a brittle shell of moon, luminescent as aged, perforated bone, is visible in the sky," he thinks. "Riding the crest of clouds fleeting and insubstantial as human thought" (141). As such comments show, Corky has a perspective—or at least a language—that we never hear from Willy. The latter's complaint about half-hidden stars develops, with Corky, into full awareness that his actions, measured against the world and the universe, are ludicrous, and that his heroic posture is pathetic. He reads, in paperbacks like *The Universe and You*, "how iron dust from the farthest stars exploded in the Big Bang millennia ago inhabits our bones. The very marrow" (143). He "figures you can't know too much about where you came from or where you're going" (187). But for all his moments of awareness, he cannot control his life or get it into focus. He feels perpetually "outside of where he wants to be" and wondering "what his life is coming to" (342).

Corky's soliloquies lead nowhere. "What goes around comes around except sometimes not," he tries. "Sometimes the turning upon itself is endless, futile. Around and around and around, the same questions, unanswered. And not that they are unanswerable, either: for somebody knows, or knew: but it's information you can't get hold of. You live with the questions, eventually you die with them, is that it?" (362). Like the characters in *Tone Clusters*, there is an appalling mismatch between the grand philosophical questions and Corky's actual experience of everyday life, in all its chaotic unmanageability. Nor, for all his awareness, can Corky control his basic instincts. The same man who ponders the universe, the next moment decides life is about "fucking, either you are, or you aren't. Bottom line" (296). As much the epitome of Schopenhauerean Will as Felix Stevick, he thinks "life is fuck or be fucked, eat or be eaten" and "he's hungry" (297). A slave to his desires, temper, appetites, prejudices, Corky's final three days, no doubt like much of his previous forty-three years, is a constant battle between these basic impulses and some hazy awareness that his life is running away from him. He is determined to remain "upbeat," to be optimistic, to be American, even as he suspects the futility of his wasted energy. But although he sporadically tries to step back to think what it is all for, or even what his life *is*, he is faced with the eternal silence of infinite spaces and has no choice but to plunge on. "Corky, what *is* your life?" Thalia asks. "My—what?" says Corky (298).

Corky wants above all to be loved, or noticed, or somehow redeemed. He wants to *belong*. He dreams of "finding himself in a public place naked, and everybody staring at him, laughing and edging away" (374). The fear of being ousted haunts him. *"They've dropped me from the head table,"* he thinks, arriving to make a speech at a fund-raising event the night he is shot (589). He is driven by a need to *be* somebody, constantly imagining himself in others' eyes, redefining himself to try to control his life. That need to be loved stems, in part, from the loss of his parents. He feels guilt at never having told his mother how he loved her and for failing to "identify his father's murderers with a simple lie—he who, all the years of his life afterward, would be capable of any kind of bullshit when it suited him" (519). But Corky is spiritually orphaned, too. He has no overarching vision that will clarify his life, no inner code, no devotion to a family, or a craft, and therefore a wholly confused sense of whatever he *is* living for. Solitary, parentless, godless, lacking discipline or more than token attempts at integrity, he seeks redemption, like the far less likeable Felix, through self-punishment. "Maybe that's all we want," he muses. "Somebody to hit us hard enough, our guilt's absolved" (425). Judgment would give a sense of order or meaning to his actions and to his world. "What goes around comes around" may be true in the world of boxing, but in life you may not even have that. A belief, too doggedly held, can be as dangerous—to oneself or others—as no belief. Doomed to bob in his oceanic chaos, Corky is—in another of the novel's metaphors—"a rat in a maze," but he has built the maze himself. A driver, too, who has turned himself into a "driven man" (280), he thinks "the one place a man's got to be in control for Christ's sweet sake is his car" (38). But while in *Black Water* and *Foxfire*, the drivers crash, Corky can go only where the road leads, and *What I Lived For* is one big traffic jam.

So on one level, *What I Lived For* is about how-not-to-live. As such, like *Black Water* and *Foxfire*, it is about degrees of perception and misperception and so, ultimately, about degrees of maturity. Seeing, at the age of eleven, his father die, Corky remains that eleven-year-old child. When he spots that his girlfriend Charlotte's new man, Gavin Pierson, is also reading *A Brief History of Time*, he "checks Gavin's bookmark and sees he's gotten to page eighty. He's sure *he's* gotten further" (429). His petty competitiveness, resentments, desire for gratification—all this is essentially childish. His form of sexism is not so much malicious as immature. His derogatory exclamations about women display his anger, his bitterness, more than actual misogyny. "He doesn't hate women," Oates has said, in response to the idea that Corky is a misogynist. "He loves them." "Certain women have had power over him and when he gets the chance to have power over a woman, he takes it."[28] This is much like Foxfire in a mirror. Specific women become generalized as WOMAN. WOMAN IS THE ENEMY is his response to a sense of grievance.

Corky is a representative American man tied to his era in a fast-changing world, and not least in terms of gender roles. His sense of racing time also has to do with his race against the tide of history (the Dostoyevskian shadow who tracks him to the end is called Teague, or Tyde). Time in *What I Lived For* is both historical and immediate. It is the day draining away from him, but also the era he once knew. "Once his America's gone, it's gone" (181). In Corky's generation, "the male's the initiator, the male's dominant, the male's *it*" (355). He is not, then, a man likely to adapt to the fluidity of a gender democracy. Kiki Zaller's deliberate sexual humiliation of him leaves "Doggy-Corky" skulking away with "his tail between his legs," feeling that he will never be the same man again (359).

Despite all this, Corky is an engaging character. As with the girls in *Foxfire*, we experience life from his perspective. We first see him as that eleven-year-old hearing the gunshots that kill his father. But he is also engaging because, boy that he may remain in some ways, his heart is often in the right place. His smile has brightened his girlfriend Charlotte's life. He cares about his stepdaughter, Thalia, albeit in a manner confused with sexual feeling. He tries to right events, even if throwing himself in the path of bullets meant for Slattery is a logical, suicidal end. There is some kind of redemption in his attempt to prevent Thalia perpetuating the vicious cycle of anger and revenge that has poisoned his own life since his father's murder. "I know you are a good man and God resides in your heart despite you," Thalia says on his answer-phone (517). His appalling traits vie with positive impulses. Nowhere are his contradictions more comically and poignantly drawn than in his racial attitudes. One moment he feels black himself because the Irish were once "considered like Negroes" (17). The next moment the black proprietor who refuses to sell him a gun is "a stunted little spade" (380).

To the extent that he is an American archetype, the novel might be read as "a powerful indictment of American culture."[29] Perhaps the novel *is* about what *not* to live for, and Oates a secular American moralist, but given Corky's manic energy it is not at all clear how he might have lived differently, or what he might have lived for. He is an extraordinarily "living" being, definable only by those who—in the spirit of *Foxfire*—might choose to label him as a MISOGYNIST, CHAUVINIST, ENEMY, MICK, MAN (MALE) CHARACTER, or any other abstraction. As for Corky himself, his constant attempts at self-definition parallel the unfocused frenzy of his life. He is a man with a thirst that grows in intensity even as it is "seemingly satisfied" (31). He is a man happiest with "pure sensation" (62). "He's forty-three years old and divorced and no kid or kids and no woman he loves or can trust" (127). "He's a man among men in the money world" (147). "Where he is he doesn't know, or why, or where he's going, but shit, he *is* here" (147). He's a man whose emotions are sometimes "so transparent, he can read them himself" (157). "He's a man who loves women and never hurts a woman deliberately" (179). "He's getting to an age he thought he'd never get to be" (218). "He's a real man seeming not to be living in his head but living through his body" (232). "He's a guy who tries to play it both ways as long as he can" (282). He's "feeling like he's ready to kick the bucket any hour now" (391). "He's a millionaire with a five-bedroom house in Maiden Vale. Living alone" (392). "He's a guy lives by his watch—Jesus, already 5:57 P.M.?" (397). He's "your basic dumb-fuck" and always lets himself off that way (430). He's a guy who hits women, "but only open-handed, never with fists" (434). He's a guy who knows "the 'past' is flying away from us into space like distant galaxies flying away from one another, all things in the universe flying away from one another after the Big Bang initiated Time," but who cannot do anything about it (440). He's a guy nobody taught "how to grow up," and by the time he does "there's no one *there*" (457). He's a guy whose mind gets blown at the thought that he's alive, but never knows "*what* alive *is*" (477). He's "*so fucking lonely*" (520). He's a guy buys a gun to protect himself then gets shot "from his own gun" (601). "He's going to die never understanding," because "what *is*" passes "so swiftly so irrevocably into what *was*" (604). He's a guy finally dying, "lying for a long time dazed suspended in relief turning over and over in his mind what has happened to him and where he is and by slow degrees feeling stronger, more in control as in fact he hasn't felt for years or possibly in his entire life until now, it takes something like this to make you *think* for Christ's sake, to make you assess your life" (607). But "that little prick Teague, or Tyde," who thinks he has something to talk about if Corky had time, has finally come to get him (607). "He's *Corky Corcoran!*" "Kiss me, America, I'm your boy" (520). Bottom line.

Oates's next-but-one novel, *Man Crazy*, is a slighter work in every sense, but is sandwiched by *We Were the Mulvaneys* and *Broke Heart Blues*, two complex, elegiac explorations of the nuances of maturity. Together with the last novels to be dealt with in this study, *Blonde* and *Middle Age: A Romance*, they show the infinite variety of the mature novelist. *Blonde* in particular pushes the boundaries of even Oates's achievements. It is about that aspect of American culture—and not just American—that fosters the cult of celebrity, not least in the iconic status of the token blonde "princess," with disregard for the personal or cultural consequences of such empty worship. As such it epitomizes Oates's dark eyes on America. Yet *Middle Age: A Romance* seems, in its way, equally significant. Oates's art, even when focused on unpalatable truths, tends toward affirmation. For this reason, *Middle Age: A Romance*, which focuses sharply on how individuals can at least discover a sense of their life's purpose, provides an appropriate end to this study.

"The place where you came from ain't there any more, and where you had in mind to go is cancelled out." So Arnold Friend tells Connie in "Where Are You Going, Where Have You Been?"[30] If all the novels in this final chapter echo that sentiment, the optimism—or meliorism—of *We Were the Mulvaneys* stems from Oates's belief in the capacity of individuals to alter their perspective or the circumstances they find themselves in. Judd Mulvaney, the family's youngest son, has to face the fact that the place where he came from has gone and that, anyway, "the story book house" (words used as the title of the first chapter) was always a communal fiction. But out of the events that led to the premature breakup of the family—specifically his sister Marianne's date rape and his father's subsequent inability to face up to having failed to protect her— Judd determines "to set down *what is truth*."[31] In doing so, he learns something of inestimable value about individual behavior, and not only in family life. "All happy families resemble one another, each unhappy family is unhappy in its own way," runs Tolstoy's opening line in Anna Karenina. The Mulvaneys, with their evolving relationships, separations, reunions, tragedies, and periods of storybook happiness, surely resemble most families in being, as the years pass, neither totally happy nor totally unhappy. But there are degrees of happiness among the individuals, and their best chance of happiness, and in some cases therefore of survival, lies with those able to evolve in the face of time and events. If Oates's view differs from Tolstoy's, the difference is partly cultural. She has no great hope that human tensions will ever change, but she holds the American pragmatist view that individuals can.

"*What is truth?*—Pontius Pilate's question," Judd muses. "And how mysteriously Jesus answered him—*Everyone that is of the truth heareth my voice.*" "Once I thought I understood this exchange but no longer" (14). The concept of truth that Judd comes up with, however, is not simply the one relative, dialogic truth—the certainty that there is no certainty—traditionally associated with the novel form, but something more definable. Truth turns out to be ever shifting, but not unfathomable. It depends on each individual's attitude toward events. The family members' reactions to a given truth (centrally, Marianne's date rape and the fact that she is then forced to live away from the family) in turn produces further truths that must themselves be dealt with in a never-ending sequence. There is no truth that does not itself have an overlay of human perception that then creates a further truth. There is no precise opposition between the idea of fabrication (as in storybook families) and the quality of truth. The individual helps to create truth, and so lives are made and destroyed by the interaction of the world and the mind. Truth, like personality or families, or indeed the family business, Mulvaney Roofing, is an active thing that *evolves* from experience to experience like a form of imbrication.

Judd's discovery of the nature of truth, in other words, is a conversion to the pragmatist's vision. "Philosophy is out of touch with real life, for which it substitutes abstractions," wrote James. "The real world is various, tangible, painful." Schopenhauer's "great popular success," he went on, was "due to the fact that, first among philosophers," he wrote the "truth about the ills of life," and James, with rather more optimism than Schopenhauer about how we might negotiate those ills, sought to do the same. Likewise, Judd's pragmatic approach, both in the telling of his family's story and in examining each individual's actions, is based on the importance of experience as the shaper and reshaper of truth. "Experience merely as such doesn't come ticketed and labelled," argued James. "We first have to discover what it is." Since for James "experience is flux" and "the essence of life is its continuously changing character," so truth, too, is ever shifting even though it can be pinned down for a given person at a given moment ("What works is true and represents a reality, for the individual for whom it works"). Crucially, our perspective therefore shapes both the present truth and future ones, for ourselves and for others. "Truth *happens* to an idea. It *becomes* true, is *made* true by events." We all "plunge forward into the field of fresh experience with the beliefs our ancestors and we have made already; these determine what we notice; what we notice determines what we do; what we do again determines what we experience; so from one thing to another, altho' the stubborn fact remains that there is a sensible flux, what is *true of it* seems from first to last to be largely a matter of our own creation." For James, as for Judd, then, "discarnate truth is static, impotent, and relatively spectral." What matters is "the truth that energizes and does battle." James's truth, for Judd, is the truth about his family.[32]

Judd's opening comments about discovering the nature of truth, and his later comments about his identity, bear directly on his narrative. "The evolving of consciousness" is not just the stuff of creativity but of life itself, of survival. In the face of one devastating truth, "not just that I would lose the people I loved, but that they would lose me," he is entirely concerned with getting to understand his family and why things have gone as they have (138). He begins—in the chapter "Family Pictures"—with a static vision: an idyllic picture of the life of a Happy Family. High Point Farm is described at the high point of the family's happiness. In this storybook house, the Mulvaneys are a coherent family entity with a seemingly stable identity. They are "the Mulvaneys of High Point Farm" (8). But even as Judd is writing, we are aware that in fact they *were* the Mulvaneys. The storybook house is "blurred at the edges as in a dream where our ever-collapsing barbed wire fences trailed off into scrubby, hilly, uncultivated land." And, of course, the Mulvaneys of High Point Farm are now "one of those haunting tantalizing dreams that seem so vivid, so real, until you look closely, try to *see*—and they begin to fade, like smoke." Getting them "into focus requires effort, like getting a dream into focus and keeping it there" (8).

"What is family, after all," asks Judd, "except memories?" (4). "*A family is a four-dimensional structure,*" to quote from "The Brothers," a story that Oates published a year earlier, "*one plane of which is Time.*"[33] But truth and transience are not oppositions. The Mulvaneys still exist for Judd, even if the cast has evolved. They are *not* mere memories, but like all human relations a tangible set of facts in constant transition. The illusion is that the family ever existed in some static storybook idyll, impervious to the invasions of time and events. "A storybook house, you're thinking, yes?" writes Judd. "Must be, storybook people live here" (12). But of course it is neither a storybook house nor a storybook family, at least in any conventional, realist sense: neither a Happy Family nor an Unhappy Family. Such a concept is itself a fiction since nothing remains one thing, but is constantly subject to time and perception. Near the end of the novel, Judd puts the events down as "just something that happened." "It's just the way families are, sometimes," he says. "A thing goes wrong," the "years pass and—no one knows how to fix it" (428). But the story he actually tells shows that, while things may just happen to the family, each family member's reaction affects subsequent events. We are engaged, as individuals, in creating the facts of our situation.

Looked at with the kind of objectivity no one in his position could be expected to have, it is the father, Michael Mulvaney Sr., not the teenage rapist, Zachary Lundt, who nearly destroys the family. Michael Senior's reaction to what happens to Marianne compounds the situation and creates new truths for the family to deal with. Like Judd, he had built himself a "sturdy personality," but in his case based on being the kind of father his own father failed to be. "Being angry, resentful—that's easier, somehow," says Judd to the middle brother, Patrick, near the end. "To a degree," Patrick replies (452). In fact, Michael Senior's anger, frustration, and resentment at his inability to be that static vision of a FATHER leads him "to dismantle it" with nothing in its place (452). He banishes Marianne just as his own father once banished him, gets banned from the Mount Ephraim Country Club for insulting members, and dies an alcoholic. "He'd had to compete with his brothers for their father's approval—his 'love,'" surmises Judd (31). A quarrel had resulted in his banishment, and as a "disowned son" he had therefore "reimagined himself as a small-town American businessman who owned property, had money and influence, was 'known' and 'liked' and 'respected' in his community" (101). His treatment of Marianne repeats his own father's treatment of him, but it does so, ironically, because his concept of fatherhood led him to a static definition directly opposed to his own father's neglect.

Another irony is that the rapist Zachary's attitude toward Marianne barely differs from her father's own attitude toward girls in his youth. "If anybody's treating a girl or a woman rudely in your presence," Michael Senior tells his eldest son, Michael Junior, "*you* protect her" (95). Yet in his own youth, his attitude toward women was "predatory" and based on a vague grudge he held against his sisters, "against his mother about whom he'd never speak," and against college girls, whom he resented "almost as much, and as unfairly, as he resented college boys." Such resentment meant that he would "just take and enjoy" without regret (126). In Judd's analysis, then, his father in youth might easily have *been* a Zachary Lundt. All his life, he has reacted to events and experiences by taking the "easier" option of being resentful. His reaction to his daughter's fate is entirely in keeping with the character he has constructed for himself. Hence his "sinking look" when he learns what has happened to Marianne: "he was a man, he knew" (133).

The Mulvaney father's self-destruction, then, is not just to do with the truth that happens to his idea, but with his failure to face the new facts that arise out of his attitude. His static belief determines what he notices; what he notices determines what he does; what he does determines what he experiences. Being angry may be easier, but it is also self-destructive. His view of life becomes solipsistic, paranoid, and embittered. He feels "cheated of the business he'd spent a lifetime building up," cheated of his farm and family, "sucked dry and tossed down like a husk. His enemies ganging together against him, bringing him to ruin" (385). But while this response leaves his "enemies" untouched, it destroys him and nearly his family. In his wife Corinne's vivid analogy, he is like a worker she has read about, "trapped in hardening concrete that squeezed him to death" (378). The more his ideal of himself and his family harden, the more his mind is "squeezed," and vice versa. His death dream of being on a white horse, surrounded by his children, "*born into the world to be father of those children,*" is that same fatherhood ideal taken to romantic extreme (397). In his determination to be an ideal father, when they most need him he ends up the very opposite. The nature of a truth depends on an individual's perspective on it, which in turn creates another truth. Michael Mulvaney Sr. allows isolated truths of given moments to dictate the behavior of a lifetime. Like Persia Courtney, and unlike Marya and Felix, he does not live to get another chance.

In contrast, Corinne Mulvaney's very different vision of life eventually reunites the rest of the family. Whether or not religion is the "comforting fantasy" that Patrick sees it as, his mother's faith reaps just as tangible results as her husband's bitterness (414). It enables her to strive for both the reunion of the family and finally a life of her own. Her conviction of providence gives her strength not only to defend her husband, where "another wife might have screamed *Bankrupt . . . Failure . . . Impotent . . .* ," but to reunite a family split apart by his demons (387). Her stance, moreover, casts light on her sons' failings as much as her husband's. Just as Michael Senior's determination to be a better father than his own ironically leads him to repeat the act of banishing one of his children, so Judd himself responds to his father's treatment of Corinne by reenacting the war between his father and grandfather. "You don't know what your story is going to be until looking back," he says (381). "We live forward, we understand backward."³⁴ The act of telling his account alters his perspective and leads to his own "hard reckoning" of how he, too, left his mother when she needed him (355). Whereas Corinne's attitude reaps positive results, Judd finally sees that his own reaction—dismissing his father as a drunk who *"doesn't give a shit"* (368) and vowing "never again" to live "under the same roof"—compounds his mother's problems (377).

What is so of Judd is also true of Michael Junior—also known as Mike "Mule" Mulvaney—and Patrick, or "Pinch." In Judd's view, Mike broke from the family out of shame for what happened to Marianne because it meant that he "no longer counted for much in certain quarters of Mt. Ephraim" (190). Mike's view of truth is that "you always know more than you say," so nearly every statement "is a lie" (96). Since he therefore assumes personal truth to be all but impossible, he relieves himself of the burden of individual responsibility by becoming a U.S. marine—because a Marine (Oates's uppercase) simply does "what his superior officer tells him to do" (392). Patrick, a "self-declared loner" who has to experiment with being "normal" (34), pursues an academic career and an independence of mind devoted to scientific truth, but "the haughty Pinch-style" blinds him to emotional truths (40). He cultivates a cold, analytical approach to protect himself from emotional vulnerability. But the "peripheral vision in his left eye" suggests his distorted perspective (211). When he learns about Marianne's rape, he escapes to Cornell, "proud of keeping the Mulvaneys at a distance" (208). Disgusted to discover that Marianne has not been invited home for Christmas, he refuses to come home himself. No less than his brother and father, then, he retreats to a place where he is "not responsible" and can forget about trying to keep up some "model family life" (219).

The particular irony of Patrick's behavior is that, as a scientist and something of an outsider, he has a sophisticated understanding of human perception. Observing his family with a scientist's eye, he sees that his father has "banished Marianne from the household and from his life so that he could banish her from his thoughts" (225). But Patrick's recognition of "hard" truth is one thing, while experience—and the malleability of experiential truth—is quite another. When he eventually rejects escapism and coerces Judd into bringing Zachary to "justice," like Legs in *Foxfire* he kidnaps his enemy (in Oates's text, his Enemy) only to discover the difference between theory and event. The cunning Zachary Lundt of his imagination turns out to be a "whimpering boy who'd wet his jeans" (297). Any catharsis is internal. Patrick's act of mercy is a refutation of bitterness, and of revenge. *"I could have let you die and I let you live,"* he tells Zachary. Judd's view that Zachary will remember those words all his life may be wishful thinking. All that we know of Zachary suggests otherwise. What matters is that Patrick and Judd can now get on with their lives.

Truth, then, remains a slippery phenomenon. It is experiential, so not necessarily found merely in analytical, objective examination. The latter can itself warp the viewers' perspective, and is highly problematic in any case. (Patrick's very pride in his supposed lack of emotion is undercut by the fact that when a girl calls him *"icy-cold"* he is "thrilled"; that is, he is experiencing a strong emotion [234].) "Truth lives, in fact, for the most part on a credit system," writes James. "Our thoughts and beliefs 'pass' so long as nothing challenges them, just as bank-notes pass so long as nobody refuses them. But this all points to direct face-to-face verifications somewhere, without which the fabric of truth collapses like a financial system with no cash-basis whatever."[35] Truth, then, is inherently personal and social. It lies in the mind's reaction to verifiable facts, because that reaction in turn creates new truths, and new facts. Truth lies not just in Patrick's judgment of his father, nor merely in the circumstances or facts themselves, but in his attitude to his father and to his family, given the facts he sees. Truth lies in his response to the circumstances, rather than in the clarity of his perception.

The subject of "it" herself, the actual physical victim, Marianne, is the silent center around which the other characters are tested. If she is "an emotional self-portrait" in some respects, Oates distances herself from Marianne's passivity. "I'm very sympathetic with the Mulvaney father, but I did identity very closely with Marianne," Oates has said; on the other hand, "Marianne wouldn't write a novel. Marianne would do everything to save her cat, but she wouldn't do anything to save herself." Marianne is initially characterized by inaction. Oates's worksheets stress Marianne's "*minuteness* of vision, experience. Her absolute lack of ambition, self-expectation, anticipation—anything. She does not direct her life, but is only 'directed.'" Her personality, which in her worksheets Oates sees as "the antithesis of her brother Patrick's" is "a Buddhist vision," "the minuteness of the divine."[36] Traumatized by the rape, she feels "*already gone,*" as if only her body remains (83). "Whatever happens to us can't be avoided," wrote Oates in her journal in 1978, "we can only control, to some extent, our attitude toward it."

Marianne cannot prevent what has happened, or her father's reaction, but she refuses to blame. Judd acknowledges the tragedy of what happens between father and daughter and frames it in that most devastating of truths about our relationship with eternity in his description of her watching from her bedroom window as her father drives away: "Smaller and smaller," his taillights are "like rapidly receding red suns (dwarf stars, Patrick called them)" until they disappear. "Strange; how when a light is extinguished," reflects Judd, "it's immediately as if it has never been. Darkness fills in again, complete" (148). An individual's religious faith can positively affect that individual's attitude and actions, but so too can a sense that there is no wider significance to human existence, let alone an afterlife. A sense of human irrelevance to a wider universe can allow us to adapt our sense of what it is we have to accept and what we choose to value. It is not merely the perception but also the perception of the perception that shapes an individual's life. Marrying the vet at the animal sanctuary where she eventually finds work, Marianne becomes a mother herself and triumphs because she refuses to allow "it" to destroy her. In this she is her mother's daughter, and the opposite of her father, who, far from helping his daughter as a victim, takes on the mantle of victim himself.

As Judd, speaking about his own account, suggests, any summing up of *We Were the Mulvaneys* would be misleading since the novel is "much more complicated than that" (355–56). What can be said, however, is that in tone as much as theme it testifies to Oates's broadened vision. There is an absence of bleakness, most particularly evident in the final family reunion. *We Were the Mulvaneys,* like *Foxfire* and *What I Lived For,* shows that maturity depends upon recognizing that one's own mind is integral to shaping and creating the emotional and in some ways the physical facts of one's existence. Rather than returning "again and again to the paradox that one can experience the world only through the self" but "cannot know really, what that 'self' is," the later Oates novels explore this paradox in terms of its practical implications for social and cultural interaction. Her view has never changed that the most profound mystery of human experience is that each of us exists subjectively and knows "the world only through the self," but her attitude toward this observation—at least in terms of the shape of her later novels—certainly has changed.

As John Searle argues, our definition of reality simply has to include subjectivity. "If 'science' is the name of the collection of objective and systematic truths we can state about the world, then the existence of subjectivity is an objective scientific fact like any other," he writes. In James's words, what we say about reality "depends upon the perspective into which we throw it."[37] Categories of happiness or unhappiness or success or failure are self-created. We cannot avoid grief, or love, or hurt, but we can shape our attitude toward both events and emotions. We cannot dictate experience, but we can decide on our attitude toward it, and in doing so we invariably help shape subsequent experiences. The vision presented in *We Were the Mulvaneys* is that truth and meaning lie in individuals' (and by implication a given society's) *perspective* on experience. Perspective shapes action, and therefore creates new facts and new truths. We will the future into being, continually. As Abelove, the leader of Marianne's commune, says (echoing Thoreau), "*past* is not 'urgent' because past cannot be changed, whereas *present* is still in the making" (317).

Much in *We Were the Mulvaneys,* then, echoes William James's arguments about the nature of truth. Of course, James could be wrong. In the 1940s, Bertrand Russell objected that since "James's doctrine is an attempt to build a superstructure of belief upon a foundation of scepticism," "like all such attempts it is dependent on fallacies." "Berkeleian idealism combined with scepticism," argued Russell, "causes him to substitute belief in God for God and to pretend that this will do just as well. But this is only a form of the subjectivist madness which is characteristic of modern philosophy." Russell's complaint, however, calls to mind Rorty's observation that truth is a quality of language. Russell's curt dismissal of James's ideas exemplifies the way an individual's assessment of anything both reflects and perpetuates that individual's worldview. Russell's vocabulary—"doctrine," "superstructure," "foundation"—is the very antithesis of the "subjectivist madness" of James's emphasis on freedom, possibility, and flux. It says more about the cultural differences between James's

American will to believe and Russell's essentially Victorian desire for order and hierarchy than about the relative value of James's stance. "That I exist at this moment—that I am a writer, a woman, a surviving human being—has very little to do with accident," Oates once wrote, "but is a direct, though remote consequence of someone's thinking; *Let us value life. Let us enhance life. Let us imagine a New World, a democracy.*"

Oates's "faith that creates faith" (in James's phrase) is never more explicitly tied to her American pragmatism. If Russell writes as an Old World skeptic critiquing New World optimism, Oates elsewhere does the same in reverse. "It is not true, as Auden so famously stated, that poetry makes nothing happen. On the contrary, poetry, or the poetic imagination, has made everything happen."[38] The proof that "the will to believe" is not merely "subjectivist madness" is evident not only in the existence of the United States, but in the objective fact of Oates's own body of writing. *We Were the Mulvaneys* shows how beliefs, with or without foundation, objectively affect behavior and circumstance. Corinne's possibly naïve faith helps her adapt where her husband's static perspective is destructive. Patrick's assessment of his father, even if correct, adversely affects the situation. You can be right about a perceived truth, but destructive in your attitude to it. You can be misguided, but create truth anyway. Either way, you contribute to the facts of your life and of those around you. Beliefs shape events. Perception of truth is never the end of the matter because your attitude toward it in turn creates new truths to react to. This, the nature of truth as dramatized in *We Were the Mulvaneys,* answers Judd's initial musings and reflects Oates's own evolving—or *imbricated*—vision. Neither happy nor unhappy, most families resemble each other. But "happiness" and "unhappiness" can themselves be perspectives. Judd's attempt to tell the truth about his family is Oates's attempt to tell the truth of human experience. "If you've been a child in any family you've been keeping such an album in memory and conjecture and yearning, and it's a life's work, it may be the great and only work of your life" (6).

The last three major novels of concern to this study, *Broke Heart Blues, Middle Age,* and *Blonde,* are about not just individual but also cultural maturity. Equally, where *Foxfire, What I Lived For,* and *We Were the Mulvaneys* dealt with our tendency to demonize, these next three novels deal with our tendency to deify. All three deal with the phenomenon of fame—two local, one global. That is to say, they deal with our cultural tendency to mythologize anyone— sometimes anything—from media personalities and film stars to enigmatic people in our locale. *Broke Heart Blues,* for instance, centers on a high school peer group who mythologize an outsider named John Reddy Heart. Heart's status as a local icon begins when, at age eleven, he arrives in Willowsville from Las Vegas with his grandfather and exotic mother, the self-styled Dahlia Magdalena Heart. It is consolidated when he becomes a teenage fugitive from justice and is then found guilty of shooting dead one of his mother's lovers. His return to school after prison, and subsequent disappearance, assures his status in absentia, even years later, as the group's "uncrowned king."[39] *Blonde* continues this exploration of fame, but on a global scale. For while it suggests how Marilyn Monroe might have seen her life in retrospect, it clearly alludes to the fate of Diana, Princess of Wales, who died—like Monroe, at the age of thirty-six—immediately prior to Oates's writing of the novel. Yet *Broke Heart Blues* and *Blonde* are both more broadly about the power of myth and metaphor to shape lives and the consequences of too deep an immersion in what amount to individual or collective fictions. Both novels probe the nature of such immersion and the possibilities open to individuals or cultures, if not to escape mythmaking, then to at least develop ironic perspectives on such systems and so discover individual or cultural maturity. *Middle Age,* in contrast, shows more pointedly the value, possibly the necessity, of myth making in helping individuals to shape and reshape their lives. All three novels triumphantly fulfill Dewey's sense of art as a tool to help us clarify contemporary issues and so usefully adjust and readjust our perspectives.

Broke Heart Blues has much in common with *Foxfire.* Again Oates's choice of battleground is American high school and its impact on adult lives. Again the perspective is that of adults looking back, but with adolescent and middle-aged perspectives melded. Again, while the novel may appear to offer no more than a bittersweet, romanticized vision of youth seen from middle age, it is a much subtler critique of the consequences of romanticism. We are initially encouraged to share the collective narrators' general nostalgia. But Oates woos her readers into identifying with flawed viewpoints only to jolt us into reconsidering our initial responses and reevaluating our perspectives. Her strategy is at once deliberately social, but also personal. As one would expect of a writer who sees novels as an evolving of consciousness on the part of both writer and reader, she is clearly aware of the limitations of her own viewpoint.

From at least *Son of the Morning* onward, there tends to be in any given novel a key character with a good right eye and a damaged left eye. To name a few: Nathan Vickery mutilates his eye with a knife. Hiram Bellefleur has a clouded eye. Kelly Kelleher suffers from strabismus. Patrick Mulvaney has weak peripheral vision on the left side. John Reddy Heart has a left eyelid that droops slightly where he was injured at the time of his arrest. In *Blonde,* Warren Pirrig, who with his wife takes in Norma Jeane but is also an abusive, threatening man, has damaged left-eye vision from his days in amateur boxing. In *Middle Age,* Adam Berendt is blind in his (for a change) right eye. A perennial theme in Oates's later novels is that we all have some degree of defective vision. "We are all in the position of Lear," as she puts it, "who, holding absolute authority over his kingdom, had 'but slenderly known himself.'"[40] But art can help improve that vision to our own and others' benefit. No attentive readers can read *Foxfire,* for example, without reflecting on their sense of the balance between idealism and realism when it comes to taking moral action against aggression, oppression, or injustice, or *We Were the Mulvaneys* without reflecting on their attitudes to problems in family life. The same is so of nostalgia for the culture of one's youth in *Broke Heart Blues.*

Instead of Maddy's dual perspective in *Foxfire, Broke Heart Blues* involves a multivoiced narration in the first and last part that focuses on the ongoing emotional significance of Heart for the classmates who never quite knew him. Meanwhile, the middle section provides his adult viewpoint. The multiple perspectives of the first and last sections are a new departure for Oates in the novel form, but an extension of an approach she had experimented with in stories, plays, and poetry. This is not least so in a *Tenderness* poem, "Sexy," which offers an altogether more charged and visceral version of the dangerously enticing outlaw—Eddy S. in the poem—familiar in Oates's novels from Shar to John Reddy Heart himself. Such a narration makes individual voices often impossible to disentangle, although in *Broke Heart Blues* distinctions can be made as the narrative progresses between an overall group mentality and a few figures—including Evangeline Fesnacht, Richard Eickhorn, and Veronica Myers—who think more independently.

The novel opens from the collective perspective of the "rich girls" of Willowsville, insiders who call themselves "good moral Protestant girls," but who have a vivid, collective fantasy about Heart taking their virginity (7). "We were virgin Willowsville girls and would remain virgin Willowsville girls all our lives," they reflect. "Though John Reddy Heart would be our first lover, our virginity would grow back. We were impenetrable. This virginity, like a curse, would persist through our brave, desperate attempts at adulthood. Through our marriages, our plunges into motherhood and adultery. Through separations, 'nervous breakdowns,' divorces, second marriages, further motherhood" (10). We then switch to the collective viewpoint of the "rich men's sons" (14). While the Willowsville girls fantasize about Heart so deeply it almost seems real, any of the boys would have been pleased to "have changed into John Reddy Heart" (15). From then on the perspective, while at times gendered, is often an undifferentiated melee from within the peer group. It is also plain from the start that the overall perspective is distanced by decades from the actual events surrounding their high school days, yet curiously close when it comes to emotional responses to the memories.

This emotional commitment to a fantasy figure and a mythic past becomes one of the novels two key subjects. The other is the human experience of time. *Broke Heart Blues* opens with several references to time, and the final part begins by describing the thirtieth reunion as "a delirious time," "a profound time. A time to celebrate," "a time for hilarity and a time for gratitude. A fun time—but also a tragic time. A time none of us is likely to forget" (307). Indeed, the group's relationship to time informs every aspect of the novel. For instance, part 1 actually takes up considerably more than half the novel, while part 2 is less than half the length of part 1, and part 3 is shorter still. For most of the characters, this equates with their emotional commitment to the times depicted. As the young Richard notes from Pascal in his journal, *"we yearn for eternity—but inhabit only time"* (206). Part 1, which depicts the mythologizing of Heart, represents the sense of time as experienced by the classmates in youth—leisurely time spilt as carelessly, Richard will later put it in a poem, as "gold coins from our pockets" (190). In parts 2 and 3, time seems to speed up as both Heart himself and the collective peer group who never quite knew him rapidly age. The losses that time delivers increasingly haunt them. It is a phenomenon of aging, they agree, that you get to experience "what absence means. That, one day, one hour, one minute, someone or something ceases to exist in relationship to you" (112).

The irony, however, is that the one thing that has in reality ceased to exist, but that most of them cannot give up, is their youth. For *Broke Heart Blues* is really about the complexities and paradoxes involved in our ongoing emotional commitment to a past that becomes little more than a fantasy. Most of the classmates speak a language past its live-by date, while only a handful discover new languages, and so new ways of being. Reunion by reunion, their collective youth dissolves. Many have empty marriages or personal tragedies or frustrated careers, and they look back on high school as the days when they were their "truest selves" (190). The majority feels that after high school everything is posthumous. While many of the girls remain in thrall to Heart's memory as older women, many of the boys feel transformed "overnight into husbands, fathers, IRS-terrorized adult citizens" (109). These physical adults have "scared kids' eyes inside rubbery adult masks" (324). They have a sense (in a typically unattributed remark) that "after the age of forty, déjà vu is as good as it gets" (322). Mainly, they are bewildered by time and by memories of their "rollercoaster" youth in which they were heedless of their teachers' advice to slow down (190). "Did you ever dream you'd get so old?" exclaims one classmate, forty-five-year-old Scottie Baskett, whose youthful idealism took him into medicine but who has become a plastic surgeon: he does valuable work on birth defects but his "bread-and-butter" is in vanity procedures. "Nobody's happy anymore," he tells his former classmates. "Nobody's happy with their bodies, or with their spouse's body. We're too old too fast." Plastic surgery, he has come to realize, is a manifestation of our attempts to deny time. "It's about stopping the clock—no, turning it back. *Unwinding* it" (46).

As so often in Oates's novels, a character dismissed by the viewpoint we are encouraged to identify with articulates a significant truth. Near the end of part 1, the collective narrators reminisce on two teachers. Their admiration for their social studies teacher, Mr. Cuthbert, or "Cuthie," seems to rest entirely on the fact that he "liked John Reddy and was respectful of him. And maybe just a little scared" (199). In contrast they despised the earnest new history teacher, Mr. Feldman, a "jerk" "headed for university teaching," who thought he could lecture them about their "souls." But just as Marya Knauer is wrong to dismiss Schwilk and Sylvester, so Feldman's views, seen independently of the group's derisive gloss, are worth listening to. "Ninety-nine percent of human beings," he tells them, "persist in believing in fairy tales and 'myths'" while one percent "reason, analyze, come to independent conclusions." He explains that it is up to them "to learn to question all assumptions, all murky thinking." "The yearning for mythic origins must be exposed as infantile," he insists, "'nostalgia' for what never was, ludicrously out of place in a civilization founded upon scientific progress, linear time, ceaseless change—*history*" (199). The pupils' collective response is summed up by "canny Art Lutz" who provides "a brilliantly timed lip-fart executed as only Art could do it" (199). Instead of reflecting on Feldman's opinions about the need for independent thought, they accept one puerile gesture of disdain as their collective response.

More significantly, they confess—as adults—that forty years later they are still "laughing" (199).

As at the beginning of part 1, so at the end. The first chapter finishes with the Willowsville girls rifling through Heart's garbage and finding an empty Coke can. They are "incredulous" that this object has touched "his actual mouth" (13). Veronica Myers, later to become a film star who summons up emotion by thinking of Heart, snatches it from oblivion to cherish it as a memento. The section's penultimate chapter ends with the group's memories of Heart's disappearance from Willowsville. One of them, Blake Wells, who kept a camera with him to preserve their "posthumous time" before graduation, managed to photograph Heart driving away in a U-Haul. But the pictures are "mere blurred snapshots" that, however they examine them, are simply "not riddles to be solved." The overall effect is "like background in a picture in which the foreground, the actual subject, is missing" (216). In the final chapter of part 1, twenty years later, Richard and Evangeline are still talking about Heart. Evangeline phones to ask why there were no fingerprints on the gun except Heart's. In the end, his innocence seems certain. The most likely (but by no means only) suspect is the gun's owner, his grandfather, Aaron, a crack shot who, as an act of penance, builds a giant trash sculpture, the Glass Ark, and wills it to his grandson, whose "sacrifice" is enshrined in it (299). But, as ever in Oates, that conventional kind of mystery is not really what the novel is about. Far more fascinating is the mystery of why these wealthy, middle-class Americans have so idolized Heart into abstraction.

Part 2 reveals that to have done so has been a mass delusion of idiotic proportions. It becomes clear that they have been in thrall to an image that is no more than a mirage. They have created a metaphor to describe a man, and then revered the metaphor. Again, wisdom comes from a marginalized source. As Tildie, the proprietor of the Glass Ark, says, "It's the idea of what it is, it *is*. Not what it's made of" (301). Just as the Glass Ark is above all reflective, so Heart's taciturn nature and outlaw status have encouraged his peer group to reflect their own ideas and desires onto him, building on what few details they get from him. Katie Olmsted, stricken with multiple sclerosis in high school, and wheelchair-bound until her years of remission, has dreamed of him as a Jesus-figure, and tells him at school one day that, like herself, he is a leper. His straightforward reply ("maybe Jesus was a leper, too") is seen as a riddle that ricochets around the community, even being taken up in a sermon by the local minister (184). Other members of the community see him as a "snake" in the gardens of Willowsville (161). For others he is a stud, and for yet others merely *"that greaser-killer-kid,"* who *"should've gone to prison for life"* (110). All things to all people, his role as hero or antihero is stretched to the point of parody when girls swoon if they pass him, and it becomes known to be "particularly dangerous to pass close by John Reddy on the stairs" (206).

In fact, now known as odd-job man MR. FIX-IT, he turns out to be an ordinary person living a not-very-successful life. Aged thirty-eight, he is in a disintegrating relationship, the latest of several temporary set-ups he has been in as he drifts around New York State. Far from discovering the heart of the mystery, we find that Heart is more mystified than anyone. The fact that the youth of Willowsville had seemed "to see some elusive promise in him" remains "one of the mysteries of his life" (294). When, at the very end of part 2, Kate Olmsted (she now refers to herself as Kate, not Katie) recognizes him at the Glass Ark, he sees her simply as "one of the rich Willowsville girls" from whom he had kept his distance (301). When she reminds him of his long-cherished "advice," he remembers none of it (302). Her invitation to him to attend the latest reunion strikes him as preposterous. Part 2 however brings out another aspect of the John Reddy Heart phenomenon. While the group fantasy has little basis in fact—being no more (as Oates's epigraph cites Pascal on life) than "a dream a little less inconsistent"—their idea of him paradoxically represents their search for authenticity. Where many of them have not even matured in adulthood, he has, after all, had to grow up in childhood—symbolized earlier in the book by his arrival in town, aged eleven, "young yet somehow not young"; sporting sideburns, "a man-sized hat" and his dead father's watch (20). He has had to take action in real life rather than indulge in the prolonged playtime enjoyed by most of his comfortably-off observers. Even in her thirties, Kate talks to him "in the cadences of a fifteen year old" (301). The same goes for their admiration of the fact that he is a rebel, whereas they are merely would-be rebels whose first concern, they admit, is "[not] to jeopardize our allowances, or cause our parents worry" (86). Like a contemporary Huck Finn, he has dealt with many of the actual dangers, fears, and heartaches—real migration, real threats to his mother, real murder—that are spared most of his more articulate, conformist counterparts, the contemporary Tom Sawyers of American white, middle-class life.

Finally, in part 3, dealing with the thirtieth reunion, we see both the consequences of overromanticizing youth and the practical possibilities for escaping such a trap. In trying to relive their adolescence, most of these adults pointedly return, not to idealism but to the pack mentality that also characterized that youth. It is not insignificant that this community is wealthy, white, and essentially racist. As one classmate, still a resident, says, Willowsville is "integrated" now. "But where exactly in the village is it 'integrated'?" (351).

As the reunion progresses, just as the insiders begin to check for braces on their teeth so they revert to the blatancies of adolescent behavior. They try to avoid "that jerk Ketch Campbell perspiring and hopeful in a maroon WHS T-shirt and new blue jeans that fitted his womanish hips oddly." Poor Ketch, it turns out, has been "faithfully attending" every reunion and they had "come to see it was impossible to discourage him," but they manage "to elude him," just as they do "other forgotten classmates" (310). "If you have to read the nametag, it's probably no one important," quips some (ironically anonymous) insider tucked near the center of the herd (324). It becomes obvious that the urge to conform that made them all elevate Heart as a lonesome hero involves as much exclusion as inclusion. They reject the "abnormal" (Ketch with his "womanish hips") and take a racist dislike to a "mean-looking, Italian-looking man" and his friends as "boorish, uninvited guests" who do not *belong* (312). When a woman named Lee Ann Whitfield turns up as a county judge, the group recall "our fat girl hunched at the misfits' table in the cafeteria." They remember "the shyly hopeful movement of her lowered gaze as we swung by, a pack of us, ignoring her, in fact not seeing her, as we didn't see the trash bins and the colored cafeteria workers behind the counter" (323). They welcome her, of course, even though "the poor woman was afraid we'd snub her. Imagine. A New York State judge, forty-eight years old. As if we aren't all adults now" (324). But that very phrase "New York State judge," and a subsequent reference to her as "our fat girl in disguise" (332), reveal the snobbery and hypocrisy beneath their civility. Reminiscent of the diners in "The Undesirable Table," one of Oates's most resonant stories of the 1990s, who are forced to sit by a window onto things they would rather not consider, they can accept Lee Ann only because she is no longer one of "the luckless creatures outside."[41]

Part 3's main motif is the class's traditional pig roast. As the reunion wears on, the "spell of the pig" kicks in, and we have, on the face of it, a bleak and disturbing vision of human appetites run riot (331). "Stuffed to the gills" with pig and pizzas, the crusts left for some "disdainful maid to clean up," the classmates dance with the ferocity of people bitten by tarantulas and trying "to sweat the poison out" (352). Two dancers are described as "slither-bumping with the frenzy of copulating insects." Another has a forehead "beaded with sweat of an eerie reddish hue," while two others dance "twined together like drowning creatures" (353). They roast the pig on a deck suspended above "a treacherous and unfathomable abyss" ("an abyss," thinks Richard, "—as of Time itself" [332]). And indeed this deck will collapse beneath their weight soon after midnight. The carcass, "stripped clean of all save gristle," presides over everything like a sacrifice (334).

As time diminishes ("Jesus. It's like you look over your shoulder and there's somebody rolling up a carpet right behind you. Brrr!" [335]), so the Schopenhauerean vision intensifies. Dancing to "Hunger, Hunger" (calling to mind Bruce Springsteen's equally apt "Hungry Heart") by their favorite band, Made in the USA, they stuff themselves in a cannibalistic frenzy even though "hunger ain't never gonna be fulFILLED" (337). A strobe light makes one dancer look like a patch of his skull is missing. Others take on the appearance of dead classmates—like Smoke Filer who died when "the T-Bird steering column had pierced him like a spit" (354). The plastic surgeon, Scottie Baskett, is all too appropriately their "carver again this year" (331). Meanwhile, one former classmate cannot help wanting to tear Veronica Myers with his teeth, while "pigged out" lip-farter Art Lutz, finally necking with Mary Louise Schultz, discovers that Mary has had a double mastectomy (332)—a twist to the padded-bra stereotype of teenage movies like *Animal House*. These former teenagers, their legs twitching to the music like "haunches hanging from sides of beef," are physical animals and subject to decay (348). Even the women get their own sacrificial pig in the end. The men stare amazed as the women bear their "buck-naked, hairy host," Willowsville mayor Dwayne Hewson, "like a pig to the spit" to the pool, toss him in "with screams of female triumph," and unwittingly trigger a fatal cardiac arrest (356).

But if *Broke Heart Blues* critiques nostalgia rather than being in itself nostalgic, it is by no means simply satire. Much of the novel's drama has been about how we create and live by artifice, albeit with practical results. Since we are all artists of a kind, we can always recreate. Toward the end, a few characters have evolved beyond the reunion mindset. In particular, Richard and Evangeline sit talking at dawn. Richard says he has only come in the hope of seeing Evangeline. A less than fully accepted member of this cliquish group, this has been Evangeline's first reunion in years, and she feels the group have "ruined it" (365). Even in youth, they rarely understood her. "I am taking 'minutes' on our lives whether you allow me to or not," she has told her classmates when, after writing minutes bearing no relation to a meeting, she fails to be reelected secretary. The minutes that count, she tells them, are not "the minutes of some silly old *meeting*. They are the great world of chance and fate that *surrounds us*" (80). Many of the concerns of the moment are trivial when set against the one, profound truth that we are subject to time. Over the years, the group have become "damned impressed by 'E. S. Fesnacht,'" but as with Judge Lee Ann Whitfield, they are impressed with "the career if not the woman" or "her peculiar prose." "What's this stuff *about?*" they ask. "What's it mean?" (345). Writers, Oates has said, "address individuals, and we posit our hope in them."[42] "You have to feel that someone cares," Evangeline tells Richard. He assures her that *he* will read anything she writes (364). Individual judgment, not the rule of the crowd or praise of the pack, is what the writer, and pragmatist, puts her faith in.

If Richard and Evangeline are the most obvious artist-figures, there are others: the painter Trish Elders; the plastic surgeon Scottie Baskett; the actress Veronica Myers, the poet Millie Le Roux; the photographer Kate Olmsted, the feminist documentary filmmaker Sandy Bangs. The Heart family themselves turn out to be deeply imbued with the ability—and need—to make their lives into art. Heart himself, of course, becomes MR. FIX-IT. His grandfather, Aaron, builds the Glass Ark. His mother has reinvented herself as Dahlia Magdalena Heart, "the White Dahlia" (240). His sister Shirleen reappears as Sister Mary Agatha of St. Anne's Sisters of Charity. His brother, Farley, becomes Franklin S. Hart, a Silicon Valley multimillionaire software tycoon. The owner of Hartssoft, he also happens to be a pioneer of a kind of Virtual Reality where you can *"click into an event from X possible points of view"* and so, much like the novel's narrative, make use of *"an infinite number of perspectives"* (276). We all create our lives by rewriting our memories, projecting our futures into being, reinventing ourselves. One of Richard's poems, indeed, is "an attempt to evoke a mood" that is less an individual passion than "something communal, collective. Our 'yearning for infinitude.'" Likewise, *Broke Heart Blues* is made of voices who all to some extent are, like Richard, continuously engaged in a "reimagining and reconstituting of the past" as if they themselves are an "epic American poem" (162).

In the final pages, various individuals awaken, as it were, from "the spell of the pig" and reevaluate their lives. Chet Halloren, for instance, wants "to discover if life is truly so random as it's come to seem in middle age. Or whether there's a pattern, a design. In which I somehow fit" (307). To recognize the significance of art in life and of the art of living is to recognize that the pattern, the design, the purpose, comes from you. Recognition that you are responsible for defining and redefining your life also implicitly involves recognizing that you are situated in time. "After the age of forty déjà vu is as good as it gets" only if you retain metaphors or modes of behavior best outgrown, and if you therefore deny time, or try vainly to shore it up. The memories of youth that can shape whole lives are, to the present moment, no more real than "the seductively lighted store windows" of Willowsville's Avenue of Fashion. They are merely "glimmering mirages," even though they have "the power to evoke in our dreams of the next forty years, and beyond, that quicksilver emotion of hope, elation, certainty and well-being perhaps found solely in dreams" (185). To mature is to develop into a life unencumbered by whatever metaphors are no longer appropriate.

For the classmates of *Broke Heart Blues*, this means, as Richard puts it, refusing to allow high school to become a "metaphor for life that devours what remains of the remainder of life" (201). "If I outgrow John Reddy Heart," Shelby Connor, another former classmate, asks her therapist while being treated for fatigue and depression, "what will I have left?" (86). When you first read the novel, her words may well read as "what will I have left to focus on?" On reflection, they may read more like "what will I have left behind?" *Broke Heart Blues* is all about individuals graduating from the first meaning to the second. What will Shelby have left to focus on? True adulthood and true maturity. What will she have left behind? A romantic myth that in later life is more likely to limit than to enhance her potential. What has to sink in for these adults is that "John Reddy Heart" has ceased to exist in relation to them, just as he has ceased to exist for the man himself. "My name is John Heart," he corrects Kate Olmsted. "That was a long time ago" (301). Equally, what has to sink in for Verrie Myers, the fading film star, is that the Coke can she has kept all these years is not a symbol, but aluminum junk. To her credit, and surely her happiness, when it falls from her handbag in a parking lot, this is exactly what happens. She places it on the sidewalk with an ironic flourish where they think Heart used to park his pink Cadillac. *"There,"* she announces. "I'm done with it" (367). Across the playing fields, dozens of sprinklers suddenly switch on, spraying a "startling iridescent play of water" that is "tinged with the colors of the rainbow." While Verrie and Trish race away across the hockey field and through the sprinklers, in the foreground the Coke can topples over and is forgotten as "mere teenage litter" (368). Whatever one's rainbow-tinted memories of high school, as Richard advises elsewhere, "you never lose what you never had" (357).

Outgrowing limiting metaphors, while it has specific implications for the classmates of Willowsville High, obviously has far wider implications for humanity as a whole. In probing a cultural and global rather than local phenomenon—our devotion to celebrities as a mass delusion—*Blonde*, Oates's mammoth novel about Marilyn Monroe, makes them explicit. For *Blonde*'s central irony is that this celebrity is just one more member of the audience, a devotee of a contemporary religion, who finds herself the latest goddess to be sacrificed, the latest pig on a spit. Using Norma Jeane's supposedly posthumous viewpoint to offer a perspective on the meaning of a life that eludes the individual in the frenzy of living it, *Blonde*'s strategy grows out of *Black Water* and *What I Lived For*. As with those previous novels, it asks us to reassess a given mode of life and a given set of contemporary attitudes. Like Kelly Kelleher and Corky Corcoran, Norma Jeane yearns above all to be loved. "Love me!" she pleads. "Already, I love you."[43] But like them she is only privileged to see the end results of her yearnings after her death. She behaves as if life were a fairy tale, but her search for the happy ending—as opposed to some measure of ongoing happiness—is of course doomed. "How relieved she was," thinks Norma Jeane before her marriage to the "Ex-Athlete," "now her life was settled!" (431). That she views herself in the third person is symptomatic of her attempt to find a stable, finite identity somehow beyond her unfinished self—unfinished because she is still living. "If I could say, There! that's me!" thinks the young Norma Jeane. "That woman, that thing on the screen, that's who I am" (10). But such stability is always elusive. "Never has she seen the final scene, never the concluding credits rolling past. In these, beyond the final movie kiss, is the key to the movie's mystery, she knows. As the body's organs, removed in an autopsy, are the key to life's mystery" (11). Whatever meanings there are must be found in the dense thicket of living, so the greatest irony of all is that Norma Jeane's pursuit of fame as the static image of Marilyn Monroe is a pursuit of that-which-is-not-life: a pursuit, then, of death.

Blonde, of course, is about much more than the story of how Norma Jeane became Marilyn Monroe. It explores the wider phenomenon of a woman rising to iconic status and being destroyed in the process. It examines how a young woman, brought up on romance, can come to be sold for her sexuality, then finally try to reinvent herself in maturity. Enamored of a certain kind of cultural romance, this time the worship of a fantasy future rather than a fantasy past, her pursuit of that myth reflects the values we hold as a society. Where once that young girl looked out at the fantasy fostered by the wider culture, now that dead woman looks back at us embalmed in countless glossy pictures, as if to bid us examine what we are up to. Yet that woman, now nothing more than an image, is no longer a symbolic ideal of a living being but a reminder of death. For another of the ironies of such a story is that the very qualities we latch onto about her are those most vulnerable to the smothering carapace of iconic fame. The icon starts out as the essence of life; she is an empathic, vibrant, adaptable, living being hoping for her Dark Prince. She ends up nailed into fame's custom-built coffin, hiding from the paparazzi and the public eye, a blonde actress imprisoned in a public image she cannot control, careering into a black tunnel from which she never emerges.

> Then the Blond Actress is in the limousine. The rear door is shut. The windows are dark-tinted, impossible to see through from the outside. Her escorts speak sharply to the crowd—"Give the girl a break, will you —She's suffering, you can see . . . "—and climb into the limousine and it moves off, slowly at first, for photographers are blocking the street; then it's gone. The crowd in its wake still clamoring for attention and cameras still flashing until the newsreel breaks off. (675)

Confused by the performance that has become her real life, she is found dying, her once-beautiful mouth "slack as a gash cut into her face," her cheek muscles twitching "as if she were trying to speak" and not just "groaning softly" where she lies (737).

Such passages show that *Blonde* is not just about Marilyn Monroe. The blonde icon phenomenon this century takes in a number of women from Eva Peron to Grace Kelly. But a 1997 *Time* article by Oates signals a likely trigger for Oates's writing of *Blonde*. "The Love She Searched For" appraises the British establishment's role in the life and death of Diana, Princess of Wales. In it, Oates describes Diana as "a virgin cynically used by the so-called 'royal family' of Britain." "By refusing to live a lie for the sake of patriarchal order," argues Oates, "Princess Diana exposed the hypocrisy of the establishment to the glare of commoners." For Oates, the hunt for Diana began when she was sought out as a young bride who would be "virginal in every sense," including being "ignorant of the very conditions of her marriage." "With the cruel logic of those fairy tales that don't end happily," she became "the intended sacrifice to the establishment."[44] There are many differences, of course, between Diana and Norma Jeane in terms of their backgrounds and their public images. But the point is less in the detail than in the critique of a cultural phenomenon.

Oates saw Diana's drama as to do with "her often desperate search for love." "This hope to be loved," Oates muses, "is in fact a wish to be loved 'for what I am.'" "The paradox of the celebrity's quest," however, "is that she must realize that her 'admirers' are drawn to her" not for herself but "for the very reasons that the crowd is drawn to her." Of Diana's alleged string of relationships with various exotic figures—said to include a Cavalry Officer, a Rugby Captain, a Prominent Businessman, and a Heart Surgeon—the last was with "an international playboy, who was clearly attracted to Diana as the most celebrated glamour-icon of our time."

Oates seemed to see in Diana a figure whose life and death, in its deeper structure rather than particular circumstances, echoed Monroe's both in the enormity and banality of her fame and in that personal need for love. The textual suggestions are myriad. "What is your name, Sweetie?" asks "the Blond Actress" of a little girl she visits in an orphanage. The girl's mumbled answer sounds like "*Donna,* maybe? Or *Dunna?*—'don't know?'" (450). She might as well have said "Diana," as if Monroe were meeting her successor while the latter was still a child. The suggestions recur in the numerous references to princes and princesses. One of her suitors, Isaac Shinn, is described as "the formidable Rumplestiltskin" asking the Fair Princess to marry him (280). And though Norma Jeane does become "exalted above the rest," she sees in the mirror "not the Fair Princess whom the world saw and marveled over but her old Beggar Maid self." A sense of unworthiness, of self-loathing, as Oates puts it in the Diana essay, dogs her every moment. *"What is this spell?"* she thinks. *"How long can it last?"* Like Diana, she finds herself being "groomed for 'stardom,'" which turns out to be "a species of animal manufacture, like breeding" (281). And when, embroiled in her relationship with the U.S. president, she steps too far, the vocabulary sounds more Old World than New. "Nobody threatens the President of the United States, lady," she is told. "That's treason" (710).

Drawing attention to such parallels, of course, is nothing new. Julie Burchill's *Diana* specifically links the two figures. "How," she asks, "did a shy Sloane kindergarten teacher from the heart of England with no visible talents come to conquer the world in a manner which would make John F. Kennedy and Marilyn Monroe look like little more than hometown heroes?" So, too, does William Heyen, in "Famous Photo," one poem among his remarkable sequence *Diana, Charles, & the Queen,* when his Diana "tongues her lip" for photographers "as she thinks of Marilyn Monroe / whose skirt gusted to her waist."⁴⁵ The Spencer family's request to have Elton John sing a rewritten version of "Candle in the Wind" at Diana's funeral echoed public instinct. Both figures played out uncannily similar roles within Western culture. "In every decade there must be a fair princess exalted above the rest," explains suitor Shinn, and Monroe's successor was plainly Princess Diana (281).

But what Oates points up is the authenticity behind the image. Abstraction and romance distort, mask, but finally give way to our realization that here are two human beings—two women—having to deal as best they can with the complexity of actual life. "In Diana, the fairy-tale princess who was cruelly awakened to the world of hurt, betrayal and humiliation," writes Oates in the *Time* article, "women of all ages found a mirror image of themselves, however magnified and glamourized. In her ordeals, in the courage, stubbornness and idealism of her attempt to reinvent herself as an independent woman, women have found a model for themselves." Similarly, what seems most authentic about Norma Jeane has everything to do with these pragmatist values of energy, inventiveness, and adaptability. "Our nature consists of motion," Norma Jeane quotes Pascal in her schoolgirl journal; "complete rest is death" (656). She might just as well have quoted James or Dewey, or Oates herself, since this is so central a tenet of Oates's career. However much a "concocted confectionary" Marilyn Monroe becomes, she is ironically her truest self through that acting, because to act is sometimes simply to live. *"It was deeper than acting,"* complain anonymous trained actors in the novel. *"It was too raw"* (202). "You feel genuine emotion, Miss Monroe . . . ," they tell her. "That's why you're a brilliant actress" (608).

As with Diana's marriage into the staidness of the British royal family, so with Norma Jeane—the tragedy is in the mismatch between the emotional openness that led her on her inspired journey and the stultifying nature of her goal. "Film is a phenomenon whose resemblance to death has been too long ignored," wrote Norman Mailer in *Marilyn*.⁴⁶ In *Blonde*, too, Oates dwells on the fact that to become a movie star is to have one's dead image projected onto the screen. Norma Jeane is embalmed into movie stardom, from her first marriage, to the embalmer Bucky Glazer, through to her final makeup man, Whitey. "Am I dead?" she asks when she starts receiving flowers from well-wishers (143). As her career develops, she receives a continual stream of cards, letters, gifts, photos. But they arrive not for the living person but for the icon, the studio invention. Ironically, they are the kind of letters she herself might have written "as a star-struck young adolescent," but they are written to "Marilyn" "as you'd write to the Virgin Mary" (419). Meanwhile, Whitey goes to ever-greater lengths to keep Norma Jeane's face looking like Marilyn Monroe, the idealized version of life, that is *not* life. Even as she strives for authenticity, her fans, admirers and followers pursue a version of her celebrity "life" through the piecemeal, rumor-laden babble of the media, and mythologize her into abstraction. The tragic paradox of our cultural determination to create icons, the novel insists, is that we condemn them to a fate that is the very opposite of what it means to be human, and healthy.

Like *Broke Heart Blues*, *Blonde* depicts one of the ways in which a society—American society specifically, but by analogy Western society in general—can compromise its own stated values. American pragmatism, after all, despite what it owes to European thinkers, grew out of American culture and articulates its ideals as formed out of the European Enlightenment. Oates's standpoint is therefore a traditionally American standpoint, even as it critiques the culture out of which it grows and the kinds of individuals that that culture tends to produce. Where *What I Lived For* shows a businessman living the kind of life warned against by Thoreau and *Broke Heart Blues* shows the ease with which we lapse into pack mentalities in thrall to a Coke can culture, *Blonde* depicts a whole culture warped by technological progress. The would-be icon has to be as wrapped up in the delusion as her fans. Diana believed in the Dark Prince and fairytale wedding. Norma Jeane is first of all a believer in the Church of Moviedom, and only then a star in its tinselly firmament. *"It is what we did together instead of church,"* she says of her visits to a movie theater with her mother. *"Our worship"* (55). The religious relics she grows up with are not plaster saints but photos and posters of the stars, "handsome glossy photos behind glass like works of art to be stared at" (52–53).

Oates's achievement in *Blonde,* then, is that she does for Western culture what elsewhere she does for individual circumstances. She dramatizes the nature and consequences of our mass delusions. Norma Jeane, this starstruck fan caught up in a historical moment, is as much an American everywoman as Corky Corcoran is an everyman. She wants to be noticed, adopted—literally adopted, at first—but then befriended, married, made love to by the world of the screen, of glamour: the seductive, delusory world of fame. In charting the absurdity of this goal, Oates quotes Freud's warning that "no one who shares a delusion ever recognizes it as such" (381). Where in earlier novels, various individuals are shown to have both blindness and insight, in *Blonde,* as on a smaller scale in *Broke Heart Blues,* it is a collective problem. We see so much of our lives in terms of, or in relation to, the produce of dream factories based in southern California, where delusion is the very air they breathe, and promote. The media of our ever-more-refined and sophisticated technologies are not real life, but in subtle and not so subtle ways we mistake them for such. "For in movie logic, aesthetics has the authority of ethics; to be less than beautiful is sad, but to be willfully less than beautiful is immoral" (90–91). And what does it do to a culture, to an individual, when they begin to confuse movie logic with life logic? This is the ultimate subject of *Blonde,* and surely a vital one for us as a global community. As the climate changes, and our awareness of our planetary fragility increases, what price will we pay for going on living and refining our mass delusions?

So dark a novel, indeed, is *Blonde* that, were it not for the last novel under consideration in this study, *Middle Age: A Romance,* one could almost come away feeling that it edges toward cynicism. How random *Blonde* makes love seem, and personality, and friendship! All such a swirl of uncertainties! By and large, the sense of human motivation we get from *Blonde* is of a self-serving, manipulative race of predatory men and vain women. "How many dozens, hundreds of birds singing," thinks Norma Jeane of Mr. Zinn's aviary, "& each song lovely & yearning & heart-rending & yet the effect of so many songs at once was that of mere noise & frantic pleading *Look at me! Hear my song! Here I am! Here!*" Effectively, Norma Jeane auditions to become one of these birds, symbolic of dead movie stars, stuffed, embalmed, brought to "life" by the flick of a switch (211). Accuracy, however, is not itself cynicism. Oates simply delineates the con-job aspects of celebrity culture—what, in an essay on *Death of a Salesman* she calls the "hypocrisy, deceit, fraud" of public relations consumerism. But, given that the vision is filtered through the posthumous perspective of Norma Jeane aka Princess Diana, we could hardly expect anything else.

Moreover, even as *Blonde* provides a dark vision of contemporary Western culture, Oates's steady gaze offers opportunities for remedy, if only through default. With such a novel as a reminder, we can always try to grow out of our collective fascination with the image, the celebrity, the sound bite, the stage-managed politics, and all other manner of contemporary delusions. We do not have to worship the cultural icons and brand names that go into shaping our global capitalist society. We do not have to be victims of our "ever more frantic, self-mesmerized world of salesmanship, image without substance, empty advertising rhetoric."[47] *Blonde,* then, like *Broke Heart Blues,* is about how we can trap or release ourselves. Movie worship and fame worship are religions of the dead rather than of the living. Norma Jeane refers to Britain as the Kingdom of the Dead and Los Angeles as the City of Sand. But they share an adherence to myths. Los Angeles might as well be known as the Kingdom of the Dead in its promotion of the all-powerful image. And to foster and perpetuate mass delusions—including the delusion of perpetuity and security—is to build a civilization of sandcastles while the tide comes in.

Middle Age: A Romance is a novel in an altogether lighter if no-less-serious vein, and perhaps the most upbeat Oates novel in recent years. "All communities are myth-making," reflects one of the main protagonists, Marina Troy, "and none more so than communities of the privileged and sequestered."[48] Like Willowsville in *Broke Heart Blues,* Salthill-on-Hudson is exactly that. And like both *Broke Heart Blues* and *Blonde, Middle Age* has at its center a person who becomes mythicized by a community. Once again, too, this figure, Adam Berendt, a junk sculptor "with no reputation beyond the local" (4), who gives most of his work away and who lives "frugally in the midst of affluent Salthill" (138), is literally and temperamentally an outsider. But unlike the previous two novels, Adam, whose hero is that protopragmatist Socrates and who seems to have "drifted in from another planet" (153), is not an essentially hollow figure like John Reddy Heart nor a cartoon-like sex symbol like Marilyn Monroe. Instead, he is—or has made himself into—a figure whose values are spiritual, rather than material, practical rather than idealized, and that demonstrably help others to live more fulfilling lives. Several of his grieving friends grope to articulate his impact, but among the best is Camille Hoffman's assertion that his "presence in the world made others feel less *futile*" (96).

The novel's prologue belongs to Adam, whose narration, like Norma Jeane's in *Blonde,* is posthumous; he has died in his early fifties of a heart attack, while attempting to save a small girl from drowning. But where *Blonde* was a novel about a form of death, this is very much a novel about life emerging *from* death. Like Heart and Monroe, Adam is mysterious when alive and takes on mythic proportions once he has gone. But unlike Heart and Monroe, his identity as Adam Berendt during his twenty-one years in Salthill has been "a sustained act of will" forged entirely by himself (2). More important still, in terms of the optimism the novel exudes, he differs from Heart and Monroe in being a figure beneficial to almost all the lives he touches. After the prologue, Adam's narration is at an end, but his full effect on others has only begun. As befits a Socrates disciple, Adam proves the immortality of the "soul"—in the approximate meaning of the Greek word *psyche:* "the inner person, one's intellectual and emotional self"—not as a physical afterlife, but in its ongoing effect on the lives of those left behind. His death resurrects the lives of his friends. Almost literally in this novel, "the living," as Socrates argued, "come into being again from the dead."[49]

In life, Adam has been the platonic—if sexually charged and charging—friend to the wealthy Salthill wives in their otherwise empty or frustrated lives (4). He has also, it turns out, been regarded by many of the husbands, too, as their only possible confidante, and by at least two of the teenage children of his friends as the only adult worth consulting. In line with Socrates' dictum "know thyself," Adam's friendship with these people has often taken the form of the Socratic method in new millennium guise (5). Lacking "all capacity for the supernatural" and able to "believe in man. Not God" (6), Adam will either just allow his subjects to talk or will quiz them about "the purpose of life" (26). All the women love him, yet it is generally known that his interests are "impassioned but curiously impersonal," and that, while "you would never get to know the man intimately," "you might get to know yourself" (26). While Adam's seeds—his words, example, attitude—find fruition in death, and while his dog, Apollo—named after Socrates' faithful friend Apollodoros—suggests Adam's ongoing presence, this is not a novel about anything supernatural. Even as he entrances women physically, he emphasizes the ephemeral nature of the body and the potentially timeless quality of the mind. It is for this reason, he argues, closely following Socrates' argument in *Phaedo* that *"the philosopher is one who practices dying, practices death, continuously"* (5). This is not because such a person wants to die, but because the fact of individual death has to be taken into account if an individual is concerned to discover lasting purpose to his or her life through its impact on others.

Separated into three parts after the prologue, *Middle Age* follows four couples (couples who either already are together or eventually will be) whose lives are dramatically affected by Adam's presence and death. These include bookshop-owner Marina Troy and Adam's lawyer Roger Cavanagh; Lionel and Camille Hoffman; Abigail Des Pres and Gerhardt Ault, and Owen and Augusta Cutler. We track these couples from their grief through to their revitalization into, for most of them, more rewarding and productive lives than they had lived while Adam was still around. Adam's prologue is entitled "Fourth of July," not only because his death occurs at an Independence Day party but also to signal the start of his friends' journey toward independence of thought and taking responsibility for their lives' significance. It is shaped something like a ballet, with each character or couple given their time in the spotlight, even as they interact with each other and, as it were, with Adam's disembodied "presence." So part 1 begins with Marina, moves to Camille and Lionel, then to Abigail, Abigail's husband Harrison and son Jared, and then Roger Cavanagh, and finally to Augusta and Owen. Part 2 follows the same choreography, as, in more condensed form, does part 3. The one alteration to this "dance" is that Marina and Roger's romance means that he joins her at the start of part 3, and they reappear in the slot originally allotted to Roger.

In part 1, Marina and Roger encounter each other as a result of Adam's death and, despite an abortive sexual encounter in Adam's house (ended when they imagine hearing his footsteps), are left with poor impressions of one another. Marina has been contacted to identify Adam's body because one of her business cards has been found in Adam's pocket, while Roger has to deal with Adam's will. Just as Marina finds it hard to match the corpse with the "man in motion," so Roger has to square Adam's private papers with the man he thought he knew (25). Viewing the corpse, Marina remembers lines from *Phaedo* that Adam had often quoted. "If you catch me and I don't escape you" are words Socrates had said to his followers about the possibility of their reaching him in the afterlife. She then reflects on her hikes with Adam and his questions that had led her to express her regret at not having pursued her vocation as a sculptress. She also looks out some sketches of Adam, but discovers that they fail "to capture the man's mysterious essence," representing only "a mannequin," a simulacrum of a middle-aged man "from which all youth, vigor, mystery had departed" (39). When she meets Roger, he seems the very opposite of Adam. He is not a man who trusts emotion. "Not his own, and certainly no one else's." He is not just a lawyer by profession, but "by nature": a man who requires "control" (52). Badly shaken by his divorce, he seems to dislike and mistrust "all women on principal." With his "eerie, reptilian" yet "curiously beautiful eyes," he seems eager to hurt (52). Both participants being grief-stricken, Marina and Roger's sexual encounter is an empty gesture of desperation—in Marina's case, a need for "a man, a sexual being, in Adam's place" (59).

The Hoffmans, meanwhile, are a decent, liberal couple who have also felt the power of Adam's "mysterious authority" over imaginations grown "romantic from disuse" (66). Lionel commutes to work long hours at the family publishing firm "out of a genuine perplexity about what, other than work, a responsible adult male was meant to do" (71). He is not a stranger to death—his younger brother has long since died of an aneurysm, aged thirty-six—but he is something of a stranger to life. Socially, he feels unconnected in any meaningful way, and remembers "*Adam as the only one he could talk to, even if he couldn't talk to him*" (76). Nor is he happy to turn his thoughts inward. In the face of Camille's grief over Adam's death, he finds himself unable and unwilling to console her.

The Hoffmans have ended up living that-which-is-not-life in an "expensive burrow marriage" from which oxygen has leaked, "leaving the air humid and stale as soiled bedclothes" (87). Camille is only too aware that "if Lionel were to interview her for Wife, he wouldn't hire her" (90). For Camille, moreover, there is no one to whom she "*can speak of such things, now that Adam is gone*" (92). Just as Marina, on viewing Adam's corpse and in her examination of the sketches she made of him, is forced to see that the essence of his being is motion beyond capture, so Camille once learned much the same from Adam firsthand when she confessed her love for him. "What is it you 'love'?" he asked her (95). When she suggested his face, he reeled off the features she must therefore be professing to love: his blind eye, psoriatic skin, bumpy forehead, Cro-Magnon skull, crooked teeth. Finally, he pulled out his penis to show her how ugly it was. Again, Adam's physical presence is not the point—not for him, anyway. In grief, both Hoffmans dream of him. Camille feels he is telling her to "*love the living*" (98), while Lionel, feeling that Adam is instructing him to face Camille and "*bring her into the light,*" in fact leaves their bed to phone his mistress, Siri (99).

In part 1 we also have Abigail Des Pres and her son, Jared, and Owen and Augusta Cutler. Where Camille is in a stale marriage, Abigail Des Pres is divorced and feels alienated from Jared. At a recent fund-raising luncheon, she has told Camille and other women friends that in the wake of her divorce and subsequent weight loss she feels "like a rubber sex doll that's been deflated and discarded" (92). As a mother, she feels a failure. Jared seems to want nothing more than "*to be average,*" a member of the pack rather than an independent being (106). Both Abigail and her son have gained from Adam's attention. "Why so intense, Abigail?" he has asked her. "You'll burn yourself out" (112). Meanwhile, Jared has admired Adam because he "mostly lets me talk" (129). But Abigail's attempts to connect with her son go horribly wrong when, drunk and upset, she crashes the car while driving Jared back to summer school from a dinner date that she has pleaded he agree to, and though only mildly injured he never wants to see her again. The Cutlers are at least together, and Augusta is at least open with her husband about the sorry state of their union. "We've lost all mystery to one another," she tells him. "We're corpses embalmed together, this is our mausoleum" (185). Owen, for his part, has always felt infuriated by this one-eyed man who always seemed right and so made the rest of them seem wrong. On first hearing of his death, he rejoices. But as with all the other relationships, Adam's death is not the end of these four people's stories, but the start.

Part 2, "And I Don't Escape You," begins with Marina in the Pocono Mountains, at a house at Damascus Crossing that she had turned down when Adam was alive but received in his will. Marina has come to realize, or believe, that Adam had loved "the Marina who was yet to be," the artist she would have become rather than the "anaesthetized" Marina of Salthill-on-Hudson (194). She has consequently begun "to think like an artist, one for whom any stray object might be an inspiration," but is as yet working only on completing Adam's art rather than embarking on her own. During her time at the house, however, she discovers not only that Adam was other than he seemed—that in fact he had once been known as Francis Xavier Brady—but also that her efforts to complete his sculptures are futile. "The fragmentary artworks Adam Berendt had left behind in this house hadn't been completed by Marina Troy," she sees, "but sabotaged. Clearly Marina Troy knew nothing of Adam Berendt, the man was finally a stranger; Marina had no access to his vision, as she'd had no access to his heart. She was only herself" (237). In other words, Marina's legacy from Adam has not been to complete Adam's work, but to discover her own independent destiny.

Meanwhile, the lives of the Hoffmans, Abigail Des Pres, Roger Cavanagh, and the Cutlers are being equally transformed. Just as Marina has broken free of her "anaesthetized Salthill life" (203), so Lionel—mistakenly in his case—has come to believe that Adam would have celebrated Lionel's particular way of awakening from his decades as a "living mummy" (246). Lionel, in other words, decides to leave his wife for his mistress, telling Camille that his life has become "mysterious and new again" and "glorious beyond belief" (268). By the time he discovers that Siri is a part-time hooker set up for him by Harrison, Abigail's husband, it is too late. Camille has transformed their burrow-like home into "a space open to daylight" and begun collecting dogs—one of which is named Apollo and all of which Lionel is allergic to. Abigail Des Pres's dependence on Adam has taken the form of Socratic dialogues with herself. Miserable at her son's rejection of her, she blurs "the invisible surveillance camera" in her kitchen with her image of Adam and talks to it while preparing her suicide. But for Abigail, too, life suddenly changes. Rejected by Jared, she sees and admires an oriental-looking girl in a red beret. After a brief, would-be romance with an ageing poet named Donegal Croom, whose "shimmering lines of poetry" are so obviously going to outlast his decaying body, she discovers that the girl in the red beret is Tamar, daughter of a suitor Abigail has been indifferent to (341). She starts to date this man, Gerhardt Ault, and so gains Tamar as a step-daughter.

In turn, Roger Cavanagh has decided, after his disappointment with Marina, to "immerse himself in the impersonality of his work" and regard himself as no more than "a money-making machine" (345). But then he meets Naomi Volpe, an independent, idealistic, energetic young woman who reinvigorates him. Thanks to files that Adam kept on the National Project to Free the Innocent, they go together to interview Elroy Jackson, an inmate of death row, and for the first time in his career Roger—revolted by Elroy's original public defender, "Boomer" Spires—finds himself "caring passionately about someone" (371). Although this person is Elroy, not Naomi, when she announces her pregnancy and finally delivers a baby to him before disappearing to start a new life, he names the boy Adam, embraces fatherhood, and awakens to a whole new way of being. Among the community, "a collective sense of panic" sets in that one of them could go "outside the tribe" and find happiness. But this is what happens. Suddenly this mistrustful man opens up to life, "now answering his friends' questions with startling candor" (390). He seems "years younger" and even begins to speak with "a new, entertaining levity" reminiscent of Adam himself (391). "Lost in awe," he finds that he has begun "to forget to feel afraid" (394). Finally, the Cutlers independently change their lives. Augusta heads west and discovers the truth about Adam Berendt (that as a teenager he was responsible for the deaths of his mother and young sister in a fire in their Montana mobile home). Owen, meanwhile, relinquishes his overriding interest in the family business and takes up reading Greek philosophy and cultivating his garden.

In part 3, Marina returns to Salthill but "at the age of almost forty" is "finally an artist" (433). She rediscovers "the rude, pushy lawyer Cavanagh" as a devoted single father. He seems "invigorated; a figure of mystery," and the two of them, self-fulfilled at last, become a couple. Particularly attached to Tamar, Abigail decides that while she may not deserve "her privileged, white-skinned American life," she nevertheless "means to live it, and to wring every drop of happiness from it, she can" (450). Even the Cutlers find a new lease of life, rediscovering one another now that Augusta has found herself out West and Owen has found some fresh interests. "Unexpectedly in Salthill, it's a season of romance" (451). Only Lionel, who has misread Adam's teachings, suffers a very different fate, savaged to death by Camille's dogs. After Abigail and Tamar have been to the theater, we are told, "The dance is ended, the final ballet" (452). But that sentence seems to stand for the novel itself. It is a romance, and as such to be read more metaphorically than we might read Oates's grittier reflections on life in modern-day America. But as a reflection on the human capacity for individual transformation—as a ballet that illustrates such possibilities—it is an appropriate work with which to end discussion of Oates's evolution of consciousness from novel to novel through four decades of extraordinary endeavor, even if that endeavor is only evolution-to-date.

Plainly, Adam is a version of the novelist-as-pragmatist. Marina is the artist-as-reader or the reader-as-artist. Each of the protagonists comes to learn that they can, independently, revise their values and so their lives. Oates's art, then, has by *Middle Age* become incontestably a pragmatist's art: rarely optimistic or pessimistic, but almost always melioristic. If Schopenhauer hovers in the shadows of all three novels—specifically in the feeding frenzy that ends *Broke Heart Blues* and in Max Pearlman's advice to Norma Jeane that Schopenhauer's vision of human nature *"is the truth of the world"* (504)—in the end, pragmatism routs pessimism. This is the central importance of Adam Berendt's epigraphic dictum, repeated several times during *Middle Age*: "life devours life, but man breaks the cycle, man has memory" (188, 313, 450). The first one-third of the statement is pure Schopenhauer. The rest is pure pragmatism: we cannot change nature. We cannot change society overnight, or even over decades. But individuals can and do, through acts of will, change for the better. This is what happens to individuals in *Broke Heart Blues* and in *Middle Age*. It cannot happen in *Blonde* because that novel is about mass delusion seen through an already dead icon. But implicitly, in the act of reading the novel, we can see the delusions for what they are. Norma Jeane herself dismisses that "old fart Schopenhauer" and his view that "life as blind will and purposeless suffering" (201). She at least sees that Schopenhauer and Max speak a certain truth from a certain perspective. Even *Blonde*, then, can be read as affirmative because, in pinpointing the nature of our mass delusions, it implies that, as individuals, we can redirect ourselves toward more productive perspectives and therefore more productive behavior.

In all three of these later novels, Oates, like other pragmatists before her, is concerned with the possibilities for revising our perceptions and rethinking our beliefs. To borrow John Stuhr's words on Dewey, Oates "criticizes the split between aesthetic experience and ordinary life, between art and everyday objects, and between creation and appreciation." She also, in all three of these novels, clearly "rejects the identification of the religious with the supernatural." For Oates, as for Dewey, "growth does not *have* an end but rather *is* an end. Accordingly, the educational process is one of continual reconstruction and self-transformation directed at no end beyond itself."[50] Far from seeing individualism and social behavior as necessarily a dichotomy, she focuses on any individual's ability not just to create a vision by which to live but to recognize that this process is controllable. Once we become conscious of the extent to which our perception of everyday life is as creative as any "artist's"—once we see that each of us is the novelist of our own life—we can recreate and adapt. We can avoid the stasis that so often characterizes individual or collective nostalgia for something that, after all, never really existed. We take charge of our choice of metaphors, of role models, of myths, all the while conscious that that is what we are doing. If we cannot help but partially fabricate memories, and people, and ourselves, we can at least adapt these fabrications. If we create large aspects of our lives, we can also recreate. We can grow aware of defective aspects of our vision.

Oates's world is a world of paradox, irony, suggestion. But as several critics have stressed, it is above all communal. This is not to say that it encourages a group mindset, but rather individuals to respond by revising their own perspectives. Above all, it is therefore a pragmatic art. Her ongoing preoccupation with identity, with her "self," personal though it may have been at the outset, ends up being a profoundly insightful analysis of just about every area of her nation's and culture's life. For identity pervades everything. What is true for an author, intrigued by the disparity between her living self and the JCO she writes into being, is just as true for the actress, the politician, the woman, the man, the cultural identity. Through the example of her own evolving of consciousness, Oates has given Americans, and many others, a series of meditations that can be used in the ongoing process of the evolving of an individual's and a nation's consciousness. She has given America a new vision of its multiple selves, but she has also revealed the current disparities between the ideals of classical American philosophy and the values that, in her view, drive many contemporary Americans. In the process of this extraordinary evolving of consciousness over four decades of watching herself, and watching America, she has made herself into the nearest thing America has to a national novelist.

> It cannot get completed because there is nothing to complete, there is only a web of relations to be rewoven, a web which time lengthens every day.
> —RICHARD RORTY, *Contingency, Irony, and Solidarity*

AFTERWORD

JOYCE CAROL OATES's national reputation has undulated since her work first appeared at the start of the 1960s, and her international reputation remains to be solidly established. But in the short term, this is unimportant. From a pragmatist's viewpoint, solidity of a static kind is deathly. It might even be said that for things to remain "up in the air," rising or falling but at least in motion, is their most positive state. An Oates story from *The Collector of Hearts* (1999), "The Sky Blue Ball," seems to say this as precisely as does anything she has written. Short, simple, and haunting, it is, on the one hand, about silence, solitude, and the imagination; on the other hand, it is about physical activity, and the hope for social engagement.

A woman—let's say Oates—tells of how a long time ago, when she was fourteen, a sky blue ball came sailing over a wall she was walking beside. It was new and spongy and very like a ball she had played with as a little girl and "long ago misplaced." She tossed it back, and over it came again. Continuing what she thought was a game, she threw it back each time, calling out "Hi, there!" but to no reply. When eventually the ball failed to return, she climbed the wall and found it amid the weeds, "no longer sky blue but faded and cracked" and smelling of nothing but the earth and her own "sweating palm." The planet-like ball seems to stand for the enigma both of life itself and of artistic—that is to say, human—activity. In motion, the ball is alive. The artist may never see the recipient, may never know the lives of others that she nevertheless reflects, records, and engages with. The artist in us all is, in some ways, only ever alone. The ball, like a childhood memory, is only ever in our imagination. But in interaction, in the living process of writing and reading, it becomes as alive as anything else on earth. Regardless of whether this interpretation of the story is Oates's, as a reading it is a version of the ball in motion. In reading and reacting to the story, I am throwing the ball back. If unread, the story would become the equivalent of the ball lying dull and cracked amid the weeds.[1]

What matters, then, is not the art object in itself, but, first, the act of creating it and, second, the act of engaging with it. As with one story, so with a whole career: a consensus is emerging not so much as to the precise interpretation of Oates's art—indeed, that would suggest the kind of stasis it seems designed to avoid—as about its value. Much of it can speak to us individually or collectively about the wonder of simply being alive. But much more of it in recent years fulfills the pragmatic task of clarifying, and so helping us to think about and discuss, the issues of our day. As Brenda Daly implies, whether a critic shows interest in Oates as "a naturalist, or a postmodernist, a crime writer or a gothic novelist," overall she "eludes such categories." Writers and critics with very different perspectives have come to agree on one thing, however: Joyce Carol Oates is not just America's most extraordinary "woman of letters" (Updike's phrase) but as significant an American writer as any of her contemporaries. Joanne Creighton cites novelist Anne Tyler's view that "a hundred years from now people will laugh at us for sort of taking her for granted." This is much the same view as Henry Louis Gates Jr. expresses in saying that a future archaeologist equipped with nothing more than Oates's collected works could piece together postwar America. Nor does Oates's significance lie in being merely an extraordinary recorder of her era. If Richard Rorty is accurate in arguing that the novel, movies, and television have "gradually but steadily replaced the sermon and the treatise as the principal vehicles of moral change and progress," then Oates's novels alone stake their claim to be part of this. But even after that, we have her stories, essays, poems, and plays to consider, all of which testify to her unyielding search for new forms of artistic expression, new ways of seeing. "Art is more moral than moralities," wrote Dewey. "For the latter either are, or tend to become, consecrations of the status quo." Dewey saw the crucial role of art as being in not just reflecting but creating and revising our visions of ourselves and of our societies. "The moral prophets of humanity," he wrote, "have always been poets even though they spoke in free verse or by parable."[2] We may not know to what extent future generations will see enduring value in Oates's work, but she will plainly have left plenty of strong material to assess.

Having herself risen through the social strata and so come to know as intimately as anyone the layers of her country, Oates is in every sense a multifaceted commentator on America. If introspection compromises the social dimension of her early work, overall her art illustrates Dewey's belief that, in Stuhr's words, "the private and the public do not stand in necessary opposition."[3] The inmost can become the outmost, as Emerson promised. This is very much in the American tradition, and since Oates is steeped in all manner of American writing, any degree of introspection, as she has artistically matured, has echoed the wider culture. From the beginning, identity, self-creation, reinvention have been major American preoccupations. From Hawthorne to Morrison, American writing has explored the relationship between authenticity and disguise and the elusiveness implicit in constant renewal of the self and the culture. Oates has sought to follow the labyrinth of her own personality to the last elusive twist in the bend, but this has simultaneously involved helping to reshape American writing, and redefine the possibilities open to the American writer. "The process of coming to know oneself," as Rorty writes, "confronting one's own contingency, tracking one's causes home, is identical with the process of inventing a new language." And to attempt to "alter the sound of American music" (in Oates's phrase) is at the heart of the culture.[4] So while Oates has continually sought to rewrite her own experiences, at the same time she has always been engaged in the ongoing collective work, the shared social effort of continually reassessing our institutions and beliefs. "Ours is the responsibility," writes Dewey, "of conserving, transmitting, rectifying and expanding the heritage of values we have received that those who come after us may receive it more solid and secure, more widely accessible and more generously shared than we received it." It is a responsibility that Oates has palpably seen as central to her life's work.[5]

But the significance of Oates's oeuvre extends beyond national boundaries. Oates is primarily an American pragmatist, but her work is also a gathering point for Western thought in general. Her evolving of consciousness has taken in not only the ideas of American philosophers and commentators, but—as with the pragmatists before her—the sum intellect of Europe and beyond. While Pascal, Schopenhauer, and Nietzsche clearly number among her favorites, her novels also reveal intimacy with the writings of just about every major Western thinker since Plato. Nor, as her Taoist-influenced readings of Kafka and others show, is she much less attuned to Eastern thought. Even within only *With Shuddering Fall,* Eileen Bender traces the ideas of Blake, Kafka, Melville, Beckett, Nietzsche, Milton, and Meredith. And if, as Daly points out, the well-read Oates lapses therein by putting implausible perspectives into the eighteen-year-old Karen's head, one ultimately startling aspect of Oates's fiction is how lightly she wears her learning.[6] You need not be well-read to read Oates, but you can hardly help *becoming* so. Or at least you can hardly help becoming acquainted with all manner of invigorating ideas, even if you think the novel is only about suburban restlessness or a doomed interracial love affair or the confessions of a girl gang or the life and death of a cultural icon. Harnessing this accumulated wisdom to a feminist pragmatism, Oates's work has given her culture, as well as a wider community of readers, a unique and generous perspective on its innumerable selves.

To describe Oates as a national novelist perhaps requires some comment on her work in the contexts of her contemporaries. Talk of contemporary American literature nowadays always dances on the edge of impossibility. Contemporary critics' sense of "the inconceivable totality of the American novel" echoes many writers' feelings over the last three or four decades that the reality of contemporary American life has outstripped the possible response of fiction.[7] Oates's first book, *By the Northgate* (1963), appeared a couple of years after Philip Roth's famous essay "Writing American Fiction." "The American writer in the middle of the 20th century has his hands full trying to understand, and then describe, and then make *credible* much of the American reality," wrote Roth. "It stupefies, it sickens, it infuriates, and finally it is even a kind of embarrassment to one's own meagre imagination. The actuality is continually outdoing our talents, and the culture tosses up figures almost daily that are the envy of almost any novelist." If writers have felt inadequate, so have the critics in tabulating the varied and numerous strands of responses. "The past exclusion of nonwhite and nonmale intellectual and artistic talent from validation and recognition," as Cornel West puts it, "is a moral abomination." But the impulse "to correct exclusion with inclusion, to democratize the falsely meritocratic, and to pluralize the rigidly monolithic" has inevitably increased the difficulty of overall conception. Only a Jamesian "willingness to live without assurances or guarantees"—without a definable canon—allows for any kind of contextual discussion at all.[8]

This is why Joyce Carol Oates's achievement is so central to contemporary American culture. Her body of work actually reflects the state of affairs articulated by Roth about American reality at the start of Oates's career and by critics about the contemporary American novel. She simultaneously embraces the realist traditions found in Bellow, Styron, Updike, and Tyler, diverse interests in, say, history, science, race, gender, and region that link her with any number of writers (Morrison, Louise Erdrich, Andrea Barrett, Ellen Gilchrist, Cormac McCarthy), and the postmodernism associated with writers as different as Doctorow and DeLillo. Oates allows her readers, over the course of her novels, to choose from the whole panoply of previous and present narrative art, as well as creating other novels unlike any that have gone before. If you wanted to illustrate any kind of fiction from the picaresque to the postmodernist, the realist to the modernist, and had only Oates's work to choose from, you would be able to do so. If you wanted to illustrate the permutations of genre permeability you could do so simply using the interplay between her novels, stories, poetry, plays, and criticism. She writes about, and often from the viewpoint of, precisely the kinds of characters tossed up daily "that are the envy of any novelist": a reform-school girl turned kidnapper, a Jeffrey Dahmeresque psychopath, a Kennedyesque senator, a Marilyn Monroesque movie princess with royal connections. Her collage-plays, such as *I Stand Before You Naked* and *The Secret Mirror* in *Twelve Plays,* express this polyphony in microcosmic form. On the one hand, her willingness to "enter the minds" of diverse protagonists signals her belief that to understand diverse American realities within an overall conceptual frame is at least possible. On the other hand, the sometimes painfully personal aspect of her art, which helps create a tension between what we assume to be acted and what we suspect is actual, provides an inherent recognition that mutually incomprehensible diversity is often the state of affairs in American society.

"Click into the event from X possible points of view. Soon your perspective will be multiplied to infinity. Limitless as the universe." Like Franklin Hart's pioneering version of virtual reality, we have had to adapt our selves and our art to our new status as beings with hugely increased exposure to multiple perspectives. We can access information from an incalculable number of viewpoints, and the narrative device of parts 1 and 3 of *Broke Heart Blues* reveal the impact of this on the possibilities for the novel form. Jurassic pockets notwithstanding, there are strong elements in American culture, too, that continually push for the acceptance of pluralism. Contrary to D. J. Taylor's opinion that Oates is "a high priestess" of political correctness, Oates's career exemplifies an Emersonian and William Jamesian rejection of rigidity or dogma-led group mentality of any kind. Moreover, the fact that she is so interested in exploring American realities different from her own, and so diversely in terms of genre and approach, means that her work provides a link between notions of an American literary canon and notions of plurality. What O'Donnell calls "the capacious, worldly, bordering yet borderless country of the contemporary American novel" is nowhere better reflected than in Oates's imbricated, ever-proliferating achievement. Just as "the proliferations of the 'American' novel over the last forty years," as O'Donnell writes, have been "rhizomic," spreading plant-like, "with multiple crossings and branchings, growing everywhere," so Oates is the most rhizomic of contemporary American writers.[9] No other contemporary writer has given voice in so sustained or varied a way to the multiplicity of concerns that define contemporary American culture. Her work is inclusive without being conclusive, and her paradoxical search for unity yet awareness of diversity should place her writing at the center of American cultural debate.

There are prolific writers; writers who have written Great American Novels and writers whose hold on the public's imagination outstrips Oates's. But the only truly comparable figure, in terms of the extent and variety of subject matter as well as some actual subject matter, is Norman Mailer. There is a sense in which Oates, even while declaring Updike a literary soul mate, has consciously or unconsciously always seen Mailer as both a literary companion and opposite—as if she were a Norma (Jeane) Femailer to his Normal Male. At first sight, they entirely contrast. The short, pugnacious, hard-drinking street fighter (as the image goes) and the willowy, self-effacing, academic teetotaler hardly look like sparring partners. The ebullient self-promoter whose "magnificent disgust" at his era led him to become not just a writer but "an actor in the cultural drama" seems the very opposite of the "invisible woman."[10] But the parallels between the two are manifold. Feminist though she is, Oates's writing also has its genderless aspects, and Oates has never been afraid to climb into the ring with male writers. Such an emphasis on the mind's androgyny echoes not only Whitman, of course ("I am the poet of the woman the same as the man, / And I say it is as great to be a woman as to be a man") but also Virginia Woolf. "One has a profound, if irrational instinct in favour of the theory that the union of man and woman makes for the greater satisfaction, the most complete happiness," writes Woolf in *A Room of One's Own*. This prompts her to ponder "whether there are two sexes in the mind corresponding to the two sexes in the body." Ambivalence toward gender orientation in one's writing—or even in *some* of one's writing—is ambivalence toward limitation. "A great mind," Woolf quotes Coleridge, "is androgynous." The genderless attitude—as an ideal—facilitates a broader perspective and greater productivity. "I would ask you to write all kinds of books," urges Woolf, "hesitating at no subject however trivial or however vast."[11] Oates, whose books range from *The Edge of Impossibility* to *Tenderness, Miracle Play* to *On Boxing, The Poisoned Kiss* to *Zombie, Blonde* to Rosamond Smith's *The Barrens*, children's books like *Come Meet Muffin!* to young-adult novels like *Big Mouth & Ugly Girl* and *Freaky Green Eyes*, is the exemplary disciple of this call. And one aspect of this is to embrace the perspective of the male's male, a writer whose own output, from *The Naked and the Dead* to *Why Are We in Vietnam?* to *Of a Fire on the Moon* to *The Executioner's Song* to *Ancient Evenings* to *The Gospel According to the Son,* not only rivals but often anticipates, parallels, or follows her own.

In a 1970s essay on Mailer, Oates argues that what had "largely been mistaken as self-display" was really Mailer's "efforts to dramatize the terror of the disintegrating identity." She describes Mailer as a kindred spirit in terms of his fascination with issues of identity, whose approach is nevertheless antithetical to her own. Though she disagrees "with nearly every one of Mailer's stated or implied ideas," she is "always conscious in reading his work that the stasis he dramatizes is a vast, communal tragedy." Mailer (like Oates) "is obsessed with the need to trust his own deepest instincts" and "to create a mythology in order to avoid being enslaved by someone else's." Both have been driven by a Nietzschean vision of self-creation, and "to fail as a poet—and thus for Nietzsche, to fail as a human being—is to accept somebody else's description of oneself."[12] While Mailer's song of himself directly contrasts with Oates's song of herself, both have been preoccupied with their public identities. The extroverted writer and the introverted writer may look poles apart, but these two stances—as Oates's novels show—are part of that same preoccupation with securing their own significance as writers, even if that significance is ultimately as reflections of their culture, rather than as individuals.

Oates's story "Naked," for instance, is concerned with women's fears of physical vulnerability, but, as Sally Robinson illustrates, it is also about identity. Like so much of Oates's writing, this identity theme works on more than one level. The woman is a faculty wife whose "uncensorious liberalism" is challenged when the black children strip her to "the undeniable privilege of her white skin." But she also seems to symbolize the authorial tension between revelation and concealment. "The terror of being discovered naked as she was, battered, bruised, disheveled as a wild animal," is "simply too much for her." She wants "only to hide and not be seen." She sees "herself, a naked, spectral figure, floating in directions parallel to but hidden from the roads" that lead home. Filled with a fear of death, she imagines the moment when "all the prior history of her life—her achievement, her winningness, her sunny smile and resolute optimism, and her love for her family and theirs for her"—will "be summarily erased" and she will "become a story, a fiction." The woman's fate seems, among other things, to parallel the fate of any writer whose work is examined by critics. Many of the attributes the woman admires in herself are traits Oates might equally admire. *"I do what I want to do,"* says the story's heroine. And the story ends with her "in the dark below the house, squatting where no one could see her," waiting naked "until such time as it would become known to her why she was waiting."[13] Whatever else—peer reaction? to be noticed?—a writer awaits readers, and not only "an ideal reader or two" but also those willing to critically assess and honor aspects of the writer's achievement. Criticism, if the writer's work is taken up, is the writer's fate, the fiction she will be turned into: *la gueule qu'on lui a fait*—"the mug that the critics have given [her]."[14]

Oates, like almost all writers, wants her work to be noticed. Her desire for invisibility has to do with her personal life, her everyday self. But for her work, she is as ambitious as any male writer. Like Marya Knauer, her career has surely always involved a "wish to compete" in the literary Game—albeit with more playfulness and more ironic distance from such a notion than Marya displays.[15] Who better to enter the ring with than Mailer? Like many male writers before him, from Byron to Hemingway, Mailer has written on boxing, notably with *The Fight* (1975), about Muhammad Ali's recapture of the world heavyweight championship against George Foreman in Zaire. Oates's *On Boxing* was commissioned as an article and draws on an interest ignited by her father, who took her to bouts when she was a young girl. So it is not so much that she competes as that she has no hesitation in entering "male" terrain, and often triumphantly. Mailer commented of *On Boxing* that it was so good "I said to myself, 'My God, *I* could have written that piece.'" Oates responded that "there's nothing like that supreme accolade—to be told that you write like a man. And not just any man, but Norman Mailer."[16] In both cases, their songs of themselves have been about siding with the outlaws. Having begun his career in a realist mode, Mailer quickly became a spokesman for the counterculture. From his essay "The White Negro" (1957), reprinted in *Advertisements for Myself* (1959), to *Armies of the Night* (1968) he both promoted himself and, in David Van Leer's words, finally "satirized his own persona."

If Oates's description of herself as an "invisible woman" superficially contrasts with Mailer's self-advertising stance, his notion of himself as a "White Negro" is echoed in Abraham Licht's description of himself as white, but outside the white race, and in Iris Courtney, who "sides with the outlaws." "I felt the thrill of the outlaw, the outcast: the object of loathing and taboo," writes the self-named Anellia in *I'll Take You There*. "My skin was 'white,' a camouflage I might wear through life." Moreover *Invisible Woman*, the title Oates gave her journal and a volume of her selected poems, is a reference to Ralph Ellison's 1952 novel, *Invisible Man*, about a black man's search for identity in a racist society. Oates's exploration of identity involves both a perceived *lack* of identity and an assertion of identity that, like Whitman and Mailer, transcends the individual to become cultural. "Through me many long dumb voices," writes Whitman. "I am not only American," writes Oates, "but a kind of cross-section of America—barring the real wealth and the real poverty. Which is most authentically myself I can't know but would guess—judging from the odd jarring sympathies I feel for even monsters like Manson—that I place myself psychologically *even below* the decent respectable working-class background of my childhood."[17]

Famously, of course, another of Mailer's subjects has been Marilyn Monroe. Quite aside from twinning Norma Jeane with Princess Diana, there are clear reasons why *Oates* would take up Monroe as a subject matter. But while the motive for metaphor in any poetic sensibility, in Oates's view, is "the ceaseless defining of the self and of the world by way of language," Oates's interest in Monroe also seems connected to her interest in Mailer as an American literary figure.[18] Among other things, Mailer shares Oates's fascination with parallel names, pseudonyms, and anagrams. Oates's retention of the extra *e* in Jeane would seem to be a way of signaling the wedding of herself with the character (just as such previous, though male, figures as Jules, Jesse, Jinx, Jerome, and Judd all have the *J* of Joyce). Similarly, in *Marilyn*, Mailer, in his doomed desire to find an intimate connection between himself and the star he never met, indulges in anagramatic fantasy. He notes that her letters ("if the 'a' were used twice and the 'o' but once") would spell his own name, "leaving only the 'y' for excess." He is sane enough to realize, of course, that "if he wished to play anagrams," she was also Marlon Y. Normie or Marolem Mamroe or Mormam Maeler, so he backs off from such verbal pleasures. Instead, he settles for "nothing less vainglorious than a novel of Marilyn Monroe," "written in the form of a biography." *Blonde*, in turn, is a quasi *auto*biography of Monroe. Like Mailer, Oates never deludes herself that she "might be telling a story which could possibly be more accurate than a fiction," since both writers are "quick to imagine the interior of many a closed and silent life." Each novelist offers "a literary hypothesis of a *possible* Marilyn Monroe."[19] But what they also offer, of course, not only in *Marilyn* and *Blonde* but in both writers' enormous body of work, are versions of America that are simultaneously biographical and autobiographical: seen from within and without on the Emersonian assumption that the inmost becomes the outmost. For Marilyn Monroe, as opposed to Norma Jean(e), was a fiction, just as America, while rooted in the real, is enraptured with itself as an idea, written into being.

In the end, this is not a contest at all, but a comparison: no more legitimately seen as a boxing bout than a love affair, a dance, a collaboration, two interweaving strands of a tapestry in the making: America describing itself to America. Yet where for years we have compared Oates with other writers, past and present, perhaps comparisons are no longer necessary. Rather, who might we compare with Joyce Carol Oates? For years now, she has lived with her particular *la gueule qu'on lui a fait*—a prolific, many-genred woman writer given to Gothicism and the "unwomanly" impulse to write about violence. But that "mug" she has tended to receive merely seeks to hold work that slides out of critical frameworks and literary precedent. In fact, the work remains very much a living subject. The main body of her readership has yet to assemble, and no definitive category may finally fit her multidimensional achievement. Yet the fact that she overflows the measure makes tracing the contours of her work all the more interesting. It has therefore seemed a reasonable task to help further articulate the significance of her novel writing in ways that complement studies ranging from G. F. Waller's *Dreaming America* in 1979 to Daly's *Lavish Self-Divisions* in 1996. If each of us inevitably distorts the material with our vision because we cannot include it all, such communal creativity is, for the pragmatist, the irreducible experience of actual life.

In her worksheets for *What I Lived For,* Oates quotes Charles Darwin commenting that "my mind seems to have become a kind of machine for grinding out general laws out of large collections of facts." She has always been a writer conscious that much of what we do we cannot explain to ourselves, let alone to others. No doubt, like Nietzsche, she must at times feel as if she were a "pen being tried out by some superior power on a bit of paper." For Oates, very often the desire to write precedes the subject, which comes into being through the act of writing. Similarly, in terms of critical approaches to her work, what matters is that we engage, as she puts it in *The Profane Art,* in "reflection upon reflection." Process is all. Oates talks of running—one of her pastimes—as if it were writing. "It has the illusion that it's timeless," she says. "I just run and there's no beginning or end, just basically running." To run—as she learned early in her life—is to survive, just as, for her, to write is to survive. "Suicide is pointless!" says Abraham Licht. "One must be a rainbow, and exult in its prismatic ever-changing colors, that live forever, and cannot be destroyed." This attitude is one reason why her work has ultimately come to reflect not merely aspects of her personal story, but something of the homogeneity, variety, but perhaps above all vibrant energy of her culture. The Americanness of Oates equally involves the fact that she is always in motion, always becoming. In Saul Bellow's *Henderson the Rain King*, Henderson, asked what kind of traveler he is, believes that "some people found satisfaction in *being*," while "others were taken up with *becoming*." "Enough!" he decides. "Time to have become. Time to Be! Burst the spirit's sleep. Wake up, America!"[20] But Henderson forgets that being *is* becoming. Becoming *is* being. Or else there is nothing. This is the heart of Oates's work, just as it is at the heart of pragmatism, and it helps explain her productivity.

To conclude, then, would not just be an end to becoming, but an end to being. It would be to consign the sky blue ball to the weeds, dull, cracked, and motionless. The point is to keep it in motion. Moreover, whether the ball throwing is an activity the artist engages in for the amusement of her own imagination or as a social activity—whether the thrower the other side of the wall exists—is not, finally, at issue. The quest for private perfection and the quest for shared endeavor may be incommensurable, but, for a writer such as Oates, they are not incompatible. She translates the religious zeal of Pascal and the pessimism of Schopenhauer, via Emerson, Nietzsche, James, and Dewey, into the meliorism of American (feminist) pragmatism or (pragmatist) feminism. Perhaps, like all of us, she has only ever slenderly known aspects of her "self." But she has not so much lost interest in her personal identity as grown interested in her writing as a repository for cultural perceptions, "a process" (as she writes in "JCO and I") "that has resulted in a sequence of texts." She has—in her writing—become an experimental pen, a machine for illustrating general laws from a myriad muddles of facts, an instrument for measuring the "seismic shudders" of her culture even as she is a catalyst for gradual or seismic shifts in consciousness by individual readers. The inward remains. But out of the inward comes the outward. Out of the personal comes the cultural. That introspective girl who retreated from a cruel environment into books and writing, in doing so projected her mind onto her country and turned those dark eyes on America. Her work is her ongoing triumph. The writings of Joyce Carol Oates, whose books will continue to be read, reinterpreted, and so kept alive, regardless of the fate of the individual who wrote them, are, as she says of America itself, "a tale still being told—in many voices—and nowhere near its conclusion."[21]

NOTES

INTRODUCTION

1. Joyce Carol Oates (hereafter, JCO), journal, 12 January 1975, quoted in Greg Johnson, *Invisible Writer: A Biography of Joyce Carol Oates* (New York: Dutton, 1998), 240; JCO, *(Woman) Writer: Occasions and Opportunities* (New York: Dutton, 1988), 5, 34; Linda Wagner-Martin, "Panoramic, Unpredictable, and Human: Joyce Carol Oates's Recent Novels," in *Traditions, Voices, and Dreams: The American Novel since the 1960s,* ed. Melvin J. Friedman and Ben Siegel (Newark: University of Delaware Press, 1995), 196–97; Ellen G. Friedman, "Joyce Carol Oates," in *Modern American Women Writers,* ed. Elaine Showalter, Lea Baechler, and A. Walton Litz (New York: Charles Scribner's Sons, 1991), 353–74.

2. American pragmatism is the philosophical movement anticipated by Emerson, christened by Charles Sanders Peirce, then articulated by William James. Classical American philosophy is philosophy in America between the setting forth of pragmatism in the 1870s and the deaths of John Dewey and George Santayana in the early 1950s. Pragmatism has been developed by figures as diverse as Jane Addams, Josiah Royce, George Herbert Mead, Alain Locke, and, more recently, Richard Rorty and Charlene Haddock Seigfried.

3. Richard Rorty, "Feminism and Pragmatism," *Michigan Quarterly Review* 30 (Spring 1991): 242; John Barth, "The Literature of Replenishment," *Atlantic Monthly,* January 1980, 66; Richard Rorty, *Contingency, Irony, and Solidarity* (Cambridge: Cambridge University Press, 1989), 7.

4. Allan Megill, *Prophets of Extremity: Nietzsche, Heidegger, Foucault, Derrida* (1985; rpt., Berkeley: University of California Press, 1987), 33; Richard Rorty, *Consequences of Pragmatism: Essays, 1972–1980* (Brighton: Harvester Press, 1982), xlii, 161, 166; manuscript page in John Dewey Papers, Morris Library, Southern Illinois University at Carbondale, 102/58/10, quoted by John J. Stuhr, "John Dewey," in *Pragmatism and Classical American Philosophy: Essential Readings and Interpretive Essays,* ed. John J. Stuhr (Oxford: Oxford University Press, 2000), 435, and Stuhr, "Classical American Philosophy," ibid., 1.

5. William James, "What Pragmatism Means," in Stuhr, ed., *Pragmatism and Classical American Philosophy,* 197; Stuhr, "Classical American Philosophy," 1; Mary Kathryn Grant, *The Tragic Vision of Joyce Carol Oates* (Durham, NC: Duke University Press, 1978), 4.

6. Stuhr, "Classical American Philosophy," 2; Eileen Teper Bender, *Joyce Carol Oates: Artist in Residence* (Bloomington: Indiana University Press, 1987), xi.

7. See, for instance, Eva Manske, "The Nightmare of Reality: Gothic Fantasies and Psychological Realism in the Fiction of Joyce Carol Oates," in *Neo-Realism in Contemporary American Fiction,* ed. Kristiaan Versluys (Amsterdam: Rodopi, 1992), 131–43. The phrase "nightmare vision" is taken from Carol Harter, "America as a 'Consumer Garden': The Nightmare Vision of Joyce Carol Oates," *Revue Des Langues Vivantes,* bicentennial issue (1976), 171–87.

8. Ralph Waldo Emerson, "Self-Reliance," in *The Norton Anthology of American Literature,* ed. Nina Baym et al. (1979; rpt., New York: Norton, 1989), 442; Joe David Bellamy, "The Dark Lady of American Letters," in *Conversations with Joyce Carol Oates,* ed. Lee Milazzo (Jackson: University Press of Mississippi, 1989), 21. Emerson's phrase does not appear in all versions of "Self-Reliance."

9. JCO, letter to the author, 20 July 1994; William James, "Faith and the Right to Believe," in *The Writings of William James,* ed. John J. McDermott (Chicago: University of Chicago Press, 1977), 739.

10. JCO, conversation with the author, Princeton, NJ, 17 July 1998; John J. McDermott, "William James," in Stuhr, ed., *Pragmatism and Classical American Philosophy,* 140.

11. David Bromwich, "The Novelists of Every Day Life," in *The Revival of Pragmatism: New Essays on Social Thought, Law, and Culture,* ed. Morris Dickstein (Durham, NC: Duke University Press, 1998), 370–76; McDermott, "William James," 144; JCO, *Do with Me What You Will* (New York: Dutton, 1973), 123; JCO, letter to the author, 20 July 1994.

12. JCO, *(Woman) Writer,* 377; JCO, "JCO and I," limited-edition pamphlet (Concord, NH: William B. Ewert, 1994); Mikhail Bakhtin, *The Dialogic Imagination: Four Essays,* trans. Michael Holquist and Caryl Emerson, ed. Michael Holquist (Austin: University of Texas Press, 1981), 292.

13. JCO, *I'll Take You There* (New York: Ecco Press, 2002), 276; JCO, *(Woman) Writer,* 6; *Ohio Review,* "Transformations of Self: An Interview with Joyce Carol Oates," in Milazzo, ed., *Conversations,* 47; JCO, "Afterword: Reflections on the Grotesque," in *Haunted: Tales of the Grotesque* (New York: Dutton, 1994; New York: Plume, 1995), 303.

14. Ralph Waldo Emerson, "Self-Reliance," in *The Complete Prose Works of Ralph Waldo Emerson,* ed. G. T. Bettany (New York: Ward, Lock, 1889), 15.

15. JCO, *(Woman) Writer,* 3–4; JCO, *You Must Remember This* (New York: Dutton, 1987), 401. In *(Woman) Writer,* Oates suggests two theories about the genesis of art: "it originates in play," and "it originates out of the artist's conviction that he or she is born damned; and must struggle through life to achieve redemption. By way of art."

16. Rorty, *Consequences of Pragmatism,* 161; JCO, introduction to *The Essential Dickinson* (Hopewell, NJ: Ecco Press, 1996), 3; JCO, letter to the author, 20 July 1994; JCO, "Delirium and Detachment: The Secret of Being a Writer," *New Yorker,* 23 June–3 July 1995, 134–37.

17. Rorty, *Contingency, Irony, and Solidarity,* xiv–xvi.

18. JCO, letter to the author, 7 January 1998.

19. Megill, *Prophets of Extremity,* 342.

20. JCO, letter to the author, 20 July 1994. "I'm an American writer keenly attuned to the world in which I live, its seismic shudders and more subtle emanations."

21. P. Sreelakshmi, *Elective Affinities: A Study of the Sources and Intertexts of Joyce Carol Oates's Short Fiction* (Madras: T. R. Publications, 1996), 10.

22. Brenda Daly, *Lavish Self-Divisions: The Novels of Joyce Carol Oates* (Jackson: University Press of Mississippi, 1996), xi.

23. Marilyn C. Wesley, "The Simultaneous Universe: The Politics of Jamesian Conversion in Joyce Carol Oates's Fiction," *Essays in Literature* 18, no. 2 (1991): 274. For early views of Oates and feminism, see, for instance, Grant, *The Tragic Vision of Joyce Carol Oates*, 28–29, whose conclusion in the 1970s was that "Oates is not a feminist writer; in fact she appears impervious to feminist concerns," and Susan Koppelman Cornillon, ed., *Images of Women in Fiction: Feminist Perspectives* (1972; rev. ed., Bowling Green: Bowling Green University Popular Press, 1973), 120, for whom Oates seemed to "fully participate in the myths of our culture about the 'basic natures' of men and women."

24. William James, "What Pragmatism Means," 195. "There is absolutely nothing new in the pragmatic method. Socrates was an adept at it."

25. Bertrand Russell, *Bertrand Russell Speaks His Mind* (New York: Bard Books, 1960), 14; William Heyen, "Open Letter to Oates," *Tri-Quarterly* 73 (Fall 1988): 89; JCO, *I'll Take You There*, 252; Friedrich Nietzsche, *Beyond Good and Evil*, in *Basic Writings of Nietzsche*, ed. and trans. Walter Kaufmann (New York: Random House, 1968), 278; JCO, *Childwold* (New York: Dutton, 1976), 137; JCO, journal entry, 1 June 1978, quoted in Johnson, *Invisible Writer*, 279; George Santayana, "The Genteel Tradition in American Philosophy," in Stuhr, ed., *Pragmatism and Classical American Philosophy*, 356.

1. MIRRORS AND WINDOWS

1. Harold Bloom, introduction to *Joyce Carol Oates*, ed. Harold Bloom (New York: Chelsea House, 1987), 2; Linda W. Wagner, introduction to *Critical Essays on Joyce Carol Oates*, ed. Linda W. Wagner (Boston: Twayne, 1979), xxiii; Mary Kathryn Grant, *The Tragic Vision of Joyce Carol Oates* (Durham, NC: Duke University Press, 1978), 11.

2. G. F. Waller, *Dreaming America: Obsession and Transcendence in Joyce Carol Oates's Fiction* (Baton Rouge: Louisiana State University Press, 1979), 29–30; Samuel Chase Coale, "Contending Spirits," in Bloom, ed., *Joyce Carol Oates*, 126; Donald A. Dike, "The Aggressive Victim in the Fiction of Joyce Carol Oates," *Greyfriar* 15 (1974): 13–14.

3. JCO, *(Woman) Writer: Occasions and Opportunities* (New York: Dutton, 1988), 75: "Once, years ago, in 1972 to be precise, when I was living in London, and I was very sick, I had a mystical vision." For more information, see Greg Johnson, *Invisible Writer: A Biography of Joyce Carol Oates* (New York: Dutton, 1998), 210, who states that the experience took place in December 1971, and that by early February Oates had drafted *Do with Me What You Will* and *New Heaven, New Earth*.

4. Bloom, introduction to Bloom, ed., *Joyce Carol Oates*, 1; JCO, *New Heaven, New Earth: The Visionary Experience in Literature* (New York: Vanguard, 1974; London: Victor Gollancz, 1976), 3. Subsequent in-text references are to this edition.

5. JCO, *The Edge of Impossibility: Tragic Forms in Literature* (New York: Vanguard, 1972; London: Jonathan Cape, 1976), 6, 182, 182, 213.

6. Waller, *Dreaming America*, 21.

7. JCO, *Invisible Woman: New and Selected Poems, 1970–1982* (Princeton, NJ: Ontario Review Press, 1982), 99; JCO, *Anonymous Sins and Other Poems* (Baton Rouge: Louisiana State University Press, 1969), 6–7, 64, 79.

8. JCO, *Anonymous Sins*, 59.

9. JCO, *(Woman) Writer*, xii; JCO, letter to the author, 20 July 1994.

10. JCO, *With Shuddering Fall* (New York: Vanguard, 1964; London: Jonathan Cape, 1965), 172; and *A Garden of Earthly Delights* (New York: Vanguard, 1967), 180, 172. Subsequent in-text references are to these editions. For the 2003 Modern Library edition, Oates revised and rewrote three-quarters of the novel.

11. Johnson, *Invisible Writer*, 114; Eileen Teper Bender, *Joyce Carol Oates: Artist in Residence* (Bloomington: Indiana University Press, 1987), 30.

12. Pamela Smiley, "Incest, Roman Catholicism, and Joyce Carol Oates," *College Literature* 19 (Fall 1991): 39, 45.

13. Dike, "The Aggressive Victim," 18.

14. See Johnson, *Invisible Writer*, 71.

15. Elaine Showalter, *"Where Are You Going, Where Have You Been?"* (New Brunswick, NJ: Rutgers University Press, 1994), 9.

16. Arthur Schopenhauer, *The World as Will and Idea*, ed. David Berman, trans. Jill Berman (London: Dent, 1995), 245; Ellen G. Friedman, *Joyce Carol Oates* (New York: Ungar, 1980).

17. Eilat Negev, "My Life with Sylvia Plath, by Ted Hughes," *Daily Telegraph*, 31 October, 1998, 4; Richard Rorty, *Contingency, Irony, and Solidarity* (Cambridge: Cambridge University Press, 1989), xiv–xvi.

18. JCO, letter to the author, 20 July 1994.

19. Walter Sullivan, "The Artificial Demon: Joyce Carol Oates and the Dimensions of the Real," in Bloom, ed., *Joyce Carol Oates*, 13.

20. Schopenhauer, *The World as Will and Idea*, 85.

21. Waller, *Dreaming America*, 12.

22. JCO, *Expensive People* (New York: Vanguard, 1968; New York: Quality Paperback Book Club, 1990), 130. Subsequent in-text references are to this edition, which includes the 1990 afterword.

23. JCO, *New Heaven, New Earth*, 46; Robert Phillips, "Joyce Carol Oates: The Art of Fiction LXXII," in *Conversations with Joyce Carol Oates*, ed. Lee Milazzo (Jackson: University Press of Mississippi, 1989), 63; Rorty, *Contingency, Irony, and Solidarity*, 192.

24. Greg Johnson, *Understanding Joyce Carol Oates* (Columbia, SC: University of South Carolina Press, 1987), 49, 50; Bender, *Joyce Carol Oates*, 32, 33, 35; Waller, *Dreaming America*, 120, 123; Joanne V. Creighton, *Joyce Carol Oates* (Boston: Twayne, 1979), 63; Sullivan, "The Artificial Demon," 11.

25. In this quotation from Oates, as in others elsewhere, italics are in the original. Because Oates uses italics so frequently, at quotations below I have not stated "italics in the original."

26. Fyodor Dostoyevsky, *Notes from Underground*, trans. Jesse Coulson (Harmondsworth, Eng.: Penguin, 1972), 16.

27. Kim Chernin, *The Hungry Self: Women, Eating, and Identity* (London: Virago, 1985), 23. For further biographical information, see Johnson, *Invisible Writer*, 172–76.

28. Brenda Daly, *Lavish Self-Divisions: The Novels of Joyce Carol Oates* (Jackson: University Press of Mississippi, 1996), 35; Sandra M. Gilbert and Susan Gubar, "Infection in the Sentence: The Woman Writer and the Anxiety of Authorship," in *Feminisms: An Anthology of Literary Theory and Criticism*, ed. Robyn R. Warhol and Diane Price Herndl (New Brunswick, NJ: Rutgers University Press, 1997), 21–22.

29. JCO, *New Heaven, New Earth*, 35.

30. Stendhal, *The Red and the Black*, trans. Catherine Slater (Oxford: Oxford World Classics, 1991), 348; JCO, *them* (New York: Vanguard: 1968; New York: Quality Paperback Book Club, 1992), 264, 266, 267. Subsequent in-text references are to this edition, which includes the 1992 afterword.

31. Bloom, introduction to Bloom, ed., *Joyce Carol Oates*, 5.

32. George Steiner, *Language and Silence: Essays, 1958–1966* (London: Faber, 1967), 87–88.

33. Sullivan, "The Artificial Demon," 11; Milan Kundera, *The Unbearable Lightness of Being*, trans. Michael Henry Heinz (New York: Harper & Row, 1984; London: Picador, 1989), 63. This part of the novel reflects Oates's own experiences with a student just prior to *them*. Richard Wishnetsky, a schizophrenic student who in 1966 shot and killed a rabbi and then himself in the Shaaray Zaneck synagogue, "impressed and alarmed" Oates with his intensity about philosophical and religious matters. "I could not understand," said Oates, "that what I as a professor talked about all the time—every teaching day—these grandiose problems of life, death, God, fate, etc., etc., were being taken in absolute seriousness by Richard. He was really living these problems out, while my colleagues and I made coin by them, so to speak"; see Johnson, *Invisible Writer*, 127–32. The effect of this incident is clear in stories like "In the Region of Ice" and "Last Days" and in several subsequent novels.

34. Rorty, *Irony, Contingency, and Solidarity*, 196.

35. JCO, "*Wonderland* Revisited," in *Wonderland* (Princeton, NJ: Ontario Review Press, 1992), 510, 507, 508; assigned to Trick Monk in the novel, the epigraphic poem appeared under Oates's name as "Iris Into Eye," *Poetry Northwest* (Autumn 1970) and in *Angel Fire* (Baton Rouge: Louisiana State University Press, 1973), 61.

36. Calvin Bedient, "Sleeping Beauty and the Love Like Hatred," and Gordon O. Taylor, "Joyce Carol Oates: Artist in Wonderland," in Bloom, ed., *Joyce Carol Oates*, 19, 24; JCO, "*Wonderland* Revisited," 509, 510; Joe David Bellamy, "The Dark Lady of American Letters," in Milazzo, ed., *Conversations*, 19–20.

37. Taylor, "Joyce Carol Oates," 33–34; Johnson, *Invisible Writer*, 119.

38. JCO, "In Traction," in *The Assignation* (New York: Ecco Press, 1988; New York: Harper & Row, 1989), 40, and "Jail-Bait," *Guardian Saturday Review*, 10 October, 1998, 1–2; Taylor, "Joyce Carol Oates," 26; Johnson, *Invisible Writer*, 124, 129.

39. Creighton, *Joyce Carol Oates*, 76; JCO, *Wonderland* (New York: Vanguard, 1971), 58. Subsequent in-text references are to this edition.

40. Johnson, *Invisible Writer*, 185.

41. JCO, *The Edge of Impossibility*, 92.

42. As several critics have noted, the novel's ending is itself unstable to the extent that Oates revised it after initial publication. In the original ending, father and daughter are adrift in a boat, and Shelley is dying, whereas in subsequent editions "nobody is going to die" (508).

43. Schopenhauer, *The World as Will and Idea*, 37.

44. JCO, *New Heaven, New Earth*, 133.

2. ABSTRACTION INTO ACTION

1. Greg Johnson, *Joyce Carol Oates: A Study of the Short Fiction* (New York: Twayne, 1994), 3, 56; JCO, "The Edge of the World," in *By the Northgate* (New York: Vanguard, 1963), 157. Each story mentioned here also appears in JCO, *Where Are You Going, Where Have You Been? Selected Early Stories* (Princeton, NJ: Ontario Review Press, 1993).

2. Harry J. Berman, "Joyce Carol Oates's 'A Theory of Knowledge,'" *International Journal of Aging and Human Development* 93, no. 4 (1992–93): 296.

3. JCO, "A Theory of Knowledge," in *Night-Side: Eighteen Tales* (New York: Vanguard, 1977), 356. Subsequent in-text references are to this edition.

4. Berman, "Joyce Carol Oates's 'A Theory of Knowledge,'" 298–301.

5. Walter Clemons, "Joyce Carol Oates: Love and Violence," in *Conversations with Joyce Carol Oates*, ed. Lee Milazzo (Jackson: University Press of Mississippi, 1989), 39; Greg Johnson, *Understanding Joyce Carol Oates* (Columbia, SC: University of South Carolina Press, 1987), 134; letter to Gail Godwin, 18 September 1972, quoted in Greg Johnson, *Invisible Writer: A Biography of Joyce Carol Oates* (New York: Dutton, 1998), 217. Johnson suggests that the period from *New Heaven, New Earth* through much of the 1970s was a time of psychological healing and the development of a new perspective. Not the least of this was Oates's "belief that personal salvation lay in escaping the illusion of the Romantic, isolated ego" and participating in what she called a "communal consciousness" (*Invisible Writer*, 210).

6. JCO, *Childwold* (New York: Vanguard, 1976; London: Jonathan Cape, 1977), 64. Subsequent in-text references are to this edition.

7. D. H. Lawrence, *Studies in Classic American Literature* (New York: Thomas Seltzer, 1923; Harmondsworth, Eng.: Penguin, 1983), 70; William Faulkner, "An Introduction to *The Sound and the Fury*," in *The Sound and the Fury*, ed. David Minter (New York: Norton, 1987), 220; Johnson, *Invisible Writer*, 246.

8. Calvin Bedient, "Sleeping Beauty and the Love Like Hatred," in *Joyce Carol Oates*, ed. Harold Bloom (New York: Chelsea House, 1987), 21; Eileen Teper Bender, *Joyce Carol Oates: Artist in Residence* (Bloomington: Indiana University Press, 1987), 72; Brenda Daly, *Lavish Self-Divisions: The Novels of Joyce Carol Oates* (Jackson: University Press of Mississippi, 1996), 90.

9. Friedrich Nietzsche, *The Birth of Tragedy*, in *The Basic Writings of Nietzsche*, ed. Walter Kaufmann (New York: Random House, 1968), 72.

10. Mary Ann Wilson, "From Thanatos to Eros: A Study of Erotic Love in Joyce Carol Oates' *Do with Me What You Will*," *Studies in the Humanities* 11 (December 1984): 54.

11. JCO, *Do with Me What You Will* (New York: Dutton, 1973), 538. Subsequent in-text references are to this edition.

12. Ellen G. Friedman, *Joyce Carol Oates* (New York: Ungar, 1980), 190.

13. Marilyn C. Wesley, *Refusal and Transgression in Joyce Carol Oates's Fiction* (Westport, CT: Greenwood Press, 1993), 117.

14. Bender, *Joyce Carol Oates*, 42; Daly, *Lavish Self-Divisions*, 89–90.

15. Wilson, "From Thanatos to Eros," 53–54.

16. Taylor, "Joyce Carol Oates: Artist in Wonderland," in Bloom, ed., *Joyce Carol Oates*, 25.
17. JCO, letter to the author, 20 July 1994.
18. Bender, *Joyce Carol Oates*, 11.
19. Samuel Chase Coale, "Joyce Carol Oates: Contending Spirits," in Bloom, ed., *Joyce Carol Oates*, 126; Johnson, *Invisible Writer*, 239–41; Joanne V. Creighton, *Joyce Carol Oates* (Boston: Twayne, 1979), 95, 100; G. F. Waller, *Dreaming America: Obsession and Transcendence in Joyce Carol Oates's Fiction* (Baton Rouge: Louisiana State University Press, 1979), 189; Daly, *Lavish Self-Divisions*, 94.
20. JCO, *The Assassins: A Book of Hours* (New York: Vanguard, 1975), 10. Subsequent in-text references are to this edition.
21. William James, *The Meaning of Truth* (London: Longmans, Green, 1909), 90.
22. JCO, *New Heaven, New Earth*, 64.
23. Daly, *Lavish Self-Divisions*, 95.
24. JCO, *New Heaven, New Earth*, 213. "[James] Dickey has said that the century's greatest phrase is Albert Schweitzer's 'reverence for life.'"
25. "I don't think I get depressed or feel emotions like other people do," Oates told Sally Quinn in a 1975 *Washington Post* interview. "I think I have worked my way through all that." Johnson, *Invisible Writer*, 243.
26. Johnson, *Invisible Writer*, 276.
27. JCO, *(Woman) Writer: Occasions and Opportunities* (New York: Dutton, 1988), 75.
28. Arthur Schopenhauer, *The World as Will and Idea*, ed. David Berman, trans. Jill Berman (London: Dent, 1995), 24.
29. John Dewey, *Knowing and the Known*, in *John Dewey: The Later Works, 1925–1953*, ed. Jo Ann Boydston (Carbondale: Southern Illinois University Press, 1981–90), vol. 16, 248; Waller, *Dreaming America*, 202, 202, 200; Creighton, *Joyce Carol Oates*, 112; Bender, *Joyce Carol Oates*, 91–92.
30. Daly, *Lavish Self-Divisions*, 103, 109; Richard Rorty, *Contingency, Irony, and Solidarity* (Cambridge: Cambridge University Press, 1989), 5.
31. Johnson, *Invisible Writer*, 268.
32. Robert Phillips, "Joyce Carol Oates," 73, 71.
33. Rorty, *Contingency, Irony, and Solidarity*, 7.
34. JCO, "The Nature of Short Fiction; or, the Nature of My Short Fiction," preface to *Handbook of Short Story Writing*, ed. Frank A. Dickinson and Sandra Smythe (Cincinnati: Writer's Digest Books, 1970), xii.
35. Lorna Sage, *Women in the House of Fiction: Post-War Women Novelists* (London: Macmillan, 1992), 190, calls it Oates's "most explicitly anti-Nabokov novel"; Daly, *Lavish Self-Divisions*, 93, calls Kasch "a tragically isolated Humbert Humbert."
36. JCO, *New Heaven, New Earth*, 24.
37. Sage, *Women in the House of Fiction*, 191.
38. Phillips, "Joyce Carol Oates," 73.
39. John J. McDermott, "William James," in *Pragmatism and Classical American Philosophy: Essential Readings and Interpretive Essays*, ed. John J. Stuhr (Oxford: Oxford University Press, 2000), 142; Daly, *Lavish Self-Divisions*, 93.

40. Mikhail Bakhtin, *The Dialogic Imagination: Four Essays*, trans. Michael Holquist and Caryl Emerson, ed. Michael Holquist (Austin: University of Texas Press, 1981), 256; Phillips, "Joyce Carol Oates," 70, 74.

41. JCO, *Son of the Morning* (New York: Vanguard, 1978), 329. Subsequent in-text references are to this edition.

42. Erik H. Erikson, *Young Man Luther: A Study in Psychoanalysis and History* (London: Faber, 1958), 236–37; Sharon L. Dean, "Faith and Art: Joyce Carol Oates's *Son of the Morning*," *Critique* 28, no. 3 (1987): 144.

43. Dean, "Faith and Art," 143–44.

44. Joe David Bellamy, "The Dark Lady of American Letters," in Milazzo, ed., *Conversations*, 19; JCO, *The Poisoned Kiss and Other Stories from the Portuguese* (New York: Vanguard, 1975), 189.

45. Dean, "Faith and Art," 145; Friedman, *Joyce Carol Oates*, 191; John J. Stuhr, "John Dewey," in Stuhr, ed., *Pragmatism and Classical American Philosophy*, 439; John Dewey, *A Common Faith*, in Boydston, ed., *John Dewey Later Works*, vol. 9, 19.

46. John Dewey, "The Significance of the Problem of Knowledge," in *John Dewey: The Early Works, 1882–1898*, ed. Jo Ann Boydston (Carbondale: Southern Illinois University Press, 1969–72), vol. 5, 21–22.

3. REWRITING THE NOVEL

1. JCO, *Love and Its Derangements* (Baton Rouge: Louisiana State University Press, 1970), 11, 13, 20, 30–31, 60.

2. JCO, *Angel Fire* (Baton Rouge: Louisiana State University Press, 1973), 5, 13, 14, 62.

3. JCO, *Fabulous Beasts* (Baton Rouge: Louisiana State University Press, 1977), 83. The poem "Dreaming America" is reprinted in *Invisible Woman*.

4. JCO, *Women Whose Lives Are Food, Men Whose Lives Are Money* (Baton Rouge: Louisiana State University Press, 1978), 17, 19, 24, 29, 37, 41, and JCO, *Invisible Woman: New and Selected Poems, 1970–1982* (Princeton, NJ: Ontario Review Press, 1982), 52; Wendell Berry, "A Homage to Dr. Williams," in *The Generation of 2000: Contemporary American Poets,* ed. William Heyen (Princeton, NJ: Ontario Review Press, 1984), 1. "What he accomplished," writes Berry of William Carlos Williams, "was a sustained and intricate act of patriotism in the largest sense of the word."

5. JCO, *The Profane Art: Essays and Reviews* (New York: Dutton, 1983), 106–7.

6. JCO, in conversation with the author, Princeton, NJ, 17 July 1998; JCO, *The Profane Art*, 107.

7. JCO, *Contraries* (New York: Oxford University Press, 1981), vii–viii, 6, 33, 86, 88, 4–5, 59.

8. Eileen Teper Bender, *Joyce Carol Oates: Artist in Residence* (Bloomington: Indiana University Press, 1987), 120.

9. Ellen G. Friedman, "Joyce Carol Oates," in *Modern American Women Writers*, ed. Elaine Showalter, Lea Baechler, and A. Walton Litz (New York: Charles Scribner's Sons, 1991), 356; Bender, *Joyce Carol Oates*, 130; Charlene Haddock Seigfried, *Pragmatism and Feminism: Reweaving the Social Fabric* (Chicago: University of Chicago Press, 1996), 39; Marilyn C. Wesley, "The Simultaneous Universe: The Politics of Jamesian Conversion in Joyce Carol Oates's Fiction,"

Essays in Literature 18, no. 2 (1991): 274; Cornel West, *The American Invasion of Philosophy* (Madison: University of Wisconsin Press, 1989), 181 (quoted in Seigfried, *Pragmatism and Feminism*, 39).

10. JCO, journal, 2 December 1977, quoted in Greg Johnson, *Invisible Writer: A Biography of Joyce Carol Oates* (New York: Dutton, 1998), 276.

11. JCO, *Solstice* (New York: Dutton, 1985; London: Jonathan Cape, 1985), 135. Recovering from trauma, the main character, Monica Jensen, comes across Marcel Duchamp's *The Bride Stripped Bare by Her Bachelors, Even Large Glass, 1915–23,* with Duchamp's quotation fixed to the wall: "There is no solution because there is no problem."

12. Richard Rorty, *Contingency, Irony, and Solidarity* (Cambridge: Cambridge University Press, 1989), 73.

13. JCO, *I Lock My Door upon Myself* worksheets, Joyce Carol Oates Archive, Department of Special Collections, Syracuse University Library. On the back of a draft of the 1990 novella *I Lock My Door upon Myself,* the entries are dated 2 March and 20 January 1975. The "evolving of consciousness" entry (cited in Johnson, *Invisible Writer,* 240) is 12 January 1975.

14. Richard Tarnas, *The Passion of the Western Mind: Understanding the Ideas That Have Shaped Our World View* (New York: Crown, 1991; London: Pimlico, 1996), 420–21.

15. JCO, *Bellefleur* (New York: Dutton, 1980), 13, 15. Subsequent in-text references are to this edition.

16. JCO, *The Edge of Impossibility: Tragic Forms in Literature* (New York: Vanguard, 1972), 195; Brenda Daly, *Lavish Self-Divisions: The Novels of Joyce Carol Oates* (Jackson: University Press of Mississippi, 1996), 148; Bender, *Joyce Carol Oates,* 116–17, 114, 111; Rorty, *Contingency, Irony, and Solidarity,* 7, 9; John Gardner, "The Strange Real World," in *Joyce Carol Oates,* ed. Harold Bloom (New York: Chelsea House, 1987), 101.

17. See Daly, *Lavish Self-Divisions,* 142–48, for a discussion of the novel's parallels and contrasts with *Wuthering Heights.*

18. Johnson, *Invisible Writer,* 289 (the journal entry is 25 January 1979); JCO, letter to the author, 20 July 1994.

19. JCO, "Afterword: Reflections on the Grotesque," in *Haunted: Tales of the Grotesque* (New York: Dutton, 1994; New York: Plume, 1995), 307.

20. E. L. Doctorow, speaking at the Cheltenham Literary Festival, England, 15 October 1993.

21. Gardner, "The Strange Real World," 103; Dale Boesky, "Correspondence with Miss Joyce Carol Oates," *International Review of Psychoanalysis* 2 (1975): 484. Oates's words are: "Since I interpret most activities that take the individual out of his claustrophobic ego-role as 'religious,' I suppose I am in some vague way a 'religious' writer, though not in any conventional sense"; JCO, "Joyce Carol Oates on Thoreau's *Walden,*" *Mademoiselle,* April 1973, 96.

22. JCO, *What I Lived For* worksheets, Joyce Carol Oates Archive, Department of Special Collections, Syracuse University Library.

23. Friedrich Nietzsche, *Beyond Good and Evil,* in *The Basic Writings of Nietzsche,* ed. and trans. Walter Kaufmann (New York: Random House, 1968), 213; Wallace Stevens, "The Idea of Order at Key West," in *The Collected Poems of Wallace Stevens* (London: Alfred A. Knopf, 1955), 128–30; John R. Searle, *The Construction of Social Reality* (Harmondsworth, Eng.: Penguin, 1996), 160.

24. José Saramago, "Erratic Odyssey: The Novel's Return Towards the Condition of Poetry," *Times Literary Supplement,* 20 November 1998, 14; JCO, *New Heaven, New Earth,* 297, 292. The quotation is from Kafka's diary entry of 16 January 1922; Saramago describes "poetic time" as the time "confined and enclosed within the novel," as opposed to, say, "the time in which we find ourselves" or "when the author was writing" or the "days it takes to read it."

25. JCO, *New Heaven, New Earth,* 3–4; Bertrand Russell, *Mysticism and Logic* (1917; rpt., London: Allen & Unwin, 1970), 10–11 (Russell is quoting Heraclitus from Burnet's *Early Greek Philosophy* [2d ed.; London, 1908], 146–56; name of publisher not supplied); JCO, *New Heaven, New Earth,* 4.

26. Marilyn C. Wesley, *Refusal and Transgression in Joyce Carol Oates's Fiction* (Westport, CT: Greenwood Press, 1993), 141; Daly, *Lavish Self-Divisions,* 152–53; Perry Nodelman, "The Sense of Unending: Joyce Carol Oates's *Bellefleur* as an experiment in Feminine Storytelling," in *Breaking the Sequence: Women's Experimental Fiction,* ed. Ellen G. Friedman and Miriam Fuchs (Princeton, NJ: Princeton University Press, 1989), 251.

27. Seigfried, *Pragmatism and Feminism,* 2, 18, 114–15; Nodelman, "The Sense of Unending," 253; Joanne V. Creighton, *Joyce Carol Oates: Novels of the Middle Years* (Boston: Twayne, 1992), 38.

28. Daly, *Lavish Self-Divisions,* 154; Elaine Showalter, "*The Dead* and Feminist Criticism," in *Faith of a (Woman) Writer,* ed. Alice Kessler-Harris and William McBrien (Westport, CT: Greenwood Press, 1988), 19; Bender, *Joyce Carol Oates,* 8; Johnson, *Invisible Writer,* 304; Linda Wagner-Martin, "Panoramic, Unpredictable, and Human: Joyce Carol Oates's Recent Novels," in *Traditions, Voices, and Dreams: The American Novel since the 1960s,* ed. Melvin J. Friedman and Ben Siegel (Newark: University of Delaware Press, 1995), 208; Allen G. Shepherd, "Faulknerian Antecedents to Joyce Carol Oates's *Mysteries of Winterthurn,*" *Notes on Contemporary Writing* 17, no. 5 (1987): 10.

29. Elaine Showalter, *Sister's Choice: Tradition and Change in American Women's Writing* (Oxford: Oxford University Press, 1991), 62. On Oates's use of *Little Women,* see also Elizabeth Lennox Keyser, "*A Bloodsmoor Romance:* Joyce Carol Oates's *Little Women,*" *Women's Studies* 14, no. 3 (1988): 211–24.

30. JCO, preface to *Where Are You Going, Where Have You Been? Stories of Young America* (Greenwich, CT: Fawcett, 1974), 9.

31. JCO, letter to the author, 20 July 1994.

32. JCO, *A Bloodsmoor Romance* (New York: Dutton, 1982), 33. Subsequent in-text references are to this edition.

33. Daly, *Lavish Self-Divisions,* 162–63.

34. JCO, *Bloodsmoor* worksheets, Joyce Carol Oates Archive, Department of Special Collections, Syracuse University Library.

35. Showalter, *Sister's Choice,* 63.

36. Cynthia Eagle Russett, *Sexual Science and the Victorian Construction of Womanhood* (Cambridge: Harvard University Press, 1989), 191–93, 203–4.

37. Deborah Gorham, *The Victorian Girl and the Feminine Ideal* (London: Croom Helm, 1982), 56, 37; Showalter, *Sister's Choice,* 63.

38. Russett, *Sexual Science,* 205.

39. JCO, (Woman) Writer: Occasions and Opportunities (New York: Dutton, 1988), 16, 4.

40. Benjamin De Mott, "The Necessity in Art of a Reflective Intelligence," in Critical Essays on Joyce Carol Oates, ed. Linda W. Wagner (Boston: G. K. Hall, 1979), 21, 22; JCO, New Heaven, New Earth, 143.

41. Henry Wadsworth Longfellow, Selected Poems, ed. Anthony Waite (London: Dent, 1996), 3-4.

42. Søren Kierkegaard, The Concept of Irony with Constant Reference to Socrates, trans. Lee M. Capel (New York: Harper & Row, 1965), 85, cited in Allan Megill, Prophets of Extremity: Nietzsche, Heidegger, Foucault, Derrida (1985; rpt., Berkeley: University of California Press, 1987), 260; Wagner-Martin, "Panoramic, Unpredictable, and Human," 208; Sharon L. Dean, "Faith and Art: Joyce Carol Oates's *Son of the Morning*," Critique 28, no. 3 (1987): 146; Shepherd, "Faulknerian Antecedents," 10.

43. Lorna Sage, Women in the House of Fiction: Post-War Women Novelists (London: Macmillan, 1992), 193; Daly, Lavish Self-Divisions, 173.

44. JCO, Mysteries of Winterthurn (New York: Dutton, 1984), 3. Subsequent in-text references are to this edition.

45. JCO, New Heaven, New Earth, 289, 268-72, 276-77, 291.

46. JCO, The Edge of Impossibility, 167; Daly, Lavish Self-Divisions, 170.

47. Jane Addams, Democracy and Social Ethics, ed. Anne Firor Scott (Cambridge, MA: Belknap Press, 1964), 9.

48. JCO, letter to the author, 20 July 1994, and journal, 26 July 1978, quoted in Johnson, Invisible Writer, 209: "Whatever happens to us can't be avoided. We can only control, to some extent, our attitude toward it."

49. JCO, letter to the author, 7 January 1998.

50. JCO, (Woman) Writer, 158; JCO, My Heart Laid Bare worksheets, Joyce Carol Oates Archive, Department of Special Collections, Syracuse University Library; Johnson, Invisible Writer, xv; Stevens, "The Idea of Order at Key West," Collected Poems, 130.

51. Joanne Creighton, review of My Heart Laid Bare, Chicago Tribune, Books, 2 August 1998.

52. JCO, My Heart Laid Bare (New York: Dutton, 1998), 368-69. Subsequent in-text references are to this edition.

53. Jonathan Swift, Gulliver's Travels (Harmondsworth, Eng.: Penguin, 1988), 158.

54. JCO, author chat transcript, Authors on the Record, Barnes & Noble.com, Monday, 15 June 1998, 7.00 p.m. ET, 2.

55. William James, Pragmatism, in Pragmatism and Classical American Philosophy: Essential Essays and Interpretive Essays, ed. John J. Stuhr (Oxford: Oxford University Press, 2000), 194, 196.

4. LOOK BACK TIME

1. Leo Tolstoy, "The Death of Ivan Illych," in The Cossacks/Happy Ever After/The Death of Ivan Illych, trans. Rosemary Edmonds (Harmondsworth, Eng.: Penguin, 1960), 159.

2. Donald A. Dike, "The Aggressive Victim in the Fiction of Joyce Carol Oates," Greyfriar 15 (1974): 13-14; Ellen G. Friedman, Joyce Carol Oates (New York: Ungar, 1980), 6; Benjamin De Mott, "The Necessity in Art of a Reflective Intelligence," in Critical Essays on Joyce Carol Oates, ed. Linda W. Wagner (Boston: G. K. Hall, 1979), 22; Susan Koppelman Cornillon, "The

Fiction of Fiction," in *Images of Women in Fiction: Feminist Perspectives,* ed. Cornillon (1972; rev. ed., Bowling Green: Bowling Green University Popular Press, 1973), 118; Horace, Epistle 1, ii, 98, quoted in *The Essays of Michel de Montaigne,* vol. 2, trans. Charles Cotton (London: G. Bell & Sons, 1913), 2.

3. *Ontological Proof of My Existence,* a version of Shelley's plight at the end of *Wonderland,* appears in JCO, *The Perfectionist and Other Plays* (Hopewell, NJ: Ecco Press, 1995), 101–27, and in *Three Plays* (Princeton, NJ: Ontario Review Press, 1980), 11–52, as does the play version of *The Triumph of the Spider Monkey* (103–57).

4. JCO, *The Time Traveler* (New York: Dutton, 1989), 62, 25.

5. JCO, *Twelve Plays* (New York: Dutton, 1995), 3, 437–38, 4, 216.

6. Ibid., 370.

7. Greg Johnson, *Invisible Writer: A Biography of Joyce Carol Oates* (New York: Dutton, 1998), 332; JCO, *(Woman) Writer: Occasions and Opportunities* (New York: Dutton, 1988), 377; JCO, journal entry quoted in Johnson, *Invisible Writer,* 333; JCO, *On Boxing* (Garden City, NY: Doubleday, 1987), 60.

8. Linda Wagner-Martin, "Panoramic, Unpredictable, and Human: Joyce Carol Oates's Recent Novels," in *Traditions, Voices, and Dreams: The American Novel since the 1960s,* ed. Melvin J. Friedman and Ben Siegel (Newark: University of Delaware Press, 1995), 198; Marilyn C. Wesley, "Father-Daughter Incest as Social Transgression: A Feminist Reading of Joyce Carol Oates," *Women's Studies* 21, no. 3 (1992): 252; Ellen G. Friedman, "Joyce Carol Oates," in *Modern American Women Writers,* ed. Elaine Showalter, Lea Baechler, and A. Walton Litz (New York: Charles Scribner's Sons, 1991), 356, 361; John Mulryan, "The Genderfication of Literature: Cross-Gender Writing in Joyce Carol Oates's *Expensive People* and Brian Moore's *I Am Mary Dunne,*" *CEA Critic* 56 (Fall 1993): 124.

9. Friedman, "Joyce Carol Oates," 356; Wagner-Martin, "Panoramic, Unpredictable, and Human," 202, 204.

10. Friedman, "Joyce Carol Oates," 365; JCO, *Where I've Been, and Where I'm Going: Essays, Reviews, and Prose* (New York: Plume, 1999), 7.

11. Robert Phillips, "Joyce Carol Oates: The Art of Fiction LXXII," in *Conversations with Joyce Carol Oates,* ed. Lee Milazzo (Jackson: University Press of Mississippi, 1989), 70.

12. William James, *The Will to Believe,* in *Pragmatism and Classical American Philosophy: Essential Readings and Interpretive Essays,* ed. John J. Stuhr (Oxford: Oxford University Press, 2000), 235; John Dewey, "The Need for a Recovery of Philosophy," in *John Dewey: The Middle Works, 1899–1924,* ed. Jo Ann Boydston (Carbondale: Southern Illinois University Press, 1976–83), vol. 10, 3.

13. John Dewey, "The Significance of the Problem of Knowledge," in *John Dewey: The Early Works, 1882–1898* (Carbondale: Southern Illinois University Press, 1969–72), vol. 5, 21–22; John Dewey, *Reconstruction in Philosophy,* in *John Dewey Middle Works,* vol. 12, 149.

14. Johnson, *Invisible Writer,* 161; Mickey Pearlman and Katherine Usher Henderson, "Joyce Carol Oates," *Inter/View: Talks with America's Writing Women* (Lexington: University Press of Kentucky, 1990), 43; Joanne Creighton, *Joyce Carol Oates: Novels of the Middle Years* (New York: Twayne, 1992), 84; Arthur Miller, *Death of a Salesman,* in *Collected Plays* (New York: Cresset Press, 1958), 161.

15. Joseph Dewey, *Novels from Reagan's America: A New Realism* (Gainesville: University Press of Florida, 1999).

16. John J. Stuhr, "John Dewey," in Stuhr, ed., *Pragmatism and Classical American Philosophy*, 439; JCO, *(Woman) Writer*, 75.

17. JCO, *(Woman) Writer*, 378. "What is most autobiographical about the novel is its inner kernel of emotion—Marya's half-conscious and often despairing quest for her own elusive self" (377).

18. Bernard Levin, "Against the Demon Voices," *Sunday Times*, 11 June 1987, 20; Marilyn C. Wesley, *Refusal and Transgression in Joyce Carol Oates's Fiction* (Westport, CT: Greenwood Press, 1993), 54; Elaine Showalter, "Joyce Carol Oates: A Portrait," in *Joyce Carol Oates*, ed. Harold Bloom (New York: Chelsea House, 1987), 137, 141; Friedman, "Joyce Carol Oates," 364.

19. See Wagner-Martin, "Panoramic, Unpredictable, and Human," 199–200: Oates's women characters "are frozen in the psychological states abuse has created for them." Wagner-Martin sees this in terms of Marya's use by, rather than of, others. One source for James's statement may be an 1870 diary entry: "My first act of free will shall be to believe in free will": William James, "Diary," in *The Writings of William James*, ed. John J. McDermott (Chicago: University of Chicago Press, 1977), 7.

20. Creighton, *Joyce Carol Oates: Novels of the Middle Years*, 63; Eileen Teper Bender, *Joyce Carol Oates: Artist in Residence* (Bloomington: Indiana University Press, 1987), 158; Wagner-Martin, ""Panoramic, Unpredictable, and Human," 197–200.

21. JCO, *Marya: A Life* (New York: Dutton, 1986), 82, 57, 39. Subsequent in-text references are to this edition; George Lukács, *The Historical Novel*, trans. Hannah Mitchell and Stanley Mitchell (1962; Harmondsworth, Eng.: Penguin, 1981), 239.

22. JCO, *(Woman) Writer*, 331. Oates is writing about her maternal grandmother, Elizabeth Bush, who refused to learn English.

23. Wesley, "Father-Daughter Incest as Social Transgression," 259.

24. Daniel Goleman, *Vital Lies, Simple Truths: The Psychology of Self-Deception* (London: Bloomsbury, 1997), 153. "Paranoid predispositions need not come from such explosive events as abuse," writes Goleman. "The same tendencies can be imprinted on the mind by less obvious forms of tyranny." But in any such cases, anticipation of hostility can evoke "the response it was meant to anticipate."

25. George Steiner, *Language and Silence: Essays, 1958–1966* (London: Faber, 1967), 86.

26. Jiddu Krishnamurti, *Krishnamurti's Notebook* (New York: Harper & Row, 1984), 80. "You are caught up in your daily practice, or ambition has you by the throat. If you are a professional of some kind, probably you never see."

27. Showalter, "Joyce Carol Oates: A Portrait," 142.

28. Wesley, *Refusal and Transgression*, 128.

29. James Baldwin, *The Fire Next Time* (New York: Dial Press, 1963; Harmondsworth, Eng.: Penguin, 1964), 42; Henry Louis Gates Jr., *The Signifying Monkey: A Theory of African-American Literary Criticism* (Oxford: Oxford University Press, 1988), 90, xxv, 53.

30. JCO, "Naked," in *Heat and Other Stories* (New York: Dutton, 1991; New York: Plume, 1992), 124; Sally Robinson, "Heat and Cold: Recent Fiction by Joyce Carol Oates," *Michigan Quarterly Review* 31, no. 3 (1992): 409–11. Other stories that provide useful comparisons on the

question of characters having to face the other to whom they are blind or that deal with the ambiguities of race and gender relations within academic life include, respectively, "An Act of Solitude," in *Will You Always Love Me?* (New York: Dutton, 1996; New York: Plume, 1997), 3–20, and "Up from Slavery," in *The Hungry Ghosts: Seven Allusive Comedies* (Santa Barbara: Black Sparrow Press, 1978), 63–76.

31. Bender, *Joyce Carol Oates*, 162; Brenda Daly, *Lavish Self-Divisions: The Novels of Joyce Carol Oates* (Jackson: University Press of Mississippi, 1996), 132.

32. JCO, journal, 26 July 1978, quoted in Johnson, *Invisible Writer*, 209.

33. Creighton, *Joyce Carol Oates: Novels of the Middle Years*, 69.

34. William James, *A Pluralistic Universe*, in *Pragmatism and Classical American Philosophy*, ed. Stuhr, 158–59; James Atlas, "An American Masterpiece," *Vanity Fair*, August 1987, 140; John Updike, "What You Deserve Is What You Get," *New Yorker*, 28 December 1987, 119.

35. JCO, *You Must Remember This* worksheets, Joyce Carol Oates Archive, Department of Special Collections, Syracuse University Library.

36. JCO, *You Must Remember This* (New York: Dutton, 1987), 391. Subsequent in-text references are to this edition.

37. JCO, *New Heaven, New Earth: The Visionary Experience in Literature* (New York: Vanguard, 1974; London: Victor Gollancz, 1976), 132, and *You Must Remember This* worksheets.

38. Johnson, *Invisible Writer*, 334: "As always, Joyce remained anything but a doctrinaire feminist, insisting that both men and women, impelled by natural and little-understood impulses, often participate in their own victimization."

39. JCO, *On Boxing*, 4.

40. Ibid., 16.

41. Ibid., 56, 77.

42. Ibid., 30.

43. Victor Strandberg, "Sex, Violence, and Philosophy in *You Must Remember This*," *Studies in American Fiction* 17 (Spring 1989): 11, 13.

44. JCO, *On Boxing*, 56, 21; Richard Rorty, *Contingency, Irony, and Solidarity* (Cambridge: Cambridge University Press, 1989), 17, 20.

45. Wagner-Martin, "Panoramic, Unpredictable, and Human," 200; William Heyen, "Open Letter to Oates," *Tri-Quarterly* 73 (Fall 1988): 92; Strandberg, "Sex, Violence, and Philosophy," 14; Dewey, *Novels from Reagan's America*, 34, 36, 35, 61, 58, 14.

46. Arthur Schopenhauer, *The World as Will and Idea* [1819], ed. David Berman, trans. Jill Berman (London: Dent, 1995), 121, 162; Strandberg, "Sex, Violence, and Philosophy," 9, 11, 7, 12, 14, 16; JCO, *Contraries: Essays* (New York: Oxford University Press, 1981), 176, cited in Strandberg, "Sex, Violence, and Philosophy," 14.

47. Dewey, *Novels from Reagan's America*, 34; Updike, "What You Deserve Is What You Get," 119.

48. JCO to Robert Phillips, 22 April 1966, cited in Johnson, *Invisible Writer*, 137.

49. JCO, letter to the author, 20 July 1994.

50. JCO, *American Appetites* (New York: Dutton, 1989), 13. Subsequent in-text references are to this edition.

51. Friedrich Nietzsche, *Beyond Good and Evil,* in *Basic Writings of Nietzsche,* ed. Walter Kaufmann (New York: Random House, 1968), 283; Schopenhauer, *The World as Will and Idea,* 80.

52. Wesley, *Refusal and Transgression,* 150; *Ohio Review,* "Transformations of Self: An Interview with Joyce Carol Oates," in Milazzo, ed., *Conversations,* 49. Ian's implied suicide is explicit in Oates's worksheets. She considered a scene where everything "would seem to be moving toward a blissful (clichéd) *happy ending,*" when suddenly he "*gets a gun,*" puts "the barrel of the pistol in his mouth," and fires. The ending opted for is something between that and another possible ending, a "speculative" scene in which Sigrid "wld. be, against all expectations, a good wife." JCO, *American Appetites* worksheets, Joyce Carol Oates Archive, Department of Special Collections, Syracuse University Library.

53. JCO, *American Appetites* worksheets. Greg Johnson suggests that this metaphor of appetite is also linked with Oates's flirtations with anorexia and her sense that "her work, rather than food," is "her primary source of nurture" (*Invisible Writer,* 355). But the worksheet comments equate appetites with desire, in general, and with the Schopenhauerean Will, in particular. "Every person has constant aims and motives in accordance with which he directs his conduct, and he can always account for his individual actions," writes Schopenhauer. "But if he were asked why he wills at all, or why he wills to exist at all, he would have no answer" (*The World as Will and Idea,* 84).

54. JCO, *New Heaven, New Earth,* 88–89.

55. JCO, "A Report to an Academy," *Invisible Woman: New and Selected Poems, 1970–1982* (Princeton, NJ: Ontario Review Press, 1982), 74, and *The Secret Mirror: A Collage-Play,* in *Twelve Plays* (New York: Dutton, 1991), 367.

56. JCO, *Because It Is Bitter, and Because It Is My Heart* (New York: Dutton, 1990), 125. Subsequent in-text references are to this edition. The title is from Stephen Crane's poem "The Creature and the Creation."

57. JCO, letter to the author, 20 July 1994.

58. JCO, *You Must Remember This* worksheets, Oates Archive, Syracuse University Library.

59. Alfred Kazin, "[On Joyce Carol Oates]," in Wagner, ed., *Critical Essays on Joyce Carol Oates,* 158.

60. Henry Louis Gates Jr., "Murder She Wrote," *Nation,* 2 July 1990, 27; JCO, *Because It Is Bitter, and Because It Is My Heart* worksheets, Joyce Carol Oates Archive, Department of Special Collections, Syracuse University Library.

61. JCO, letter to the author, 20 July 1994.

62. Rupert Brooke, "Peace," *The Collected Poems of Rupert Brooke* (New York: Dodd, Mead, 1927), 111; Edward Lucie-Smith, *American Realism* (New York: Harry N. Abrams, 1994), 69.

63. JCO, *Because It Is Bitter* worksheets, Oates Archive, Syracuse University Library. In the worksheets, Oates elaborates on parallels between Jinx and the artist, in particular his creation of a "world to live in."

64. JCO, *On Boxing,* 34; Gates, "Murder She Wrote," 28.

65. Gates, "Murder She Wrote," 28; David Germain, "Author Oates Tells Where She's Been, Where She's Going," in Milazzo, ed., *Conversations,* 177. "I'm more or less of the school of the writer as witness."

5. DARK EYES ON AMERICA

1. JCO, letter to the author, 7 January 1998.

2. JCO, "A Manhattan Romance" and "Murder-Two," in *Faithless: Tales of Transgression* (New York: Ecco Press, 2001), 209, 220, 222.

3. Greg Johnson, *Invisible Writer: A Biography of Joyce Carol Oates* (New York: Dutton, 1998), 334–35.

4. JCO, *Where I've Been, and Where I'm Going: Essays, Reviews, and Prose* (New York: Plume, 1999), 37, 38, 44, 45.

5. Ibid., 51, 37; JCO, *Twelve Plays* (New York: Dutton, 1991), 436.

6. Henry Louis Gates Jr., "Murder She Wrote," *Nation*, 2 July 1990, 29. The Balzac comment was made to Walter Clemons, "Joyce Carol Oates; Love and Violence," in *Conversations with Joyce Carol Oates*, ed. Lee Milazzo (Jackson: University Press of Mississippi, 1989), 33.

7. "Not All Men's Fault: Not Quite," *Economist*, 14 August 1993, 87; Johnson, *Invisible Writer*, 383; Gates, "Murder She Wrote," 27.

8. William James, "A World of Pure Experience," in *Pragmatism and Classical American Philosophy: Essential Readings and Interpretive Essays*, ed. John J. Stuhr (Oxford: Oxford University Press, 2000), 192.

9. JCO, *What I Lived For* worksheets, Joyce Carol Oates Archive, Department of Special Collections, Syracuse University Library. It is not unusual to find notes for one Oates novel written on the drafts and worksheets of another, but for all their surface difference, *Black Water* and *What I Lived For* seem particularly connected ("How to join it with Corky C.?" runs a typed note concerning the image of the drowning girl. "A mistake . . . ?"—and scrawled in parenthesis is the addendum, "Yes, what a mistake it wld. have been!").

10. JCO, *Black Water* (New York: Dutton, 1990), 93. Subsequent in-text references are to this edition.

11. Johnson, *Invisible Writer*, 382; Jean-Paul Sartre, "Time in the Work of Faulkner," *Literary and Philosophical Essays*, trans. Annette Michelson (London: Rider, 1955), 79–87.

12. JCO, letter to the author, 20 July 1994.

13. Johnson, *Invisible Writer*, 330, 383. "It was no accident that he allowed his passenger to drown," she wrote Johnson. "Imagine—he didn't report the accident for nine hours." Oates's worksheets suggest, however, that the Senator's liberal "decency" is part of her concern. "To what extent do we 'forgive' our friends for their crimes, simply because they are our friends?" she writes. "Conversely, to what extent do we wish to punish our enemies/non-friends, simply because they are not our own . . . ?" JCO, *What I Lived For* worksheets.

14. Andrew Sullivan, "Monica Catches Out the Semi-Moral Majority," *Sunday Times*, news review section, 30 September 1998, 6; Johnson, *Invisible Writer*, 169.

15. JCO, conversation with the author, Princeton, NJ, 17 July 1998; Johnson, *Invisible Writer*, 396; D. J. Taylor, "Cunning Little Vixens," *Sunday Times*, 15 August 1993, books section, 6.9; Michiko Kakutani, "Girls Who Hate Men and Act Accordingly," *New York Times*, 16 July 1993, C-18; Lance Morrow, "Are Men Really That Bad?" a *Time* article cited in Ray Waddle, "Is Fatherhood under Attack?" *Saratogian*, 22 March 1994, xerox copy in the Oates Archive, Syracuse University Library; Johnson, *Invisible Writer*, 393; JCO, letter to the author, 20 July 1994. Not un-

like *Huckleberry Finn*, banned by the Concord Public Library in 1885 and more recently dropped from some school reading lists for its controversial language, *Foxfire* has been banned from some lists because parents' groups found "its language and subject matter offensive" (Johnson, *Invisible Writer*, 393).

16. Brenda Daly, *Lavish Self-Divisions: The Novels of Joyce Carol Oates* (Jackson: University Press of Mississippi, 1996), 216; Lynn Karpen, "Legs Sadovsky Goes Mythic," *New York Times Book Review*, 15 August 1993, 6.

17. JCO, *Foxfire: Confessions of a Girl Gang* (New York: Dutton, 1993), 197. Subsequent in-text references are to this edition.

18. Daly, *Lavish Self-Divisions*, 217.

19. Clemons, "Joyce Carol Oates," 126; William James, "What Pragmatism Means," in Stuhr, ed., *Pragmatism and Classical American Philosophy*, 194.

20. Daly, *Lavish Self-Divisions*, 212.

21. Robert Phillips, "Joyce Carol Oates: The Art of Fiction LXXII," in Milazzo, ed., *Conversations*, 76; JCO, "Bound," *New Yorker*, 22 and 29 April 2002, 202.

22. JCO, *New Heaven, New Earth: The Visionary Experience in Literature* (New York: Vanguard, 1974; London: Victor Gollancz, 1976), 291.

23. Johnson, *Invisible Writer*, 389; JCO, *New Heaven, New Earth*, 105.

24. JCO, *What I Lived For* (New York: Dutton, 1994), 540. Subsequent in-text references are to this edition.

25. Henry David Thoreau, *Walden, Or Life in the Woods* (New York: Norton, 1960), 65.

26. JCO, *Where I've Been, and Where I'm Going*, 325.

27. Arthur Miller, *Death of a Salesman*, in *Collected Plays* (New York: Cresset Press, 1958), 60.

28. JCO, conversation with the author, Princeton, NJ, 17 July 1998.

29. Johnson, *Invisible Writer*, 389.

30. JCO, "Where Are You Going, Where Have You Been?" in *The Wheel of Love and Other Stories* (New York: Vanguard, 1970; London: Jonathan Cape, 1971), 52.

31. JCO, *We Were the Mulvaneys* (New York: Dutton, 1996), 14. Subsequent in-text references are to this edition.

32. William James, *Some Problems of Philosophy: A Beginning of an Introduction to Philosophy* (London: Longmans, Green, 1911; Lincoln: University of Nebraska Press, 1996), 26; idem, *Pragmatism* (London: Longmans, Green, 1907), 172, 178; idem, *A Pluralistic Universe* (London: Longmans, Green, 1909), 253; idem, *The Meaning of Truth* (London: Longmans, Green, 1909), 243; idem, *Pragmatism*, 201, 255; idem, *The Meaning of Truth*, 202.

33. JCO, "The Brothers," in *Will You Always Love Me? and Other Stories* (New York: Dutton, 1996; New York: Plume, 1997), 243. The story was first published in 1995 in *Ellery Queen's Mystery Magazine*.

34. Peter Jones, "William James, 1842–1910," in *American Philosophy*, ed. Marcus G. Singer (Cambridge: Cambridge University Press, 1985), 60. The remark is attributed to Søren Kierkegaard.

35. James, *Pragmatism*, 207–8.

36. Johnson, *Invisible Writer*, 45; JCO, conversation with the author, Princeton, NJ, 17 July

1998; JCO, *We Were the Mulvaneys* worksheets, Joyce Carol Oates Archive, Department of Special Collections, Syracuse University Library.

37. JCO, *The Poisoned Kiss and Other Stories from the Portuguese* (New York: Vanguard, 1975), 189; John R. Searle, *Minds, Brains, and Science* (1984; rpt., Harmondsworth, Eng.: Penguin, 1989), 25; James, *Pragmatism*, 245.

38. Bertrand Russell, *A History of Western Philosophy* (1946; rpt., London: Simon & Schuster, 1996), 772; JCO, *New Heaven, New Earth*, 246.

39. JCO, *Broke Heart Blues* (New York: Dutton, 1999), 212. Subsequent in-text references are to this edition.

40. JCO, *(Woman) Writer: Occasions and Opportunities* (New York: Dutton, 1988), 34.

41. JCO, "The Undesirable Table," in *Will You Always Love Me?*, 216.

42. JCO, letter to the author, 20 July 1994.

43. JCO, *Blonde* (New York, 2000; London: Fourth Estate, 2000), 83. Subsequent in-text references are to this edition.

44. JCO, "The Love She Searched For," *Time*, 15 September 1997, 58. Subsequent in-text references are to this source and page number.

45. Julie Burchill, *Diana* (London: Orion, 1998), 1; William Heyen, *Diana, Charles, & the Queen* (Rochester, NY: BOA Editions, 1998), 50.

46. Norman Mailer, *Marilyn: A Biography* (London: Hodder & Stoughton, 1973; London: Spring Books, 1988), 177.

47. JCO, *Where I've Been, and Where I'm Going*, 325.

48. JCO, *Middle Age: A Romance* (New York: Dutton, 2001; London: Fourth Estate, 2001), 34. Subsequent in-text references are to this edition.

49. Plato, *Phaedo*, in *The Last Days of Socrates*, trans. Hugh Tredennick and Harold Tarrant (Harmondsworth, Eng.: Penguin, 1993), 99, 125.

50. John J. Stuhr, "John Dewey," in Stuhr, ed., *Pragmatism and Classical American Philosophy*, 441.

AFTERWORD

1. JCO, "The Sky Blue Ball," in *The Collector of Hearts: New Tales of the Grotesque* (New York: Plume, 1999), 3–7.

2. Brenda Daly, *Lavish Self-Divisions: The Novels of Joyce Carol Oates* (Jackson: University Press of Mississippi, 1996), 223; John Updike, "What You Deserve Is What You Get," *New Yorker*, 28 December 1987, 119; Joanne V. Creighton, *Joyce Carol Oates: Novels of the Middle Years* (Boston: Twayne, 1992), 106; Richard Rorty, *Contingency, Irony, and Solidarity* (Cambridge: Cambridge University Press, 1989), vi; John Dewey, *Art as Experience* (New York: Putnam, 1958), 348.

3. John J. Stuhr, "John Dewey," in *Pragmatism and Classical American Philosophy: Essential Readings and Interpretive Essays*, ed. John J. Stuhr (Oxford: Oxford University Press, 2000), 442.

4. Rorty, *Contingency, Irony, and Solidarity*, 27; JCO, *My Heart Laid Bare* (New York: Dutton, 1998), 452.

5. Stuhr, "John Dewey," 441; John Dewey, *A Common Faith*, in *John Dewey: The Later Works*,

1925–1953, vol. 9, ed. Jo Ann Boydston (Carbondale: Southern Illinois University Press, 1981–90), 57–58.

6. Daly, *Lavish Self-Divisions*, 12.

7. Patrick O'Donnell, introduction to "The Late Twentieth Century" section of *The Columbia History of the American Novel*, ed. Emory Elliott (New York: Columbia University Press, 1991), 514.

8. Philip Roth, "Writing American Fiction," *Commentary* 31 (March 1961): 224; Cornel West, "Postmodern Culture," in *The Columbia History of the American Novel*, ed. Elliott, 519; O'Donnell, introduction to "The Late Twentieth Century," 514; William James, *The Meaning of Truth* (London: Longmans, Green, 1909), 229.

9. JCO, *Broke Heart Blues* (New York: Dutton, 1999), 276; D. J. Taylor, "Cunning Little Vixens," *Sunday Times* books section, 15 August 1993, 6.9; O'Donnell, "The Late Twentieth Century," 514, 513.

10. Roth, "Writing American Fiction," 226.

11. Walt Whitman, "Song of Myself," in Whitman, *Leaves of Grass*, ed. Sculley Bradley and Harold W. Blodgett (New York: Norton, 1973), 48; Virginia Woolf, *A Room of One's Own/Three Guineas*, ed. Morag Shaich (Oxford: Oxford University Press, 1992), 127–28, 142.

12. JCO, *New Heaven, New Earth: The Visionary Experience in Literature* (New York: Vanguard, 1974; London: Victor Gollancz, 1976), 179, 180, 185; Rorty, *Contingency, Irony, and Solidarity*, 28. An even earlier discussion of Mailer appears in JCO, "Out of the Machine," *Atlantic*, July 1971, 42–45.

13. JCO, "Naked," in *Heat and Other Stories* (New York: Dutton, 1991; New York: Plume, 1992), 124, 126, 128, 129, 136, 138.

14. JCO, letter to the author, 22 July 1994; JCO, *(Woman) Writer: Occasions and Opportunities* (New York: Dutton, 1988), 384. Oates is quoting Polish writer Witold Gombowicz (via Romain Gary): "There comes a day when a writer is held prisoner by 'la gueule qu'on lui a fait' ('the mug which the critics have given him')—an appearance which has nothing to do with his work or himself."

15. JCO, *Marya: A Life* (New York: Dutton, 1986), 70.

16. Greg Johnson, *Invisible Writer: A Biography of Joyce Carol Oates* (New York: Dutton, 1998), 338.

17. David Van Leer, "Society and Identity," in *The Columbia History of the American Novel*, ed. Elliott, 493; Whitman, "Song of Myself," 52; JCO, "Delirium and Detachment: The Secret of Being a Writer," *New Yorker*, 23 June–3 July 1995, 137; JCO, *I'll Take You There* (New York: Ecco, 2002), 212. Oates makes the link with Ellison's title explicit in Robert Phillips, "Joyce Carol Oates: The Art of Fiction LXXII," in *Conversations with Joyce Carol Oates*, ed. Lee Milazzo (Jackson: University Press of Mississippi, 1989), 80.

18. JCO, *(Woman) Writer*, 156.

19. Norman Mailer, *Marilyn: A Biography* (London: Hodder & Stoughton, 1973; London: Spring Books, 1988), 20.

20. Friedrich Nietzsche, letter to a friend, quoted in Bryan McGee, *The Great Philosophers* (Oxford: Oxford University Press, 1988), 247; JCO, *The Profane Art: Essays and Reviews* (New

York: Dutton, 1983), 2; JCO, conversation with the author, Princeton, NJ, 17 July 1998; JCO, *My Heart Laid Bare* (New York: Dutton, 1998), 406; Saul Bellow, *Henderson the Rain King* (New York: Viking, 1959; Harmondsworth, Eng.: Penguin, 1981), 150.

 21. JCO, "JCO and I," limited-edition pamphlet (Concord, NH: William B. Ewert, 1994); JCO, *(Woman) Writer*, 371.

SELECTED BIBLIOGRAPHY

Works by Joyce Carol Oates

Novels and Novellas

With Shuddering Fall. New York: Vanguard, 1964; London: Jonathan Cape, 1965.
A Garden of Earthly Delights. New York: Vanguard, 1967.
Expensive People. New York: Vanguard, 1968; New York: Quality Paperback Book Club, 1992.
them. New York: Vanguard, 1969; New York: Quality Paperback Book Club, 1992.
Wonderland. New York: Vanguard, 1971; Princeton, NJ: Ontario Review Press, 1992.
Do with Me What You Will. New York: Vanguard, 1973.
The Assassins: A Book of Hours. New York: Vanguard, 1975.
Childwold. New York: Vanguard, 1976.
The Triumph of the Spider Monkey. Santa Barbara: Black Sparrow Press, 1976.
Son of the Morning. New York: Vanguard, 1978.
Cybele. Santa Barbara: Black Sparrow Press, 1979.
Unholy Loves. New York: Dutton, 1979.
Bellefleur. New York: Dutton, 1980.
Angel of Light. New York: Dutton, 1981.
A Bloodsmoor Romance. New York: Dutton, 1982.
Mysteries of Winterthurn. New York: Dutton, 1984.
Solstice. New York: Dutton, 1985; London: Jonathan Cape, 1985.
Marya: A Life. New York: Dutton, 1986.
You Must Remember This. New York: Dutton, 1987.
American Appetites. New York: Dutton, 1989.
Because It Is Bitter, and Because It Is My Heart. New York: Dutton, 1990.
I Lock My Door upon Myself. New York: Ecco Press, 1990.
The Rise of Life on Earth. New York: New Directions Books, 1991.

Black Water. New York: Dutton, 1992.
Foxfire: Confessions of a Girl Gang. New York: Dutton, 1993.
What I Lived For. New York: Dutton, 1994.
Zombie. New York: Dutton, 1995.
We Were the Mulvaneys. New York: Dutton, 1996.
First Love: A Gothic Tale. Hopewell, NJ: Ecco Press, 1996.
Man Crazy. New York: Dutton, 1997.
My Heart Laid Bare. New York: Dutton, 1998.
Broke Heart Blues. New York: Dutton, 1999.
Blonde. New York: Dutton, 2000; London: Fourth Estate, 2000.
Middle Age: A Romance. New York: Dutton, 2001; London: Fourth Estate, 2001.
Beasts. New York: Carroll & Graf, 2002.
I'll Take You There. New York: Ecco Press, 2002.
The Tattooed Girl. New York: Ecco Press, 2003.
Rape: A Love Story. New York: Carroll & Graf, 2003.
The Falls. New York: Ecco Press, 2004.

BY ROSAMOND SMITH (PSEUDONYM FOR OATES)
Lives of the Twins. New York: Dutton, 1987.
Soul/Mate. New York: Dutton, 1989.
Nemesis. New York: Dutton, 1990.
Snake Eyes. New York: Dutton, 1992.
You Can't Catch Me. New York: Dutton, 1995.
Double Delight. New York: Dutton, 1997.
Starr Bright Will Be with You Soon. New York: Dutton, 1999.
The Barrens. New York: Dutton, 2001.

BY LAUREN KELLY (PSEUDONYM FOR OATES)
Take Me, Take Me with You. New York: Ecco Press, 2004.

STORY COLLECTIONS
By the North Gate. New York: Vanguard, 1963.
Upon the Sweeping Flood and Other Stories. New York: Vanguard, 1966.
The Wheel of Love and Other Stories. New York: Vanguard, 1970; London: Jonathan Cape, 1971.
Marriages and Infidelities. New York: Vanguard, 1972.
The Hungry Ghosts: Seven Allusive Comedies. Santa Barbara: Black Sparrow Press, 1974.
The Goddess and Other Women. New York: Vanguard, 1974.
Where Are You Going, Where Have You Been? Stories of Young America. Greenwich, CT: Fawcett, 1974.

The Seduction and Other Stories. Santa Barbara: Black Sparrow Press, 1975.
The Poisoned Kiss and Other Stories from the Portuguese. New York: Vanguard, 1975.
Crossing the Border. New York: Vanguard, 1976.
Night-Side: Eighteen Tales. New York: Vanguard, 1977.
All the Good People I've Left Behind. Santa Barbara: Black Sparrow Press, 1979.
A Sentimental Education: Stories. New York: Dutton, 1980.
Last Days: Stories. New York: Dutton, 1984.
Raven's Wing: Stories. New York: Dutton, 1986.
The Assignation: Stories. New York: Dutton, 1988.
Oates in Exile. Toronto: Exile Editions, 1990.
Heat and Other Stories. New York: Dutton, 1991.
Where Is Here? Hopewell, NJ: Ecco Press 1992.
Where Are You Going, Where Have You Been? Selected Early Stories. Princeton, NJ: Ontario Review Press, 1993.
Haunted: Tales of the Grotesque. New York: Dutton, 1994.
Will You Always Love Me? and Other Stories. New York: Dutton, 1996; New York, Plume 1997.
Demon and Other Tales. West Warwick, RI: Necronomicon Press, 1996.
The Collector of Hearts: New Tales of the Grotesque. New York: Plume, 1999.
Faithless: Tales of Transgression. New York: Ecco Press, 2001.
I Am No One You Know: Stories. New York: Ecco Press, 2004.

ESSAYS

The Edge of Impossibility: Tragic Forms in Literature. New York: Vanguard, 1972.
"The Hostile Sun": The Poetry of D. H. Lawrence. Los Angeles: Black Sparrow Press, 1973.
New Heaven, New Earth: The Visionary Experience in Literature. New York: Vanguard, 1974; London: Victor Gollancz, 1976.
Contraries. New York: Oxford University Press, 1981.
The Profane Art: Essays and Reviews. New York: Dutton, 1983.
On Boxing. Garden City, NY: Doubleday, 1987.
(Woman) Writer: Occasions and Opportunities. New York: Dutton, 1988.
George Bellows: American Artist. Hopewell, NJ: Ecco Press, 1995.
Where I've Been, and Where I'm Going: Essays, Reviews, and Prose. New York: Plume, 1999.
The Faith of a Writer: Life, Craft, Art. New York: Ecco Press, 2003.

UNCOLLECTED ESSAYS CITED

"The Nature of Short Fiction; or, The Nature of My Short Fiction." Preface to *Handbook of Short Story Writing*, edited by Frank A. Dickinson and Sandra Smythe. Cincinnati: Writer's Digest Books, 1970, xi–xviii.

"Out of the Machine." *Atlantic*, July 1971, 42–45.
"Joyce Carol Oates on Thoreau's *Walden*." *Mademoiselle*, April 1973, 96.
"Disguised Fiction." *PMLA* 89 (May 1974): 580–81.
"The Dream of the Sacred Text." In *The Generation of 2000: Contemporary American Poets*, edited by William Heyen. Princeton, NJ: Ontario Review Press, 1984, 204–6.
"'JCO' and I." Limited-edition pamphlet. Concord, NH: William B. Ewert, 1994.
"Delirium and Detachment: The Secret of Being a Writer." *New Yorker*, 23 June–3 July 1995, 134–37.
"The Love She Searched For." *Time*, 15 September 1997, 58.
"Jail Bait." *Guardian Saturday Review*, 10 October 1998, 1–2.
"Words Fail, Memory Blurs, Life Wins." *New York Times*, 31 December 2001, 11.
"Bound." *New Yorker*, 22 and 29 April 2002, 202.

POETRY

Anonymous Sins. Baton Rouge: Louisiana State University Press, 1969.
Love and Its Derangements. Baton Rouge: Louisiana State University Press, 1970.
Angel Fire. Baton Rouge: Louisiana State University Press, 1973.
The Fabulous Beasts. Baton Rouge: Louisiana State University Press, 1975.
Women Whose Lives Are Food, Men Whose Lives Are Money. Baton Rouge: Louisiana State University Press, 1978.
Invisible Woman: New and Selected Poems, 1970–1982. Princeton, NJ: Ontario Review Press, 1982.
The Time Traveler. New York: Dutton, 1989.
Tenderness. Princeton, NJ: Ontario Review Press, 1996.

PLAYS

Miracle Play. Los Angeles: Black Sparrow Press, 1974.
Three Plays. Princeton, NJ: Ontario Review Press, 1980.
Twelve Plays. New York: Dutton, 1991.
In Darkest America (Tone Clusters and *The Eclipse)*. New York: Samuel French, 1991.
The Perfectionist and Other Plays. Hopewell, NJ: Ecco Press, 1995.
New Plays. Princeton, NJ: Ontario Review Press, 1998.

EDITED BOOKS

Scenes from American Life: Contemporary Short Fiction. New York: Vanguard, 1973.
Night Walks: A Bedside Companion. Princeton, NJ: Ontario Review Press, 1982.
First Person Singular: Writers on Their Craft. Princeton, NJ: Ontario Review Press, 1983.
The Best American Essays, 1991. New York: Ticknor & Fields, 1991.
The Sophisticated Cat. New York: Dutton, 1992.
The Oxford Book of American Short Stories. New York: Oxford University Press, 1992.

The Essential Dickinson. Hopewell, NJ: Ecco Press, 1996.
American Gothic Tales. New York: Plume, 1996.
Tales of H. P. Lovecraft. Hopewell, NJ: Ecco Press, 1997.
Telling Stories: An Anthology for Writers. New York: Norton, 1998.
With Shannon Ravanel. *The Best American Short Stories, 1979.* New York: Houghton Mifflin, 1979.
With Boyd Litzinger. *STORY: Fictions Past and Present.* Lexington, MA, 1987.
With Dan Halpen. *Reading the Fights.* New York: Henry Holt, 1988.
With Janet Berliner. *Snapshots: C20th Mother-Daughter Fiction.* Boston: David R. Godine, 2000.
With Robert Atwan. *Best American Essays of the Century.* Boston: Houghton Mifflin, 2000.

YOUNG ADULT BOOKS

Big Mouth & Ugly Girl. New York: HarperTempest, 2002.
Freaky Green Eyes. New York: HarperTempest, 2003.
Small Avalanches and Other Stories. New York: HarperTempest, 2003.

CHILDREN'S BOOKS

Come Meet Muffin! Hopewell, NJ: Ecco Press, 1998.
Where Is Little Reynard? New York: HarperCollins, 2003.

Secondary Sources

BOOKS

Allen, Mary. *The Necessary Blankness: Women in Major American Fiction of the Sixties.* Urbana: University of Illinois Press, 1976.
Bakhtin, Mikhail M. *The Dialogic Imagination: Four Essays.* Translated by Michael Holquist and Caryl Emerson, edited by Michael Holquist. Austin: University of Texas Press, 1981.
Baldwin, James. *The Fire Next Time.* New York: Dial Press, 1963; Harmondsworth, Eng.: Penguin, 1964.
Bastian, Katherine. *Joyce Carol Oates's Short Stories: Between Tradition and Innovation.* Bern: Peter Lang, 1983.
Bender, Eileen Teper. *Joyce Carol Oates: Artist in Residence.* Bloomington: Indiana University Press, 1987.
Bloom, Harold, ed. *Joyce Carol Oates.* New York: Chelsea House, 1987.
Borges, Jorge Luis. *Labyrinths: Selected Stories and Other Writings.* Edited by Donald Yates and James Irby, 1964. Reprint; Harmondsworth, Eng.: Penguin, 1987.
Burchill, Julie. *Diana.* London: Orion, 1998.

Chernin, Kim. *The Hungry Self: Women, Eating, and Identity.* London: Virago, 1985.
Cornillon, Susan Koppelman, ed. *Images of Women in Fiction: Feminist Perspectives.* Bowling Green, OH: Bowling Green University Popular Press, 1972; rev. ed. 1973.
Creighton, Joanne V. *Joyce Carol Oates.* Boston: Twayne, 1979.
———. *Joyce Carol Oates: Novels of the Middle Years.* Boston: Twayne, 1992.
Daly, Brenda. *Lavish Self-Divisions: The Novels of Joyce Carol Oates.* Jackson: University Press of Mississippi, 1996.
Dewey, John. *The Essential Writings.* Edited by David Sidorksy. New York: Harper & Row, 1977.
———. *John Dewey: The Early Works, 1882–1898.* 5 vols. Edited by Jo Ann Boydston. Carbondale: Southern Illinois University Press, 1969–72.
———. *John Dewey: The Middle Works, 1899–1924.* 15 vols. Edited by Jo Ann Boydston. Carbondale: Southern Illinois University Press, 1976–83.
———. *John Dewey: The Later Works, 1925–1953.* 17 vols. Edited by Jo Ann Boydston. Carbondale: Southern Illinois University Press, 1981–90.
Dewey, Joseph. *Novels from Reagan's America: A New Realism.* Gainesville: University Press of Florida, 1999.
Dostoyevsky, Fyodor. *Notes from Underground.* Translated by Jesse Coulson. Harmondsworth, Eng.: Penguin, 1972.
Dickstein, Morris, ed. *The Revival of Pragmatism: New Essays on Social Thought, Law, and Culture.* Durham, NC: Duke University Press, 1998.
Elliott, Emory, ed. *The Columbia History of the American Novel.* New York: Columbia University Press, 1991.
Emerson, Ralph Waldo. *The Complete Prose Works of Ralph Waldo Emerson.* Edited by G. T. Bettany. New York: Ward, Lock, 1889.
Erikson, Erik H. *Young Man Luther: A Study in Psychoanalysis and History.* London: Faber, 1958.
Friedman, Ellen G. *Joyce Carol Oates.* New York: Ungar, 1980.
Gates, Henry Louis, Jr. *The Signifying Monkey: A Theory of African-American Criticism.* 1988. Reprint; Oxford: Oxford University Press, 1989.
Gilbert, Sandra M., and Susan Gubar. *No Man's Land: The Place of the Woman Writer in the Twentieth Century.* New Haven: Yale University Press, 1988.
Gorham, Deborah. *The Victorian Girl and the Feminine Ideal.* London: Croom Helm, 1982.
Grant, Mary Kathryn. *The Tragic Vision of Joyce Carol Oates.* Durham, NC: Duke University Press, 1978.
Hamalian, Leo. *D. H. Lawrence and Nine Women Writers.* Cranbury, NJ: Associated University Presses, 1996.
Heyen, William. *Diana, Charles, & the Queen.* Rochester, NY: BOA Editions, 1998.

James, William. *A Pluralist Universe*. London: Longmans, Green, 1909.
———. *The Meaning of Truth*. London: Longmans, Green, 1909.
———. *Pragmatism*. London: Longmans, Green, 1907.
———. *Some Problems of Philosophy: A Beginning of an Introduction to Philosophy*. London: Longmans, Green, 1911; Lincoln: University of Nebraska Press, 1996.
———. *The Varieties of Religious Experience*. London: Longmans, Green, 1902.
———. *The Will to Believe*. New York: Dover Publications, 1956.
———. *The Writings of William James*. Edited by John J. McDermott. Chicago: University of Chicago Press, 1977.
Jardine, Alice, and Paul Smith. *Men in Feminism*. London: Routledge, 1987.
Johnson, Greg. *Invisible Writer: A Biography of Joyce Carol Oates*. New York: Dutton, 1998.
———. *Joyce Carol Oates: A Study of the Short Fiction*. Boston: Twayne, 1994.
———. *Understanding Joyce Carol Oates*. Columbia, SC: University of South Carolina Press, 1987.
Kessler-Harris, Alice, and William McBrien, eds. *Faith in a (Woman) Writer*. Westport, CT: Greenwood Press, 1988.
Kowaleski, Michael. *Deadly Musings: Violence and Verbal Forms in American Fiction*. Princeton, NJ: Princeton University Press, 1993.
Krishnamurti, Jiddu. *Krishnamurti's Notebook*. New York: Harper & Row, 1976.
Lawrence, D. H. *Studies in Classic American Literature*. New York: Thomas Seltzer, 1923; Harmondsworth, Eng.: Penguin, 1977.
Lercangée, Francine. *Joyce Carol Oates: An Annotated Bibliography*. Preface and annotations by Bruce F. Michelson. New York: Garland, 1986.
Loeb, Monica. *Literary Marriages: A Study of Intertextuality in a Series of Short Stories by Joyce Carol Oates*. Bern: Peter Lang, 2002.
Longfellow, Henry Wadsworth. *Selected Poems*. Edited by Anthony Waite. London: Dent, 1996.
Lucie-Smith, Edward. *American Realism*. New York: Harry N. Abrams, 1994.
Lukács, Georg. *The Historical Novel*. Translated by Hannah Mitchell and Stanley Mitchell. 1962. Reprint; Harmondsworth, Eng.: Penguin, 1986.
McGee, Bryan. *The Great Philosophers*. Oxford: Oxford University Press, 1988.
Megill, Allan. *Prophets of Extremity: Nietzsche, Heidegger, Foucault, Derrida*. 1985. Reprint; Berkeley: University of California Press, 1987.
Menand, Louis. *The Metaphysical Club*. New York: Farrar, Strauss, Giroux, 2001.
Mickelson, Anne Z. *Reaching Out: Sensitivity and Order in Recent American Fiction by Women*. Metuchen, NJ: Scarecrow Press, 1979.
Milazzo, Lee, ed. *Conversations with Joyce Carol Oates*. Jackson: University Press of Mississippi, 1989.

Nietzsche, Friedrich. *The Basic Writings of Nietzsche*. Edited and translated by Walter Kaufmann. New York: Random House, 1968.

Norman, Torborg. *Isolation and Contact: A Study of Character Relationships in Joyce Carol Oates's Short Stories, 1963–1980*. Goteborg, Sweden: Acta Universitatis Gothoburgensis, 1984.

Pascal, Blaise. *Pensées*. Translated by A. J. Krailsheimer. Harmondsworth, Eng.: Penguin, 1995.

Pearlman, Mickey, and Katherine Usher Henderson. *Inter/View: Talks with America's Writing Women*. Lexington: University Press of Kentucky, 1990.

Plato. *The Last Days of Socrates: Euthyphro, The Apology, Crito, Phaedo*. Translated by Hugh Tredennick and Harold Tarrant. Harmondsworth, Eng.: Penguin, 1993.

Rorty, Richard. *Consequences of Pragmatism: Essays, 1972–1980*. Brighton: Harvester Press, 1982.

———. *Contingency, Irony, and Solidarity*. Cambridge: Cambridge University Press, 1989.

———. *Objectivity, Relativism, and Truth*. Cambridge: Cambridge University Press, 1991.

Russell, Bertrand. *Bertrand Russell Speaks His Mind*. New York: Bard Books, 1960.

———. *A History of Western Philosophy*. London: Simon & Schuster, 1996.

———. *Mysticism and Logic*. London: Allen & Unwin, 1970.

Russett, Cynthia Eagle. *Sexual Science and the Victorian Construction of Womanhood*. Cambridge: Harvard University Press, 1989.

Sage, Lorna. *Women in the House of Fiction: Post-War Women Novelists*. London: Macmillan, 1992.

Schopenhauer, Arthur. *The World as Will and Idea* [1819]. Edited by David Berman, translated by Jill Berman. London: Dent, 1995.

Searle, John R. *The Construction of Social Reality*. 1995. Reprint; Harmondsworth, Eng.: Penguin, 1996.

———. *Minds, Brains, and Science*. 1984. Reprint; Harmondsworth, Eng.: Penguin, 1989.

Seigfried, Charlene Haddock. *Pragmatism and Feminism: Reweaving the Social Fabric*. Chicago: University of Chicago Press, 1996.

Severin, Hermann. *The Image of the Intellectual in the Short Stories of Joyce Carol Oates*. Frankfurt: Peter Lang, 1986.

Showalter, Elaine. *Sister's Choice: Tradition and Change in American Women's Writing*. Oxford: Oxford University Press, 1991.

———, ed. *"Where Are You Going, Where Have You Been?"* New Brunswick, NJ: Rutgers University Press, 1994.

Singer, Marcus G., ed. *American Philosophy.* Cambridge: Cambridge University Press, 1985.
Sreelakshmi, P. *Elective Affinities: A Study of the Sources and Intertexts of Joyce Carol Oates's Short Fiction.* Madras: T. R. Publications, 1996.
Steiner, George. *Language and Silence: Essays, 1958–1966.* London: Faber, 1967.
Stevens, Wallace. *The Collected Poems of Wallace Stevens.* London: Alfred A. Knopf, 1955.
———. *Opus Posthumous.* New York: Alfred A. Knopf, 1957.
Stuhr, John J., ed. *Pragmatism and Classical American Philosophy: Essential Readings and Interpretive Essays.* Oxford: Oxford University Press, 2000.
Tarnas, Richard. *The Passion of the Western Mind: Understanding the Ideas That Have Shaped Our Worldview.* New York: Crown, 1991; London: Pimlico, 1996.
Tolstoy, Leo. *The Cossacks/Happy Ever After/The Death of Ivan Illych.* Translated by Rosemary Edmonds. Harmondsworth, Eng.: Penguin, 1960.
Wagner, Linda W., ed. *Critical Essays on Joyce Carol Oates.* Boston: G. K. Hall, 1979.
Waller, G. F. *Dreaming America: Obsession and Transcendence in the Fiction of Joyce Carol Oates.* Baton Rouge: Louisiana State University Press, 1979.
Warhol, Robyn R., and Diane Price Herndl. *Feminisms: An Anthology of Literary Theory and Criticism.* New Brunswick, NJ: Rutgers University Press, 1997.
Watanabe, Nancy Ann. *Love Eclipsed: Joyce Carol Oates's Faustian Moral Vision.* Lanham, MD: University Press of America, 1998.
Weinstein, Arnold. *Nobody's Home: Speech, Self, and Place in American Fiction from Hawthorne to DeLillo.* Oxford: Oxford University Press, 1993.
Wesley, Marilyn C. *Refusal and Transgression in Joyce Carol Oates's Fiction.* Westport, CT: Greenwood Press, 1993.
Woolf, Virginia. *A Room of One's Own/Three Guineas.* Edited by Morag Shaich. Oxford: Oxford University Press, 1992.

ESSAYS AND REVIEWS

Atkins, Christine E. "This Is What You Deserve: Rape as Rite of Passage in Joyce Carol Oates's 'Naked.'" *Women's Studies* 31, no. 4 (2002): 433–45.
Atlas, James. "An American Masterpiece." *Vanity Fair,* August 1987, 140.
Barth, John. "The Literature of Replenishment." *Atlantic Monthly,* January 1980, 65–71.
Barza, Steven. "Joyce Carol Oates: Naturalism and the Aberrant Response." *Studies in American Fiction* 7 (1979): 141–51.
Bender, Eileen Teper. "The Woman Who Came to Dinner: Dining and Divining a Feminist 'Aesthetic.'" *Women's Studies* 12, no. 3 (1986): 315–33.

Berman, Harry J. "Joyce Carol Oates's 'A Theory of Knowledge.'" *International Journal of Aging and Human Development* 93, no. 4 (1992–93): 293–302.

Berry, Wendell. "A Homage to Dr. Williams." In *The Generation of 2000: Contemporary American Poets*, edited by William Heyen. Princeton, NJ: Ontario Review Press, 1984, 1–14.

Boesky, Dale. "Correspondence with Miss Joyce Carol Oates." *International Review of Psychoanalysis* 2 (1975): 481–86.

Bonds, Diane S. "Joyce Carol Oates: Testing the Lawrentian Hypothesis." In *D. H. Lawrence's Literary Inheritors*, edited by Keith Cushman and Dennis Jackson. London: Macmillan, 1991, 167–87.

Brace, Marianne. "Menace, Molestation, and Murder." *Independent*, Monday review section, 31 August 1998, 10.

Burwell, Rose Marie. "*Wonderland*: Paradigm of the Psychohistorical Mode." *Mosaic* 14, no. 3 (1981): 1–16.

Carroll, James. "He Could Not Tell a Lie." *New York Times Book Review*, 2 October 1994, 7.

Colakis, Marianthe. "The House of Atreus Myth in the Seventies and Eighties: David Rabe's *The Orphan* and Joyce Carol Oates's *Angel of Light*." *Classical and Modern Literature* 9, no. 2 (1989): 125–30.

Crowley, John. "Outlaw Girls on the Rampage." *New York Times Book Review*, 15 August 1993, 6.

Dean, Sharon L. "Faith and Art: Joyce Carol Oates's *Son of the Morning*." *Critique* 28, no. 3 (1987): 135–47.

Dike, Donald A. "The Aggressive Victim in the Fiction of Joyce Carol Oates." *Greyfriar* 15 (1974): 13–29.

Ditsky, John. "The Man on the Quaker Oats Box: Characteristics of Recent Experimental Fiction." *Georgia Review* 26 (Fall 1972): 297–313.

Early, Gerald. "The Grace of Slaughter: A Review-Essay of Joyce Carol Oates's *On Boxing*." *Iowa Review* 18, no. 23 (1988): 173–86.

Fossum, Robert H. "Only Control: The Novels of Joyce Carol Oates." *Studies in the Novel* 7 (1975): 285–97.

Friedman, Ellen G. "Joyce Carol Oates." In *Modern American Women Writers*, edited by Elaine Showalter, Lea Baechler, and A. Walton Litz. New York: Charles Scribner's Sons, 1991, 353–74.

Gates, Henry Louis, Jr. "Murder She Wrote." *Nation*, 2 July 1990, 27–29.

Goodman, Charlotte. "Women and Madness in the Fiction of Joyce Carol Oates." *Women and Literature* 5 (Fall 1977): 17–28.

Harter, Carol. "America as a 'Consumer Garden': The Nightmare Vision of Joyce Carol Oates." *Revue Des Langues Vivantes*, bicentennial issue (1976): 171–87.

Hebel, Udo J. "Breaking through the 'Suburban Wasteland': Transgression as Affirmation of the Self in Joyce Carol Oates's *Expensive People.*" *Arbeiten Aus Angustik Und Amerikanistik* 16, no. 1 (1991): 13–29.

Heyen, William. "Open Letter to Oates." *Tri-Quarterly* 73 (Fall 1988): 87–92.

James, Eric. "Seeing Two Things at Once: Misinterpretations of the Pluralism of William James." *Times Literary Supplement,* 23 June 2000.

Kakutani, Michiko. "Girls Who Hate Men and Act Accordingly." *New York Times,* 16 July 1993, C-18.

Kapp, Isa. "In Defense of Matrimony." *New Leader* 55 (December 1972): 8–10.

Karpen, Lynn. "Legs Sadovsky Goes Mythic." *New York Times Book Review,* 15 August 1993, 6.

Keyser, Elizabeth Lennox. "*A Bloodsmoor Romance:* Joyce Carol Oates's Little Women." *Women's Studies* 14, no. 3 (1988): 211–23.

Krystal, Arthur. "Ifs, Ands, Butts: The Literary Sensibility at Ringside." *Harper's Magazine,* June 1987, 63–67.

Levin, Bernard. "Against the Demon Voices." *Sunday Times,* 11 January 1987, 20.

Manske, Eva. "The Nightmare of Reality: Gothic Fantasies and Psychological Realism in the Fiction of Joyce Carol Oates." In *Neo-Realism in Contemporary American Fiction,* edited by Kristiaan Versluys. Amsterdam: Rodopi, 1992, 131–43.

Markmann, Charles Lam. "The Terror of Love." *Nation,* 14 December 1970, 636–37.

Mulryan, John. "The Genderfication of Literature: Cross-Gender Writing in Joyce Carol Oates's *Expensive People* and Brian Moore's *I Am Mary Dunne.*" *CEA Critic* 56 (Fall 1993): 17–25.

Nodelman, Perry. "The Sense of Unending: Joyce Carol Oates's *Bellefleur* as an Experiment in Feminine Storytelling." In *Breaking the Sequence: Women's Experimental Fiction,* edited by Ellen G. Friedman and Miriam Fuchs. Princeton, NJ: Princeton University Press, 1989, 250–64.

Petite, Joseph. "The Marriage Cycle of Joyce Carol Oates." *Journal of Evolutionary Psychology* 5 (1984): 223–36.

———. "The Marriage Cycle of Joyce Carol Oates II." *Journal of Evolutionary Psychology* 6 (1985): 16–27.

Quinn, Sally. "Joyce Carol Oates: A Life Within." *Washington Post,* 30 April 1975, B1, B2.

Radin, Victoria. "Under the Skin." *New Statesman,* 22 February 1991, 34.

Redmon, Anne. "Vision and Risk: New Fiction by Oates and Ozick." *Michigan Quarterly Review* 27, no. 2 (1988): 203–13.

Robinson, Sally. "Heat and Cold: Recent Fiction by Joyce Carol Oates." *Michigan Quarterly Review* 31, no. 3 (1992): 400–14.

Rorty, Richard. "Feminism and Pragmatism." *Michigan Quarterly Review* 30 (Spring 1991): 231–58.

Roth, Philip. "Writing American Fiction." *Commentary* 31 (September 1961): 223–33.

Salholz, Eloise. "Gothic Horrors." *Newsweek*, 6 February 1984, 79.
Shepherd, Allen G. "Faulknerian Antecedents to Joyce Carol Oates's *Mysteries of Winterthurn*." *Notes on Contemporary Writing* 17, no. 5 (1987): 8–10.
Shone, Tom. "A Leap Out of the Dark." *Sunday Times*, 2 April 1995, sec. 10, pp. 6–7.
Smiley, Pamela. "Incest, Roman Catholicism, and Joyce Carol Oates." *College Literature* 19 (Fall 1991): 38–49.
Stout, Janis P. "Catatonia and Femininity in Oates's *Do with Me What You Will*." *International Journal of Women's Studies* 6 (1983): 208–15.
Strandberg, Victor. "Sex, Violence, and Philosophy in *You Must Remember This*." *Studies in American Fiction* 17 (Spring 1989): 3–17.
Sullivan, Andrew. "Monica Catches Out the Semi-Moral Majority." *Sunday Times*, news review section, 30 September 1998.
Tayler, Christopher. "Miss Golden Dreams." *Times Literary Supplement*, 21 April 2000, 22.
Taylor, D. J. "Cunning Little Vixens." *Sunday Times*, 15 August 1993, books section, 6.9.
Teel, John. "Venturing into Genre (and Pseudonym): Joyce Carol Oates and 'Rosamond Smith.'" *Journal of American and Comparative Cultures* (Fall–Winter 2002): 390–94.
Updike, John. "What You Deserve Is What You Get." *New Yorker*, 28 December 1987, 119–23.
Viner, Katharine. "Toni Morrison—Voice of America." *Guardian*, 24 March 1998, 2.5.
Wagner-Martin, Linda. "Panoramic, Unpredictable, and Human: Joyce Carol Oates's Recent Novels." In *Traditions, Voices, and Dreams: The American Novel since the 1960s*, edited by Melvin J. Friedman and Ben Siegel. Newark: University of Delaware Press, 1995, 196–209.
Wesley, Marilyn C. "Father-Daughter Incest as Social Transgression: A Feminist Reading of Joyce Carol Oates." *Women's Studies* 21, no. 3 (1992): 251–63.
———. "Reverence, Rape, Resistance: Joyce Carol Oates and Feminist Film Theory." *Mosaic* 32, no. 3 (1999): 75–85.
———. "The Simultaneous Universe: The Politics of Jamesian Conversion in Joyce Carol Oates's Fiction." *Essays in Literature* 18, no. 2 (1991): 269–75.
Wilson, Mary Ann. "From Thanatos to Eros: A Study of Erotic Love in Joyce Carol Oates' *Do with Me What You Will*." *Studies in the Humanities* 9 (December 1984): 48–55.
Wynne, Judith. "Profile of a Prolific Writer: Joyce Carol Oates." *Sojourner*, 7 March 1983, 4.

WEBSITE

For further, regularly updated information, see Randy Souther's website on Joyce Carol Oates, *Celestial Timepiece*, at http://jco.usfca.edu/

INDEX

Abrahams, Billy, 178
"Act of Solitude, An" (story), 254–55n30
Addams, Jane, 123, 241n2
Adventures of Augie March, The (Bellow), 94–95
Adventures of Huckleberry Finn (Twain), 183, 187, 210, 256–57n15
Advertisements for Myself (Mailer), 236
"After great pain, a formal feeling comes" (Dickinson), 138
"After Sunset" (poem), 94
AIDS, 136
Alcoholism, 169–70, 173, 190, 198
Alcott, Louisa May, 110
Ali, Muhammad, 236
Alice in Wonderland (Carroll), 51, 90, 97
America: academia in, 152, 168; business in, 177; capital punishment in, 112, 179, 182; celebrity in, 17, 94, 204; class in, 83, 136, 150, 161, 164, 174, 188–89, 210; consumerism in, 53; culture of, 9, 17, 90, 170, 177, 195, 204, 232, 234; depression-era, 31, 36, 47, 80, 143; in the eighties, 183; in the fifties, 50, 53, 167–74, 178; fraternities in, 187; high school in, 177, 205–17; history of, 17, 89, 90, 100, 132–33, 231, 232, 234; immigrants to, 81, 136; industrial, 154–55; inner city in, 41; landscape of, 91, 93; and language, 3; and law, 58–67, 104; and medicine, 45–53, 104; military in, 200; in nineteenth century, 92–133; and nostalgia, 16, 155, 204–14; places in, 48, 50, 55, 91, 94, 149, 162, 163, 205, 213, 221, 225, 226; politics in, 112, 114, 136–37, 151, 177–83, 217; post-Vietnam, 82; postwar, 41, 53, 155, 172, 230; prison system in, 48, 178; regions of, 62, 84, 103–107, 168–70, 210, 211, 219, 232; rural, 84, 180; science and, 112, 113, 117, 232; in the sixties, 41, 46–47, 50, 53, 64, 167–74, 178, 183; small-town, 155; society in, 16, 30, 46–47, 54, 126, 140, 170, 178; sororities in, 146, 151, 187; suburbia in, 137, 140, 161, 232
American Appetites, 11, 16, 133–34, 137, 138, 141, 161–68, 174, 255n52
"American Expressway" (poem), 91
American Holiday (play), 14
"American Independence" (poem), 94
"American Tradition, An" (poem), 93
Ancient Evenings (Mailer), 235
"And So I Grew Up to Be Nineteen and to Murder" (poem), 24
Angel Fire (poems), 90
Angel of Light, 6, 16, 67, 96
Anna Karenina (Tolstoy), 196
Anonymous Sins and Other Poems, 14, 22, 23, 90–91
Anorexia, 179, 255n53
Anti-Semitism, 123, 156, 188
Apollo, 17, 60–63, 169

"Approaching the Speed of Light" (poem), 93
Aquinas, Thomas, 99
"Are Men Really That Bad?" (Morrow), 184
Armies of the Night (Mailer), 236
"Art and Ethics?—The(F)Utility of Art" (essay), 176
As I Lay Dying (Faulkner), 68
"As Time Goes By" (Hupfeld), 154
Assassins, The: A Book of Hours, 6, 9, 15, 26, 59, 64, 67–73, 83, 95, 104, 147, 153
Assignation, The (stories), 47, 134, 135
Atlas, James, 154
Atom bomb, 112, 156
Auden, W. H., 204
Aurelius, Marcus, 28
Austen, Jane, 113

Baker, Norma Jean. *See* Monroe, Marilyn
Bacon, Francis, 70
Bakhtin, Mikhail, 8, 84, 149
Baldwin, James, 149
Balzac, Honoré de, 178, 256n6
Barrens, The (Oates as Smith), 235
Barrett, Andrea, 233
Barth, John, 3, 37
Barthelme, Donald, 37
Bastian, Katherine, 13
Bateson, Gregory, 98, 106
Beasts, 175
"Because I could not stop for Death" (Dickinson), 25
Because It Is Bitter, and Because It Is My Heart, 16, 25, 26, 133, 149, 151, 161, 167–74, 177, 178, 255n63
Beckett, Samuel, 231
Bedient, Calvin, 46, 60, 64
Bellamy, Joe, 88
Bellefleur, 2, 3, 6, 12, 13, 15, 16, 56, 59, 60, 68, 83, 90, 95–110, 115, 117–21, 127, 128, 130–31, 138, 140, 141, 161
Bell-Jar, The (Plath), 38
Bellow, Saul, 185, 232, 239
Bellows, George, 135, 172

Bender, Eileen T., 11, 26, 27, 60, 63, 67, 74, 96, 99–100, 110, 119, 142, 152, 231
Berkeley, George, 203
Berman, Harry, 56–58
Berry, Wendell, 94, 248n4
Big Bang, 195
Big Mouth & Ugly Girl (young adult), 235
Bigotry, 151, 186–89, 193–94
Birth of Tragedy, The (Nietzsche), 60
Black (play), 137, 151
Black American writing, 149
Black Water (novel), 6, 14, 16, 177–83, 190–91, 193, 206, 215, 256n9, 256n13
Black Water (play), 14, 135
Blake, William, 95, 231
Blonde, 5, 11, 16, 94, 175, 177, 195, 204, 205–206, 215–21, 235, 237–38
Bloodsmoor Romance, A, 15, 90, 96, 98, 109–18, 122, 128, 131
"Bloodstains" (poem), 92
Bloom, Harold, 19–20, 43
Bluebeard's Last Wife (play), 136
Borges, Luis Jorge, 7, 46
"Bound" (essay), 187
"Bride Stripped Bare by Her Bachelors, Even Large Glass, 1915–23, The" (Duchamp), 249n11
Brief History of Time, A (Hawking), 193
Britain: 220; royal family, 216–18
Broke Heart Blues, 3, 16–17, 175, 177, 195, 204–14, 219–20, 221, 227, 233
Bromwich, David, 6, 131
Brooke, Rupert, 172
"Brothers, The" (story), 11, 197
Brothers Karamazov, The (Dostoyevsky), 94
Brown, Bundini, 158
Brown, John, 106
Buddenbrooks (Mann), 100, 106
Burchill, Julie, 217
Bush, George, Sr., 180
By the Northgate (stories), 55, 232
Byron, George Gordon, Lord, 236

Camus, Albert, 28
Catcher in the Rye, The (Salinger), 38
Chandler, Raymond, 176
Chappaquiddick, 178–79
Chaucer, Geoffrey, 38
Chekhov, Anton, 14, 40, 56, 165
Chernin, Kim, 39
Childwold, 3, 9, 15, 17, 59, 67, 73–83, 85, 88, 90, 140, 141
Cisoux, Hélène, 109
Civil rights, 62, 168
Civil War, 173
Classical American philosophy, 2, 5, 83, 109, 161, 228, 241n2. *See also* Pragmatism
Clemons, Walter, 58
Clinton, Bill, 182
Coale, Samuel, 19–20, 67, 84
Cold War, 47
Coleridge, Samuel Taylor, 234
Collector of Hearts, The (stories), 229
Come Meet Muffin! (children's book), 235
Communism, 156, 188
Confessions of Nat Turner, The (Styron), 85
Contraries (essays), 90, 95–96
"Contrary Motions" (poem), 92
Cornillon, Susan, 134, 243n23
Crane, Stephen, 255n56
"Creation of the World, The" (Michelangelo), 164
"Creature and Creation" (Crane), 255n56
Creighton, Joanne, 37, 48, 67, 68, 74, 109, 129, 142, 153, 230
Crime and Punishment (Dostoyevsky), 163
Crossing the Border (stories), 56
Crosswicks Horror, The, 16, 96
Cybele, 89

Dahmer, Jeffrey, 233
Daly, Brenda, 7, 15, 31, 40, 63–64, 68, 70, 71, 74, 83, 99, 108–10, 111, 119–20, 122, 152, 186, 230, 231, 238
Darwin, Charles, 238
De Mott, Benjamin, 117, 134

De Quincy, Thomas, 120
"Dead, The" (story), 56
Dean, Sharon, 84–85, 88–89, 118
Death Festival (working title for *The Assassins*), 68
Death in Venice (Mann), 190
Death of a Salesman (Miller), 140, 191, 220
"Death of Ivan Illych, The" (Tolstoy), 133, 138, 148, 162, 168, 190
"Death Throes of Romanticism, The," (essay), 21
DeLillo, Don, 233
"Delirium and Detachment" (essay), 10–11
Derrida, Jacques, 3, 118
Descartes, René, 10
Detective fiction, 118–27
Dewey, John, 2–4, 11, 74, 88, 89, 123, 139–40, 165, 205, 218, 227–28, 230–32, 239, 241n2
Dewey, Joseph, 140, 159–60
Diana (Burchill), 217
Diana, Charles, & the Queen (Heyen), 217
Diana, Princess of Wales, 11, 17, 176, 205, 216–20, 237
Dickens, Charles, 38, 145
Dickinson, Emily, 10, 25, 123, 138, 150
Dike, Donald, 19–20, 27, 39, 133
Dionysius, 60–63. *See also* Apollo
Do with Me What You Will, 7, 15, 20, 58–67, 68, 75, 90, 95, 104, 107, 243n3
Doctor Faustus (Mann), 99
Doctorow, E. L., 100, 233
"Does the Writer Exist?" (essay), 134
Don Quixote (Cervantes), 44
Dostoyevsky, Fyodor, 38, 50
Double Delight (Oates as Smith), 11
Douglass, Frederick, 113
"Dreaming America" (poem), 93, 248n3
Dreaming America (Waller), 238
Dreiser, Theodore, 19
Duchamp, Marcel, 97, 249n11

Eakins, Thomas, 172
East of Eden (Steinbeck), 30–31

Eclipse, The (play), 136
Edge of Impossibility, The, 20, 25, 121, 235
"Edge of the World" (story), 55, 56
Einstein, Albert, 135
Ellison, Ralph, 237, 259n17
Emerson, Ralph Waldo, 2, 4–5, 9, 49, 54, 57, 76, 112, 124, 231, 233, 238, 239, 241n2, 242n8
Epicurus, 87
Erdrich, Louise, 233
Erikson, Erik H., 84
Euripides, 145
Europe: 101–102, 231; Enlightenment in, 219; History of, 136
Executioner's Song, The (Mailer), 235
Expensive People, 6, 15, 19, 36–41, 44, 68, 69, 156, 176

"F——" (poem), 94
Fabulous Beasts (poems), 90, 92, 93
Faithless (stories), 175
Falls, The, 131
"Famous Photo" (Heyen), 217
Faulkner, William, 59, 68
Feminism: 1–2, 15–16, 56, 60, 64, 83, 96–142 passim, 159, 161, 183, 213, 234, 239, 243n23, 254n38; anti-feminism, 113, 138, 156; and pragmatism, 5, 15–16, 64, 96–97, 99, 109–10, 115, 139, 232
"Feminism and Pragmatism" (Rorty), 3
Fight, The (Mailer), 236
Fire Next Time, The (Baldwin), 149
First Love, 116
Flaubert, Gustave, 38
"Flight" (poem), 93
Foreman, George, 236
"Former Movie Queen, Dying of Cancer . . . " (poem), 93
Forster, E. M., 129
"Forty-Two Kids" (Bellows), 172
Foucault, Michel, 3
Foxfire: Confessions of a Girl Gang, 16, 132, 175, 177, 183–90, 193, 194, 195, 201, 202, 204–206, 256–57n15
Franklin, Benjamin, 112
Freaky Green Eyes (young adult), 235
Freud, Sigmund, 219
Friday Night (play), 136
Friedman, Ellen, 1, 30, 61, 88, 96, 133, 138, 139, 141–42
Frye, Marilyn, 3

"Gala Power Blackout in New York City, July '77" (poem), 94
Garden of Earthly Delights, A: 19, 25, 26, 30–36, 38, 40, 46, 53, 80, 103; revised and rewritten 25, 244n10
Gardner, John, 100, 104, 109, 116–17
Gary, Romain, 259n14
Gates, Henry Louis, Jr., 149, 168, 170, 173, 177, 178, 183, 230
Gemini (working title for *Blonde*), 11
Gender issues, 15, 31, 40, 70, 83, 86, 109–10, 137–39, 142, 183–90, 193, 232, 234
Germain, David, 255n65
Gilbert, Sandra, 40
Gilchrist, Ellen, 233
"Girl at the Center of Her Life, A" (poem), 23
"Giving Oneself a Form Again" (poem), 91
Goddess and Other Women, The (stories), 56
Gödel, Kurt, 105
Godwin, Gail, 58, 70
Goleman, Daniel, 145, 253n24
Gombowicz, Witold, 259n14
Gorham, Deborah, 114
Gospel According to the Son, The (Mailer), 235
Gothicism, 100, 102
Goya, Francisco, 68
Grant, Mary Kathryn, 4, 19, 243n23
Grapes of Wrath, The (Steinbeck), 30, 36
"Grave Dwellers, The" (poem), 91
Great Expectations (Dickens), 143
Great Gatsby, The (Fitzgerald), 42
Greensleeves (play), 136

Gubar, Susan, 40
Gulf War (play), 137
Gulliver's Travels (Swift), 130

Habermas, Jürgen, 11
Hamlet (Shakespeare), 123
"Happy Birthday" (poem), 94
Harter, Carol, 242n7
Hawthorne, Nathaniel, 166, 231
Heat (stories), 134, 135, 150
Hegel, Georg Wilhelm Friedrich, 99
Heidegger, Martin, 3
Hemingway, Ernest, 236
Henderson the Rain King (Bellow), 239
Heraclitus, 106, 108
Here She Is! (play), 170
Heyen, William, 17, 159, 217
Higginson, Thomas Wentworth, 113
Hobbes, Thomas, 145
Hollywood, 186, 215–21
Holocaust, 136
"Holy Saturday" (poem), 94
Homer, Winslow, 135
Hopper, Edward, 135
How Do You Like Your Meat? (play), 136
"How Gentle" (poem), 92
"How I Contemplated the World from the Detroit House of Corrections . . . " (story), 56
Hughes, Ted, 30
Hungry Ghosts, The (stories), 56
Hungry Self, The (Chernin), 39

I Lock My Door upon Myself, 249n13
I Stand Before You Naked (play), 136, 233
I'll Take You There, 8, 17, 25, 151, 175, 187, 237
I'm Waiting (play), 136
Imperial Presidency (play), 14, 136–37
"In the Region of Ice" (story), 245n33
"In Traction" (story), 47
"Insomnia" (poem), 92
"Internal Landscape, An" (poem), 23
Interview, The (play), 137

Invisible Man (Ellison), 237
Invisible Woman (poems), 15, 27, 90, 92–94, 135, 237
"Iris into Eye" (poem), 92

James, Henry, 21, 40, 54, 56, 67, 78, 107
James, William: and American writing, 232–33; and *Childwold*, 76, 79–80, 83, 88; conversion theories of, 96; and empathy, 15, 123; feminine style of, 109, 120; influence of, 2, 15–17, 43, 136, 139, 218, 239; and *Marya: A Life*, 142–44, 152, 154, 253n19; pragmatism of, 2–6, 56, 68, 75, 131, 241n2; and radical empiricism, 40; in a story, 56–58; and *We Were the Mulvaneys*, 196–97, 201, 203–204; and *You Must Remember This*, 160–61
Jane Eyre (Brontë), 111
"JCO and I" (essay), 7, 239
"Jigsaw Puzzle" (poem), 91
Johnson, Annie, 135
Johnson, Greg, 13, 37, 38, 47, 48, 49, 55, 58, 67, 68, 75, 97, 101, 110, 128, 137, 156, 176, 184, 190, 246n5, 256n13
Johnson, Samuel, 122
Joyce, James, 14, 40, 56
Juvenal, 39

Kafka, Franz, 43, 56, 82, 106, 118–21, 125–26, 167, 231
"Kafka's Paradise" (essay), 120, 126
Kakutani, Michiko, 183–84
Kant, Emmanuel, 99, 131
Kelly, Lauren. *See* Oates, Joyce Carol
Kennedy, Edward M., 178, 180, 233
Kennedy, John F., 53, 217
Kierkegaard, Søren, 118, 163, 257n34
King Lear (Shakespeare), 94–95, 191, 206
Kopechne, Mary Jo, 178
Korean War, 47, 155
Koresh, David, 85
Krishnamurti, Jiddu, 146, 253n26

Kristeva, Julia, 108–109
Kundera, Milan, 44

"Lady with the Pet Dog, The" (story), 56
Language and Silence (Steiner), 43–44
"Last Days" (story), 245n33
Lavish Self-Divisions (Daly), 238
Lawrence, D. H., 8, 21, 36, 37, 54, 59, 69
Levin, Bernard, 141–42
Lewinsky, Monica, 182
"Lines for Those to Whom Tragedy Is Denied" (poem), 23
Little Women (Alcott), 110
Lives of the Twins (Oates as Smith), 11, 134
Locke, Alain, 241n2
Loeb, Monica, 13, 55
Lolita (Nabokov), 76, 78
Longfellow, Henry Wadsworth, 117–18
"Love and Its Derangements" (poem), 91
Love and Its Derangements (poems), 90–92
Love and Money (working title for *them*), 41
"Love Letter, with Static Interference from Einstein's Brain" (poem), 135
"Love She Searched For, The" (essay), 216
"Lovers, The" (poem), 94
"Lovers Asleep" (poem), 94
"Loving" (poem), 91
Lucie-Smith, Edward, 172
Lukács, Georg, 143, 154, 168

Madame Bovary (Flaubert), 41, 43–44
Mailer, Norman, 38, 218, 234–38, 259n12
Man Crazy, 116, 175, 186–87, 195
"Manhattan Romance, A" (story), 175–76
Mann, Thomas, 99, 113, 190
Manske, Eva, 242n7
Manson, Charles, 237
Marilyn (Mailer), 218
Marriage of Heaven and Hell, The (Blake), 95
Marriages and Infidelities (stories), 40, 55
Marx, Karl, 11, 145
Marya: A Life, 7, 13, 16, 25, 133–34, 137, 138, 141–54, 171, 174, 178

McCarthy, Cormac, 233
McCarthy, Eugene, 156
McCullers, Carson, 46
McDermott, John, 6, 83
Mead, George Herbert, 241n2
Megill, Allan, 3, 12, 118
Meliorism, 5, 43, 139, 195, 227, 239
Melville, Herman, 231
Meredith, George, 231
Metafiction, 15, 40, 89
"Metamorphosis" (story), 56
Michelangelo, 164
Middle-Age: A Romance, 6, 16–17, 177, 195, 204–206, 220–27
Mill, John Stuart, 11, 113
Miller, Arthur, 191
Milton, John, 231
Miracle Play, 14, 134, 151, 235
Modernism, 75, 79, 82, 89, 129, 233
Monroe, Marilyn, 11, 205, 215–18, 221, 233, 237–38
Montaigne, Michel de, 252n2
Morality: 82, 111, 139–40, 159, 183, 230; moralizing narrators, 114, 194
More, Thomas, 145
Morgan, Pierpoint, 130
Morrison, Toni, 231, 233
Morrow, Lance, 184
Mozart, Wolfgang Amadeus, 160
Mr. Sammler's Planet (Bellow), 185
Mulryan, John, 138
"Murder-Two" (story), 175–76
My Heart Laid Bare, 16, 96, 127–32, 237, 239
Mysteries of Winterthurn, 13, 15, 20, 90, 98, 109–10, 118–27, 136, 137–38, 141, 147, 152, 153, 187, 190
Mysticism: 10, 86, 105, 108, 117; Eastern, 166

Nabokov, Vladimir, 11, 247n35
"Naked" (story), 150–51, 235
Naked and the Dead, The (Mailer), 235
National Book Award, 15, 59
Negative (play), 137, 151, 170

Neurology, 9, 46, 98, 139
New Heaven, New Earth (essays), 14, 20–21, 24, 30, 53–54, 58, 67, 108, 120, 156, 166, 176, 243n3, 246n5
New Plays, 14, 135
Nietzsche, Friedrich, 2–4, 8, 11–12, 17, 43, 60, 99, 105, 131, 152, 159, 162, 231, 235, 238–39
Night-Side (stories), 15, 56
Nodelman, Perry, 109
Nominalism, 57
"Notes on Failure" (essay), 95

Oates, Carolina, 128
Oates, Frederic, 128
Oates, Joyce Carol: aestheticism, 8, 12, 15, 43, 77; on art and artists, 20, 67, 95–96, 98, 118; artistic maturity of, 12, 13, 16, 116–17, 204; and biographical issues, 7–8, 11, 16, 19, 39, 45, 71, 84, 97, 140, 236–37; on consumerism, 220; essays of, 13, 15, 16, 55, 94, 134, 175–76, 230, 233; on experience, 251n48; and experimentation, 3–7, 12–13, 15, 36, 62, 75, 100; on failure, 7; on gender, 139; on history, 41; and introspection, 9–15, 24, 45, 55, 58–59, 68–72, 80, 82, 90, 97, 104; as Lauren Kelly, 11; on maturity, 95; merging genres, 14, 132, 135; and moral vision, 5, 43, 58, 67, 96; mystical vision of, 20, 50, 58, 72, 243n3; plays of, 3, 13–14, 16, 82, 134–37, 140, 151, 175–77, 206, 230, 233; poetry of, 3, 13–14, 15–16, 55, 82, 90, 134–35, 140, 175–76, 206, 230, 233; on readers, 5; on religion, 77, 104; return to realism, 137–40; as Rosamond Smith, 129, 134, 175–76, 235; on the self, 7–9; as social commentator, 9–15, 19, 24, 45, 53–58, 74, 80, 104, 109, 138, 168, 173, 175; stories of, 3, 13, 55, 82, 140, 175–76, 206, 230, 233; and twins and doubles, 11, 50; on writers, 10, 21–22, 36, 53–54, 78, 259n12; on writing, 7, 8, 9, 21–22, 24, 30, 38, 43, 47, 76, 98, 255n65
O'Connor, Flannery, 46

O'Donnell, Patrick, 233–34
Of a Fire on the Moon (Mailer), 235
"Of the Violence of Self-Death" (poem), 23
On Boxing, 134, 138, 156–58, 173, 235, 236
Ontological Proof of My Existence (play), 14, 134, 137
"Out of the Machine" (essay), 259n12

Pascal, Blaise, 2, 4, 5, 82, 98–99, 207, 210, 218, 231, 239
Passion of the Western Mind, The (Tarnas), 98
"Peace" (Brooke), 172
Peirce, Charles Sanders, 56, 241n2
Perfectionist, The (play), 137
Perfectionist and Other Plays, The, 14, 16, 135, 137
Peron, Eva, 216
Phaedo (Plato), 222–23
Phillips, Robert, 76, 84, 161
Phillips, Wendell, 113
Philosophy: 4, 57, 87, 136; American, 231; Eastern, 231; Greek, 226; traditional, 9, 74; twentieth-century, 99, 203. *See also* individual philosophers
Picaresque, 233
Picture of Dorian Gray, A (Wilde), 96
Pilate, Pontius, 196
Plath, Sylvia, 21–22, 26, 30, 38, 76, 156
Plato, 231
"Playlet for Voices" (poem), 135
Pluralism, 2, 5, 88, 99, 109, 233
Poe, Edgar Allan, 38, 118
Poirier, Richard, 133
Poisoned Kiss, The (stories), 56, 88, 235
Pollock, Jackson, 69
Postmodernism, 37, 41, 89, 97, 100, 168, 171, 174, 230, 233
Poststructuralism, 3, 128
Pragmatism: 2–18; characteristics of, 4–5, 241n2; and criticism, 238; in early work generally, 54, 67; in essay collections, 95–96; and experimentation, 5–7; and feminism, 15–16, 64, 96–97, 99, 109–10, 115;

Pragmatism (*continued*)
  in later work generally, 25, 137, 141, 152, 174, 176, 230; in novels (early), 30, 43, 73–75; 82–83, 88–89; (pivotal), 98–105, 115–16, 120, 123; 125–26, 131; (later), 143, 152, 154, 159–61, 174, 196–97, 203–204, 213, 227–28; in other genres, 56–58, 176, 230; and poststructuralism, 3; terminology, 185; and Western culture, 219
Profane Art, The (essays), 90, 95, 238
Proust, Marcel, 38
"Psalm of Life, A" (Longfellow), 117
Psychic, The (play), 137
"Public Outcry" (poem), 94
Pynchon, Thomas, 118

Quinn, Sally, 247n25

Rabbit at Rest (Updike), 191
Race issues: in early poetry, 23; in *Invisible Woman*, 232; in novels (early), 30; (pivotal), 106–107, 123, 130; (later), 139, 148–51, 156, 166–74, 177–78, 180–81, 186–89, 193–94, 232; in plays, 135–37, 151; racism, 123, 135–37, 148–51, 166–74, 180–81, 186–89, 193–94, 211; in stories, 150–51, 235, 253–54n30
Radical empiricism, 40, 41, 49
Ragtime (Doctorow), 100, 102
Rape: A Love Story, 131, 175
Raven's Wing (stories), 134
Reagan, Ronald, 160, 179
Realism: Mailer and, 236; new realism, 16, 140, 160–62; in novels (early), 12, 19, 25, 31–36, 38, 41, 55, 62–64, 74, 76, 156; (pivotal), 89, 128; (later), 129, 131, 137, 143, 154, 161–74 *passim*; traditional, 16, 75, 80, 82, 233; versus romance, 184, 188–89
Red and the Black, The (Stendhal), 41, 44
Rehearsal, The (play), 137
Religion: 28, 31, 57, 85–89, 105, 144, 187, 203, 209, 215; and art, 85–86, 105; Buddhism, 202; Catholicism, 26, 156; and fanaticism 84; Henotheism, 104; Judaism, 151; and movies, 219; Pantheism, 104, 160; Protestantism, 206; Puritanism, 183; Taoism, 120–21, 231
"Report to the Academy, A" (play/poem), 14, 167
Rise of Life on Earth, The, 175
"Rising and Sinking and Rising in My Mind, A" (poem), 23
Robinson, Sally, 150–51, 235
Rockefeller, John D., 130
Romanticism, 21, 108, 111, 154, 184, 188, 205
Room of One's Own, A (Woolf), 234–35
Roosevelt, Franklin D., 188
Rorty, Richard, 2–4, 6–7, 10–12, 22, 30, 37, 45, 74, 75, 97, 123, 159, 203, 230, 241n2
Rosenberg trial, 156
Rossetti, Christina, 176
Roth, Philip, 232
Rothko, Mark, 74
Royce, Josiah, 241n2
Russell, Bertrand, 17, 108, 203–204
Russett, Cynthia Eagle, 112–13, 115

Sage, Lorna, 79, 119
Salinger, J. D., 38
Santayana, George, 18, 241n2
Saramago, José, 106, 250n24
Sartoris (Faulkner), 59
Sartre, Jean-Paul, 179
Scarlet Letter, The (Hawthorne), 166
Schopenhauer, Arthur: in *American Appetites*, 162, 164–65; on art, 12, 20, 29, 160–61; as inspiration, 231, 239; on introspection, 54, 73; in *Marya: A Life*, 145; and pessimism, 99, 197, 239; in a poem, 94; and pragmatism, 2–5; and Universal Will, 25, 33, 48, 131, 165, 192, 212, 227, 255n53
Schweitzer, Albert, 247n24
Searle, John, 106, 203
Secret Mirror, The (play), 233
Seduction, The (stories), 56
Seigfried, Charlene Haddock, 2, 15, 96, 109, 120, 241n2
"Sexy" (poem), 206

Shakespeare, William, 38
Shepherd, Allen, 110, 119, 120, 122, 126
Showalter, Elaine, 110, 112, 114, 117, 141–42, 147
"Sky Blue Ball, The" (story), 229–30
"Sleeping Together" (poem), 92
"Small Avalanches" (story), 56
Smiley, Pamela, 26, 30
Smith, Rosamond. See Oates, Joyce Carol
Social Darwinism, 130
Socrates, 17, 99, 221–23, 225, 243n24
Soldier's Pay (Faulkner), 59
Solipsism, 21–22, 24, 39, 49, 54, 68, 80, 85, 106, 141, 145–46, 152, 154, 199
Solstice, 13, 15, 20, 25, 131, 137–38, 141
Son of the Morning, 9–10, 14–15, 58, 59, 67, 68, 75, 83–89, 90, 104–105, 110, 118, 139–40, 205
Soul/Mate (Oates as Smith), 11
Sound and the Fury, The (Faulkner), 59, 68, 179
Spinoza, Baruch, 160
Sreelakshmi, P., 13–14, 55
Starr Bright Will Be with You Soon (Oates as Smith), 175
Steinbeck, John, 33, 46
Steiner, George, 43, 145
Stendhal (Henri Beyle), 38, 42, 46
Stevens, Wallace, 21, 89, 105, 128
Stevenson, Adlai, 155
"Stone Orchard, The" (poem), 94
Strandberg, Victor, 159–61
Stuhr, John J., 4, 5, 88, 227, 231
Styron, William, 85, 232
Sullivan, Andrew, 182–83
Sullivan, Walter, 32, 37, 44
Swift, Jonathan, 130
Swimming Hole, The (Eakins), 172
Syracuse University, 18

Take Me, Take Me with You (Oates as Kelly), 11
Tarnas, Richard, 98–99, 106
Tattooed Girl, The, 131, 175
Taylor, D. J., 183, 233

Taylor, Gordon O., 46–48
Tenderness (poems), 14, 206, 235
Tennyson, Alfred, Lord, 37
them, 15, 17, 19, 36–37, 38, 41–45, 46, 59, 63, 66, 85, 103, 245n33
"Theory of Knowledge, A" (story), 15, 56, 58, 68, 84
"There Are Those Who Die" (poem), 94
Thoreau, Henry David, 76, 77, 126, 145, 190–91, 203, 219
"Three Dances of Death" (poem), 24
Through the Looking Glass (Carroll), 72
Time magazine, 17, 184, 216, 218
Time Traveler, The (poems), 14, 134–35
To the Lighthouse (Woolf), 89
Tolstoy, Leo, 38, 58, 133, 138, 148, 168, 196
Tone Clusters (play), 136, 190, 192
Transcendentalism, 112
Triumph of the Spider Monkey, The (fiction/play), 14, 134
"Turn of the Screw, The" (story), 56
Turner, Nat, 85
Twelve Plays, 14, 16, 134–37, 177, 233
Tyler, Anne, 230, 232
Tyson, Mike, 134

Ulysses (Joyce), 159, 161
Under/Ground (play), 170
"Undesirable Table, The" (story), 211
Unholy Loves, 89
"Unmailed, Unwritten Letters" (story), 56
"Up from Slavery" (story), 253–54n30
Updike, John, 154, 161, 191, 230, 232, 234
Upon the Sweeping Flood (stories), 55

Van Leer, David, 237
"Vanity" (poem), 23–24
Victorians, 114, 171, 204
Vietnam War, 47, 81, 141, 171, 173
"Vision, A" (poem), 93

Wagner-Martin, Linda, 1–2, 14, 19, 110, 118–20, 138, 142, 159, 253n19
Walden (Thoreau), 77, 191

Waller, Gary, 19–20, 21, 33, 37, 68, 74, 238
Washington, George, 171
We Were the Mulvaneys, 6, 16, 25, 175, 177, 195–204
Wesley, Marilyn C., 16, 62, 96, 108–109, 138, 141, 144, 148, 162
West, Cornel, 97, 232
"What Has Not Been Lost in the Deserts of North America?" (poem), 93
What I Lived For, 6, 11, 16, 105, 175, 177, 190–95, 202, 204, 215, 219, 238, 256n9, 256n13
Wheel of Love (stories), 28, 55
"Where Are You Going, Where Have You Been?" (story), 28, 32, 51, 56, 195
Where I've Been, and Where I'm Going (essays), 176, 191
"White Negro, The" (Mailer), 236–37
Whitman, Walt, 10, 234, 237
Why Are We in Vietnam? (Mailer), 235
Will You Always Love Me? (stories), 11
William, Don, 186
Williams, William Carlos, 248n4
Wilson, Mary Ann, 61, 64
"Winter Suite, A" (poem), 135

Wishnetsky, Richard, 245n33
With Shuddering Fall, 14, 19, 25, 26–30, 31, 35, 40, 45, 53, 80, 89, 156, 231
(Woman) Writer (essays) 8, 9,128, 134, 137, 242n15
Women Whose Lives Are Food, Men Whose Lives Are Money (poems), 90, 93–94
Wonderland, 11, 14–15, 19, 26, 45–53, 58, 59, 62, 66, 67, 88, 90, 92–93, 104–105, 134, 156, 176
"Wonderland Revisited" (afterword), 46
Woolf, Virginia, 21, 54, 79, 89, 111, 234
World as Will and Idea, The (Schopenhauer) 5
World War I, 82
World War II, 34, 47
"Writing American Fiction" (Roth), 232
Wuthering Heights (Brontë), 94, 100–101

Yeats, W. B., 8, 21, 46
You Must Remember This, 6, 9, 16, 25, 133–34, 139, 140–41, 154–63, 165, 168, 187, 190, 192, 199

Zombie, 175, 235

www.ingramcontent.com/pod-product-compliance
Lightning Source LLC
Chambersburg PA
CBHW050433240426
43661CB00055B/2361